There have been countless people who have supported me, as Rainbow Diner evolved from an idea twelve years ago, to the completed book that it is today. I am forever grateful.

I want to give special thanks and acknowledgement to the following people:
Bruce Silvey, Renee Rosenburg, Elizabeth Bremner, Ginger Bhakti, Nick Parker, Tess Urton, Karen Aiken, Julie Ricks McClintic, Susanne Sherman, Mark H., Steven Whitacre, Lynn Burchfield, Dena Moes, Marty Thompson, Michael Riedeman, Alysia Abbott, Joan C., Kerry Breen, Nina Blasenheim, every single member of The Recollectors--and my three amazing sons, who rooted for me the whole way.

Eternal gratitude to my family, who I would never trade in for a *normal* family--without you, I wouldn't have my stories.

Back and front cover design by Astrid's brother, Benny.
Cover photo: young Astrid, from "the shoot."
Back cover cities and rainbow illustration by Astrid.

Rainbow Diner is the true story of my childhood, written from memory and from the content of my childhood journals. I have been diligent about telling the story with utmost accuracy. However, human memory is flawed and subjective, and someone else may remember the events differently. Additionally, dialogue from the distant past cannot always be recalled word-for-word and––as such––has been recreated in some instances, while keeping the scenes and the essence of the characters intact. All names have been changed to protect the privacy of the people in this book.

For my brother.

San Francisco, 1995
The Last Day

Dad died of AIDS in 1995, when I was twenty-six. He told me he was HIV-positive in June of 1991 and died three years and nine months later. One day he had no symptoms, the next he was tired and soaking the sheets, then he couldn't work, then he was on hospice care at home.

In my mind's eye––no matter how sick he became––Dad was in his favorite Manhattan disco in 1979. He was in his tight Calvin Kleins with his shirt unbuttoned, outdancing everyone. It seemed only yesterday we were there; I wanted to encapsulate Dad's glory days, or transport him back there somehow. But in a flash he was gone. My dashing, flamboyant, elegant father was gone.

Growing up with Dad was like starring in a mesmerizing, R-rated off-Broadway hit that kept going without intermission. He ruined ordinary for me. How could the life be so markedly evacuated from someone so vivacious? The world would be so boring without him.

Dad offered reasons and explanations, but he never offered an estimation of time left, and I was too afraid to ask.

"It's called Wasting Syndrome," Dad's doctor explained to me, "It's really lucky that he hasn't had Kaposi's sarcoma or pneumocystis pneumonia. It's amazing," he added, as if he were sharing good news. But this wasting syndrome wasn't lucky. No, to me it was worse than the opportunistic conditions Dad might have acquired. My polished, sophisticated father was literally slowly disintegrating in the ugliest way. The name of the condition fit so well. Little by little, Dad was being stripped of his style and finesse, his good looks, his charm. Beauty had always been so important to him. He always wore the best cologne, used the best skin cream; he wore the latest fashions and most of his jewelry was nothing less than pure gold and silver. Dad knew what to say in a room full of people so that everyone turned his way. Now all of what made him a star would be shrinking and spoiling like a rotten peach for all to see.

    Dad knew what to expect. He had been watching all his friends suffer and then drop like flies, one by one. He became an R.N. in 1985, just after he and his partner moved from New York to San Francisco. San Francisco was the epicenter of the AIDS pandemic, and my father had been on the front lines––he worked on the AIDS unit in a San Francisco hospital. He told stories about the gaunt, dying men alone in their hospital beds––abandoned by their families––and stories about all the heartbroken partners and friends.

    As Dad's HIV advanced to AIDS, a memory kept coming to mind over and over, of a weekend in 1989 when I stayed with him and his domestic partner in their S.F. apartment. I replayed the image in my mind of Dad right after a long nightshift. He was smoking a cigarette in his little kitchen in the early morning, still wearing his starchy white nursing uniform (Dad liked to wear white scrubs, even though I'm pretty sure he wasn't required to). Dangling from his pocket full of pens was a plastic I.D. badge that bore a small photo of him smiling and looking proud–– obviously taken when he was sharp and alert and *not* at the end of a twelve-hour nightshift. Below the photo on the badge was his name in all caps, followed by the well-earned "R.N."

I adoringly watched him as he made me eggs over easy and white toast, knowing he had to be exhausted. The way he cooked for me had not changed since I was a kid––always in a tiny, tidy apartment kitchen, and always making any old meal seem like gourmet cuisine.

As I ate my breakfast, Dad sat at the table smoking his Kool with big dark circles under his eyes, telling me about opportunistic infections and purple skin lesions. *God, I hope he never gets it*, I repeated in my head over and over.

In another impressionable memory of him, Dad said off the cuff, "I wonder how *I'll* end up going." It was during a visit just a few years later, when he was HIV-positive, but not sick yet. I wondered whether it was more daunting or *less* daunting to have such acute knowledge of all the terrible possibilities. *Wasting syndrome.* This was it? Dad was literally going to just slowly waste away in the end? How could this happen?

Why did the level of panic come as such a surprise those last few months? The uncontrollable bargaining and grief could not be paced; I wasn't in control of it. I couldn't do a thing about the imminent AIDS that was about to engulf my father; I couldn't make it stop. I felt trapped in the claustrophobic edgy fret of wondering *when* Dad would die. Time. I wished I could talk to the sickness and tell it to hold on a minute. What was once a wide-open plain for the diversity of my feelings had become a shriveled space. If I wanted to clear anything up with Dad, I needed to do it very soon.

As a little girl, I was willingly and rapturously my father's project—he designed the blueprint for the type of woman I'd become. Who was I without him? He acquired me when I was about to be fatherless, taking on the project of my mother, who was alone and impregnated by a married man. After I was born, he consummated our adoption with an all-consuming, faithful love.

Mother was eccentric, unpredictable and beautiful, but ultimately did not line up with what he thought was female. It was tricky being both her daughter and his apprentice.

My father showed me how to dress, how to talk, how to dance, how to hold a martini glass. He told me who to ignore. He knew everything about how a woman ought to act. When he introduced me to his friends or colleagues, it was more of an announcement, an unveiling: "Dear folks, I'd like you to meet the most beautiful young woman on the face of the earth: My princess, my beloved daughter." I was one of the top-of-the-line products in Dad's life that set him above the rest.

I had craved this man, my father, with a hunger that could only be equated with that of a ravenous, obsessed lover. How big would be this vacancy. I was so used to reaching out to grab hold of him—he was always almost in reach, but not quite. At times I felt ashamed at how much I wanted his approval. I hated the way he could be so curt and sharp and vulgar. Dad had a way of shutting the door in my face just when I thought I no longer needed to knock.

Six days before he died, I had sat vigilantly beside my father's bed in his fancy Diamond Heights apartment in San Francisco. He dipped in and out of consciousness, his breathing rattled and pausing with apneic spells. His vanishing body filled the room with a thick sweet scent that I will never forget. He had become nothing but thin, opaque skin on bones. He looked so small and vulnerable under his quilt--his cheeks and eyes sunken in--with every edge of his clavicle bones discernible. I thought he might turn to ash in front of me. The parts of Dad that remained unchanged stood out—the hazel of his eyes, his fine white hair, his voice, the baby soft underside of his forearm, which I dared let myself touch that day.

Sunlight came through the sliding glass door in his bedroom, and it landed on the open closet full of suits and dress shirts. My father had been--what I called--a Three Piece Suit Man. He was a man who could do anything, a man who was faultless and irresistibly charming. I wanted to go inside of that closet and take in his smell, wrapping myself up in the sleeves of Dad's shirts. This is what I used to do in his closet when I was a little girl. If I thought of the way he was when I was a little girl––even for a second––the thorny pain was so great, I had to make the thought go away. I couldn't bear to see him this way. And yet the day wore on, minute by minute.

  I had struggled with what to say to my father on this day, which was most certainly our last day together. I lived in small town called Arcata, about 300 miles north of San Francisco, so I had to plan out my trips to see him. I had talked with my therapist about the impending last visit. I was glad for the therapist, as I didn't have many people to turn to regarding the consuming knotty heartache of losing my father when I was just twenty-six.

  I was a stay-at-home mom of two little boys while most of my friends were either still in college or were busy launching out into life after graduating. People had peculiar reactions when I dared share that my father would soon die of AIDS. AIDS was still something you heard about happening to someone outside of your circle, to those who belonged to unfortunate statistics on the news. AIDS was still mostly associated with gay men. People didn't know what to say to me. Sometimes I simply said, "My dad is sick," but every now and again someone would ask, "With what?"

  Brother Ben was three years younger than me, and would only come to see Dad when I was in town. He had made it to the other side of a very turbulent adolescence, which had culminated in a terrible motorcycle accident that nearly took his life. He still struggled to manage his budding masculinity in the shadow of a provocative gay father. Being around Dad was still very difficult for him.

  My husband was well-intentioned. But he had taken to drinking pretty heavily after his own father had died of brain cancer two years before. He was so young––a father too soon––prematurely pushed into a life of working forty hours a week at a hardware store. Other than my therapist and my journal, I kept things inside most of the time. Sometimes, I'd startle in the night out of breath and panic-stricken right at the moment of waking. In that moment came a brief awareness that Dad was dying and my marriage was disintegrating. But then the next minute the feeling was gone, like when you wake from a bad dream and only remember a flash of the details.

On the last day with Dad, I struggled to remember the *tools* given to me by my therapist—stay in the moment, breathe, take time-outs, keep your truth. More than anything, I wanted so much to have a good talk with him. I wanted poignant words between us that might stick with me forever, lines out of a Meryl Streep movie. No points of conversation between us were completed. Most of his dialogue was fragmented in single sentences or words.

"Dancing––" he said, looking past me toward the sliding glass door to the patio and extending his thin arm so that it slid off the side of his bed. I took his cool hand.

"Dad, you were the best."

He closed his eyes while I described his days of dancing ballet in New York––the bright stage lights hot on his face and the exhilaration he must have felt while waiting behind the curtain. I talked of his days of practice and his sore, taped feet.

I recalled for him the two of us dancing at Ones Discotheque in Manhattan when I was barely twelve, and the way he lit up the dance floor. I could tell he was there under his eyelids by his fervent smile—that he could see the lights and hear the music and feel the pulse of the New Yorkers dialing him in.

I wondered how I could handle another minute of recalling the good times for my dying father. It seemed that the years had whipped by; I was disoriented and disorganized beside his bed. I held his bony, stiff hand and kept talking, tears running down my face. I felt the urgency to climb into the bed with him, as I did every night when I was a little girl. But I couldn't.

Time was an odd thing on that last day with Dad. A large silver-framed clock hung on his bedroom wall and I could hear it ticking. I wanted to remove it and put it into a closet or into another room. The ticking sound indicated to me too perfectly that time was my enemy. Moments were slipping away, running through my fingers like water. Not only was I helpless against the time that was flying forward, but I would never be able to do anything about the time that had already gone by--moments, hours, days and months that I had so longed for with this dying man lying there on a bed. Every tick of the clock sounded out one less moment I had left to get my Dad to see me as dear, cherished, and successful.

Somewhere between the hours of nine and ten o'clock, on the morning that I sat at Dad's bedside, I decided to use his big clock in a way that would be to my advantage. In the same way that it cut a sharp line between gone and next, I thought that the decisive hand might offer a sense of precise order, a way out of this disorienting predicament. Starting at 10 a.m. sharp, and on the hour thereafter--and I mean right on the dot--I momentarily left Dad's bedside to go to the little bar in the living room to pour myself another glass of vodka.

I wasn't sure if Anton noticed me dipping into the booze. Anton was Dad's partner of fourteen years. The two had assured Ben and I that Anton was somehow HIV-negative. Knowing this brought me some comfort, and I hoped they didn't just say it to spare us more heartache--I wasn't entirely sure it was true.

Anton had always been fun and silly and stylish to my brother Ben and I. We adored him. Maybe we related to him so easily in part because he was eighteen years younger than Dad--we were always joking, horsing around and having heart-to-hearts. As kids we loved spending time with his large gregarious Cuban family whenever we were in Queens.

On this visit Anton was sullen. His already pale skin was ashen against his thick black hair. I walked by him in the living room as I fetched my next glass of vodka, where he sat half-slumped on the grey couch, talking on the phone and smoking cigarettes much of that afternoon. He was speaking Spanish, probably to his relatives. The television was on non-stop. If I attempted to catch Anton's attention that day, he was immediately animated and calling me princess with a smile that was not his usual smile––big circles under his eyes.

Halfway through the afternoon, as I sat clutching my glass with both hands, Dad turned his head to me with one eye closed and one eye open and said weakly, "You could put a little gin in that glass."

"It's vodka, Dad."

"Vat's a girl," he slurred.

He turned to face the ceiling again, letting out a long breath and closing his eye with apparent relief, as if he had needed the comfort of knowing that his daughter had her own medicine against his illness. Dad startled me when shot his hand up in the air a few moments later. He appeared to be holding out an imaginary glass.

"*A martini...*" he whispered.

I cried quietly and felt myself go back in time as Dad slept. Time––once expendable––seemed no longer sequential or linear. I was disoriented by the fact that the past became more accessible the closer Dad came to death. The present was blurred by my memories–– memories that were steadily growing more and more vivid as Dad was moving further and further away.

As I sat beside his bed, I returned to when it all began––back to a little house in Long Island, a communal home in Vermont, and back to the turbulent flip-flopping between New York and California. I could see my little brother Benny so well, excitedly looking out a round airplane window as we flew between our polar-opposite parents––equal only in their eccentricities, and each on either side of the country.

Carle Place, New York--The Early Days

Our home was full of music and artistic creations in the early '70s--when I was between the ages for three and six, and we lived in a little house on a busy street in a New York hamlet called Carle Place. While Dad was at work, little brother Benny and I did elaborate art projects with our mother--plaster of paris and watercolor paint; melted crayons and clay. Mother baked bread and carved witch faces out of apples. She placed the apple witch faces on the kitchen windowsill, where they grew more and more wrinkly and realistic. She'd roll a giant spool of newsprint across the hardwood floor, so that there was one long piece that went from one end of the dining room to the other. We covered our bodies with paint, and slipped around on the paper, laughing about our butt prints.

Mother played The Beatles, Carole King and The Supremes on the record player, singing her heart out. Dad loved the theater. He took the family to see *Jesus Christ Superstar* on stage and also the Broadway production of *Hair*. He said his love for the theater started early--he had been dancing ballet since his early teens. He had even danced on stage in New York City and Connecticut as a young adult. He liked to brag about his *Broadway days*, showing off his newspaper clippings and old show bills.

Mother looked like Snow White. She was petite with a head full of thick, long, dark ringlet curls. She was blessed with high and round rose-colored cheeks, and perfect red lips that stood out against her fresh, fair complexion. She had a compelling quality about her; she was both lovable and tragic, and easy to want to save. She had been a writer long before she met Dad. Mother's poems were passionate, fatalistic, and hard to understand.

Mother was also an artist. Our house was full of her pastels and charcoals, and her watercolor and oil paintings. Something I always suspected about my mother: that she felt misunderstood all her life, and wondered if she perchance had been born into the wrong family, or was switched at birth. Perhaps Dad had felt this way about his family, too. Perhaps he wanted to save her in the same way that *he* wanted to be saved.

Dad was raised in Stanford, Connecticut, and was the middle child of three in a heavy-handed Irish Catholic family. He was the smallest, skinniest one of the siblings--and ultimately a fragile and lonely adolescent with a proclivity for ballet, which his father openly despised.

Dad's parents came from Ireland by boat in the 1930s, making a life for themselves in the United States. His father had been a brewer for Guinness, and both he and Dad's mother had a substantial drinking problem. Allegedly, our grandfather repeatedly beat all three kids on a regular basis. Dad said he spent his childhood wishing he could save his mother and little sister from the beatings, and that this was why he entered the field of social work--because he wanted to save people. I always thought that he must have wanted to save Mother early on.

I was not my dad's biological child. My biological father was a married man--a musician--with whom my mother had a passionate affair. Mother was alone and pregnant with me in 1968 when she met Dad, who adopted me after I was born.

Mother has told me the story of the night she and Dad met many times. She was going to a party with friends in the little town of Brattleboro, Vermont. It was summer and the evening was warm and balmy. She was twenty-five years old and pregnant, but not showing just yet. Someone at the party announced the anticipated arrival of a well-liked friend, Neil Arlen. He was twenty-eight––a handsome artistic and kind social worker from Connecticut––and a dancer who was both funny and charming. Mother has always said that she turned to her friend and announced confidently, "I am supposed to meet Neil Arlen."

Neil arrived in a VW Beetle. She said she *knew* it was him when the Beetle pulled up, when she watched him from the upper balcony as he got out of the car and put his keys in his jeans pocket. He was skinny with brown wispy hair to his shoulders. "He moved like a dancer," Mother said about the way he walked, "he was light-footed."

She says he was smiling with such a welcoming presence when he reached the top of the stairs.

"She was the most beautiful woman I had ever seen," Dad said on several occasions over the years about meeting Mother––a statement that grew increasingly odd to hear coming from him.

The two were not romantic right away, but rather close friends. Dad became her support and confidant, moving into her home and cooking her meals and rubbing her feet during the pregnancy. Soon they were a couple.

My parents married and Dad legally adopted me when I was a baby. Apparently, this was a happy time. We lived in a small rustic bathroom-less cottage in Townsend, Vermont. The two owned an antique shop in Brattleboro, and Dad tended bar at night. A little over two years later, Mother was pregnant with my brother, and we moved to Carle Place, New York.

Dad and I had slept beside each other since I was an infant, and I could not imagine sleeping any other way. Creeping into my parent's bedroom every night and sleeping next to him in Carle Place is one of my earliest and most comforting memories. I laid awake staring at the shadows on the wall until enough time had passed, before tip-toeing down the dark hall to my parent's bedroom. I stood at Dad's side of the bed, watching his silhouette in the sliver of light from the crack in the doorway. Every time, without so much as a grunt, he lifted the covers for me to get in. I climbed in the bed--wrapping my arms and legs tightly around his warm body--and burrowed my head into his chest. I loved to bury my face in Dad's soft nest of chest hair. Dad and I were one under the quilt in the twilight hours. Sleep came easy.

On the other side of the bed was my mother with her back turned to us. I didn't crave her like I craved my father. As an adult, Mother would give me pages of poems and passages that she had written around this time. In one poem, written in fevered and seemingly manic handwriting, she wrote of a deep loneliness at night. She described an empty spot where her husband ought to have been, a husband stolen by her daughter. I was disturbed by the poem and wished that she had never showed it to me.

My brother Ben was born in 1972, two days after I turned three. Unlike me, Benny was Dad's biological child.

Dad took me to our favorite diner on the day of Benny's birth. Though I was only three, I still remember our lunch that day.

"My princess, guess what?" Dad was bouncing up and down across the table at our large booth, making a drum-roll with his hands on the formica. He was beaming and smiling ear-to-ear, his face bright red. "You have a baby brother."

Baby brother. Baby brother. I practically climbed up on the table to get to him, my knees sticking to the red vinyl of the booth bench. I was picturing a bundled pink baby in a baby carriage. *Baby brother.*

Dad told me to order whatever I wanted, calling it a special day.

"Lady, do ya' got any hotdogs and baked beans?!" I yelled to the waitress, who was a couple tables over. I had never seen Dad laugh so hard. We joked about my diner order for years, jabbing each other in the sides, and saying in a hillbilly accent, "Hey lady, do ya' got any hotdogs and baked beans?!"

Baby brother Ben. Little did I know, that squirming perfect little baby would come to mean the entire world to me.

My parents enrolled me in a kindergarten just up the street. Dad said that the teacher had commented that I was "gifted" with a high I.Q. I have fond memories of this school, where I did the usual things kids do at normal schools, like writing the alphabet on paper that came with lines, wearing a smock while painting at an easel, and playing on the monkey bars. I don't think I finished the year, as my next memory of school is of going to another school close by, something my parents called a free school.

"You're too smart for bells and desks. Kids need to be *free* to learn," Mother explained one morning at the breakfast nook table. I heard her talking to Dad about grades, using words like "rigid" and "uptight." As far as saying goodbye to the kindergarten class and the school, I only recall feeling sad about the crossing guard that stood by the stop sign, who smiled and gave me a warm hello every day.

The free school was held in a large house, with every room on the first floor being used for the school. Rich––with long, bushy hair past his shoulders–– and a hippie lady named Suzette were the founders, and they lived in the upstairs. Kids ran amok with no shoes, and often no clothes. Art supplies and half-finished projects lay on every surface. Music—mostly The Beatles—played in the background much of the time.

There were no traditional instructions or lessons at the free school. If I wanted to go outside, I went outside; if I wanted to eat, I ate. *Teachers* all went by first names and hung out in clusters together, talking and helping kids with art projects, woodworking, and rehearsals for plays without scripts.

Little brother Benny got to go to the free school too, even though he was only two. Like everything else at the free school, there seemed to be no rules about grades or ages. One kid was a teenager and did magic tricks for everyone; another kid wore diapers. But Benny was only there *sometimes*, when Mother brought him.

Mother spent a lot of time at the free school. I'd be playing in the tree fort up the hill or swinging on the big swing next to the house in the late morning and catch a glimpse of her--her green wool sweater or her long brown skirt with a gothic alphabet print. I'd spot her walking into the yard, through the grass, approaching the house. Mother fit into my free school with a snugness; she belonged to everyone there, but she mostly belonged to me. She rinsed paintbrushes and cleaned cuts. She danced to *The White Album* in the basement with the older kids, knowing all the lyrics.

The grown-ups at the free school seemed to just love my mother. Really, *everyone* loved her. I liked to watch her in the sun, sitting in the grass by the big swing set. Her curls caught the light in such a radiant way--all copper and caramel and molasses. I liked to watch the way people gravitated to her, intently listening to what she had to say. Just about everything she described had a mystical quality, sometimes talking so quietly that you had to get real close to hear her. She'd talk about past lives and souls and right brain and left brain. She was compassionate and gentle with bugs and animals and small children.

No one demonstrated how much one could love my mother more than Allen. Allen hung out at the free school a lot, even though he didn't have any kids. He was a quiet man, but kind and helpful--he pushed me on the swings a lot. He helped with projects and drove kids on school excursions in his little compact car. He was always asking me questions about my mother, like what was her favorite color, and what was her favorite song.

One time, Allen was driving a me a few other kids to the traveling carnival, when a song came on the radio that made him cry. It was that one by Charlie Rich, that went, "Hey, did you happen to see the most beautiful girl in the world?" He started singing along pretty loudly. At first, he was singing just fine; he knew all the lyrics. The next thing I knew, he was crying like a child would cry, but still singing. The words came out long and howling. He pulled over on the side of the road and removed his large black-framed glasses. He rubbed his eyes, and ran his hands through his thick messy black hair, wailing right there in the car, as he called out, "Katherine, Katherine," over and over. All of us kids stayed quiet, glancing at each other awkwardly. I was embarrassed--my face burning--feeling that this scene was all on account of me, because I was part of my mother. I could see Allen in the rearview mirror--his red face full of tears and snot, and his eyes looking all shrunken and beady without his coke-bottle glasses.

"Astrid, I don't think your mother knows how much I love her," he blubbered, catching my eyes in the rearview mirror.

"Yes she does," I confirmed like it was a good idea.

Allen turned around and shot me a squinty look. I immediately regretted saying this. My mother had told me about--what she called--"silly love poems" she was receiving from Allen. She told me not to pay any attention if he carried on about her, that it was no big deal. I could tell that she felt sorry for him; she hugged him a lot.

The first thing that started to go wrong in our little happy family was that something was changing about Mother--she started a food co-op in our basement, went vegetarian, and stopped buying milk. These things we sort of handled, but when she announced that she hated TV, we got a little worried.

One evening, as Dad and I sat watching *The Partridge Family* in the front room, she poured a whole pitcher of water down the back of the TV set.

"What the hell!?" Dad yelled as he jumped up off the couch.

Her expression was blank and unchanging as she slowly turned her back to us and walked away with the empty pitcher swaying at her hip, leaving a trail of small water drops on the hardwood floor. Sparks and hisses flew from the dying television, but she just continued walking calmly out of the room and down the hall as if she had just shot an injured animal in the head.

Mother took off a lot by herself--usually to Pennsylvania or Vermont in our rusty brown clunker--leaving for days at a time. Every now and again, she brought Benny and I along with her.

"We're going on a trip to Vermont without your father," Mother said one morning without warning. She rallied me and Benny into the car for the three or so hour drive. On a trip with Dad, I got the sense that the grown-ups knew what was next. And I had his voice and his soft forearm and his chest. Mother's trips were circus-like, with surprises and unpredictable acts.

As we drove along a rural road, a pickup truck pulled in front of us with a dead buck strapped to the back. His limp body was tied tight with a thick rope--his eyes fixed and wide open--and his neck was slack with the weight of his enormous antlers. Mother pulled over to the side of the road like one would pull over to vomit, like a detour of physical necessity--urgent and without choice. She dropped her forehead to the steering wheel and began to sob, her shoulders heaving in rhythm with her wailing.

"*Why, why, why--*" she cried, the sound of her voice muffled by her hands, and by the dark curls that covered her face. Who was she asking?

"Mommy what's wrong?" Benny asked, standing up in the backseat and leaning over to touch her shoulder.

I knew she wouldn't answer. It wasn't that she didn't love us, she was just too sad. I knew it was best to be quiet and wait it out. It felt like a long time that we stayed on the side of that dark country road listening to our mother's mournful weeping.

It seemed that I might have been able to catch her sadness with my little hands, except Mother's sad sounds left her and disintegrated like our foggy breath in that cold car. Her gloom was a shroud of fog or mist or smoke that I swiped at over and over, the vapors translucent through the spaces between my fingers. Wishing I could chase away or capture my mother's sadness was like in a dream, and it wasn't the first time I'd had this dream. I knew there were demons inside of her––I had seen them before. Mother's demons could not be caught or chased away; I was insignificant against them. She was in a world of her own, with her own rules and her own tragedies. My mother was so far away and all alone, even though I was right there behind her in the backseat.

The other thing that started to seem off in our family was that Dad had begun slipping out of the house more than he used to. Only, his disappearing acts were much shorter than Mother's––he'd usually only be gone for an hour or two. His seeming urge to leave the house started with his purchase of a big red '60s Buick convertible.

"I don't see why we have to have that thing," Mother complained about the Buick from the front porch, her hands on her hips, "It's too big."

I did think that convertible looked like a giant boat. Dad took every chance he got to ride off in the Buick; he seemed to want to escape. He was my very favorite person in the world, so I tried to tag along whenever he'd allow it––these were stolen moments I relished. Sometimes, our stolen moments were in the guise of a trip to the grocery store for milk or to the hardware store for a tube of wood glue.

"Let's keep going, princess, shall we?" he'd say as he lit a Kool cigarette from behind the big steering wheel after taking the convertible top off. The rest of the world disappeared when Dad took me away for a ride. He turned up the radio so loud, it drowned out the motor, the traffic and the wind whirling through the open car. Blurry trails of Long Island swished past as we wiggled our bodies in the seat and sang out hearts out to "Afternoon Delight," and "Rubberband Man," and "Kung Fu Fighting." I felt like I was flying––like I was hardly fixed to the car at all––with my hair whipping wildly in my face. I was so small in that big white vinyl bench seat. I'd curl into Dad's lap as much as I could, wrapping my hands around his right arm. I took in his smells––cigarettes and musky armpit odor mixed with soap, cologne and department store.

Of all the songs Dad liked to sing in the car, the one he seemed to especially love was "Seasons In The Sun," by Terry Jacks. He listened to the song on the record player at home, too. Dad's Terry Jacks record went along with his America and Glen Campbell records because he played one or all three when he was in a serious, quiet mood. Just like with "Seasons In the Sun," I thought the America and Glen Campbell lyrics were strange––about a horse with no name, alligator lizards and a man who called himself a lineman. Why did Dad like this music? It wasn't like the music we played together. These records were old and more like rock-and-roll and reminded me that Dad had a life before I was born. There was a part of him that I'd never get.

I watched Dad's face intently when he sang along to that Terry Jacks song in the car. He knew all the lyrics––about dying and birds singing. I felt uneasy and tried to figure out what the song really meant. Just *why* did Dad love it so much? He looked straight ahead at the road, one hand on the big steering wheel and the other bringing his cigarette to his mouth in between verses. The dark lyrics about death to the cheerful tune gave me an eerie, distrustful feeling, like things weren't really what they seemed, and like there was something I wasn't catching onto. I didn't know whether I should be happy or scared when I heard that song.

Back to Vermont

We were six and three in 1975, when our parents decided they didn't want to live together anymore. Mother took Benny and I to Vermont straightaway when she left Dad, to live with her new boyfriend named Clark. Clark was only nineteen, or so Dad said. This was most likely an exaggeration, but probably only by a few years. I wondered how she knew this man so well, well enough to pack up and take us to live with him. Allegedly, Mother had been having an affair with Clark, driving to Vermont to visit him toward the end of her marriage with Dad.

Clark was tall with long brown hair that he wore in a ponytail. I liked him right away because he seemed more like a kid than a grown-up, always laughing when I was silly, and wanting to play outside. He sang and played guitar and kept his red cottage warm with a wood stove, which never seemed to burn out.

Our introduction to Clark was presented like a fun surprise, as if to say "taaa daaa!" Mother was flying high and rapturous over her new boyfriend and over moving into his little cottage––and so I was, too. At least I thought I was, but I couldn't quite tell for sure. Deep down it seemed there was something in the happiness and excitement that I wasn't fully understanding.

I believed this new life to be a little vacation, a brief time that would surely come to an end. As an extension of my mother, I blended into her landscape without even trying. I loved to see her happy––she made her whims seductive and contagious, able to convince just about anyone around her that her fun was everyone's fun.

If you knew her—if you *really* knew her—you wanted to keep her from her dark moods. At six-years-old I knew this. So Vermont was an adventure.

In the background of everything though, was an ache for Dad and my house in Carle Place. I missed Dad so much I felt sick. I was used to cuddling up to him when I was scared and now I was scared because he wasn't there. I cried quietly at night, thinking about Dad's voice and soft arms and about my cat Henry's smooth yellow fur. I tried my darndest to accept Mother's affections toward Clark, this instantaneous replacement of my beloved father. It seemed that the kissing and holding hands and everything else that goes along with being a couple must be easily interchangeable from one man to the next.

Clark's one-room cottage was on the outskirts of a town called Newfane, in the secluded Vermont countryside, apart from neighbors and away from paved roads. We came to live with him just as winter was turning into spring. We spent the afternoons and evenings going on walks with Mother and Clark. The countryside was ripe with blooming wildflowers, and barren trees were sprouting green leaves and blossoms. Insects were coming out of their nests and underground burrows. Mother and Clark lifted my shirt after romps in the outdoors to brush off the large ants that had crawled up my legs to my back. I spent hours catching grasshoppers and salamanders, making them homes out of old boxes or rocks, and letting them scurry through my fingers and up my arms.

We walked across old covered bridges, the cracked planks under our feet spaced apart so that we could see the river or creek below. Other times we walked deep into the woods, tramping through the thicket with burrs attaching to our clothes, toddler Benny clumsily and tiredly pulled along, his little sweaty fingers slipping from my palm.

Eileen was Mother's new good friend in Vermont--a free-spirited woman with long stringy brown hair and a pretty face. The best thing about Eileen was that she had three daughters close to my age. She and Mother spent hours listening to Jimmy Cliff and Cat Stevens at Judy's house while us kids played. I loved playing with the sisters in their attic. I had to climb up a rickety pull-down ladder to get to the big roomy attic where they slept and where they kept their many dolls with doll outfits. We'd play house up there––Benny was always either the baby or the husband––while our mothers laughed and danced and smoked pot downstairs.

At first, I seemed to be taking a break from school––then I was going some of the time. Mother started occasionally sending me to the school place that the sisters attended, keeping Benny home with her. There was a nice play yard and a teacher sort of person who I barely remember, other than that she was very kind. What stayed with me the most was a circle time outside in the grass one afternoon. I was sitting cross-legged, wearing a dress with no underpants. The teacher walked over to me and said in a hushed voice that I really ought to wear underpants to school and won't I please close my legs. This was embarrassing to me, mostly because I hadn't known there was a rule about wearing underpants to school, and I could tell by her concerned tone that this was something *everyone* knew.

In a few months, Mother moved us out of Clark's cottage and into a communal home called the Fortmack House. I have no recollection of packing things up or of any big fights between Mother and Clark; I don't remember a goodbye scene. The only thing I recall about leaving Clark behind is of driving out to his cottage in late fall with Mother and her friend after we had already moved out. I didn't know why we were going there. Mother and her friend were all fired up and saying nasty things about Clark, so I got the feeling it wasn't good.

All the leaves on the trees were red and orange when we drove back out to Clark's cottage. Clark was not home and we were standing outside in the cold--there was a sting of crisp wind that hit my cheeks and lips. Would we wait for Clark to get home to say hello? Benny was squatting in the dirt, whining about being hungry. Mother and her friend were cheering and laughing and saying to each other that Clark was a motherfucker and an asshole. The next thing I knew, Mother hoisted a big log up over her head and drove it through the front window, glass shattering to the ground and inside the cottage. My stomach sank and my mouth went dry. I wanted to get away before Clark returned. We did get out of there lickety-split, Mother and her friend cheering in the front seat. As we drove away, I wondered if I would get in trouble for the broken window.

I cried quietly at night, even though I had *both* Benny and Mother in the same bed with me at the Fortmack House. The nighttime was when I thought of Dad the most--his voice and soft arms and my cat Henry's yellow fur. Having moved to house number two in Vermont, I was afraid we might *never* return to him.

Mother had started out energetic and jubilant over her new life in the country. She taught me how to make angels in the snow after the first big winter storm hit. I lay next to her in the powdery snow facing the big white sky, snowflakes on her lips and eyelashes--her cheeks crimson--as she smiled at me sideways. We made clouds in the air with our laughter as we waved our arms and legs to form wings. Could there ever be a more enchanting mother? I was certain we'd fly away--swirling from drift to drift--me and my angel snow mother.

However, Mother appeared unable to leave the daybed in the front room shortly after winter began. Maybe her desire to lie under the covers had been developing over time, but I blamed it on one single afternoon. I thought she was just too cold.

It was snowing on the afternoon that I blamed for Mother's chill. Mother--who loved to walk in the snow--led me and Benny and a group of the Fortmack adults into the snowy woods for a long walk. I pulled along three-year-old Benny as we followed behind. Mother suddenly stopped and told everyone to close their eyes and listen to the sound of the river a little way off.

"Let's go," she whispered.

We all marched ahead--Mother leading the way--our boots making crunching sounds on the fresh powder as we brushed past snow-covered bush and branches and knocked down sharp icicles. My feet and ears ached; I bit my mittens to wake my numb fingers. As we walked, I could hear the burble of the river growing louder. Benny was being a good sport, with frozen snot running down to his top lip.

When we got to the river, I immediately noticed that the banks had frozen, while the center still flowed fast. Underneath the clear ice lay mucky earth, brown leaves and rock. I pressed my boot to the ice, making just a crack, but not going all the way through. Suddenly, I heard my mother howling.

"Wheeeeeeeeeeew!!" she hollered. I turned to see her rip her coat off and throw herself—boots and all—into the icy river. She went in with a crash, ice breaking like glass under her boots, her body hitting the rush of freezing water. My body hurt to watch. I felt an uneasy pressure to laugh or take part, as her screams were the kind a person lets out when they've been sprayed with the garden hose—playful, shocked, delighted, childlike. But I wasn't getting it. *Why is she doing this?* I wondered. My mother was in ice and so far from home. Benny jumped up and down and clapped, heading toward the edge, seemingly wanting to join her. Someone grabbed his arm.

"Katherine, *no*..." the adults begged. Even these groovy Fortmack settlers knew that *this* was nuts. Her apparent glee had already stopped before she got out, when she was wading in the icy water, looking at the bank with faraway eyes like she didn't know how to get there. "Grab onto my arm!" a man called out.

It seemed that my mother had been beguiled by that icy river. When she got out--all rigid and stuck--she looked past me and Benny. All her liveliness and sparkle seemed to have been drained out. I watched in silence as the fretful grown-ups fawned over her, biting my lip so I wouldn't cry. Benny ran over and grabbed onto her wet leg, saying "Mommy?"

As we made our way home, our mother's snow pants grew stiff with ice. The walk was probably only fifteen minutes, but it felt like an eternity. Her teeth chattered and her lips were blue and her hair hardened like a stiff sheet around her hat. At the house, in front of the wood stove, the adults helped Mother peel off her hardened clothing, her whole body shaking. They ran their hands across her bright red flesh and blew on her palms while one of them drew a hot bath. I was frightened by the expression in her eyes, which was serious and faraway.

Mother was in the bath for an eternity. I figured it must be taking a long time for her to thaw. After the bath, she went to the small daybed in the front of the house and slept. She lay on the day bed for days. Benny and I stood on chairs in the kitchen, assisting with the grinder and juicer and helping to wash vegetables, as other adults pitched in to care for us.

Over and over, I visited my sleeping mother, who lay covered in thick down quilts. I put my head on her chest, playing with the curls of her hair and tracing my fingers around the various patterns on her quilts. Sometimes, I just watched her, wondering what she was dreaming and how enticing this long sleep must be. Would Mother ever wake up? I wanted her so badly. I wished that she had never jumped into the icy river. She had gotten too chilled that day. I worried my mother was terribly ill. I worried my mother might die.

One snowy gray afternoon, while Mother lay on the daybed, Dad pulled up the drive of the Fortmack house in a large dark green clunker he had bought. Watching from the window, I didn't know it was him until I saw him step out of the car.

"Daddy!" I screamed, "It's Daddy! It's Daddy!"

It seemed like a dream that Dad showed up. Benny and I ran out the front door and through the snow to get to him--with no jackets--jumping into his arms and hanging on him like baby monkeys.

When we came back inside, I figured to get our things, Mother walked slowly with her head down. She rose so infrequently during her sleepy sad time, that it was often a shock to see her upright. Not as much because she was up, but because she didn't look like herself—her hair was all matted and her back bent over like an old lady. She was gathering our things and handing them to Dad with tears rolling down her cheeks. They didn't say much to each other. The other Fortmack residents must have stayed away from this scene because I don't recall any of them being present.

After a pawing, sobbing goodbye from Mother, we piled into the vast backseat of Dad's new car--a Plymouth Fury. Relief filled every part of me that had hollowed from worry and wanting. I imagined returning to the house in Carle Place, back to my cat Henry, back to my room and yard--the breakfast nook table. We were with Dad. Everything was going to be okay.

Dad got into the driver's side and immediately turned around to face us.

"Kids, first things first."

"What's first? What, what?" We were bouncing up and down.

"Let's get you some *real* food ASAP."

"Real food" meant junk food. We cheered in the back seat.

We stopped at the first possible burger joint and scarfed down burgers, fries, and Cokes. It was the first meat we'd had in a long while. My whole body felt warm. Having Dad show up in his Plymouth Fury to fetch us had me in a state of euphoria. I was drunk with the junk food and with the fact that I was with my dad in the flesh. We were going back to Carle Place.

Hempstead, New York

I was turning seven. One of my top front teeth was hanging by a thread. I played with the raw gums underneath, sticking my tongue under the wiggly tooth to feel the sprout of a new tooth pushing through. I was watching TV in the Carle Place living room with my dad, curled up in his lap on the antique white wicker couch, rubbing the hairless underside of his forearm.

"Just as soon as you lose those first couple teeth," Dad announced, "I'm taking you to a modeling agency."

"You see her?" Dad pointed to the girl in the toothpaste commercial, not moving his eyes from the television. "It looks easy, but she had to work her hind end off to get there."

He said this modeling enterprise could not be carried out until my baby teeth were gone, that I'd have my *true smile* after I lost my teeth, and we'd see just how much it was going to be worth. He asked if I was ready for this leap, as it was going to take a lot of hard work and dedication.

"Can I be in a movie?" I asked, bouncing on his lap.

Truthfully, I was afraid of losing my tooth. Not only was part of me falling off, but it looked like I was going to be a new kind of me, even though I had only just turned seven.

"Let's aim for Miss America," he said excitedly, rubbing his nose to my nose, "or at least the best damn stewardess in the sky. You're the most beautiful girl in the world, princess. Get used to it."

He said I'd better watch it because boys might start wanting to jump my bones. Dad liked to use that expression, which always made me think of boys jumping out of nowhere, rattling my arm and leg bones like I was a Halloween skeleton.

    A few days later, when the tooth finally fell out, Dad took me to the five and dime in the Fury. On the way there he talked it up about how I'd be the next Farrah Fawcett. I knew Farrah Fawcett from watching *The Six Million Dollar Man* with Dad, and it was hard to imagine that I might look like her—she was so tall and sophisticated and wearing lots of makeup.

    "Now *that's* what you call a sex symbol, princess," Dad had explained, pointing at Farrah on the television. "Jesus H., can we say *tits*, people?" (Dad loved to put the word *people* at the end of his pronouncements, like a question, or like he was taking a vote.)

    We stayed in the car for a few minutes when we pulled into the parking lot of the five and dime while Dad smoked the rest of his Kool.

    "I want to remember this forever," he said as he looked down at me and held my chin between his thumb and forefinger.

    I held onto his big palm as we walked through the parking lot. He marched me through the entrance to the small photo booth there and ushered me inside.

    "Smile big to show off that missing tooth, princess!" he called out, letting the heavy velvet curtain fall closed. I took a seat on the small wooden bench inside. I was alone in that booth, my reflection faint in the dark glass.

    Poof! Flash! went the snapshot camera and then again for the next pose and the next…

    I wondered if Mother was all right back in Vermont. I talked to her on the phone and she asked whether I was doing any art projects and how was the free school. I was afraid to tell her just how glad I was to be back at Carle Place; I was nervous that I'd let it slip out. I tried to not sound *too* happy. So I'd mention a scuffed knee or being stuck at the free school all the way till five, when Dad got off work. The truth was, I loved that we weren't sharing our house with a bunch of other people and that Benny and I had our own room and we each had our own bed (even though I still crept into my dad's bed every night); I loved that I knew when I was going to school and when I'd come home. I loved Dad's seemingly undivided attention and his fawning over my movie star looks.

In a few months, Mother came out of her sadness and moved back to New York—to a town called Hempstead, just a short drive from Carle Place. It was the spring of 1976—I was seven and Benny was four. Like at the Fortmack House, Mother lived with several adults in one big house. We lived with her about half the time, switching back and forth between her house and Dad's Carle Place house every couple days. The going from house to house was a new, somewhat topsy-turvy adjustment. It seemed I'd always forget some important item when I made the switch—my favorite doll, my favorite dress or shirt, my pen set, underpants.

Food was different at each house, which was hard to get used to. It was tough not to prefer Dad's when we got Cokes and potato chips and Skippy peanut butter. Dad always took us through the McDonald's drive-through as soon as he picked us up after not seeing us for a few days. Mother served brown rice and vegetables with miso paste, which I was always picking through to weed out the vegies I hated. Benny would sometimes sit in front of his rice and vegetable concoction and cry. The crying would occasionally turn into him throwing his fork and yelling, "I hate you!" Mother often attempted a timeout in this case, which usually required her staying with him and holding him down as he thrashed about. Sometimes, she'd just fix him some toast. I was aware of a tension in me, just under the surface—a fear that our mother would feel rejected or overwhelmed and become sad and tired.

We shared Mother's upstairs bedroom when we stayed with her. In her room were half-finished sketches and oil paintings, some etched on large drawing pads of quality paper, others on actual canvas fastened to large wooden frames. Tubes of oil paints, pastels and pieces of artist's charcoal lay scattered all over her multi-colored braided rug. Her room was like a kid's room in that, aside from the art supplies, she had many dolls that she had kept since her childhood. It seemed that—no matter where I stood in Mother's room—the dolls were staring at me with their realistic wide-open glass eyes.

It was in the Hempstead house that Mother met and fell in love with Tom Brown. Tom was twenty-two, with big blue eyes and long lashes, and wispy dark blonde hair to his shoulders. He had a sulky, mysterious quality about him. He didn't talk much to Benny and I at all, which made him hard to like. However, Mother seemed happier than I had seen her in a while, so I went along with Tom like he was a good idea.

Mother wrapped herself around Tom, curling up on his lap in the grass out in back of the house. In the living room, the two sat on the couch kissing with their arms around each other, laughing and smoking with the other grown-ups.

Adults came and went at the Hempstead house and kids came and went, too. I liked this busy in-and-out, social habitat. Everything changed, new experiences cropped up— life was never dull. It seemed like *all* the adults were heavy talkers, always in the living room or out back in the grass, smoking and drinking beer and getting all fired up about this and that.

Sometimes I got lucky, and the adults brought their kids. I liked to show them my *dares*, like eating ants, and licking earthworms, and climbing the backyard tree lickety-split. I was particularly proud of my creativity in the kitchen. I'd pull up a chair to the stove, turn on the burner until the little blue flame popped up, and fry myself a big chunk of butter. The butter melted and started to scald, hissing and spitting, giving me little burns on my arms and hands. I poured the greasy treat into a mug and ate it with a spoon, relishing the salty grease.

"Mmm, want some?" I'd say to the other kids, like it was the best treat, and we'd pass it around.

Benny seemed to need Mother more than ever— clinging to her skirt like a distressed kitten and throwing his body on the floor, kicking and screaming if she didn't pick him up or take him in her arms. I felt both annoyed and sorry for him, aware that he was neither a baby nor a full-fledged kid. Benny wasn't going to get all of Mother like he so wanted—he wasn't even going to get part of her. In no time at all, she announced that she and Tom were moving to this faraway place called San Francisco.

  We stayed in Carle Place with Dad when Mother left for San Francisco—it was still 1976. She sent us letters describing a big red bridge and a lovely park where bands played and people read their poetry out loud and sold their own art. I imagined my mother in this sunny place by the ocean, working on her paintings in the sand.

  Soon, she wrote that we would get to come stay with her in San Francisco. She had taken a job at a linen shop, and told me about how she had to fold napkins and tablecloths just right. Along with her letter, she sent me a delicate and feminine cloth napkin with tiny yellow flowers embroidered around the hem. I put it to my nose and tried to smell Mother in the fabric—imagining her picking it out and touching it with her hands. I ran my fingers over every surface of the white small and starchy square napkin, tracing the little embroidered yellow flowers. I rubbed it across my cheeks. I placed it under my pillow, and thought about visiting Mother in San Francisco as I lay in bed, trying to fall asleep.

  Benny and I had no clue of what was ahead—we didn't realize our life was about to change so dramatically. Mother's move from New York to San Francisco had thrust into motion a bicoastal back-and-forth of flying across the country between our parents.

San Francisco

  Benny and I flew on an airplane for the first time in 1977—he was five and I was eight. We left Dad to go stay with Mother in California, flying by ourselves. I had been terrified of the giant plane, and the roar of the engine, finding it seemingly impossible that something so big and made of metal could lift off into the sky. Despite these fears—and the fact that I knew I would miss Dad terribly—I was so excited about seeing this place called San Francisco.

Mother and Tom lived in a sunny Victorian apartment on Frederick Street, with giant front windows. Benny and I shared a bedroom with two slabs of foam on the floor for beds. Mother kept a white dove in the apartment that she had named Petey-Tap-Tap. She explained that Petey-Tap-Tap had suffered an injured wing, and that she had saved him from an untimely death. The dove was free to roam the apartment, hopping from one ledge to another and scurrying across the kitchen table, leaving droppings behind. Mother lovingly pet Petey, fed him breadcrumbs and talked to him as though he were one of the family. I woke in the mornings to his low, stuttering call.

Mother took us to Golden Gate Park, which was right across the street from her apartment on Frederick Street. We explored every single part of the park, including secret, less frequented nooks. We hugged redwoods and played with water bugs in the tiny streams off the path. We sipped tea at the Japanese Tea Garden when Mother had enough money for it, crunching on soy sauce crackers served in a tiny bowl. We watched the koi in a pond from a small wooden bridge, tourists clicking their cameras.

Mother had taken a job as a sandwich lady for a deli. She walked around the San Francisco business district selling sandwiches, hard-boiled eggs and fruit from a large basket she carried on her hip. I loved when she took me and Benny with her. We first stopped by the small deli in the morning to pick up the prepared items for her basket.

"You have to display everything just right, so people can see all your loot," Mother explained, as she prepared her basket before we set off to the streets. I loved to watch her as she bit her lip and narrowed her eyes while gingerly arranged the turkey, egg salad and roast beef sandwiches in such a way as to not hide the hardboiled eggs, cookies and fruit.

The streets were littered with people taking up space and going places fast. There were business people with suits and little, short Chinese ladies wearing tiny plastic shoes––and all kinds of people standing in clusters outside of stores and at bus stops. The trolleys rolled by on Market Street, ringing *clangity-clang*, with greasy metal brakes and gears grinding in a way that made my teeth hurt. People stood up on the trolleys, hanging onto the bars like monkeys as they whipped past.

Mother walked quickly in her weathered brown leather sandals, wearing her flowing floral skirt and thin white peasant top. She kept part of her full dark hair back, away from her face, which was naturally lovely without makeup. I thought she looked so beautiful––the way she smiled at everyone while flawlessly balancing the large wicker basket on one hip. I felt proud to walk beside her, sure that every passer-by wanted something out of her basket.

We took elevators up to offices where Mother had what she called *regulars*. Business men in suits and women in polyester slacks or skirts and white blouses lit up when they saw our mother, The Sandwich Lady.

"Steven always wants the tuna on rye," she said with a confident little smile, hiding the tuna sandwich between the pound cake and the ham and cheese, "so we just tuck it away a little so no one else snags it." She cleverly created a tetris of carefully stashed favorites in her basket, so that no one would ever be disappointed. I loved Mother's Sandwich Lady persona––she was nurturing, resourceful, careful, lovely, and kind. I clung to this memory of her for a long time, sometimes placing an imaginary basket of sandwiches on her hip whenever I was hit with doubt.

Mother and Tom said they referred to themselves as political activists. They'd sit in the sunny living room with other San Franciscans--their voices raised with purpose and drive--as they spoke of these things they called nuclear power, fascism, The Arms Race and inequities. The getting stoned was all part of the mumbo-jumbo, which was nothing new, as Mother and Tom had smoked pot at the Hempstead House in New York. The sentences came out with periods in the wrong spots when they were smoking a joint--their cheeks puffed out with a toke held in, smoke leaking out of their nostrils.

Bits and pieces stuck, fragmented and unconnected, yet all jumbled together in a grab bag of fight the power, don't mess with mother nature, women are just as powerful as men, nuclear power kills, prejudice is bad—Jimmy Carter this and Jimmy Carter that. Occasionally, I mixed up non-political current events from the grown-up's conversations with their political talk, such as Elvis's death that year (he was referred to as *The King*, and so I pondered if Jimmy Carter was a replacement). When we flew in from New York--much to our horror--we witnessed a dead man being pulled out of a van at the airport. "I think he was an illegal alien," Tom had remarked, and so I wondered why the man looked so human.

One sunny afternoon, Mother and Tom took us to Golden Gate Park for what they called a peace demonstration. Mother had been talking it up for several days--she was in an up mood.

"Let's paint our faces for this," Mother said excitedly at the kitchen table--a piece of sourdough toast in her hand--the morning of the peace demonstration, "we'll make more of an impact."

She tore through the small dresser in our bedroom, after announcing her other idea--for us to go dressed as clowns. She was looking for red clothes because we didn't have actual clown costumes.

"Are you *sure* people are dressing up for this?" Tom asked in the doorway of our room. Mother swung around and shot him an irritated look.

"Does it matter what *other* people are doing, Tommy?" she snapped. "Does it?"

"There will be plenty of people dressing up," she said under her breath, turning away from him to continue looking through our clothes.

I didn't care much whether or not others would be wearing costumes to the peace demonstration. Mother told us that the people in costume would be regarded as the most dedicated––I wanted to be one of *those* people.

Mother got out the Crayola paint set––the kind with the little color circles that comes in a plastic case with a skinny plastic paintbrush. Benny and I took turns sitting in front of her at the kitchen table as she carefully painted our faces. She used the little paintbrush at first, but soon realized her finger was more efficient. Next, Mother painted *her* face with bright, swirly designs.

"What are you, Mommy?" Benny asked.

"I am ME!" she beamed, pulling him into her arms.

Benny and I wore as much red as Mother could find, and she wore a colorful flowing dress. I felt exhilarated by our outward display of commitment––I couldn't wait to get to the park.

"Signs," Mother announced, holding up a finger, "We will need signs." She cut up a cardboard box and broke a yardstick in half, and then left it up to us to decide what message to write on our signs.

"You should have your own voice," she said.

In sloppy watercolor, I wrote one sentence: BABIES ARE BORN WITHOUT ARMS AND LEGS.

I had been horrified one night, when I heard the conversation among the grown-ups that went something like, "Fuck man, if you live anywhere around their nuclear testing zones, you've got your babies born without arms and legs…" I had sat there, mute in their smoky circle, pondering just how far off *we* were from one of these zones. I pictured helpless, pathetic babies, wailing to be picked up––their little bodies nothing but trunks (this was appalling. This was something to protest, for sure).

Benny's sign didn't have any words, only a simple painting he did with the Crayola set.

"Right on!" Mother cheered, bending down to squeeze him and kiss his cheek.

"We should have made these last night. We don't have time to wait for glue to dry," Mother said as she started attaching the broken pieces of yardsticks to the poster boards with a big roll of packing tape.

There were thousands of people in Golden Gate Park that day, or so it seemed. Heads turned our way when we approached the demonstration, and people stopped to look at our painted faces. Mother had been wrong about the countless costumed supporters. As far as I could tell, we were the only ones in costume.

"Told you," Tom immediately sneered.

"You guys are far out," complimented a smiling man who looked a lot like Santa Claus.

I couldn't help it––I gave Tom a satisfied grin with my nose in the air. But he looked away, not making eye contact, and seeming to pretend he didn't hear the man.

Benny and I held our signs above our heads as we walked into the crowd, each on either side of Mother. The park was scattered with pockets of what Mother called demonstrators, some with microphones and amps for open-mic discussion. There were wooden platforms for musicians who played just yards apart, their guitars and drums and vocalists intermingling and combining, while colorful people with long, flowing hair and gauzy clothes swayed their bodies to the sound. Clusters of barefoot people sat laughing and kissing and smoking joints on the grass or on blankets. Some people held signs like ours, while others quietly sat at booths with petitions to sign.

The familiar scent of marijuana wafted by and commingled with the smell of falafels and shish-kabobs. People sat on chairs or blankets selling their handmade jewelry, art and painted clothing. People noticed me and Benny, asking us about our signs and even snapping photos of us as we passed. My mother had made me a celebrity.

Mother walked away, saying that she would be back, leaving Benny and I to run around and play. I watched her and Tom quickly disappear into the thick crowd, feeling half-anxious and half-exhilarated to be left alone to our own devices at the peace demonstration. One lady gave us each a helium balloon, and then a man with a mean look on his face quickly popped Benny's with his lit cigarette. Benny started crying, so I grabbed his hand.

"Let's pretend this is another planet and we're invisible!" I said as I pulled him to run with me and dodge the adults.

We became bored with pretending to be invisible visiting aliens, and dizzy from the sun and the weaving in and out of bunches of sweaty, fanatical adults. We were hot and thirsty and tired, and wishing we had money for an ice cold soda. We found a dumpster in the shade and climbed on top. We sat there holding up our signs, our clown faces running down our faces a bit by this point. I got the idea to have our own little demonstration there on top of the dumpster.

"Do it like this," I instructed Benny, as I stood up and waved my sign above my head and shouted, "NO NUKES!"

Benny seemed to get a real kick out of being able to yell as loud as he pleased. He even took it up a notch by adding cuss words, screaming, "Fuck you nukes!" and "No more fucking asshole nuclear powers!"

That's when people started snapping our photo, which encouraged us to keep hamming it up as much as possible.

"Let's count how many people take our picture!" I said after about the fifth person stopped to take our photo. We lost count. I do not recall the exact number of people who photographed us that day, but I do remember that it was a lot.

Not only did many people take our picture--we were interviewed on top of that dumpster by a news or radio station.

"Tell me about babies being born without arms and legs," the reporter asked. She looked like the stewardesses on the T.W.A. airplane we had flown in on--dressed in a polyester suit, and the ends of her shoulder-length brown hair flawlessly curled under.

Somewhere, in someone's stack of old pictures--or maybe even in a journal or a book--there is a photo from 1977 of Benny and I as clowns, holding up our sloppy signs on top of a dumpster in Golden Gate Park. I would give a lot for that photo.

We left San Francisco and moved to Berkeley in the fall, into an older Victorian off San Pablo Avenue. This was—and still is—a bad part of town.

Everything was in boxes and we were doing load after load across the Bay Bridge in the van. Mother and Tom were passing a thermos of coffee back and forth, and playing their Jackson Browne tape. Mother was singing along, with her jeans rolled up to her knees and a red scarf tied tightly around her head, dark fluffs of hair sticking out of the sides.

When we pulled up to the white Victorian that afternoon, I immediately noticed the white lace cloth Mother had already placed over the three large bay windows. I sighed, looking at the steep row of stairs to the front door, thinking about how much stuff we had to carry.

"Look guys, your room!" Mother cheered, walking down the short hallway with a big box in her arms, clothes and stuffed animals spilling out. She dropped the box on the dark green shag carpet with a grunt. I ran my hands over the rough-textured wallpaper, which had a faded swirly yellow and green flower design, and was peeling in some spots. Mother quickly went to stacking blue and gray plastic milk crates, making a pseudo-bookshelf.

"Art supplies, books—" she was listing out loud, a little out of breath, as she adjusted the crates and started cramming our belongings inside, "…projects, collections, you name it."

Mother and Tom's bedroom was "The lion room." At least, that's what I called it, because it was dark and covered with wild orange paisley wallpaper that had actual velvet fuzz on the designs. Like Benny and I, they also had a piece of foam on the floor for their bed, brought over from the San Francisco apartment.

"The front room is a bedroom, but I'm making it the living room," Mother declared later that evening, as she placed her old braided rug on the front room floor, along with a bunch of over-sized pillows. I took immediate notice that the record player was placed in this room.

Mother enrolled us in a public school called Thousand Oaks, where I attended Mrs. Bent's second grade class. Thousand Oaks was *not* a free school. Up to this point, I had not yet gone to a regular kind of school, other than my brief stint of kindergarten in Carle Place. I tried to acclimate to the bells and the desks and the having to raise my hand. I liked the lunchroom because there was chocolate milk, and sometimes pudding. I struggled to keep up with the other students, who had mastered the fundamental scholastic building blocks prior to second grade, having attended public school regularly. Spelling was especially a challenge. Mrs. Bent read a list of words out loud in slow exaggerated annunciation, and I struggled to write them out on the small lined piece of paper on my desk.

Somehow, enrolling in the public school brought on a pining for Dad that was so deep, it hurt to think about him. Summer in San Francisco had been a vacation. When we moved to Berkeley and started a new school, I wanted to say, "Ok, times up. It's been nice, but let me go home now, please." I hadn't expected the move. What would happen next? At night, I lay in bed and thought of Dad.

I daydreamed a lot in my classroom, not taking the lessons too seriously. I was thinking about how we'd be leaving for New York before the end of the school year. Any friends I made would be left behind, a fact that seemed to linger in the back of my mind whenever I felt a friendship starting to blossom. I envied Benny, who got to be in the kindergarten class, which was *surely* easier and more fun than the second grade. Sometimes, we spotted each other on the playground at recess or at lunch and we'd come together and play on the bars or sit side-by-side on the outskirts of the grass. I liked being next to Benny in the schoolyard. We didn't have to say a word; we knew that the other one would stay put when everyone else––and everything––was changing.

  Benny and I did leave California. We flew from San Francisco to New York as 1977 was coming to an end, when it was about to be winter, with my eighth birthday right around the corner. We would be with Dad for the next six whole months. I have no recollection of being sad to leave the second grade classroom. Mrs. Bents announced that I was moving to New York, and had all my classmates make little handmade goodbye cards.

  The morning of the day we left for the airport, Mother cried silently as she knelt down beside me on my foam slab bed and handed me a small blue velvet pouch with a drawsting closure. I didn't want to acknowledge that she was crying—mostly because I didn't feel sad at all, rather I felt so much *joy* about leaving for Dad—so I kept my eyes from her as I opened the little pouch. I emptied four shiny stones onto the palm of my hand.

  "They are fire, water, earth and air," Mother explained, tears dripping off her chin. "Keep them with you."

  The stones were the colors red, blue, brown and white, and had the texture of smooth glass washed up on the beach. They sounded like my marbles, with a pleasing jangle when I rolled them together in my hands. I stashed the little blue velvet bag full of stones in the front pocket of my carry-on backpack.

  "Ma'am…excuse me, ma'am, you may not enter the

plane—" the rather severe-looking, makeup caked ticket-taker was warning.

I was nervous and embarrassed when Mother ignored the ticket-taker and pushed her way right on to the plane anyway.

"Too bad," she snapped with a heartbroken defiance, tears running down her face, "I'm not going to see my kids for six months." This was Mother's zealot persona, the one that came out when she brought us to the peace demonstration in San Francisco.

After Mother helped us find our seats—the clucking stewardess trailing behind her—Mother got on her knees right in the aisle, buried her face in my lap, and proceeded to sob out loud. I stroked her messy curls—embarrassed that everyone was staring, and ashamed that I wasn't crying too.

Normal in Centereach, New York

"I want you two to have a nice, normal life," Dad said proudly in the green Fury after he picked us up at JFK airport. I liked the sound of the word *normal*.

He had left Carle Place and moved to an upstairs one-bedroom apartment in Centereach, New York—a town on Long Island, about thirty miles from where we used to live in Carle Place. The apartment community had a private drive and young, newly planted trees, some in big planters and some with redwood chips at the base. There were pruned shrubs outside the doors and patios and a swimming pool in the middle of it all. Across from the apartment were dozens of evergreen trees, which gave the place a semi-rural appeal.

Dad was obviously proud of his choice. He said that it was a long commute to his work and to the free school where he had re-enrolled Benny and I, but it was worth the trouble for us to have a nice home with enough room to play. Just like Mother seemed happier than ever in San Francisco, it seemed that Dad had really found his niche in Centereach.

It was nighttime when we pulled up to the apartment for the first time. Winter was coming; my nose and hands stung in the cold. When Dad unlocked the front door, he bowed and stepped to the side to let us run up the carpeted stairs, saying, "Voila!" We ran passed him as he lugged our suitcases up the stairs. Right away, my yellow tabby Henry ran over to say hi. I picked him up and twirled him around in my arms, saying, "Henry! I'm back!"

Just like in Carle Place, Dad's home looked kept and clean, which made it seem spacious and palace-like, even though the dining area and the living room were one space. Shag carpet—in multiple shades of green—covered every inch of the apartment. I thought Dad's new place was classy and fancy because he had art hanging on the walls with actual frames, and a table with chairs that matched.

"People, people, go see your room," Dad ushered, pointing to the doorway of the only bedroom in the apartment. (His bed was a foldout sofa in the living room, which he converted back to a couch during the day.) We ran through the tiny hallway to the bedroom, where we found two twin beds a few feet apart with bona fide, matching blue and red striped bedspreads. Beside each bed was a bedside table and a talking alarm clock—Batman for Benny and Raggedy Ann for me. Things seemed pretty regular in Dad's new home—*normal*.

The school year was already half over. Dad started us up again at the free school we had attended when we lived in Carle Place, and I was overjoyed to be back with my old friends. The free school had moved from the location in an old house to an actual building in a town called Mineola, on Long Island, only a short distance from the old place. The school took up a few rooms in the otherwise office building. Occasionally, people in three-piece-suits and pleated business skirts entered our area to complain about the noise.

The free school philosophy was do what you want when you want—that had not changed. We continued without any formal education at all. There were no lessons and no instruction. Artwork and woodworking projects were scattered everywhere. The Beatles, Donovan and Cat Stevens were always on the turntable—along with the progressive, unprecedented record, *Free to Be...You and Me,* that was released in 1972.

Dad complained about the fact that we "aren't learning anything," as he put it, and he even threatened to switch our school, but we begged him not to. For a short while, he trotted down to the free school a few mornings a week to teach. I have to give it to Dad for making an attempt to give us kids some kind of academic training—he even whipped out a real live green chalkboard, writing out math problems with white chalk. I intently watched him from my spot on the floor like he was a star. I was half-embarrassed and half-awestruck as the other kids squirmed on the rug with blank eyes, picking their noses and talking to the kids next to them before ultimately walking away. Dad gave up.

Judy and Tim were the only "teachers"—both single parents with kids who attended the school. Allegedly, they were lovers, making out in closets and the back room, even though Judy had a live-in boyfriend for at least part of that year.

Judy's son, Justin was my best friend at the free school, though he could not relate to my preoccupation with R-rated movies and disco. I was a real tomboy around him. We made bike ramps and played cops and robbers and Spider Man. Justin had big chipmunk cheeks, and wispy, straight brown hair that went halfway down his back. He frequently wore girl things, such as multiple barrettes in his long hair, even though we mostly played so-called boyish games. These were the kind of little plastic barrettes that came in bright colors, shaped as baby duckies and rabbits and hearts. Other times, Justin wore about twenty little tiny ponytails randomly placed all over his head. He liked to try on my slinky white slip when I wore it to school, even though Dad said a slip was not meant to be worn as a dress, but rather *under* a dress.

Justin and I did many overnights at his family's apartment. His place felt familiar, as it reminded me of Mother. Their apartment was cluttered with artwork, instruments, and broken toys. Like my mother, his mom dressed in flowing skirts and scruffy jeans and wore her hair down, which was just like Mother's hair, only it was orange. She smoked pot and had a boyfriend with long dark hair who played guitar in a band. Sometimes during overnights, I'd lay in bed listening to Justin's mother laughing with her boyfriend, smelling the pot smoke from their living room.

I felt a little like I was with my mother when I was around Justin's mother. Did Dad notice the similarities? I could see none of the female qualities in my mother that Dad seemed to want in me. She was not sophisticated or theatrical or into fashion; she was not trying to turn heads while saying no in a cocky way. I imagined her soft skin and her head of wild curls; being in her arms and trying to see my face in the tiny mirrors sewn on her over-sized shirt. Being at Justin's apartment was the closest I came to my mother because I missed her more there than at any other place.

We went camping in Maine and on Fire Island with the free school that year. I loved Maine for the streams and the tadpoles and the frogs, but Fire Island was my favorite––lined with reeds, cheery trees and shadbush trees, it was a magical place with stretches of boardwalks that led to the beaches and the small beach communities. I had fond memories there, having visited a few times with my parents when they were still together. Fire Island was a vacation hotspot for New Yorkers; a place Dad came to frequent when we were away in California.

We hoped on the ferry, hauling our totes, backpacks, sleeping bags and tents, and set up camp as soon as we got there. I spent the full two days getting splinters on my bare feet as I ran wild through the Sunken Forest of Fire Island with boys Justin, Nate, and Daniel, exploring every maze of boardwalk, unaware of what led to what. We were secret agents, tribal children and scientific explorers. We became sunburned raw as we played in the gentle waves on the beach for hours––with or without the adults––our eyes stinging from the salt water.

We went through the tedious task of packing everything up when it was time to leave. Judy and Tim seemed tired and ready to get home, with weak one-word commands and answers.

"Come on, come on, we're gonna be late," Judy coaxed in a panic as we practically ran down the boardwalk to catch our ferry, schlepping our half-wrapped sleeping bags and our partially-zipped backpacks with belongings spilling out.

"Come on guys, hurry up," Tim also ushered as we tried to keep up.

"NOOOOO!" we heard Judy suddenly wail from up ahead and around the corner. It was in a horrible, blood-curdling pitch––you could probably hear it for miles.

We saw our ferry. It had left the dock and was sailing away in the distance.

"WAIT!" Judy yelled, dropping the large bags she was carrying. She tried to run after the ferry, waving her arms in the air. But it was to no avail; the ferry was long gone.

When we caught up with Judy, she was in a ball on the boardwalk, crying like a baby.

"*No, no, no,* please no. We're all out of food," she cried with her face in her hands. *What an adventure! Starving castaways!* was my first thought.

Benny squatted on the wooden planks right there, refusing to budge.

"I wanted to go home," he was complaining and starting to cry.

"Come on, Benny, we have to set up our camp again––it will be fun," Tim promised unconvincingly.

"No," Benny protested with his lip out.

Finally, it took both Judy and Tim to grab Benny up--one at each side of him--and get him to walk along with the group.
     Judy and Tim took some time gathering up enough change for the payphone by the dock to call all our parents. While Judy made the calls, we walked back to the campsite and tiredly set up our tents again. Next, Tim took a handful of us with him to ask strangers for food. He said he would have better luck if he had kids with him.
     "Look sad and hungry," he instructed.
     Justin and I and a few of the other kids walked with Tim to the wealthiest side of the Island--an affluent beachside community that looked a lot like Nantucket. Tim explained that this was where rich New Yorkers parked for summer weekends. The houses were architectural works of art--at least to me they were--set up high for spectacular views, with long stairways leading right to the sandy beach.
     Tim had a burly black beard and was wearing dirty cut-offs and sandals while sporting a huge shoulder-length head of wild, curly black hair. I knew that he was horribly out of place and that he would probably scare the hoity toity vacationers that lived there. Not to mention that we looked like urchin children--greasy, dirty, sunburned, and hardly wearing any clothes.
     We stood in back of Tim as he approached the large homes. It was an adventure to see what items we might get. The food given was different at every door--a can of vegetables, a box of crackers, a jar of peanut butter. The *same* was the look of the donator at every house. People with fresh haircuts, dressed in tucked in pastel-colored polo shirts or designer sundresses, appeared smug and shocked and--if we were lucky--seemingly sorry for us. One lady handed Tim some money.
     That night, we sat around our campfire eating an odd assortment of foods that didn't really belong together on the same plate--corn and tuna; crackers and peanut butter with beans. Tim and Judy quietly sat at the

fire looking morose. The miss-matched meal made the castaway experience even more exciting, and eating it with pleasure was a testament to our endurance as stranded island children.

We made it back home the following day, having survived our starving castaway experience unscathed, but I do not recall anything beyond our castaway meal.

Music was still a big deal with Dad—we listened to and danced to music constantly. He took me to a little music store in Centereach almost every Saturday to pick out a new 45 rpm record. I had a large collection of these smaller single-song records, with about a hundred little yellow plastic disks to insert in the center so they would play on the record player in the living room. The man behind the counter at the record store knew our names and would show me the Top 20 list each week. He offered suggestions, but I usually had my mind set already, with a dance routine in my head to go with it. I had many favorites—Fleetwood Mac, Queen, E.L.O. and Andy Gibb, the Bee Gees and Boston, among many others.

Dad's records were the larger 33 rpm kind called *albums,* which I also liked to listen to. His collection included Diana Ross and Donna Summer, George Harrison, Neil Diamond and—two of his all-time favorites—Dionne Warwick and Anne Murray. Benny's favorite of Dad's albums was Queen's *News of the World.* He liked to run around the living room singing "We will, we will ROCK YOU!" and raising his fists to the air to "We are the Champions" like a boxer or a famous weight lifter.

Dad had his own dance routines. He liked to play his Diana Ross album in the living room, moving his hips back and forth with his eyes closed. His dancing looked professionally choreographed, the way his feet moved so gracefully and flawlessly. He often stuck his right middle finger in his ear while singing so that he could better hear his voice, like Robin in the Bee Gee's. Sometimes he held a pretend microphone in one while listening to Diana Ross—running his other hand through his fine brown hair—singing about the "sweetest hangover" and hissing that he doesn't want a cure for *thisss*.

I loved the record with Donna Summer's "Love to Love You Baby," but I stopped asking Dad to play it. The song broke out into sexual moaning that sounded a lot like Mother's moans when she and Tom were in their bedroom with the door closed. Dad usually got really carried away—sometimes it was amusing, sometimes I thought he took it too far.

Aside from disco, Dad and I were big into Broadway. We played the *A Chorus Line* Soundtrack album over and over, singing every line of every song, and rehearsing the dance numbers. Sometimes, we put together an impromptu performance by standing at opposite ends of the room and taking turns singing lines, or we sang the lines together as a duet.

When Dad really got into it with the Broadway songs, he looked passed me as if I weren't in the room, seemingly drawn into the lyrics, as if they had deep personal meaning to him. He'd be lost in his dancing in the living room, wearing his tight designer jeans and white T-shirt, running his fingers slowly across his chest with his eyes closed––one hand on his hip. He got his whole body involved, turning his head with his chin cocked upward like a ballet dancer, and stretching his arms out with his fingers pointed elegantly. I loved to watch him do the *One* routine, growling, "One singular sensation, every little step she takes. One thrilling combination, every move that she makes––" He kicked just like a Rockette, with his leg high in the air and his calf rotated, his toe pointed, and hips turned just right. I thought he was such a star––so talented and handsome, and so sexy. *No girl has a dad like mine.*

Dad often got sad when talking about how he loved to dance when he was growing up. His passion to learn ballet had sent his father spouting off cruel and unsupportive comments like "fairy" and "sissy." I knew he was singing about his father when he went "on stage" in the living room and sang with tears running down his face.

The Arlens

Aside from going to Fire Island and Maine with the free school, Benny and I also spent some time away when Dad would take us to visit his mother in Stamford, Connecticut. Sometimes we only stayed for just a brief visit, other times Dad left us there with her for up to a week. We dreaded our time with Grandma Arlen because we didn't get to do fun things, and we thought she was mean and grumpy. I wondered why Dad left us with her when he seemed to dislike her so much. I felt betrayed when he'd drive away.

Our grandmother had lived a very rough life. She immigrated to America from Ireland with her parents and many siblings when she was a girl (Grandma was the oldest). Her mother became ill and died when Grandma was still very young, leaving her to be—as Dad called it—the woman of the house. Her father beat her until she moved out to marry a man who also beat her.

Dad said that Grandma Arlen's home had not changed since he was a boy in the '40s and '50s. Above the dining room table hung a large painting of Jesus.

"I had to look at that thing every time I ate, people. It made me positively want to vomit," Dad would joke with his hand on his cheek, feigning nausea and shaking his head.

Grandma Arlen, sat all day on her old brown La-Z-Boy chair in front of the TV, drinking weak coffee and chain-smoking cigarettes. She looked and dressed like an old lady, though she was really only in her sixties. According to Dad, she drank a lot of booze in secret, putting some into her coffee and into other drinking receptacles no one would notice. In her thick Irish accent, she snapped at us gruffly about her dissatisfactions, and there were many of them.

She used expressions and vocabulary seemingly reserved just for grandmothers. For instance, pants or jeans were dungarees. Underwear were britches and my shirt was not a shirt, but a blouse. There was no such thing as a bra, only a brassiere. Our sneakers were always Keds, no matter the brand.

If we had to venture out in the rain, Grandma Arlen fastened a tight see-through plastic bonnet around her head that tied under her chin. She totted a wire carriage along for wheeling her groceries home (she didn't drive, never did). Her entire basement was full of canned foods; Dad told me some cans were dated from the 1950s.

Anyone who was not family was referred to by last name, even friends. She had an array of funny little Irish sayings and gestures. If you sneezed, she said "God bless you" on the first sneeze, "God save you" on the second sneeze, but if you sneezed a third time, she threw her hands up and snarled, "Ah, the devil'l take ya," which sent me to faking that third sneeze just to hear her say it.

Dad was the middle child of three. His younger sister was a nun who had left the convent. Whether she had left on her own or was booted out, I never knew for certain. Dad said she had problems that he referred to as mental problems. She had been Sister Ruth, but had changed her name to Madgie. Dad told me once that his sister "had all of her female parts ripped out by her doctor," stating that she hated these parts of herself. I wondered how she ever went pee. Later, I realized that Dad must have been referring to a hysterectomy.

Dad's older brother Robert was tough, macho, and rich. He lived close to Grandma with his wife and three kids. I loved visiting him because I idolized my older cousin Debby and because they had a swimming pool.

Dad said that Uncle Robert had been what he called a greaser in the fifties, carrying a switchblade and driving crazy in his car. According to Dad, Uncle Robert had spotted our petite, blonde Aunt Beth behind the counter at the movie theater and said, "I'm gonna marry that girl," and then he "knocked her up in no time flat." Dad explained that *he knocked her up* meant that he got her pregnant.

Uncle Robert was loud and gregarious and drank a lot of booze. There was an edge about him that made me feel a little nervous, and I didn't understand my own mannerisms— I giggled a lot but I had no idea what was making me laugh. I couldn't pin down where he was coming from or what he'd do next. He pinched my cheeks hard and tickled me until it hurt or he grabbed me up in his arms without warning. I liked my uncle's seemingly playful roughhousing, but was simultaneously scared of him. Maybe I was a little scared because Dad had shared with me that his brother was sometimes pretty mean to my cousins and to Aunt Beth. According to Dad, Uncle Robert had threatened to kill Aunt Beth a few times—he said he had even put a gun right to her head once when he was drunk, and that she had cried and pleaded for him to stop.

Grandma Arlen had been attending the same Catholic Church since Dad was a little boy. The church was only a few blocks away, and she took us with her if we happened to be visiting on a Sunday.

"How are you doing today Mrs. Arlen?" well-dressed people greeted her when we walked up the steps, "I see your grandchildren are visiting."

I got the feeling that Grandma's church was like an elite club. Once inside, the sermon seemed endless. It seemed quite possible that the enthusiastic, red-faced vigor expressed by the older priest might very well cause him to collapse at any moment. With furrowed brow and sweaty face, he professed of love and devotion and sin with the appearance that he was about to spank a bare bottom.

I kept my eyes on the many stained glass windows during the long service. I enjoyed the way the sun illuminated the colors of the artistic portrayals of Jesus with his staff and of Mary's sweet face, her eyes to her lap. The colors changed as the morning wore on--shifting the yellows, blues and reds to different pews--moving from the front to the back.

In her gruff Irish accent, Grandma Arlen snapped that we were *not* allowed to join in communion because our parents had not baptized us. She complained that this was an atrocity and how God keeps records. I wished that I could join in. Not because I was afraid of going to hell, but because I was usually hungry--and was definitely bored--and the small round white wafer looked tasty. I wondered whether that wafer was sweet, crunchy or salty. I imagined it sticking to the roof of my mouth and having to use my tongue to soften the gluey texture.

I was sure that everyone in the church was noticing that Benny and I were not joining in communion. I watched longingly as the people stood silently in line, shuffling slowly while looking at their feet. These people were part of a club of which Jesus was the most honorary member. I was confused by my desire to be part of something that did not appear very fun. There was clearly something I was missing.

Occasionally, if I pissed Grandma Arlen off--often times, I could not put my finger on exactly *what* I had done--she reminded me that Dad adopted me, and that I was not her actual kin.

"Ye know yer' not my flesh n' blood now," she'd growl--a jab which definitely stung. It was the fact that she had dared to hit me so far below the belt that hurt me, not the truth of it. It never bothered me that I was adopted by my father, especially since I had known this fact for as long as I could remember.

Grandma Arlen also spanked us on the regular--with a wooden spoon, even. Once she caught me swearing in the kitchen and pulled out a big knife, and began waving it in front of me, and telling me she'd cut my tongue off if I swore again.

"I'll come back as a ghost after I die and haunt ye, you'll see," she warned, unsmiling, which scared me to death.

Grandma Arlen frowned on a dirty child, and saw to it that her grandkids were squeaky clean. She insisted that Benny and I bathe in the bathtub together in the upstairs bathroom, even though we no longer bathed together at this point. She also insisted on washing us herself, which felt very uncomfortable. (I always figured she had us bathe together because she was thrifty about every single thing she did. She would bark that we were to use only *one* square of toilet paper when we went to the bathroom.)

"I'll not have dirty grankids," she complained, "come on now, git in the tub."

We got to spend a little time in the bath water while Grandma Arlen sat on the toilet (lid down) and smoked a cigarette. Sometimes, she'd hang wet clothes on the clothesline, which was attached to the bathroom window, and went all the way down to the yard, with a pully contraption for her to fetch the clothes when they were dry.

She always wore one of her stained cotton aprons for the bath, stuffing the giant pockets with her box of cigarettes and lighter, and many clothespins. She stood beside the tub and got ready to clean us by dipping the washcloth in the water and rubbing it aggressively with a bar of Ivory soap. We dreaded the way she then scrubbed our skin so forcibly, until our skin stung––always including our privates––which felt very strange and embarrassing, given our ages.

One time, Dad called during a one-week stay with Grandma Arlen. I stood a few feet from the dining room table, where Grandma sat talking to him, pretending to be interested in the Fisher Price Hot Wheels garage with Benny. My blood boiled as I listened to her painting a rosy picture of our visit.

"Yer father wants to speak to ye, Astrid," she called out to me in an irritated tone, turning around, thinking I was further away. I tried to hide my glee, as she stared me down, holding the phone close to her bosom so that I had to awkwardly step closer to take it from her.

"Princess, tell me the truth," Dad said in his most earnest voice on the other end, "Do you want me to come pick you up now, or do you want to stay the rest of the week?"

I gripped the receiver, biting my lip, and glanced at Grandma Arlen, who continued to stare me down. She was giving me the look of warning; I *knew* I was going to get it if I told Dad to come get me. My heart was racing. I decided in that moment that I would take whatever she had in store for me--it was worth it.

"I want you to come get us. Can you come *now*? Today?"

As soon as I hung up, Grandma Arlen slapped me right across my face with a strength and speed I didn't know she possessed. It happened so quickly, I just stood in shock, my face burning. Benny looked up from the Hot Wheels garage with wide eyes, dropping his jaw in silence. I didn't cry. I stood by the dining room table with my arms crossed, looking at the floor. *I don't care. I'm going home, I'm getting out of here. I hate being here, and now you know it.*

Dad came to fetch us in only a matter of a few hours. I told him about the slap across the face as we stood in line at Carvel's ice cream parlor, where he took us straight away after leaving Grandma's. He never left us alone with Grandma Arlen again.

"Daddy, Play Your Dad"

Grandma Arlen's husband, our grandfather—who had been a bona fide brewer for Guinness in Ireland—had died before we were born. Dad grew very sad when he spoke of his father, telling us how his father would beat him, his siblings, and his mother. When Dad's father came home from work, his mother reported the kids' bad behavior for the day. He would then stand over them, unhook his belt and pull it slowly from his belt loops, before whipping their backs and rear ends over and over. Dad said his little sister would go unconscious in the middle of beatings.

Dad often acted out this belt-whipping scene with his own belt when he told us the story. He was so good at it—so theatrical and realistic—that we egged him on. "Daddy! Play your dad! Play your dad! Come on, do the belt!"

Dad's face changed when he played his father—his eyes became serious and menacing and his jaw grew tight. He removed his leather belt quickly and folded it in half, gripping it at each end. It sounded just like a whip when he quickly snapped it together again and again. Benny and I watched intently, bouncing up and down.

"Neil, you're gonna get it this time, get over here—" Dad snarled.

It took us several tries to get it just right when Dad taught Benny and I how to snap a belt this way. He got pissed off when he was rushing for work and he couldn't find his leather belts, rummaging through our room, and yelling, "For chrissakes, if you're gonna play your grandfather, you have to put my belts back!"

Dad told us that he didn't believe in adults hurting kids. He said it was done to him so he would never do that to us. He liked to call kids "people" and "human beings." He even used the term "peoplesitting" instead of babysitting. But every now and then, something came over Dad and he acted like somebody else.

He liked to take naps during the day on the weekends, especially if he had gone out and left us with a peoplesitter the night before. He'd shut the blinds in the living room, pull out the sofa, and lie down all day long with the brown afghan pulled tightly to his chin, his thin hair stuck to the side of his face.

"Children should be seen and not heard," he moaned weakly from the sofa, "your father has a screaming headache, let me be." We *knew* something was off whenever Dad referred to us as children.

Every blue moon, Dad really scared me when I accidentally woke him during one of his all-day weekend naps. I was on the terrace with Benny one afternoon, laughing about a drawing I'd made. The next thing I knew, Dad was coming through the sliding glass door looking all snarly and haggard with scar-looking indents all over his face from his pillowcase. He grabbed me by the arm and swung me around, picking me up off the ground by my armpits. It seemed like a bad dream, it all happened so fast. Next, he hit me against the dining area wall, knocking my wind out with a thud.

"I'm gonna nail you to the fucking wall," he growled between his teeth in a voice I didn't recognize at all.

He dropped me to the floor and I watched in disbelief as he went back to the sofa and pulled the afghan over his head. I ran to my room to cry. I lay on my bed and wondered if Dad's father had said the nailing to the fucking wall thing to *him*, and I wondered if he was playing his father like he played his father with the belt. I imagined he'd have a long talk with me when he woke up, apologizing profusely. But he never mentioned what happened. I wondered if he forgot.

On the rare occasion, when Dad looked disheveled on a weekend, he ordered me into the bathroom for a spanking if I managed to piss him off badly enough. This was a great betrayal in my eyes—something he'd promised he would never do. The worst part was that it was done with my pants down.

"Pull your pants down," Dad ordered through clenched teeth, not looking at me. I tried to catch his eye—hoping to snap him out of it—hoping he'd see the *you're not really going to do this, are you?* look on my face. He sat down on the toilet and bent me over his knees, which was really awkward. I knew I was a little too old to be bent over my dad's knee with my bare bottom exposed. This made the act really humiliating. He brought his hand down hard with a sharp sting two or three times before letting me up. Pulling up my pants was just as bad as getting spanked.

Because he had the same expression and the same voice as when he acted out the belt beatings from his father, I had the feeling that deep down Dad enjoyed spanking me in the bathroom, like he was playing a part. I also surmised that he probably hated himself for doing this terrible thing every now and again that perhaps he just couldn't help.

    I always felt as though I wanted to protect my dad. The only way I could do that was to try to keep him happy and build him up when he was down. He had moods the same way that Mother had moods—from demons that were seemingly stuck inside him. I felt helpless against the big demons that had showed up way before I was even born. It seemed that someone else possessed Dad from time to time. I blamed his mean parents because they were the ones he usually cried about.
    Grandma Arlen sometimes called Dad "Girlie" and would bark at him in her Irish accent over the women that he had—as she called it—let pass by, including our mother.
    "Why'd yeh ever let 'er run away? A *real* man doesn't let his woman git away. Yer pa's a dancin' fairy kids."
    Grandma often took to slapping Dad upside the head when she'd mock him this way. She whipped him good with the back of her hand as she grumbled Girlie this and Girlie that. Dad covered his head with both hands and ducked, which took her to whacking him on the shoulder blades.
    Dad's resentment of his bullying mother seemed to leak out in various ways, mostly in his own mockery, which could be quite humorous. He frequently referred to her when we'd see a ghoulish creature on TV: "Oh my gawd, it's your grandmother!" he'd say at Godzilla or the Incredible Hulk and the three of us would share a good laugh. Other times, he referred to her cooking with the back of his hand on his forehead like he was about to faint: "Oh, people, her cooking will be the death of me."
    Still, Dad seemed to honor some kind of requirement to making sure that Grandma Arlen was all right.
    "Her life was a living hell," he explained, as if this were a disclaimer that stipulated the go-ahead for her

ongoing nastiness.

One time, we came back from the fair with Dad and Aunt Madgie to find Grandma Arlen passed out on the floor of the bathroom with vomit all over the front of her dress and all over the toilet. Dad cleaned her up, saying that she had the flu, and tucked her into her bed. A few years later, he shared that she hid bottles of booze all over the house and I put it together that she was probably drunk that night.

No matter how you cut it, Grandma Arlen had it tough. She just plain had a hard life and this fact gave me a certain amount of sympathy for her. I got the feeling that there was some kind of curse on the family, some dark cloud. I always thought this accounted for Dad's sad moods.

Sometimes, when Dad was in his sad mood, he just stayed in bed all afternoon drinking wine or martinis. I'd snuggle up next to him and run my hand up and down the soft inside of his arm.

Other times, he cradled me and Benny on the sofa with his arms wrapped tightly around us. He put Roberta Flack on the record player and sang along to "Killing Me Softly with His Song" with tears rolling down his cheeks. He kissed our necks; smelled our hair. He whispered, "I love you, baby," into my ear and whispered French words to Benny that were reserved just for him.

"If it weren't for you kids, I'd be dead by now," he always said when he was in his sad mood. "You'll hate me when you grow up, you'll see."

The two statements went together and made me feel as though my father were at the bottom of some pit and I was unable rescue him.

"No, Daddy, I will *never* hate you for as long as I live," I reassured him every time.

"Daddy, I love you forever," Benny promised.

As far as his being dead if it weren't for us, I was just glad that I could keep him alive.

A Woman to Talk To

"Princess, you're becoming a woman. You should have a woman to talk to," Dad announced one afternoon as we sat on the terrace. He had been voicing concern that I didn't have a woman around while I lived with him.

He took me down to the Big Sisters headquarters. We had an interview with one of the facilitators there, and I filled out a questionnaire about myself and talked to her about my interests. Under *What is your favorite thing to do?* I answered, "Look for frogs and tadpoles." I kept going back and forth between bugs, frogs and tadpoles, and disco. At the end of the interview, the woman gently explained that it might take a while to find a Big Sister who shared such diverse interests.

"I'm sure that there are plenty of Big Sisters who would love to do disco, but the bugs and tadpoles may be a bit of a challenge—" she said as she scanned the questionnaire like there was something she missed. I was mortified.

"You have wonderful interests. There are plenty of young women with the same interests as you," Dad defended me angrily when we got back into the Fury.

For one reason or another, I never did get a Big Sister. While I did miss my mother, I never really did feel a void where a female should have been. For the first few months in Centereach, Victoria Dobrowski was the main woman in my life. Dad knew Victoria through a single parent support group that Dad had joined, and she and her two girls––Shelby and Amber—lived in the apartment unit below us.

Dad and Victoria had found the apartments together––moving at the same time—while Benny and I were still in California. Dad and Victoria toted us four kids to the single parent meetings, where we would play wildly in a back room with other kids while the adults sat around in a circle talking this and that about the challenges of the single parent life.

Victoria was thin and tall and wore all of the latest

trends, like tight bell bottomed jeans with zippers at each hip, and lots of makeup and hair spray. If there was a void for a female in my life, Victoria was filling it. She took a special interest in me, which I ate up, on account of the fact that my own mother was across the country, and because I thought Victoria was so glamorous. She was the ideal woman—the woman I had wished my own mother resembled. Victoria became an icon that I would soon take to calling "The High Heeled Woman."

    Victoria brought me into her enchanting bathroom full of cosmetics and perfumes, shutting the door behind us. In front of the large mirror, she taught me how to apply makeup—that the lighter eye shadow goes just above the liner, and the darker shadow goes on the crease of the lid, extending out like a wing. She tested various colors of rouge on me, explaining that pink would suit me best because of my age. When testing the colors, she looked at me in the mirror, rather than face-to-face—and not in the eye—cocking her head to the side and pursing her lips before decidedly saying, "No, that's not it."

    "Oh no, no, no," she tsked, shaking her head, when I took her Chanel perfume and sprayed it heavily onto the front of my T-shirt. She then taught me to spray just a tiny bit on my wrist and apply that to the delicate skin behind my ear.

    Victoria took me to the salon once. "Make her hair just like mine," she said to the stylist, giving me a wink. I was flying high, as I loved Victoria's hairdo. Her shoulder length straight brown hair curled under in a perfectly round way, like Dorothy Hamill. I was a miniature Victoria when we were through. I did not hide my conceit, gazing at my reflection in the side-view window of Victoria's car and in passing store windows as we walked to the restaurant where she took me to lunch after our salon appointment.

    During these times her own girls, both overweight and not very pretty, were seemingly cast out—they were not allowed in the bathroom for makeup lessons and were not allowed to join in our outings. I felt a combination of awkwardness, guilt, and privilege. While Victoria praised me and singled me out, she said things to her own girls like,

"You stink," "Get away from me," and "You're disgusting." I felt sorry for them. I felt increasingly guilty about my selfish relishing of her favoritism toward me.

Dad debriefed us about Victoria behind closed doors. He said that, although Victoria was his good friend, he did not agree with the way she talked to her girls, and that the girls would have big problems as grown-ups. He said that, while Victoria completely starved herself, she overfed her daughters on purpose and that this was why they were both fat, while she was skinny as a rail. He explained that she did this so they would never look prettier than her. I found this extremely shocking and odd.

Victoria and Dad sometimes drank wine and smoked cigarettes together in the evenings—alternating apartments—while we kids played. They sat across from each other at opposite ends of the couch with their shoes off and their legs tucked under. They held out their wine glasses like they were about to say "Cheers" while singing along to Dionne Warwick, Anne Murray, and Roberta Flack.

The two became less animated as the hours approached midnight, and the wine bottles stood empty on the coffee table. They lay soggy on the couch with arms and legs draped in odd positions—Victoria's feet at Dad's head and vice-versa. After awhile we'd find them asleep, with the needle on the arm of the stereo stuck at the end of the record, making a repetitive scratchy static sound. Us four kids stayed awake, raiding the kitchen and then finding our own way to bed, whichever apartment we were in.

Gay Means Happy

Dad and Victoria were becoming closer and closer friends. The two apartments were like one big apartment; I came and went as I pleased between Victoria's apartment and ours. One morning, Benny and I were playing with Shelby and Amber in their room while Victoria and Dad went out shopping. Victoria came home with her arms full of groceries seemingly on cloud nine, twirling around.

"Neil's gonna marry me, Neil's gonna marry me," she was singing happily. I was ecstatic. Shelby, Amber and I hurriedly talked of how it will be to be sisters—where we'll live, room arrangements, last names and so forth. We were interrupting each other, slapping our hands together and bursting out in high-pitched shrills, bouncing up and down on the bed. *Sisters*, I thought. Benny sat silent with his arms crossed on one of the girls' twin beds, seemingly disgruntled and horrified.

Dad's face grew long and serious when I ran upstairs to our apartment to ask Dad about the wedding plans.

"Oh no. I was afraid of this," he said quietly, seemingly very worried about something. He told us that there was to be no such wedding—Victoria had misunderstood him. *Misunderstood? How could she have gotten it wrong?* I was greatly disappointed, and worried about how Victoria would receive the rejection. Dad then went out the terrace, closing the sliding door behind him like he wanted to be left alone. He sat out there smoking one cigarette after the other, and staring straight ahead for— what seemed like—a few hours.

"Dad?" I tried sheepishly, tapping on the sliding door as dinner time approached. "Are you coming in?"

"Let me be, princess. A little longer."

I had never seen Dad like this. Later that same evening, he went down to Victoria's apartment.

"Stay home, this is a private talk," he ordered, with the same serious look on his face as when he was outside on the terrace. A bit later, shortly after he returned from the talk, Victoria came flying through our front door without knocking and ran up the stairs as we sat watching TV. I gasped at the sight of her. She was disheveled and looking like a sad clown—hanging onto the banister with one arm at the top of the stairs—with mascara and eye shadow running down her wet face.

"I'm calling the police! They'll come take your kids away!" she shouted at Dad, pointing her finger at him. I froze on the sofa as I craned my neck to look at her, my heart racing and my stomach in my throat. *Why* was she doing this?

"You have no right to have these kids!"

"Kids, kids, go to your room—" Dad ordered, sounding panicked, and begging Victoria to *please stop*.

"Don't you come near my daughters *ever* again!" she yelled as Benny and I entered our room and reluctantly closed the door.

My heart sank. *Why is she saying these things?* Victoria had warped into a haggard, frightening creature, a transformation that made me think of science fiction movies––of blood sucking and werewolves. Benny and I darted to our room and stared at each other from across our beds in silence and disbelief. Would I no longer be doing hair and makeup with Victoria? My heart was pounding.

Dad came to our bedroom and asked us to come out to the living room for a special talk after the yelling stopped and I heard Victoria going down the stairs and out the front door. He was pale; his jaw tight. What was Dad going to say? We were full of questions about Victoria's threats of the police and having us taken away. After assuring us that she was just upset and that this would never happen, Dad began to explain this thing that he needed to say. He pulled a chair from the dining area and sat opposite us from the couch. The pitch of his voice was unfamiliar with lots of stuttering and pausing. It was what adults called beating around the bush. I was getting worried.

"I'm gay," he said, finally.

I sat in confusion over Dad's struggle to tell us something good. Benny and I squinted at each other with our heads half-cocked. *Gay means happy.*

But Dad continued, educating us about the *other* meaning for the word gay.

"I prefer to be with men," he explained, talking slowly and appearing clammy and shaky.

I still didn't get it, though. *Of course* he preferred hanging out with boys, those who are the same sex as him—it made sense. *I* liked hanging out with girls. Why did Dad seem so uncomfortable? I didn't really get it until Tweetie

Bird Man.

That winter, Dad had a new friend who my brother and I called Tweetie Bird Man on account of his little Tweetie Bird toy hanging from the rearview mirror in his small car. I don't have the slightest recollection of his real name. He was a very quiet man who hardly said a word to Benny or me and did not come around very often. I took the Tweetie Bird toy as a signal that he was all right, and perhaps even fun.

Dad made a big deal about Tweetie Bird Man buying the three of us tickets to the Ice Capades. He said that his friend got the tickets because he wanted to do something fun for us, and he knew dad loved the stage.

There was a terrible snowstorm on the night of the Ice Capades, when Tweetie Bird Man drove us there in his little yellow car. We got stuck for hours after the show, and were rescued by some firemen, who brought us to the fire station. We—along with a load of other stranded folks—were taken home in an ambulance close to dawn. We felt like we knew Tweetie Bird Man a little better after that.

Shortly after the Ice Capades snowstorm night, Tweetie Bird Man came to our house late, after we had gone to bed. Benny and I were awake, whispering to each other with the lights out. Our heads shot up simultaneously when we heard the knock on the front door and the footsteps of a visitor, sparking our curiosity and our desire not to miss any fun.

"Who is that?" Benny whispered. I could see the outline of his head in the moonlight.

"I don't know, let's go sneak to find out."

After several minutes had passed, we tiptoed out of our room and crept through the short-carpeted hall to peek around the corner at our dad and his visitor in the living room. There was Dad and Tweetie Bird Man on the sofa kissing with long and passionate kisses, their arms and legs intertwined. Why was Dad kissing Tweetie Bird Man like that? Maybe it was because I was uncomfortable, or maybe because I just thought it was pretty silly—I got a terrible case of the giggles right there, my face burning hot. Benny started giggling too, so I elbowed him to make a beeline for our bedroom.

We tiptoed fast with our hands over our mouths, and burst into fits of hushed laughter when we got to our dark room, falling onto my bed. I couldn't see Benny's face; I could only see his silhouette and his hair shining in the light of the streetlamp outside our window. It was strange not being able to see his expression after what we had just witnessed. I grabbed hold of Benny's arm and put my face on his chest, trying to muffle my giggles. It was as though we had witnessed a naked person walking across a busy street, or a store clerk in his underwear.

"He was kissing him like a girl," Benny whispered. "Why was he doing that?"

We decided that we must have seen the picture wrong. We wanted a second look to be sure, so we crept out of our bedroom again. Seeing Dad and Tweetie Bird Man still necking all over the sofa—this time with shirts off, hairy chest to hairy chest—we could not hold back our out-loud nervous laughter. That's when Dad caught us. Tweetie Bird Man immediately darted his head under Dad's afghan as Dad sprung off the sofa, and ran over to us with a terrible look on his face, ushering us toward our room.

"Go, go, go people—" he ordered, corralling us back to our room by gently but firmly pushing our shoulders. I craned my neck to attempt another glimpse of Tweety Bird Man—he had come out from under the afghan, and had his head in his hands.

"Move it—" Dad snapped through clenched teeth, pushing at my back. Benny and I darted to our beds.

"You two need to stay in bed and let me have some privacy," Dad said sternly, standing in between us in the glow of the streetlamp. I asked him why he was kissing Tweetie Bird Man like that.

"That is what I meant about being gay," he explained, as if reminding me of the fine print. "We can talk about it tomorrow."

He leaned in to give me a goodnight kiss. When his mouth touched my cheek, I thought about how he was just kissing Tweetie Bird Man. I watched his silhouette bend down to give Benny a kiss too, and then he left the room, closing the door.

I lay in my bed that night, unable to sleep. A little light went off in my head as I recalled Mother telling us about gay in reference to those who have romantic relationships with the same sex. I couldn't remember what she called it, as it had seemed so insignificant at the time. I tried and tried to recall the conversation, regretting that it must have went in one ear, and out the other. I was wishing that I had paid better attention when Mother told me about "gay"—maybe there was more to it that I wasn't getting.

I wondered how long Tweetie Bird Man might stay that night. I was used to going to Dad's bed every night, burrowing my face into his chest. He was my sleeping pill, my warm cup of milk. I couldn't stand one night without him.

After waiting for what felt like forever, staring at the wall, I crept into the living room, only to find him cuddling with Tweetie Bird Man. My heart sank low. It was a long, hard night. *Gay.* I kept repeating it in my head like a question and an explanation at the same time.

"My dad is gay!" I randomly blurted loudly that week at school. I wanted to see what other kids would do and say, like a litmus test for gay.

The reactions weren't subtle. Eyes darted quickly in my direction. The older kids put their hands over their mouths and laughed.

"You probably should watch where you say that. People can be very judgmental," Judy warned with a serious look, pulling me to the side discreetly.

"Judy said we shouldn't talk about gay too much," I reported to Dad in the Fury later that day, on the way to the grocery store. I was sitting in the front with my arm around him and my legs tucked under my bottom. Dad turned and gave me a sweet look, kissing my forehead, before lighting a Kool with one hand.

"Gay people are singled out and picked on," he said,

facing the road. He looked a little beaten down, nursing on his cigarette. "Sometimes gay people are even beat up just because they're gay."

"*What?*" I gasped. This sounded like terrible bullying. I imagined Dad getting beaten up, wondering how they would find him. Where would it happen? In the apartment?

"There's a bunch of assholes out there," he explained, "a bunch of repressed bigots." (My mother had used the word *bigot*, too. I thought it sounded like a dried fruit or the name for a bug, but I knew it meant something bad.)

"Those people are fuckers," Benny chimed in from the backseat.

"I know, Pooh, but we can't go around saying that, ok?" Dad warned, straining to reach an arm around to tap Benny on the knee.

Dad pulled into the grocery store lot and parked the car. He sat there for a few minutes, and shared that he had been going to a group where gay people met to talk about the unfairness, and that it was helpful to have friends like him. He told us that he met Tweetie Bird Man at the group.

"You people stay in the car, I'll be out in no time."

I watched Dad head into the grocery store, tossing his Kool to the ground before putting it out like he always did, like a dancer—with a graceful quick twist of his foot mid-stride. I got an idea.

"Let's have a protest right here in the parking lot!" I said to Benny, who had a case of the wiggles, standing up with his hands clutching the back of the big, green vinyl bucket seat.

"What do you mean?"

"You know, like in San Francisco—a rally," I explained eagerly, "for gay people. Anyone who beats up gay people are stupid assholes."

"Yeah!" Benny shot excitedly before beating on the big silver door handle to get out of the car.

We stood on an island covered in snow in our hats and boots, in the busy part of the parking lot, right next to the Fury. We began yelling and clapping and raising our fists in the air.

"WE LOVE GAY PEOPLE!"
"GAY PEOPLE HAVE RIGHTS!"
"GOOOO GAY PEOPLE!"

People were shooting us scowling, frowning looks. They were dropping their jaws and shaking their heads. Were *they* some of the ones who didn't like gay people?

I was so excited when I saw Dad coming out of the grocery store carrying two full paper bags.

"Here he comes!" I cheered to Benny, grabbing his elbow.

We yelled even louder, for Dad's benefit: "YAYYY GAY PEOPLE!" I imagined that Dad would be so proud; he might even join in. But Dad didn't smile. He immediately doubled his pace and started booking it really fast to get to us.

"Stop, stop, be quiet!" he demanded through clenched teeth as soon as he was in earshot.

"*What?*" I blurted, frozen in my spot with my arms out, shocked that Dad was seemingly upset.

"Get in the car, get in the car—" he ordered, pushing at us with his body, the groceries topsy-turvy in his arms. A few groceries spilled out onto the concrete when he scrambled to open the back door of the Fury. A small crowd of three or four onlookers had gathered. I darted a quick look at them—there was a scowling woman in a knitted hat, a man was laughing. I wanted to call them names.

"Get off me!" Benny yelled when I fell on top of him as we dove into the backseat. I hadn't even had time to run around to get in the front, like usual. Dad shoved the groceries in next to me, tossing the fallen items haphazardly into the car, and jumped in the driver's seat to start the ignition.

"Daddy, what? *What?*" I pressed, a lump forming in my throat. *Please no, I can't cry.*

"Don't ever let me catch you doing that again," Dad snapped out of breath in a very serious, scared tone as he pulled the gearstick into reverse and tore out of there lickety-split.

"I thought you'd like it," I said, tears starting to fall.

"I *knew* it was stupid," Benny shot, his arms crossed at his chest.

I turned around to give Benny a look, pissed off because *he* had been excited about the protest idea, too.

"It's ok Pooh, I know you two were trying to stick up for your dad," Dad said lovingly, "I just don't want you to get hurt. People will call the police or—worse—they'll punch your lights out."

Dad reached an arm around to tenderly touch my cheek with his fingertips.

This *being gay* business was not as simple as just a man who likes men. It certainly wasn't as simple as Mother portrayed when she was teaching me sex 101. It was obvious that this thing Dad called gay was a way of being that came with an array of conditions that affected everything, including me. I thought all the hubbub was stupid. *What's the big deal?* How could anyone in the world ever want to hurt my dad?

Dear John T.

Now that dad had told us about being gay, he started being open with his crushes on men. Number one was Captain Kirk. He stood in front of the television during *Star Trek* and said in a slow drawl, "Ummm, ummm...lookin' good, boy, lookin' good," drawing out the *good* by extending the "O's." Sometimes, he shook his hips fast in a side-to-side motion saying, "Baby, you are hot!" while thrusting his pelvis forward in time with the *hot* and pronouncing the "T" as a second syllable. Dad especially loved *Star Trek* because of the outfits.

"Mmmm hmmm, would you look at all those tights, people?"

Dad's other word for gay was faggot. I thought the word sounded nasty because it rhymed with maggot. He said that Captain Kirk was *really* a faggot. Dad taught us that people who are not gay—people who want to kiss and marry the opposite sex—are called straight. *Straight* sounded boring because it made me think of a board or a rod—something cold and stiff and inanimate.

"Beautiful faggot," he said under his breath as he walked past the television while tidying up about any male who looked remotely handsome.

"Dad, he likes girls," I protested, annoyed.

But Dad claimed that he could tell who was gay and who was straight. The two of us sat on the sofa watching TV, and battled over who was on *his* team and who was on *my* team. This was a game of the gay vs. the straight, sort of like a competition. According to Dad, David Cassidy was gay, as well as Neil Diamond, and Barry Manilow. I put my foot down when he brought up John Travolta.

Saturday Night Fever had come out that December of 1977, when I was about to turn nine. I was completely spellbound by the film, which Dad took me to see twice. I was all lit up about the flashy star, John Travolta—I had such a big crush, which Dad both teased me about *and* encouraged.

"Oh my gawd, there she goes again about John Revolting," Dad taunted in my direction, rolling his eyes and waving his hand in the air.

Dad finally gave in and bought me the *Saturday Night Fever* soundtrack after I bugged him about it over and over. I learned the lyrics to all the songs, as well as most of the dance moves from the movie.

Our living room became a mini disco club, with Dad and I constantly dancing to the soundtrack. The ends of my hair touched the green carpet when Dad dipped me slowly toward the floor in his big strong arms as we practiced "The Hustle" and the "More Than a Woman" routine.

One evening, as he downed the last few drops of his third martini at our favorite Chinese restaurant in Minneola, Dad brought up the idea for me to write a letter to John Travolta. I was thrilled to no end.

"First, we have to make a plan, some kind of invitation," Dad cajoled with a twinkle in his eye while Benny and I picked at what was left of the giant pupu platter.

I decided that I would invite John to dinner. The three of us planned and then re-planned the John Travolta dinner over the following days. We were sitting at the small dining room table—enjoying bowls of ice cream—when Dad grabbed a pen and paper to write out our first draft of *the dinner*.

"Ok folks, let's plan the John Revolting dinner menu, shall we?"

"Skettios!" Benny cheered, his face covered in strawberry ice cream. The canned culinary classic Spaghettios—or "Skettios"—happened to be one of Benny's all-time favorite foods.

"No Benny, definitely *not* Spaghettios," I snarled, rolling my eyes.

"Dad!" I shot, "Can we do minute steak and baked potatoes?"

I was bouncing in my chair about the thought of serving John T. my very favorite meal.

"Princess, I think that's a fine idea," Dad answered in his trying-to-be-elegant voice with his nose turned up.

"Awe, I wanted Skettios," Benny whined, dropping his dirty spoon in his bowl and crossing his arms in front of his chest in a huff.

"Pooh how about this—how about we have Skettios tomorrow night? You get to pick: meatballs or no meatballs."

"But the movie star won't be here tomorrow," Benny pouted, hamming up his big pink ice cream frown.

"Benny, Astrid gets to pick this dinner because John Travolta will be *her* special guest." I loved the sound of *that*.

After Benny made an angry beeline for our bedroom, and Dad followed after him to make things right, I sat at the table daydreaming about what we would do after the dinner. Dancing with John Travolta in the living room to the *Saturday Night Fever* album was the first image that immediately came to mind. What would I wear? I thought that all of my dresses were too little-girlish and so I decided I would wear my bell-bottomed jeans.

"You'll need to act like a lady at the table," Dad warned.

I was nervous about cutting my steak the right way, as Dad usually scoffed at my manners—which he blamed on my mother—calling me "positively barbaric."

I wrote and then rewrote the invitation letter a couple times. I detailed the plan for our evening, right down to the butter and salt and pepper on our potatoes, before folding the letter and putting it in the envelope. Dad had taken the trouble to find the address of where to send it. We talked excitedly of how it will be to have John Travolta right there––in our house—sitting at our table, eating minute steak with us, and then actually *dancing* with us.

"Dad, you should invite Captain Kirk!" I blurted out while Dad stood at the kitchen sink washing dishes.

It was not so much that I wanted to see Captain Kirk, I was just worried that Dad might try to steal all the conversation and the dancing time, being that he always took up the whole room in every situation.

"Maybe him and John Travolta are friends cause they're both movie stars," I added, thinking I had come up with a really a great idea.

"Yeah!" Benny shouted, jumping off his chair and hopping up and down. "Can he bring his spaceship?"

"Maybe, my princess, maybe," Dad said, not answering Benny and not looking at me as he continued to wash the dishes.

"Can I write a letter about the spaceship?" Benny chirped, coming behind Dad and grabbing hold of the belt loops on the back of his jeans.

"Sure Pooh, let me finish the dishes first," Dad said half-annoyed, arching backwards from Benny's weight.

I imagined sitting at the table with Dad, Benny, John Travolta and Captain Kirk (I had no idea of the actor's name, and really could not imagine him with any other persona, other than that of Captain Kirk). It hit me that we'd need one more chair, and thought to myself that I'd better not forget to remind Dad about that.

I pictured the five of us chatting up a storm, John dressed in a slinky shirt with his chest hairs showing, and Captain Kirk wearing his tight yellow space shirt.

I felt that my life had taken a new turn when I nervously put the letter into the mailbox. Next came the agonizing wait for John's response. In preparation for the acceptance of my gutsy invitation, I went over the dance moves with Dad, imagining that he was John Travolta. I imagined confidently swinging open the refrigerator door and showing John our large selection of soda pop, letting him choose a flavor. I thought of what we might discuss at the dinner table. I pictured how he might cut his steak and wondered how much butter he would put on his potato. I would ask him all about the making of *Saturday Night Fever* and about the other cast members. I'd tell him about my school—my life—and he would sit in awe and in complete attention.

After dinner, we would throw on the soundtrack and dance in the living room, while Dad watched proudly from the sofa, hopefully with Captain Kirk sitting beside him. John Travolta would be amazed at my sharp disco style. He would dip me slow, looking deep into my eyes, just like he did to Karen Lynn Gorney in the movie.

"You got a response, Astrid!" Dad called out a few weeks later, when he checked the mail at the postal area of the apartment complex after an outing, Benny and I waiting in the Fury with the engine still running.

"Lemme see! Lemme see!" I called out, crawling across the seat to the driver's side when he got back in the car with a large manila envelope.

I leapt at him, trying to grab it out of his hands. He slapped the envelope repeatedly and waved it above his head and then pulled it behind his back with a big smirk on his face.

"*Daaaad! Come on!*"

"What is that? Is it from Mommy?" Benny asked, having forgotten all about the letter to John Travolta.

"Drum roll, princess," Dad announced, pulling the envelope from behind his back. I immediately snatched it from his hands.

"It's from John Travolta, Pooh," he explained to Benny, who then let out a disappointed sigh.

I tore it open, my mind spinning with the burning question: when was John Travolta coming? I reached my hand inside the big envelope and pulled out an 8x10 photo of the "More Than A Woman" scene from my living room disco dancing fantasy. Only John—as Tony Manero—was dipping Stephanie instead of me. In ballpoint cursive, on the lower right hand corner of the photo was written: "Dear Astrid, Best Wishes, John." I whisked my hand in the empty envelope, looking for a letter from John, acknowledging my invitation. Nothing. My heart sank. I stared at the photo, feeling slightly humiliated and greatly disappointed. *This is it. He isn't coming.*

"I'm sorry, princess, maybe he's working on a movie," Dad said, kissing the top of my head and saying how special it was to receive—what he called—an "autograph" from John.

We framed the signed photo called an autograph, hanging it on the wall. Many times, I stared at it, even kissing John's image a few times. I traced my finger over his writing, remembering our date and vowed to always love John Travolta, scoffing whatever Dad had to say about it.

Sometime later that year, a boy at the free school threw a baseball full-bore indoors and it landed right smack on the record player that was spinning with my *Saturday Night Fever* album, and damn if it wasn't record one. Broke it right in half.

Around the time that I was preparing for my date with John Travolta, Dad started talking about this thing he called jumping your bones. He was saying that I was a good dancer and still the prettiest girl in the world.

"You'd better watch your buns. Boys are gonna start wanting to jump your bones," Dad warned at the table, pointing a finger at me.

"Princess you tell em' this," he instructed in a southern accent with his eyebrows raised, as he got up from the table in one of his I'm-on-stage modes. "Excuse me? I said *excuuuuuse* me? Hell no, Nah ah," he sassed, waving his finger as if to say *no-no*. Then he stuck his hip out and put his finger on his ass and said, "See this? you ain't gettin' *anyyy* of this."

I'd practice saying no to the bone jumping advances in the bathroom, or I'd have Benny play a guy asking me out and I'd turn him down Dad style.

"You'd better learn to kiss right," Dad said with his eyebrows raised and his hands on his hips.

I remembered the way he kissed Tweetie Bird Man––like he was slurping up big long pieces of spaghetti with sauce. Mother kissed Tom that way too (but I never did see my parents kiss that way when they were together).

Coppertone

The swimming pool opened that spring of 1978 in Centereach, a few months after I turned nine. I spent every possible waking moment in that pool. My Aunt Annette took me to Macy's and bought me a fabulous Wonder Woman bathing suit when I went to visit her in Connecticut one weekend. I got so tan that spring and summer that I looked like an Aborigine, with blonde hair and dark, dark skin.

I was not a very good swimmer. Dad spent several days in the water, teaching me the basics. He also taught me how to dive by standing behind me and holding my hips, instructing me to bend my knees and spring from my feet.

I lived to show off for the handsome lifeguard at the pool named Dave. Dave was twenty-one years old and incredibly tan, with an athletic build, and always with a thick layer of zinc oxide on his nose. He sat on a chair by the pool, listening to his big portable radio/tape deck. Sometimes I got lucky, and he'd play my favorite disco station. Otherwise, he'd be playing *his* favorite music—Boston, Foreigner, Kansas, Gerry Rafferty and the like. There were usually at least two women sitting around Dave, giggling at his jokes and asking him to lather them with tanning oil. Dad whispered that these women were lonely, bored housewives and they were what he called looking to get laid.

"What is 'get laid'?" I asked Dad in the kitchen.

"To have sex," he laughed.

I thought that most of the terms adults used to describe sex were odd. *Get laid* was strange because it made the routine sound dull and lifeless, like they were wanting to take a nap. *Screwing* made me think of a screwdriver.

I curiously watched Dave the lifeguard when he fraternized with the lounging "bored" ladies, memorizing the mating dance of men and women, jealous that I was too young to join in. I hated when the women were there and waited as long as it took for them to leave. When they weren't around, I had Dave's full attention. I begged him to come into the pool with me.

"Please, please, pretty please," I pleaded with a smile, my head cocked to the side, pulling his heavy slack arm as he played up some good exaggerated bellyaching.

Finally, he'd quickly grab me, lifting me over his shoulder while I screamed, before spinning me around and throwing me into the water. If I was lucky, he jumped in the water to play. He'd dunk and splash me, the two of us laughing in the hot sun, our slippery slow-motion bodies brushing under the water. I felt exhilarated by the flirtations––alive, drunk. The way that Dave the lifeguard interacted with the older women looked much less fun, compared to the way that he was with me. I was *sure* that he preferred me over them.

One evening, when we were alone at the pool, Dave the lifeguard challenged me to an arm wrestle. I sat on the white folding chair at the patio table, a rivulet of pool water dripping from my wet suit and down the plastic. The mood was tipped by the familiar smells of poolside evenings—warmed pavement wet with chlorine, my parked watermelon Jolly Rancher ring pop, the faint smell of laundry detergent off a damp towel, and the baby oil on Dave's skin. These smells were imprinting in my brain so that I would later be struck with an intense flash of *Centereach Poolside* when a trace randomly wafted by, like a little PLAY button had been pressed inside me.

I settled in for an arm wrestle with the muggy evening sky behind us. Barry Manilow's "Copacabana" played on the radio. Dave and I placed our elbows on the table with our hands clasped tightly together. I was waiting for him to say *ready, set, go* when his hand became loose and soft around my hand. My stomach dropped as he started to inch his way over, and came in toward my chair. Our faces were so close; I could hear his breath. I didn't know where to focus my eyes—all I could see was my own reflection in his shiny mirrored sunglasses.

"You're a very pretty girl," he said very quietly.

He pulled my hand in closer to him, inching me off the chair toward him. My heart raced as my body turned to Jell-O, and my face grew hot.

Without any thought at all, I quickly and impulsively withdrew my hand from his, bolted off the chair, and plunged into the pool with a huge cannon ball. I swam clear to the other side, gasping and coughing frantically when I came up for air.

I later agonized over what I had done. For days, I rewrote the arm wrestle experience over and over in my head. I imagined telling Dave that he was sexy and then kissing him, instead of running into the water. I imagined him taking me into the pool shed to get laid, fumbling with the tie on his suit, my hands slippery on his oily body. It was what was under that suit that had scared me. I plainly did not know what to do with a grown man's penis, nor did I *want* anything to do with it. Furthermore, I was terrified of what he might want to do with my privates. All of my daydreams involving Dave the lifeguard, John Travolta or any man consisted of disco dancing, staring into eyes, holding hands and little, brief kisses or *pecks*. I liked to act out humping with boys my age, but the truth was, I was deep down frightened of having my bones jumped.

The one shot chance with Dave the lifeguard was gone. I had blown it. I felt that I had failed in my competition with the women who vied for him. I had choosen me, after all the times that I had shown off for him, trying to win his attention in my Wonder Woman suit, and then I couldn't handle it.

It was awkward for a while with Dave after that day.

The distance between us—which had been dismissed for a minute or two—was then wider than it ever was.

The movie *Grease* came out that June and I was even more transfixed than I had been over *Saturday Night Fever*. I was in love with John Travolta all over again, only more so now that he showed a boyish flare as Danny. I wanted to be exactly like Sandra Dee, with her perfect blonde hair and fifties-style dresses that showed off her waistline. As with *Saturday Night Fever*, I acted out the scenes of *Grease* in the living room over and over, pulling anyone who would participate into my performances. I came to bribing Benny to play Danny, then barking at him to be more realistic.

"Oh my gawd, if I have to sit through Olivia Fig-Newton and John Revolting one more time, I will positively vomit," Dad said after the second viewing, holding his hand to his cheek.

And so, for the remaining four times I would see the film, Dad paid for my ticket and then came to pick me up after the show.

Dad *did* get me back for making him endure *Grease*. He brought Benny and I along to sit through *The Turning Point*—not once, but twice. I had to endure his whispering this and that about the sexy male dancers who leapt and twirled their way through the film.

"Mmm, mmm, mmm, that is one beautiful faggot," he purred at the sight of Mikhail Baryshnikov. In the same way that I acted out *Grease* scenes to no end, Dad became a Russian ballet dancer in the living room for the days following *The Turing Point*. I'd walk into the kitchen for a soda and see him gavotte in his elegant way that I admired so much.

The Shoot

Dad arranged for a photo shoot that summer in Centereach, saying that he wanted to work on making me a star. He said his photographer friend had commented on my beauty.

"This could be *it*, princess," he announced at the pool, as he lay covered in oil on a lounge chair, not opening his eyes. "He's got some leads in the modeling business. Step one is creating your portfolio."

I was mindlessly watching Benny traveling around the periphery of the shallow end as he held tight to the sides with floaty devices on his arms.

"What's a portfolio?" I asked, making a visor with my hand. Dad kept with his face toward the sun, not opening his eyes.

"It's a package of professional photos you show to modeling and casting agencies. The *very* best photos, so we must," he declared, turning to me and opening his eyes while pointing a finger at my face, "I say my darling daughter, we *must* make these count."

I was beyond ecstatic. I imagined doing television commercials and toothpaste ads for magazines, and maybe even starring in a movie. Dad said that I would need a special dress for what he called the shoot.

"No store is going to carry a dress beautiful enough for my princess. Let's design one ourselves," Dad said as he grabbed me in his hot, oily arms from his lounge chair, kissing the top of my head.

My mind was spinning with thoughts of an exotic gown, or a Saturday Night Fever dress with a slit.

Dad took me to the fabric store the following Saturday. He was in his weekend mode, wearing his old white T-shirt and tight faded jeans. We held hands as we walked up and down the aisles, looking through spool after spool of different types of fabrics. Benny was trailing behind, punching occasional spools and shouting "POW!" I ran my hands through silk, rayon, lace and polyester. Dad was just as invested, telling me that it needs to be just right.

"Princess," he called me over, rubbing a fabric between his thumb and forefinger, "we're talking about a fabric that will make you feel like a million bucks." It was so hard to decide.

For some reason—for why I do not recall—I chose a slinky thin polyester with a wild green and white print. Dad suggested detail, saying, "You need to stand out," so together we chose a thick band of four or five inch black tassel to hang off of the neckline.

Dad got right to work, creating the dress himself. He spread the fabric across the small dining room table before using a pair of shiny scissors to painstakingly cut it into the shape of a small dress.

Next, Dad got on his knees beside me as I held the fabric against my body. He held several push-pins tightly between his lips, removing them one-by-one to pin the fabric to my height at the hem. I was afraid he'd stick me in the shin or the knee, but he kept telling me through his clenched lips, "Hold on, be still, I'm not gonna stick you, just a few more."

I watched Dad closely, his face just below mine—the focused concentration in his hazel eyes, the old acne scars on his cheeks that he hated, his sideburns and the weekend stubble on his jaw. It was times like these that I was hit with the depth and enormity of love for my father. *There will never be another love greater than this. I love him more than anything in the entire world. I never, ever want to be without him.*

Later that night, Dad sat poised on the sofa listening to his Dionne Warwick record—the fabric draped across his knees—as he painstakingly sewed my dress with a needle and thread. I watched the way he gracefully pulled the needle through the fabric, the way his hand came around quickly— from the back and then to the top of the fabric—pulling the thread through. I loved the sound of the thread slipping through the fibers as he pulled it tight, which I tried to hear through the Dionne Warwick by sitting real close to Dad, and putting my ear close to his knee. This went on for hours. I grew tired of watching and eventually went to bed with Benny. I came out a few hours later to sneak into Dad's bed, only to find him still at it, sewing the tassel to the neckline.

"Preview, preview, preview!" Dad sang out the next day, bouncing on his toes and clapping. I quickly ran to my room and slipped it over my head with ease. I made my entrance, waltzing into the living room, making circles and swinging my hips like I was on stage. The one-of-a-kind dress was beautiful and unique, with a sleeveless flapper-style cut.

"Bravo! Bravo!" Dad yelled, clapping, "Beautiful, beautiful, absolutely beautiful." I noticed that he had big tears in his eyes when he proudly walked over to me to take my hands in a dance.

Dad's photographer friend named William showed up at our apartment on the day of the big *shoot*. I watched from the top of the stairs as Dad let him in and said hello, and the two hugged like good friends. William looked more like one of Mother and Tom's friends, rather than one of my dad's friends—with a ponytail and old jeans, and wearing an embroidered, bohemian peasant-like blue top. He was tall, with thick, dark hair and black-rimmed glasses.

"There's the movie star! Are you ready?!" William called up the stairs, spotting me right away. Dad quickly helped him carry his big tripod and hefty leather camera bag.

At the kitchen table, William unloaded his camera bag that looked more like a suitcase. With care, he pulled out a big, fancy camera, various lenses and multiple rolls of film. This looked like the real deal.

William was very enthusiastic, giving me praise for my green and white dress. He surveyed the apartment for what he called "the spot." He stood in front of the small scratchy olive green couch by the terrace for at least a minute, scratching his chin and looking at the sliding glass door. My cat, Henry was sitting in the sunny spot of the couch, not seeming to care one bit about what was going on.

"The light is just right here," he said, telling me to sit on the couch while he set up his camera on the tripod. Dad stared at me with a big grin, his hands clasped under his chin. Benny was playing his Star Wars disco compilation record and running around the carpet in circles making shooting sounds with a make-believe gun.

"Pooh, be careful not to bump into William, okay?,"

Dad cautioned, but Benny seemed oblivious and continuing to be lost in battle.

    I settled in next to Henry, and William stood about ten feet in front of me, looking through his camera while he talked, explaining that he would just keep snapping photos while we chatted. He called me his "subject," which made me think of Mrs. Bent and my stint at the public school called Thousand Oaks in Berkeley.

    "It's more natural if we just keep talking while I'm taking pictures," he said with his camera in front of his face, "tell me about your cat."

    I told William all about Henry getting his head cut open and my mother sewing the cut back together herself; I told him how Henry sleeps with me every night and how he sometimes disappears for two whole days. All the while, William's camera clicked over and over again in rapid succession. I was amazed at his dexterity and balance. Without looking up, he bobbed up and down and left to right, with one eye squinting through the camera lens and the other eye focused on me. Every now and again, he pulled his head away from the camera, repeatedly blinking and giving me directions, like "Can you move a little closer to the arm rest?" or "tell me something funny." I wondered how I could be so interesting and what it was that I was doing when he occasionally said, "Great, great, perfect, right there, *hold it...*"

    William asked me to change into what he called a "casual outfit," which Dad explained to be pants and a top. I went to my bedroom to change into my pale blue bellbottoms and a T-shirt, and saw that Benny had moved from his Star Wars fantasy game to building blocks in our bedroom—he appeared deep in concentration and did not look up when I entered the room.

    Dad had made martinis during the pause in the shoot. He and William laughed and drank while I struck one funny pose after the other. I loosened up quite a bit, sticking my tongue out and kicking my leg high in the air while William kept on clicking his camera.

    Dad had said I would "feel like a million bucks"

during the shoot, explaining that "to feel like a million bucks" meant to feel like a big movie star. Dad was right. I *did* feel like a movie star; I did feel like a million bucks. I didn't want the photo shoot to end—the electrifying first step toward my stardom. The days following the shoot seemed to drag on forever, as I anxiously waited on the developed photos. I must have asked Dad one hundred times whether he had heard from William with an update on my portfolio.

"I have the photos!" Dad finally announced about a week later, when he picked me up at the free school after he got off work. He dangled the large manila envelope in front of him from behind the big steering wheel with his eyebrows raised, chirping "chaa-chaa-chaa!"

"Let me see! Let me see!"

I leapt at him from the passenger side and tried to grab the envelope. Dad raised it above his head and said, "Hold it, hold it! Cool your buns!"

Benny shot up in the back, standing behind Dad to watch what was going on.

We sat side-by-side in the Fury as Dad pulled out a thick glossy sheet that smelled of developer. It was an 8x10 black-and-white of me and Henry. He then pulled out about ten or twelve more photos—some in the dress, some in the bell-bottoms and T-shirt.

"Where's the rest?" I asked, going for the manila envelope.

"We only develop the best ones," Dad explained.

I was a little disappointed. Where were the hundreds of other photos taken that day? I stared at the black and white 8x10s, remembering my conversations with William. *This is me.*

"What about the modeling agencies and the TV channels?" I pressed.

"I'm working on it princess, I'm working on it."

I imagined Dad and William sitting in an office, drinking martinis and talking to what Dad called an "agent." I pictured the agent in a fancy suit, approvingly reviewing my photos and making plans for a TV commercial. The agent would be nodding his head and saying something like, "Oh yes, she's got it, she's got it folks."

A few weeks later, I was looking for something in the curio cabinet when I saw the manila envelope stashed underneath some papers. I grabbed it—looking over my shoulder to make sure Dad was nowhere in sight—and pulled out the many photographs inside. *My portfolio!* But No. The picture on the top was one of my dad sitting on the same couch where I had been photographed. I was taken aback, as I did not know that there had been a photo shoot of Dad. I wondered what they talked about while the camera clicked. Was Dad creating his own portfolio? Did he hope to be a star, too?

I began leafing through the pile of 8X10s, looking for the rest of my photos. I removed the second photo from the top and instantly froze. It was a provocative naked photograph of Dad. I immediately took my eyes off the photo and stared out the window as I felt all the blood drain from my face. However, unable to stop myself, I anxiously peered down and unveiled the next image, and then the next—not because I wanted to *see* Dad's naked photos, but because I wanted to get to the place in the pile where the photographs returned to normal. He lay on his side across the scratchy olive couch, the sun shining on his tan skin and illuminating his brown chest hairs, his penis hanging against his upper thigh. I had already seen Dad's privates; he sometimes walked around the house naked. But I was taken aback by his eyes—the eyes of someone I didn't know, a look on him that I had never seen. It stung that perhaps there was a part of Dad I'd never get. I continued to go through the pile, searching for Dad's regular eyes, for Dad's warm smile, his familiar worn jeans—a modest pose.

Underneath my naked father were what Dad had called proof sheets—glossy, stiff 8X10 prints, each crowded with multiple miniature images of me and Henry.

"You choose the best photos from the proof sheets and only develop those," I remembered Dad explaining shortly after the shoot, when I was carrying on about how long it might take until we got to see the images. I didn't know what he meant until this moment—I hadn't been able to visualize a "proof sheet." I thought he was referring to some kind of proof of worthiness or prettiness.

    I splayed the proof sheets across my knees and the couch cushions and scrutinized the shots that had been deemed *not the best ones*, looking for imperfections. My images seemed so small after all, so insignificant and lackluster. Had the photo shoot *really* been about Dad? I tried to remember what I did when my photo shoot was over. Did I go outside with Benny? When and how did Dad's shoot take place? Embittered and confused, I gathered the scattered photographs from my lap and one by one returned them to a tidy stack. I placed the stack into the manila envelope and tucked it into the curio cabinet exactly as I had found it, vowing to try my best to pretend I never saw the photographs. I didn't mention the naked pictures to Dad, and I never brought up the shoot, the portfolio, William, or modeling again.

Chipped Polish

    That summer, we spent many afternoons at the beach. The beaches in New York were crowded with people on towels. There were snack bars with loud music playing and the smell of tanning oil. We almost always went to the Stony Brook beach close to where we lived, but occasionally Dad drove us all the way to Jones Beach in New Jersey.

    Just like he did at the pool, Dad poured Coppertone oil all over himself, and lay back on his towel with his eyes closed. I thought this looked incredibly boring and wondered how he could stand not spending most of the day in the water, like I did. When he got sick of my begging, he'd finally take a dip, holding me in his arms, with the gentle waves lapping at our chins. Back at the blanket, I rested my head on his tanned belly, my wet salty hair sticking to him and soaking up Coppertone so that I smelled it for days.

Dad liked to give me his special advice at the beach—maybe this was because we had lots of free time on our hands there, or maybe because it was a place where he was extra aware of the importance of looks.

"Did you see the way she looked at your fingers?" Dad snapped as we walked away from the snack bar one day, after I had handed change to the lady behind the counter for our ice cream.

I looked at my fingers, small amounts of sand in the creases, and pink nail polish chipped half way down the nails.

"*What?*" I asked, my stomach dropping as I tried to play dumb. I *knew* what Dad was talking about. He was talking about the chipped polish that I had so lazily ignored. He stopped walking and grabbed my hands, rubbing his fingers over my nails and holding them up to my face.

"It's trashy to wear chipped nail polish like this and you know it."

Dad announced a new rule as we ate the ice cream at our blanket: I may wear nail polish, but only if I do not let it chip. He had already told me I ought not let it chip, but had not made this a downright rule. When he bought me my very first bottle of nail polish that summer—a light pink ("red comes later," he said at the drugstore)—he also purchased a bottle of nail polish remover.

"Take it off and re-do it as soon as it chips, princess," he instructed as we browsed the many colors of nail polish. My heart sank at the beach that day to see Dad so disappointed in my failure with the pink nail polish.

"Go on a date with nails like that and he'll think you're a hussy," he snapped, not looking at me while he rubbed more oil on his chest. Dad explained that "a hussy" was a low-class, cheap hooker.

"What's a hooker?" Benny asked—suddenly interested in the conversation—as he squinted at Dad with the sun in his eyes, his lips and chin crimson red from his popsicle.

"A hooker is called a hooker because she *hooks* men

into paying money for sex," Dad explained.

"She has a hook? Like a fishing man?"

This made Dad laugh. I actually had the same image of the fishing hook in my mind, but I didn't say so.

"No, no Pooh. I meant she tries to look sexy so men will pay her money to do the nasty."

Benny stared blankly for a few seconds, before licking his hand clean of the melted popsicle that was going all the way down his wrist.

"It's positively sloppy, just sloppy," Dad said curtly in my direction, rolling his eyes and shaking his head.

I imagined raising my glass with chipped nail polish to toast my future date as I sat across from him at a fancy restaurant. I pictured him frowning in disgust, thinking that I'm a hussy-hooker.

Dad's opinion about nail polish was just one of many among his lessons on how to "avoid *le trash*," as he called it.

"Sister, if you want to act like a lady who's got any class at all, you'll listen," he said in that hillbilly accent he used when he talked about turning men down.

I hated when Dad called me *sister*. It was as if I weren't his daughter—like suddenly I was another relation, and I didn't know him. Still, Dad's code could be handed down at any time, and I didn't want to be trashy, so I listened with eager ears.

Dad also told me that men would eventually think of me as plain and unsophisticated if I did not eat these two things called caviar and escargot.

"You tell him, 'I eat French, thank you very much,'" he said with his hip out, pointing a finger at an imaginary date. I asked what was caviar and escargot.

"Fish eggs and snails," he said very matter-of-fact like it was no big deal.

"*Gross!*" I spat.

"Yeah, gross," Benny chimed in.

Dad called caviar and escargot "cultured foods" and had names to go with a woman who might eat these things on a date—class, elegance, maturity.

"But I *hate* fish. And I don't ever want to eat a snail,"

I complained, sticking my tongue out and mime-vomiting. I wondered how I would ever make myself eat these things, worrying that I would be labeled as boring in the eyes of my male callers. Dad acted me out on a date, making a sour face, batting his eyes and talking in that hillbilly accent: "I'll take a hamburger and fries, *anything* to avoid a fork, thank you very much."

Dad said that long hair must be kept free of tangles (I squealed in pain as he tirelessly combed out my knots with Johnson and Johnson's "No More Tangles"); he said that a slip should be worn under a special dress, and that cheap drugstore makeup is tacky. The image of my mother entered my mind —the most important woman in my life. She showed none of the traits that my father professed to be feminine. In fact, my mother was just about the opposite of who Dad said I ought to be. How was this? And what did this mean for me as her daughter?

Across The Country

Mother and Tom drove their Dodge van all the way from Berkeley, California to Centereach, New York to pick us up that August of 1978—I was nine and Benny was six. I had been excited about the prospect of a drive across the country, and about seeing Mother. But when that van pulled up in front of our apartment—when I saw Dad carrying our suitcases and boxes down the stairs with his eyes low and his jaw tight—I got a terrible case of butterflies. I thought I might throw up. This feeling was superimposed with joy at seeing my mother, who was wearing faded jean cutoffs—her mane of dark hair looking fuzzier than ever. She was giggling and hugging me and Benny over and over with tears in her eyes, saying how tall we had gotten. Benny clung to the side of her leg, hopping and stepping on her toes while looking up at her.

We were squinting and shielding our eyes with our

hands in the bright morning sun. The air was already humid––there were wet spots on the armpits of Dad's white T-shirt. Smells of the van interior immediately escaped when Tom rolled the heavy side door open with a grunt—wood and vinyl and oil and something sort of like cooking spices.

It was time to say goodbye to Dad. I uncontrollably ejected what I was trying to hold back when he grabbed me up to hold me in his arms in a long hug. I began crying out loud as I clung to him, limp and infantile. I wished I knew how to apologize to Mother for this. I looked past Dad's shoulder to see her hurt expression, and Tom standing with his arms crossed, looking at the sidewalk. Benny wasn't crying; he was still happily clinging to Mother.

Even though I understood that he had to do it—even though I knew the agreement was that we were to spend the school year with our mother—there had been some sense of disloyalty when Dad pried my arms off him to give me over to my heartbroken mother. Benny and I climbed inside the van and crawled on top of the big slab of plywood that had been made into a bed with a large piece of foam on top (there were no seats in the back). The final goodbye seemed even more dramatic when Tom rolled the side door to a loud close. I watched Dad disappear out the back windows as we drove away.

It took us twelve days to drive across the country. Our belongings were crammed into every space imaginable in that van. I was glad for Tom's built-in radio/tape deck, however there were no Bee Gee's or E.L.O. or Andy Gibb—there was flat-out *no* disco at all. I got used to—and even enjoyed—the "Casey Jones, watch your speed," and the "time waits for no one, and it won't wait for me" and the "knock-knock-knockin' on heaven's door."

We mostly camped in undesignated spots, setting the Coleman stove on a dry patch of ground to make dinner. Sometimes we'd use a tent, sometimes not. I liked to sleep under the stars with Mother—just our faces and the sky and the dirt, no tent. The cold, deep midnight blue night sky went on forever, with thousand and thousands of stars so crowded they touched each other. It was one of the most magnificent sights I had ever seen.

I felt that the space dividing my parents shrunk a little when I looked at the sky; I saw the same stars and the same moon and the same sun that Dad saw. Sometimes at night, I'd look up at the stars and wonder what Dad was doing at that very moment. I longed to be sleeping next to him on his pullout sofa and hoped he wasn't too sad.

Mother taught us all about the constellations, tracing the star configurations with her finger in the air. There were the obvious favorites—the Big Dipper and the Little Dipper. Mother's voice was melodic and small under the giant universe, saying, "Look at Pegasus, the winged horse" and "See the kite? That's Libra." There was Taurus, The Bull, Cancer and Hercules. It seemed that the vast sky was a playground for mythical creatures. They almost appeared to be moving—sword fighting and music making, and with bows and arrows.

We slept in the van along the roadside some nights, the whole van rocking with a sucking force and then a release every time a big rig drove by. The smell inside the van was car oil and earthy, musty wool blankets that had been wet then dried, then wet and dried over and over again, like laundry but without the soap. There was the smell of pot. Some smells were magnified by the heat—the hard plastic on the dash and center console, and the black rubbery seal around the windows, which seemed to melt in the day and turn hard again at night. There was snoring and farting and Mother's furball hair.

We camped by a colossal dry lakebed in the Great Salt Lake Desert in Utah. This was my favorite stop during our drive across the country. Mother and Tom took us on a long, hot mountain hike, where there were giant spectacular rocks and red dirt against a sky the most striking of blues. The hike was great, but all Benny and I wanted to do was explore the dry lake.

We spent a good chunk of an afternoon by ourselves in the stifling heat, exploring the maze of prism-like cracks where there had once been water. Strange dry plants miraculously grew in the light-colored dirt that was hard as rock and the consistency of hardened clay from a hot kiln. The ground was *white* in many spots, which I assumed to be salt because of the word "salt" in the name of the location. I imagined bending down to take a pinch to sprinkle on my food.

Benny seemed to be on a mission when he ran ahead of me in his blue jeans and T-shirt, jumping to avoid the cracks on the ground as if he were playing a game of hot lava. He was carefully selecting a walking stick among the many pieces of rounded and desiccated pale wood that lay strewn about. Once he finally picked a stick--smooth and light and taller than he was--he never let go of it the entire day. Mother had tied a red handkerchief around his head that morning, saying that the sun was going to be "very intense." Benny looked so wise--like a seasoned mountaineer--walking along the endless dry ground in the desert heat with his walking stick in his hand and his handkerchief around his head.

We searched the ground for evidence of life--hoping to find fish bones or turtle shells--awestruck to be standing on a place where water had been over our heads. I tried to imagine the huge transformation of the lake in my mind. I pictured the giant lake suddenly sucked up in a reverse waterfall that went to the sky--frightened fish struggling and dying in the evacuation. But Mother explained that it took months and months--years, even--and that the fish and plants died over time.

At the end of the day, when the sun went down and the temperature went from shockingly hot to quite cold, Mother pulled her large Georgia O'Keeffe book from a box in the van. She lay on her side on the plywood bed and settled in with her book as Benny and I rummaged through the snacks in the cooler.

"Come here," she said, holding the flashlight to the book, "Look at this, don't these paintings look like the desert we saw today?"

Benny and I took the box of crackers and crowded next to her, our heads bumping together as we intently studied the Georgia O'Keeffe paintings.

"See the ground?" Mother traced the page with her finger, "It's like the ground we saw today. And, here––the mountains."

The paintings *did* look kind of like the desert and the dry lakebed. But there were scary animal skulls in some of the Georgia O'Keeffe paintings––with colorful and ornate flowers. I stared at the images, trying to interpret the meaning of having skulls and flowers together in the same painting.

"How come we didn't see any bones?" Benny asked, cracker crumbs falling from his mouth as he wiggled and bumped into the book.

"They're out there, believe me," Mother said matter-of-factly, not taking her eyes off the images. "We just didn't see them today, but they're there."

"People bones?" he pressed.

"Maybe. Definitely animal bones, *maybe* people bones."

Without thinking about it, I bent down to smell the book, taking a big whiff where the pages met the spine.

"You're a book sniffer, honey," Mother giggled and grabbed me. "Always having to smell the books, I love you so."

We stopped in Illinois because Tom had a good friend there, and he wanted a place to park the van while he did some repairs. He wanted to make a little sunroof in the back because the exhaust smell was pretty bad, and Mother was complaining that it was toxic for me and Benny.

Benny and I liked Illinois because we got to watch TV in the living room while the adults hung out and Tom made the sunroof. We were watching the TV in the afternoon when in walked a few Native American kids with their family. The adults walked past, joining the other adults in the back of the house, while the kids stayed with us in the living room. They didn't say a word--the silence was awkward as they stared at the TV and at us.

"What's that?" the boy asked, pointing to the TV set (he seemed to be about ten years old).

Did he really not know what a TV was? I imagined this boy and his family living out in the wilderness in a teepee, away from civilization.

"It's called a TV," I said as I got off the couch and walked over to change the channel a few times to demonstrate how it works. "You can watch shows on it."

The boy looked at the other kids with a smirk and they all started laughing. I realized then that I was just the brunt of a joke. The kids still didn't say a word, even though we spent a fair amount of time together in the same room that afternoon.

Mother explained that the kids and their parents were part of this thing called "The Longest Walk."

"They're walking across the whole country. They're activists for Indian rights."

I couldn't believe they were *walking* across the country, as I thought about how driving across the country was long enough. How could they walk all that way? I was astonished by their dedication, remembering Mother explaining the word *activist* back in San Francisco, when she took us to the protest dressed as clowns.

It seemed that the drive would never end. But then, one night—it did. It was past midnight when we finally pulled up to the old white Victorian. I had been sleeping when Mother shouted, "Kids! Kids! We made it! We're in Berkeley!" She and Tom were cheering loud hoorays.

I was eager to get inside, schlepping along behind Mother and Tom, carrying as many things up the steep stairs as I could in one load. Mother turned on the hallway light, and I got a peek of the old table through the doorway to the kitchen. Even though I had seen this house before, I was looking at it with new eyes. *This is where my mother has been*, I thought, looking at the blue phone on the floor next to the old worn brown couch. I imagined her talking to me from that very spot all those times we spoke on the phone when I was in New York.

"Your room has been waiting for you!" Mother sang out, bouncing on her toes, as she opened the door to our room off the kitchen and fumbled inside for the light switch. We dropped our heavy belongings down as soon as we made it in our room with the green shag carpet and the yellow and green wallpaper. Benny started looking through the milk crate shelves, probably checking to see if he could find any of his old comic books or tickets.

Even though we arrived after midnight, Mother made us chamomile tea with honey and buttered toast, and we sat together at the orange-painted wooden table in the dining area next to the kitchen, sleepily talking about how it would be when school started.

"I'm so glad you're here," Mother said over and over. "This is a new beginning."

Hot Tomatoes

It's hard to pin down the one thing that started the trouble at the Berkeley Victorian that fall of 1978. In my mind, it seemed to begin with what Mother and Tom referred to as *parties*, though the gatherings didn't seem like parties to me. If I had a party, I would have had ice cream and pin-the-tail-on-the-donkey and balloons, the Bee Gees and Electric Light Orchestra. To them, parties simply meant groups of adults hanging around for hours, talking their boring talk and smoking pot and drinking beer, while sitting cross-legged on the floor listening to the Grateful Dead and the Doobie Brothers.

Mother still had a way of making things fun, even when you had a sneaking suspicion that something was amiss or even dangerous. One afternoon, Tom was having a get together, and his friends lay splayed out across the big pillows on the old rug in the front room. Mother appeared beaming and radiant in the doorway of Benny and my bedroom.

"Come on, come on, come on," she ushered as she took my hand in hers to pull me up off the floor, my colored pencil dropping, my drawing pad left open to a half-done drawing. Benny was so enmeshed in his superhero drawing; he just stayed put without even looking up.

It seemed as though a surprise were about to happen when Mother pulled me into her room by the hand.

"Let's dress up and serve those guys like waitresses!" she coaxed in a girlish whisper with her hands clasped under her chin.

Her giddiness was contagious. Out of her closet we pulled hangers draped with gauzy dresses and flowing skirts, tossing them to the floor. Next, we went to her dresser, raiding the contents like pre-schoolers in a game of dress-up. We were having fun—great fun. After plenty of high-pitched giggles and trying on various outfits, we chose bathing suits. I can still see my mother standing half-naked in her pink string bikini against the dark psychedelic orange, red and black wallpaper of that bedroom; I can see her big toothy smile and her teased-out mane.

"Two things go together for men," she said, looking in the mirror, and holding up one finger for each male penchant to make her point, "women in sexy outfits and food."

I felt that Mother was letting me into her world, passing down special secrets. I felt like a grown woman.

"Let's make it a show! It will be a fun surprise," she proposed.

I was thrilled. I stood next to my mother in the mirror, the two of us giddy and looking at our bodies in sexy poses. My breasts weren't really breasts at all yet—I was quite flat compared to my mother, with her round, full jugs that barely fit under the little triangles of her bikini top.

We left the orange bedroom and crept down the hallway in single-file to prepare an assortment of fruits. We ransacked the fruit bowl, standing side-by-side at the kitchen counter, making a juicy mess on the big wooden cutting board. We sliced up oranges and peaches, my elbow hitting her bare hip, juice running down our wrists. Mother pulled out a colorful, large ceramic platter and we began to arrange the fruit in a fancy pattern, clapping and laughing nervously. She laced the outer edges of the platter with sliced apples and then dried her hands off with a dishrag while she admired it from a step back, announcing, "Ta-da!"

    We took a moment to compose ourselves outside of the front room door, before stepping inside to surprise the men with our hospitality. Mother stood in front, holding the platter of fruit, me in the back. I felt a wave of apprehension, which felt something like dread. The dressing up was fun, but I wasn't so sure about the next part of the game. Were we doing a dare? Why did I get the feeling we were playing with fire?

    Mother opened the door and proudly waltzed in, swaying her hips in that bikini while balancing the tray of food in one hand like a sexy game show attendant. I suddenly felt naked and shyly followed close behind her, thinking the men might not be able to see me as well if I stayed just a few inches behind my mother, who was *really* the star. About seven or eight men were gathered together on the dirty braided rug in a semi-circle, the record player going with Van Morrison "Domino." The afternoon sun was filtering through the lace-covered windows and hitting the wall in slants, illuminating the smoke that hung motionless in the air. The men made horns with their hands and began howling to show their appreciation. *It really worked,* I thought, watching in amazement at how well my mother had pegged their reaction. I loosened up with the approval as they started taking food off the tray.

    A little mirror lay on the rug and one of the men was doing the thing with the white powder stuff—dividing it up carefully on the mirror with a razor blade to form straight lines, like a special art project. I had seen Tom and his friends making shapes with this white powder a few times. It seemed like an hors d'oeuvre, only they ate it through their noses instead of their mouths, which I thought was pretty weird. I had formulated a comparison to it, and that was of the sugary dip in my Fun Dip candy. I imagined taking my little sweet candy stick and dipping it into one of their white powder lines for a taste. Would it taste like that treat I remembered from Centereach? But, somehow, I got the picture that you'd never want to mess up those perfectly dissected lines, it would be like wrecking someone's sandcastle or knocking down someone's house of cards.

I was standing there by the powder mirror when I felt a little tickle in the palm of my hand. I looked down to see a man with curly dark hair and a black beard and mustache, lying on his side with his head propped on his elbow. His index finger had tickled its way through my fingers and into my palm.

"Hot as a red tomato, just like your mother," he said slowly and quietly with a wide grin, his eyes all slanty and bloodshot.

I gasped without sound and held my breath, my eyes darting to my bare feet as I quickly withdrew my hand from his. I thought of a large ripe tomato on a vine, warm from the sun and with its zesty, sweet smell. Did my mother and I resemble a tomato? *Was this a compliment?* I looked up at Mother then, just inches from me. She stood laughing and smiling, bending down to take a doobie from Tom, and pinching it between her fingers. I figured she hadn't heard what the man with dark hair said. Or maybe she was happy that we were warm, red tomatoes; maybe that was just what we were supposed to be.

I was starting to feel very afraid the men might jump my bones or try to get laid or do the nasty. Was this what Mother wanted? I flashed to the way my dad taught me how to reject men. The sassy, cocky dismissal seemed like it would be so easy when the time came. But I could hardly swallow my own saliva, much less say even one word.

A few minutes in, the men seemed like hungry wolves. I worried that they would become out of control; it seemed we had set them off and that we wouldn't be able to tame them. The white powder snorting sound reminded me of a bull snorting, with hoofs scrapping the ground, dust in the air. I wanted my mother to stop parading and leave the room with me. But I don't remember us leaving that smoky room––I only remember wanting to leave.

The next morning, Mother and I sat at the orange table quietly having our toast and tea. We were the only ones awake; Benny wasn't even up yet. Mother was resting her cheek on her naked knee, her blue robe falling loose around her chair. She seemed morose, staring expressionless out the kitchen window.

"There's a man from last night that wants a wake-up call," she broke the silence, continuing to look out the window, and not at me, "He's in the front room, on the floor. Please go wake him up for me." My stomach dropped. Was it the same man who said I was a tomato?

"Why me?" I asked, definitely *not* wanting to go near this strange man.

"Because I had to wake him up before, and he tried to grab me."

"I don't want to," I said reluctantly.

I was sheepish and quiet and ashamed when Mother pressed on, finally turning to face me, asking me why I would *ever* want to put my mother in that position.

"He's going to try to kiss me, he did last time. It's one simple favor, Astrid." She held up her pointer finger in front of her face. "One. One favor."

"But what if he does it to *me*?"

"He *won't*," she shot with a sharp look, rolling her eyes.

Mother was growing irritated and impatient, a state I strived to keep her from. I looked at the floor and considered going to wake the man. I thought of how he would be sound asleep. I imagined creeping over to him and tapping his shoulder. He would have morning breath and look disheveled, his matted-down hair all greasy and looking like caveman hair. I imagined that it would be difficult to wake him; I would have to shove him harder, get my body closer to him. I imagined he'd try to do the nasty like Dad warned. I pictured his large, hairy arms reaching out for me from under the covers, pulling me to him.

I searched for a better answer than, "*I don't want to.*" I felt guilty at throwing Mother to the front room instead of me. How could I explain *why* I just couldn't bear to go wake the sleeping man? No words came. I just sat there frozen waiting for something to happen—an okay from her.

"Thanks a lot," she snapped.

I felt so helpless as Mother walked away, toward the front room in her blue terrycloth robe. My mother would be grabbed at because of me. *I should have gone.* It would have been simple enough; maybe he wouldn't have grabbed me, like she said.

I waited outside the room in case she needed me, standing in the quiet and tossing my relief and my guilt. When Mother came out of the room a minute or so later, she whipped so closely past me that her blue robe brushed my knee. I waited for her to tell me about the man, but she wasn't talking. It was like I wasn't there.

Private School

Mother had taken a job at a little school in Marin. She assured us that it was *not* a public school--but she said it was not a free school, either. Benny and I got to go for free because she was the assistant kindergarten teacher there.

"It's a private school, " she declared, announcing, "There *will* be rich kids there," rolling out the L's in the word "will" like a warning. She said there would be some rules and maybe even bells, and definitely lessons. No pens were allowed—only pencils, beeswax crayons and watercolors. Also, nothing made of plastic was allowed; everything was mostly wooden.

"And there's no TV allowed," she cautioned with a ring in her voice like no TV was a good thing. I envisioned a little red schoolhouse and *Little House on the Prairie*, which Mother had read to us the year before. I was a bit on edge.

"It's a *really* good deal that you guys get to go there for free. This is one pricey school."

Mother had bought herself a light blue VW Bug. We rode the Bug across the San Rafael Bridge to the private school Monday through Friday. To get to the San Rafael Bridge, we had to drive Northwest, through the city of Richmond. Richmond was an ugly place with industrial tanks and buildings that lined the expressway. The slums and the land of the *elite* were separated by the Richmond bridge, which took a mere ten minutes or so to cross. It seemed like another country once we got to the other side.

Everything was pretty in Marin County. Quant little streets were laced with well-pruned trees and large welcoming homes with flowerpots on the front walk. White people wore sunglasses as they drove their rich-people cars to work, humming along in the pre-nine o'clock traffic. These were the people that bought fancy cheese and went to R.E.I. and North Face and shopped at FAO Schwartz at Christmas.

There were only a few girls in Mr. Schwartz's fourth grade class who were kind enough to tolerate being my friend as––for the most part––other kids did not associate with me and Benny much at all. I was the kid who tried to weasel my way in, rather than being invited. I was acutely aware of the differences between my brother and I and all the other kids. The rich kids *had* to think I was weird––arriving in a VW Bug with my mother always in her hiking boots with wild skirts and shawls, and me in my Salvation Army clothes or my New York clothes that were getting too small. I wasn't in their circle––*that* was plain as plain.

All the children had gone through the previous grades together in Mr. Schwartz's fourth grade class. The program built on itself in the private school, and the children stayed in the same classroom––with the same teacher––throughout elementary school. Mr. Schwartz often grew frustrated at me for not understanding what he seemed to think was simple instructions. Having come from the free school in New York, I did not know my times tables or how to write in cursive. Greek mythology was new to me, and there was plenty of it at this school. I repeatedly drew or painted angels when I was told to illustrate a scene from one of the stories. Mr. Schwartz snapped that not every story was about angels, and that not all *good* ought to be illustrated in the form of a yellow angel. It seemed that I was always missing some key piece of information, or some part of the puzzle that everyone else caught onto so easily.

My throat was swelling up, or that's what I thought. It seemed that, if I thought too much about Dad and Centereach, my tongue got big and rubbery or my voice box wouldn't work right. So I tried to block out thoughts of Dad—his chest, his voice, the smell of his shirt. I blocked out my room in Centereach and the smell of the pool, my cat Henry. The trouble was that trying not to think about Dad made me believe that, somehow, I was bringing him bad luck. There was a voice in my head, like some kind of bad character, saying, *You're going to make Dad go away because you're trying not to think about him.* I'd actually respond out loud, sort of like a prayer, saying, "I love Dad," three times or, "Dad will live forever." But then I was still thinking about him.

I remembered the scene on the pullout sofa in Centereach, when he said very matter-of-factly, "If it weren't for you two kids I'd be dead by now." I imagined him crying alone in the living room, only a matter of hours—or maybe even moments—before he actually died from us being gone. In my thoughts of him dying, there was no accident or illness, rather Dad simply closed his weeping eyes and quietly died on the couch. This thought led me to having to repeat "I love Dad" three times again or saying, "Dad will never die," or "Dad will live forever," and then the cycle would repeat all over again. I figured that trying to prevent Dad's demise from so far away could only be done through concentration or magic.

I tried to save the little crying I allowed for when I was in bed at night with the lights out. There were so many miles between me and Dad but I had to try to stay put. In the staying put—the longer the time went on in Berkeley—the more I clung to Benny. Benny was proof that Dad existed; he was part of Dad. Benny would return to New York in a matter of months and that meant that I would, too. Also, Benny was solid in the way that he was constantly there, always beside me and—for the most part—he was unchanging and always himself. That I could count on.

Benny and I kicked and elbowed and cursed at each other during the day, but I had taken to cuddling him on the foam mattress at nighttime. I wrapped my arms around his small bony body and ran my hand over the dry skin on his arms. His head fit perfectly in the crook of my neck—his fine, dirty-blonde hair smelling like hay, with tiny a hint of soap.

I wasn't sad because Mother wasn't loving, because she could be so sweet. She read to us every night just as she always did--with each of us on either side of her on the foam mattress in hers and Tom's orange paisley bedroom. Mother had an incredible knack for storytelling, the tone and speed of her voice changing at just the right moment. We hung onto her words that captured the essence of each story.

We read the *Chronicles of Narnia* that year. In my mother's voice, I could taste the Turkish delight and hear the snow crunch under Lucy's feet.

Our mother could also make up fairy tales right off the top of her head. The storyline flowed flawlessly, as if she were reading right out of a book. I remember one story about a brother and sister who had many adventures in the woods and then in a magical bubble that floated up to the sky. The story went on for several days, with her picking up where she had left off each night. I couldn't wait to hear what would happen next.

Mother told stories this way in her kindergarten classroom, as I witnessed when I snuck in sometimes during my recess. The small children sat in a circle around her, with three or four of them vying for her lap. Those children who had been wild at play sat quiet and hypnotized, held by my mother's musical voice. I loved to watch her storytelling; I loved to watch other people soaking up the good in her. This was my proof that I wasn't the only one enraptured by the magical part of my mother. This part of her was real life. Knowing this made up a little for the bad times.

Ballet Pink

Mother signed me up for ballet lessons that year as a special surprise. The atmosphere of the dance studio was the same as the private school, even though it was held in north Berkeley, and not Marin. The teacher, Madam Lochet, was a grouchy short French woman in her sixties who wore thin wrap-around sweaters over her shoulders, and giant broaches that sometimes drooped off of her leotard top. Her stern discipline--which radiated through the sunny studio lined with mirrors and wooden ballet barres--was something that I simultaneously longed for *and* feared. My heart raced as she staggered my way with her yard stick, spitting, "Straaaaight!" I adjusted my posture quickly, but the madam made it clear that it was too late to adjust once she had noticed. I took respect in the influence of that stick, believing the quick sting to my upper thigh might change me in a flash--*bad to good, wrong to right, rags to riches.*

All the other girls wore ballet pink and silently practiced demi-plies, grand-plies and pirouettes while elegantly holding onto the ballet barres. I *knew* I stuck out like a sore thumb in my forest green tights and maroon leotard--the inescapable mirrors pointed out this detail with every move.

"Is it Christmas?" one of the girls snickered, sending the class into a chime of cackles and a chanting of "Ho-ho-ho."

I loved ballet pink. It seemed that this shade was the key to success, the shade of untarnished perfection, and of faultless obedience and *getting it right*. Mother had explained that she couldn't afford both the ballet pink get-up *and* the classes, and scoffed that I shouldn't want to be like everybody else, anyway.

Madam Lochet's twelve-week ballet class was to culminate in a recital. About six weeks in, we all excitedly sat around in a circle when she slapped a fat catalogue on the hardwood floor, announcing, "It's time to pick the outfits, girls."

Page after page displayed the most exquisite little ballet outfits any nine or ten-year-old girl could dare to dream of having. We were all to agree upon one little ensemble for which to wear at our recital. I remained quiet while the other girls squealed and shrieked over one tutu after the other, pushing at each other and arguing over which one was prettier. I already felt the swell of worry as I imagined informing my mother of the need to write a check for the costume, which would be matching nine others. I had my own favorites--squealing silently--but I *did* love the one that was finally agreed upon. The bodice was full of glitter and clung tightly, with hints of sparkly powder-blue mixed with a brighter pink--with silver edges around the full tutu. The models in the photo held wands with stars on the end with chiffon drapery attached, and I wondered if these came with the outfits.

We practiced our routines in the weeks leading up to the recital. Each girl had her place in swan like lines and configurations. With each passing Saturday, more checks were being handed to Madam Lochet for the recital costumes. A note had been sent home regarding the costumes, with the amount required. I turned my head to look the other way when I handed my mother the note in the car that day.

"I can't afford this! She never said anything about outfits for the recital! This is ridiculous!"

When all the girls except me had paid for the lovely tutu outfit, Madam Lochet started to call my house, informing my mother that we were only two weeks away from the recital and that she needed the money. Madam had paid for the outfit herself, assuming my mother would reimburse her. Aside from the phone calls, the delinquency was announced at each class, so that I began dreading to go.

"I don't have it!" Mother barked into the receiver of the phone in the hallway, when Madam Lochet called for the tenth time. I stood around the corner where she couldn't see me. There, I heard my mother tell that Madam Lochet just where to get off and that her daughter would *not* be part of the dance recital. Click.

The following Saturday, at one O'clock, I imaged those nine girls in their puffy pink, blue and silver outfits looking as lovely as can be, cameras clicking at the sides. I wondered if the hole left by the tenth girl was obvious, or if Madame Lochet had craftily patched that up.

Mother's Funks

There were certain days with Mother that were cast with an unusual sorrow and gloom. We woke to find her disheveled and tearful. We never really knew *what* had initiated her funk, only that we ought to tiptoe around her carefully and try to make her feel better. If she were going through a particularly bad spell, she'd regress to a childlike state. She'd wail or curl into the fetal position. On these days, she called herself "Sally."

When Sally came out, I just wanted to calm her. She was lost and ruined. Holding Sally up was a big job, as *nothing* seemed to make her happy. The terrifying fact that the person who was supposed to be the most strong and able were neither of those things was magnified on these days.

I remember one Sally Day when Mother was curled up on the big chair in the dining area of the kitchen, crying. Nothing was right. Benny was on one side of her, and I on the other.

"I'm the baby, *me*. It's my turn today," she was sobbing in a soggy kind of way. Her face was wet with tears and she was wiping her nose on the sleeve of her big lavender shirt. "Does anybody ever think of *me*?"

Benny was cooing to her, saying, "Mommy, *we* think of you, *I* love you, *I* do––" He was stroking her face, trying to get in her lap, only she wasn't taking him.

"No, no, no," she shook her head and held her hands over her eyes like she didn't want any *mommy this* and *mommy that*; she seemed to be blocking out my brother, me, the house, her life.

What stood out the most on this particular Sally Day was that I wasn't wearing any pants or underwear. I don't recall whether I had taken a bath or was getting dressed when Sally showed up, causing me to abandon myself on the spot. Tom walked in and saw us, stopping to stand in the doorway. I was kneeling and so I tried to cover my bottom with my shirt, but couldn't because my arm was around my mother.

"What's wrong with *her*?" he snapped in an *I'm-tired-of-it* sort of tone.

I was filled with shame and humiliation. I was exposed and raw—caught coddling my baby who was my mother, and I was naked doing it.

After our attempts to sooth Sally proved to be futile, as she usually receded to her room where we'd hear her sobbing much of the afternoon. This was loud, guttural wailing--the kind of wailing you'd hear from a child. Sometimes, I dared to open the door to that orange paisley bedroom, to find her curled in the fetal position, unkempt and frayed. Sometimes, I adjusted her pillow or asked if she wanted some tea. Other times, I just put my hand on her shoulder. It always seemed as though I wasn't there.

    I didn't *always* try to comfort her. Sometimes, I tried to block her out with loud music or by leaving the house all together. Tom never really did anything to try to stop her, as far as I could tell. Usually, our mother was back the next day and we would carry on as if Sally had never been our unfortunate guest. It was hard to understand what could make Mother so disabled in her funk. One thing I *did* know: there was only so much space and time for a person to fall apart in our house. Our mother held the reservation for falling apart. If someone else needed to be the baby, they had better find another place to do it.

    I generally tried to avoid what I thought might be the culprit to Mother's gloom. She usually lost her cool when Benny and I fought in the car, which was often, unfortunately. One time when we were fighting, she skidded the VW Bug to a slamming halt along a rural road somewhere outside Santa Rosa, and burst out of the driver's side door. She ran up the untamed hill, leaving the car door open, and disappeared into the briars. This *did* put an end to the quarrelling between my brother and I. We fell completely silent and stared at each other there a bit slack-jawed. Usually, the vanishing of our mother put an end to our fighting and led to alliance.

    Sometime later, maybe fifteen minutes--it might have been thirty--we saw Mother's figure reappear, eyes low and hair full of burrs. She got back into the car and we drove off without saying a word.

    On another occasion--one gray foggy day with a steady drizzle--Benny was hitting me in the backseat, and I was screeching. Mother complained several times, but we weren't listening. The car came to a sudden stop on the side of the freeway, Mother's foot hitting the brake so hard that we flew forward. She tore out of her seat--the motor still running--and whipped around to Benny's side. It all happened so fast; we had no time to react. She was screaming this and that about how she can't stand our fighting and how she was going to "put an end to it." She dragged Benny out of the car by his arm in a whirlwind and pulled him to the side of the road, his little spaghetti legs scrambling to keep up.

"Mom...what are you doing?" I half-pleaded--panic-stricken--as she quickly got back in the Bug, leaving Benny on the side of the freeway.

She didn't answer. My heart sank as the car moved forward. I began to cry. I was watching her eyes in the rearview mirror, looking for some semblance of regret, a resolve, guilt--something that would make her stop the car and roll into reverse to fetch my brother. She just stared straight ahead. I turned around to the back window to see Benny's little body running after the car with his arms out, wailing. He disappeared in the drizzle as she sped off.

"Mom! Please! Don't! Go back! *Please!*" I begged. She remained silent though, speeding down that freeway like she had somewhere to go urgently. I was in horror, my thoughts racing, as I searched for why. *Why did I fight? Why won't she turn around?* I struggled to come up with some trick phrase to make her turn around. *Benny might die on the road.*

In one minute, maybe two, maybe five, we were turning around, en route to pick up my little brother. The time that had passed seemed like an eternity. Mother remained silent, her eyes unblinking in that rearview mirror.

When we got to Benny, he was in a heap on the side of the road, crying hard. I can see him in the car beside me after we picked him up, shivering and trying to stifle his crying--his breath fogging the windows. I can smell the sweet, sweaty scent of his wet hair. This was the same kid I was hating ten minutes before, and now I was loving him more than anything, curling my arm around him with my shirt damp from his.

The windshield wipers clicked back and forth. I realized that I had not noticed the sound of the wipers *or* the rain before the stop on the highway, when Benny was driving me crazy. Now those sounds seemed magnified. Mother kept quiet the rest of the way home, her eyes fixed in the rearview mirror.

Just as Mother's dark moods could have such a monumental impact on us, so could her bright, upswing moods. Along with reading to us just about every night in her whimsical, songbird reading voice--and doing pastel and charcoal artwork with us--Mother made sure we had our fair share of real life experiences.

Harvey Milk was assassinated that year, on the 27th of November. Mother and Tom were all fired up in the kitchen about it that day, Mother crying with her face in her hands. I had never heard of Harvey Milk. Mother said he was a city supervisor for San Francisco, and that he had done all this work to ban discrimination. I had only a marginal understanding of what all that meant, but it sounded to me like this Harvey Milk had stood up for people, and wanted everything to be fair-square.

"He was the first gay person in office, he did so much for gay rights," Mother told us, sniffling and nodding her head. "It's such a loss."

My stomach dropped as I immediately thought of Dad, and all the times he talked about the bullying of gay people. Was Harvey Milk shot and killed *just* because he was gay? Were there killers out there, starting to actually *shoot* gay people? Panic set in, and I wished--more than ever--that I could get to Dad. How could I know he was safe?

The very evening of the day that he was shot and killed, Mother and Tom took us to San Francisco for a candlelight vigil held for Harvey Milk. The crowd was enormous. Benny held onto one of Mother's hands, and I the other, as we joined the hundreds of people holding candles with little Dixie cups attached to catch the melting wax. It seemed the whole city was turned upside-down--the streets blocked off--and I was being consumed by the intensity. We slowly and quietly shuffled elbow-to-elbow with the mourners--some with glowing pearly tears rolling down their cheeks.

I knew everyone was sad about Harvey Milk, but all I could think about was Dad. The hundreds of long and shadowy candlelit faces were spooky, and matched so well my morbid worry. I had been missing Dad so much--the magnitude of the vigil matched my heartache and offered a deposit for the longing. At some point, Joan Baez led "Amazing Grace." I do not recall this part of the story, but I am certain my mother was both crying and singing.

Somehow, Benny and I got separated from Mother and Tom. Panic-stricken, I frantically swiped at the air with my arm as I held on tightly to Benny with my other arm, calling out, "Mommy! Mom!" I jumped up and down, trying to see past the people in front of me, while trying to not bump into the hot candles. Benny started to cry. It must have been only about five minutes or so--Mother appeared, looking just as panicked as we were. She immediately threw her arms around both of us and held us tightly there in the middle of the crowd.

My sister, Kimberly

I told Benny I would give him my only two bucks if he would dress up as a girl and pretend to be my sister. I was beyond ecstatic when he accepted without hesitation, immediately assigning him the name Kimberly.

That same day, Mother gave us her pocket change to spend at the Salvation Army a few blocks away, on San Pablo Avenue. I didn't tell her that my plan was to buy Benny a girl outfit. The Salvation Army was one of our very favorite places to go, we could spend hours rummaging through all the thrifty finds. Mother often didn't mind giving us a dollar or two—I think it was a cheap price to pay for keeping us occupied for so long. The measly pocket change went a long way at the Salvation Army.

Like a dream come true, Benny even agreed to dress like a girl for the Salvation Army excursion. My green and red Christmas dress was much too big for him, but he didn't seem to mind.

Benny trotting along the sidewalk the four or five blocks in the oversized dress and his beat-up sneakers.

"Remember, you're my *sister*," I told him, "try to act like a girl, ok?"

"What do I do to act like a girl?"

"I don't know…you know. Just be like a girl, don't go look at the trucks and cars. Look at the necklaces at the counter or the dolls."

"This is stupid," he whined as he trudged alongside me to San Pablo Avenue, throwing his head back and slumping his shoulders.

"Well, you haven't gotten the money *yet*. You'd better keep your promise," I warned in a bitchy tone.

"This is my sister," I announced to the older woman behind the counter when we walked through the door at the Salvation Army. This was the same woman that was there nearly every time we came in—I thought she wouldn't recognize that it was Benny. The dress would *surely* be so very disguising.

"Oh—" she said, scanning Benny up and down doubtfully, "What's her name?"

"Kimberly," I replied with confidence, sure that everyone in the vicinity was overcome with jealousy and awe over the fact that *I* had a little sister. Benny stood quietly being a good sport in the green and red dress.

We scanned the aisles over and over for the perfect

Kimberly outfit. I was frustrated that Benny kept wandering over to the toys, seeming not at all as rapt up as I was in the quest for sister clothes. Finally, I found the ah-ha get-up: a long yellow polyester dress with a white lace yoke and white ruffles at the bottom. It would fit Benny just right.

"This will be perfect!" I cheered, as I ran over from the little girl aisle to the toy section, where Benny sat on the floor with an old board game that he had opened. He was putting all the plastic pieces in a line beside the open box.

"Stand up!" I ordered.

Benny rolled his eyes, and stood up begrudgingly, still holding game pieces in his hand. He quietly went along with the sizing up routine, eyeing the bikes and the skateboards behind me. I held the yellow dress to his scrawny body to check for size. It would be a little long, but it would do. I loved that the dress was so overly feminine. Benny did not say a word as I placed the thin, gauzy arm of the dress over his floppy, uncooperative arm.

We had plans that evening with Mother and Tom to go see Cheech and Chong's *Up In Smoke* at the funky warehouse-turned-theater on Gilman called the Rialto. Because the movie had the word smoke in the title, I thought maybe the movie was about a genie with disappearing powers, or maybe it would be like the movie *Smokey and the Bandit,* which we saw with the free school, when Tim and Judy took us as a field trip.

Mother was making stovetop popcorn in the large cast iron skillet, like she always did for the exciting treat of a night out at the movies. She was standing in front of the big white stove, putting her whole upper body into shaking the skillet vigorously back and forth on the burner.

"I'm not paying an arm and a leg for popcorn, when I can make it myself," she announced proudly as I was putting on my shoes. "Besides, they use shit butter. And it doesn't come with soy sauce and yeast flakes!"

"You're really gonna let Ben go like that?" Tom was asking Mother by the stove, referring to Benny's yellow dress. She completely ignored him.

"We're bringing a six-year-old kid *in drag*? In drag."

He pointed at Benny as if he weren't standing right there—motionless with his lip out—looking at the floor. "Can't you say something to him?"

What was *drag*? Mother liked to use the phrase "it's a drag" about things that were a bummer, and sometimes she and Tom called a toke on a joint a drag. I never knew there was such a thing as a drag outfit.

"Get real," Mother snapped, still not looking at Tom, as she continued to shake the iron skillet, popping kernels wildly escaping the lid and flying to the floor. "If he wants to go to the movies in a dress, who cares. So be it."

"*I* care," Tom said with his arms out to the sides. "I'm not sitting with him."

As he walked away toward the bedroom, he mumbled something about Benny being a fag like his dad. I was worried Tom's reaction was going to make Benny change his mind about pretending to be my sister. But Benny still went along with it.

Mother angrily divided the popcorn into two used brown paper grocery bags, smothering it in butter, soy sauce and nutritional yeast flakes.

"So I *really* can't sit with my kids at the movies?"

"If you want to go with me, you can't."

I almost thought we weren't going to go. But we did make our way Rialto in the Bug that night. Tom stuck to his word about not sitting with us, and he and Mother sat a few aisles up in the theater. I didn't care that they weren't sitting with us; I was preoccupied with the joy of sitting next to my *sister*, Kimberly. Walking into the Rialto with "her" was such a treat—I almost believed it myself that Benny had turned into a girl. I turned my head around a few times during the movie to peek at Mother and Tom. They seemed to be having a great time—laughing, smoking pot and munching on their brown bag of homemade popcorn.

The movie was pretty boring—and was not at all about genies with magical powers, and it had nothing to do with Burt Reynolds' role as Bandit. It turned out *Up in Smoke* was in about a bunch of grown-ups who reminded me of Tom's friends—driving around in an old van like Tom's, and smoking a lot of pot.

I handed Benny the two bucks when we got home, after he immediately tore off the yellow dress. He never did pretend to be my sister again.

Cloud Pillows

Mother's funks often seemed to correlate with money and our lack of it. I guess her income was low enough to qualify us for some kind of public assistance. She usually totted us along with her to the welfare office, where we'd wait in a long line with unhappy, down-and-out looking people. Mother's voice was sharp and distracted when we were headed there—it seemed like we were in trouble for something, all three of us. It was understood that any extra money was not to be mentioned at the welfare office, and Mother instructed me to wear my oldest, most ripped-up pants.

"Remember, don't say a word about Tom. He doesn't exist, *get it?*" she warned. I was afraid they were going to find out somehow and throw us all in jail.

Mother told us to be on the lookout for what she referred to as well-dressed pigs that might come snooping around the house asking questions. Apparently, they could show up at any time. Whenever a decent-looking car pulled up on our street, my stomach dropped for a second, watching through the window to see who got out, terrified it was a well-dressed pig coming to interrogate me. The fear of being caught was always in the back of my mind.

Mother's assistant teaching job didn't bring in much money, so she was always into some kind of creative moneymaking scheme to supplement our income. The schemes and ideas felt like secret missions. We brainstormed about ways to make money on the side as we sat together at the orange table. We lit up with enthusiasm over one idea after another.

Many of our ideas went with the dust under the couch, too fantastic to be played out. But the cloud pillows *did* play out.

"Wouldn't people just love to have huge soft, floppy pillows shaped like clouds?" Mother gushed as though this was the most fantastic idea since ice cream was invented.

She spent hours sewing together large cut out cloud-shaped pieces of light blue and purple fabric. I thought she was so inventive.

One day bags and bags of fluffy pillow stuffing appeared in the front room.

"You got it!" I was clapping, proud of Mother, who had said she didn't know how she was going to afford the stuffing.

"Well, I had to cop it," she confessed, looking over at Tom instead of me, laughing and adding, "That warehouse had too much anyway."

My stomach lurched. I hoped Mother wouldn't get arrested. When had she done it?

While Mother made cloud pillows in her spare time, I made little pincushions to sell. The two of us sat together on the foam mattress in her bedroom, sewing beneath the glow of her paisley orange wallpaper. Even though she shared the room with Tom, to sit in this room was to be surrounded by Mother, amongst her stuffed animals, musical instruments, and the smell of amber incense.

Benny popped in every now and again, coming in from the yard or from rearranging his keepsakes. He had tried to sew once, when Mother handed him a needle and thread and a patch of fabric, but he had stuck himself in the finger, and made a fuss that sewing was stupid.

We had gotten a big fluffy cat that I named Scotty. He loved to curl at our feet and tried to get in our laps in Mother's room while we sewed.

Once we had finished several cloud pillows and pincushions, we loaded the merchandise into the Bug and set out to make money. Benny and I were very excited, imagining what we were going to do with all of this money. We would live like we had never lived before--we'd go out for pizza, buy new clothes, go to the Exploratorium—the possibilities were endless. We were on an adventure, entrepreneurs ready to show the world our product.

  The drive was a tad uncomfortable. The pillows were bulging out of the small back area of the Bug and crowding our heads. We arrived at the ferry station, where we would carry our golden parcels on board and sail to Sausalito.

  "Sausalito is crawling with rich people who love to shop and spend money," Mother apprised, "they will just *love* our cloud pillows. Someone might even spot us on the ferry and buy one right there."

  I felt self-conscious when we lugged our giant cloud pillows on board the crowded, full ferry. Everyone was staring as we tried to keep up with our vigilante mother, the warrior of industry with her head held high--nose up, arms full of moneymaking goods. Her butt shook with each step in her faded Levi's jeans, her old brown hiking boots slapping the wet metal floor.

  The pillows were stuffed into big trash bags and awkward to carry. Benny and I snapped at each other, arguing over who had to carry more. He was starting to complain that this was a stupid idea.

  The weather was cold and foggy when we got to Sausalito. We schlepped our goods for what seemed like a long time, before finally setting up a place to sell by the water, close to some fancy shops. We placed our blanket on concrete and strategically placed the merchandise in an appealing fashion--this was my favorite part, sort of like decorating a Christmas tree. We had nowhere to sit with the pillows taking up just about the whole blanket, so we squatted on the sidewalk or vied for the few inches of blanket on the periphery.

People came and went, passing our spot. The passers glanced at the large pillows before taking a quizzical look at the three of us. Then they kept on strolling. Occasionally, someone picked up a pillow or pincushion or bent down to touch one or the other with a pointed finger. But not one sale. I could tell we were out of place--that Telegraph Avenue in Berkeley would have been such a better choice. I wondered why our mother always had to do everything so *big*. This wasn't the right clientele--I was nine-years-old and I could see that, why couldn't she?

Benny--both cranky and hungry--teased me about how nobody wants my stupid little pincushions. Mother sulked while Benny and I played on the dock, waiting for the ferry home--amid the redolence of sea slime and fish guts--our potential pot of gold lying on the damp wood in the trash bags. I skipped and hopped with Benny, the wooden planks slick under my sneakers, tasting the salt on my lips. I played with my miniature Hello Kitty sewing kit on the splintery ledge of the dock. One of the pins fell out of my hand and I watched it sink below the dark green water.

For years, those cloud pillows followed us, from one home to the next. They became dirty and worn, with stuffing falling out. They were great for pillow fights, for sitting on, for lying on, or whatever else one might want to do with them. To me, those pillows represented the part of my mother that was both magnificently creative *and* going off the deep end--the part of her with her head in the clouds.

Mr. and Mrs. Perez

That year at the Berkeley Victorian––when I was nine-turning-ten and Benny was almost seven––we spent a lot of time with our neighbors, Mr. and Mrs. Perez, a Mexican couple in their sixties. I enjoyed being in their home and the attention the couple gave me. I especially liked their little black-and-white short-haired dog and their bunny rabbits.

It was within this time period that I started to ponder God and whether God may be of help to me with my chaotic home life. Mr. Perez was affiliated with the church up the street and gave sermons there. I watched the other children in the neighborhood going to church––mostly Mexican and black children. They parked on my block on Sundays, or walked from their homes and apartments. During the week, these children wore their usual second-hand pants and old sneakers like me; they even had tangled up hair. But on Sundays, they wore shiny hard-bottomed shoes that clapped the pavement as they walked, their dutiful mothers pulling them by the arm.

I wondered if we were having bad luck because of our lack of devotion to God and for not being normal. Were we being punished? Perhaps all the fighting in our home, Mother's sorrow, our poverty and my bottomless longing for my father were all due to the fact that we didn't pray or go to church. I imagined God sitting on a cloud––an angelic man with long hair and a staff in his hand. I hoped he looked down on me with pity.

I took to carrying a pocket-sized bible with a smooth red cover that I got at the Salvation Army. The writing was very small and there were a lot of words that I could not make out. I liked to take a big whiff of the little ancient Bible by putting my nose inside and flipping the pages. The pages were so thin, they were like tracing paper. I felt that maybe the Bible brought me good luck and would keep me from evil. I even stuck it in my coat pocket when I went to my very-first-ever dentist appointment that year, terrified that I'd get a shot with a needle right in the mouth.

I felt closer to this magical person called God when I was at Mr. and Mrs. Perez's house because of Mr. Perez being some kind of preacher. This made him glamorous—he had influence, people would come to listen to him. He was a star in my eyes, like Donny Osmond or Sonny Bono. He and his wife prayed and had many framed pictures of Jesus in their home. They listened to the religious channel on their transistor radio. The radio preacher spoke in Spanish, so I couldn't understand his words, but I could hear the passion in his voice. I imagined what he might be saying—a dark-skinned version of the minister at my grandmother's church, speaking with steadfast assurance that the robed rock-and-roller was our savior. (Until this point, my number one association of Jesus was that of the portrayal of him in the Broadway hit *Jesus Christ Superstar*.)

I was very excited the day that Mr. and Mrs. Perez invited me to join them at church. I wanted to see what *their* church looked like inside––and where all of the best-dressed children go every Sunday. Would it be very different from Grandma Arlen's church? (I hoped so).

Benny didn't want to go. Mother was in a rebellious rage on the morning that I was to go to church with the Perez family for the first time.

I argued with her, telling her that I really just wanted to see where all of my neighborhood friends were going. I promised that I wouldn't believe what they said. *My first lie against God,* I thought. *Points are being counted.*

I felt a little like I was betraying Dad, who called himself an "atheist." When I asked him what's an atheist, he said, "It's someone who doesn't buy into all that Jesus Christ religious garbage."

We laughed our heads off when Dad acted out people praying, namely his once-was-a-nun sister: "Oh Jeeeezzus, pleeeease do save me," he'd say on his knees, his hands clasped together in the prayer pose. I imagined him finding out that I was about to attend church on my own volition, how he'd probably use one of his favorite sayings: "Over my dead body you will."

I was getting ready quickly, dressing in my forest green dress and green tights. Mother continued her protest, following me to my room, saying she wondered where in hell I got this notion to join what she called the Bible thumpers, it certainly wasn't from *her*. I dashed out the front door without brushing my hair or tying my shoes.

Mrs. Perez welcomed me with a warm smile. We had some time before church was to begin. She was finishing the bun in her grey hair, with one hand holding all her wiry hair back, and talking through bobby pins in her teeth. I had never seen her without her bun and even seeing her with a bun-in-progress felt taboo.

"Aren't you pretty," she said with her accent. Did she notice my ratty hair?

Mrs. Perez did not look all that different from her everyday look, only in that she did not wear a dirty cotton apron. She wore a matronly polyester housedress that looked like a waitress's uniform with big pockets. Her dark tan pantyhose were a little shiny and made squeaky sounds when she walked. The years of hard work had taken an obvious toll on her appearance. Her fingers were worn, leathered and cracked, and shaped like little chubby sausages with dirt under the nails. I wondered if there was ever a time when she was pretty or wore pretty things.

Mrs. Perez worked around her dusty but not-so-dirty home with purpose. She was always making one kind of soup or another in her large stovetop kettle, out of pieces of meat that always seemed to be unnamed or indescribable. I thought of these concoctions as witch's brew and would dread having to politely accept a bowl. I guessed it was because of these concoctions that the Perez home always smelled of some kind of heavy, greasy broth. She seemed out of place in her old two-story house in Berkeley. She should have been way out in the woods with her kettle and axe, living in some sturdy but sideways-drooping cottage with a big smokestack coming out of it.

Mrs. Perez ushered me in to have a seat in front of the television while she finished her hair.

"Shirley Temple is on," she said with a smile before she disappeared into the back bathroom.

I took a seat on Mr. Perez's used-up, soft brown La-Z-Boy chair, directly in front of the big television. The armrests were worn down so that the leather felt and smelled like old cowboy gear. I kicked my feet back and forth, making the chair rock as I watched Shirley Temple. The episode with "The Good Ship Lollypop" was on. I loved Shirley Temple.

"Oh my gawd, would you look at her?" Dad had said once when we saw her on TV, "Can we say *disgustingly perfect*, people?" I knew then that I wanted to be exactly like her. She was cute and done-up and always wearing really, really shiny shoes that made tap-tapping sounds.

I turned my head toward the staircase when I heard footsteps coming down from the second floor. Mr. Perez appeared, stopping midway, apparently just to look at me. I felt awkward being caught in his special chair and stopped rocking. He was immediately kind though, telling me how happy he was that I'd be joining them for church. He slowly made his way down the rest of the stairs–– holding onto the banister the whole way––and took a seat across from me on the couch. We made small talk while he adjusted his big black tie. I marveled at seeing him in his white-collared shirt and black slacks, as his usual dress was either grease-stained coveralls or Ben Davis work pants with suspenders and a dirty T-shirt.

Mr. Perez was a man of few words who smiled a lot. He was always fixing something, though he walked with a limp. He was often short of breath even though he hadn't been running. He had a big belly with a stocky build, and his balding hair was gray.

Shortly, Mrs. Perez entered the room carrying a comb and hair things, with her hair pulled into a tight bun. She lovingly told me to sit on the floor and let her sit in the La-Z-Boy while she did my hair. I was thrilled. Mrs. Perez took the comb to my hair with swift, diligent strokes. My eyes watered and I winced in agony, trying to hide my pain. I could hear her loud sighs and tsks as she tackled the neglected baby-fine, dirty blonde white-girl hairs. Having someone brush my hair made me miss Dad. I thought of the way he would spray my hair with Johnson's *No More Tangles* before taking a brush to it while I cried out in pain, him snarling, "Would you *stop* carrying on?"

I could feel the fibers of Mrs. Perez's rubbery pantyhose creating static with the back of my polyester green dress while she did my hair. She smelled of sweat and gristle and baby powder. The more she worked at my knots, the more winded she became. I felt loved by her motherly torture. Soon the comb was running through my long hair with smooth straight strokes and she was clipping it back with barrettes, the loose skin on the back of her large doughy arms brushing the sides of my head. This was routine to Mrs. Perez, as she could work her hands through my hair to make the snarls go away while she held a conversation, looking the other way. To me, the act was far more engrossing––definitely beyond Shirley Temple.

It was a cloudy morning my first day at church with the Perezes. I walked up the steps beside them feeling proud of my green dress, and proud of my smooth, snarl-free hair. This Sunday I would join the other children. I was bathed in colorful sweaty polyester as I sat sandwiched between Mrs. Perez and another large woman, both holding hymnbooks in their pudgy hands.

It took my breath away when Mr. Perez got up to speak. Just an hour before, I was in his living room, sitting on *his* chair, and now he was speaking in front of all of these people. He talked with fervor and vehemence, just like the preacher on the radio. His Spanish words rolled off his tongue as he stood with confidence and charisma. He kept looking at me, but I shyly kept turning my eyes away from his. I was sure that I was the envy of everyone there.

I continued to occasionally attend church with the Perezes. I liked to go to their house early Sunday morning for Shirley Temple and hair combing before the service. I wore my green dress and green tights every time.

I felt like one of the family in the Perez home. Benny and I came to know their three grown children and their grandchildren. We became ornaments in their home--we were the Caucasian misfits amongst a tight-knit Mexican family. If we weren't at their home on our own accord, they were babysitting us while Mother and Tom went out.

The warmth of the Perez house was a refuge when Mother and Tom were fighting, which was frequently at this point. I felt embarrassed when I heard the yelling and screaming clear into the Perez yard. There was relief in their discount of the obvious turmoil. Mrs. Perez brought us into her kitchen, closed the door and offered us sweet things to eat. I watched her face closely for signs of disapproval. She graced us with her smile, but I could see her eyes frowning. *Thank you.*

The Hexed Jumpsuit, and Other Reasons

Mr. Perez started touching my private parts sometime during the fall of that year. The first time he did this was on his big brown La-Z-Boy chair. I was sitting on the couch watching TV.

"Come over here," he said, waving for me to come to him on his chair. This did not seem odd, as he had become very affectionate. I looked forward to his attention, because I craved fatherly love and because I thought he was such a celebrity in my community.

I walked over to him and sat on his lap, and we began to rock back and forth. He let me fall between his legs, pulling me into him so that I wouldn't fall forward off the chair. The rocking became more energetic as his hands slipped in between my legs. I was wearing my bellbottomed jumpsuit made of faded jean material. This beat-up, high-water outfit had become too small, and was far too tight. Mr. Perez's fingers burrowed deep in the crotch of my jumpsuit, and he pushed from there to make the chair rock faster, driving me deeper into him. It hurt. *This has to be a mistake. He means to hold me by my waist and he just missed.* Mr. Perez was good. He was a messenger for Jesus, so Jesus *had* to be on his side. Jesus may have been a half-naked rock-and-roller, but the Perezes led me to believe that Jesus was a savior who was looking out for me.

Soon I became aware of a hard thing sticking into my back. I focused on the rocking and assured myself that I was having fun. His breath became heavy behind me. I thought of being on an edgy ride at a traveling carnival in Carle Place, remembering Dad saying, "Princess, just wave if you want to get off and he'll stop." I felt dizzy and sick, like I might throw up. I didn't want to hurt Mr. Perez's feelings. *I walked over to him, I wanted to be on the chair.*

Benny sat on the couch mindlessly watching television and I wished that I were him. My brother was experiencing something so ordinary right there in the same room, just a few feet away. The same show kept playing on the TV; nothing else had changed in the room. Mr. Perez's suspender buckle began painfully digging into my back--I focused on that buckle instead of the feeling in my private parts. I saw that big metal buckle in my mind's eye, adding more teeth to it--imagining it as jagged and rusty--digging into my skin like a claw. I tried to ignore the sensation of the hard lump in Mr. Perez's pants that was up against the top of my butt, but the buckle just wasn't sharp enough. In an instant, I involuntarily sprung up, off the chair and out of his grasp.

Once I got to my feet, I really didn't know how I'd gotten there. Mr. Perez hadn't fought me. I quickly sat next to Benny on the couch and focused on the TV, keeping my face turned away from Mr. Perez. I could see in the corner of my eye that he was watching me. I tried to stay composed. I could hear my own breath, which I tried to steady. There were no words in my mind to describe what I was feeling, only physical sensations in my body—chilled, shaking, cotton-mouth, butterflies.

Once off the La-Z-Boy chair, I had a heightened awareness of my body and of the jumpsuit digging deep into my crotch--so much that it hurt. A light bulb went on as I discreetly wiggled to loosen my pants. *That jumpsuit had become too small and dug into my crotch whenever I wore it!* (American slang calls this having a case of "camel toe".) *It's because of the jumpsuit!* I had been dancing around the living room with Benny earlier that day. My doggone too-small jumpsuit was making men want to jump my bones. *I should have known!*

When I went home later that night, I stood on top of a chair in front of the bathroom mirror in my jumpsuit for a long time. I put my arms up, turned to the side, bent over. I tried to see what Mr. Perez saw; I tried to see what part of me made him do what he did. In the mirror, I turned my head and waved my finger *no way Jose* like Dad had taught. I thought of Dad pointing to his ass, saying, "See this? I said seeeee this? Nuh-uhh, sweetheart, you ain't gettin' none of this." Why hadn't I been able to turn down Mr. Perez Dad-style when he came at me? How come I didn't even see him coming? It was like nothing I had pictured; nothing like Dad ever depicted. My heart sank. How I wished I could talk to Dad.

I wondered what I ought to do with the jumpsuit--if I should never wear it again or if I should try it out on somebody else. That same week, I wore it to school, thinking very deliberately that I might try it out on a boy that I liked. During stretching exercises, where we all stood in a circle and stretched our arms above our heads, I watched David to see if he noticed my crotch. I unexpectedly became overwhelmed by the feeling that the too-small-jumpsuit had turned into some kind of weapon--something alive, something bigger than me. What if it attracted my teacher, Mr. Schwartz? I threw my arms down and sheepishly slunk around for the rest of that day. I never wore that jumpsuit again.

Soon, it became clear that it was *not* the jumpsuit that had caused Mr. Perez to touch my privates. I didn't stop going over to the Perez home after the incident on the La-Z-Boy chair, as I continued to love him and Mrs. Perez.

One afternoon, Mr. Perez gathered Benny and I for a game of doctor when Mrs. Perez was away at the grocery store. He cleared some papers and things off the dining room table and told me to lie down right on top. I was going to be the patient. I had always loved to play doctor--I played doctor all the time with my friends in New York. However, I felt the same fluttering in my stomach as I had that day on the La-Z-Boy chair, just a week or two before.

I tried to enjoy the doctor game as I attempted to override the anxiety of intuition. I hated when he did it in front of Benny.

"I need to check all the parts. Benny, you be my assistant," Mr. Perez instructed in his gruff accent.

My head turned to Benny as he stood next to me--his eyes just above the level of the table--seemingly waiting for the instructions on his part in the game. He was looking up at Mr. Perez.

"This seems okay," Mr. Perez said like he was talking to himself, as he lifted my arm. "Open your mouth and say 'ahhh.'"

He put his face right up close to mine as I reluctantly stuck out my tongue and said "ahhh" like he told me to. He had little beads of sweat on his forehead, and his dirty white T-shirt smelled like when Tom changed the oil in the van.

Next, Mr. Perez was tapping my belly. I thought that my butterflies might just hatch right out of my belly button and fill the room.

"And here--" he mumbled as he put his fingers on my privates and started to rub. Benny's eyes locked with mine. I watched the question mark show up on his face— his eyes squinty with his forehead all furrowed, biting his bottom lip. I could see speckles of green and brown in the irises of his eyes, something I hadn't really noticed before. Benny's eyes were like two tiny glass mirrors that held my reflection. I had the sudden urge to explain to him--to lie, to make something up--to make him think this was truly just a game of doctor. No words came. I had to turn my head away from him.

While Mr. Perez kept his hand on my privates, I looked at the balls of dust on the floor that lay opposite Benny, wanting to pilot us both out of there. I was imagining myself a miniature person playing in the dust balls. The dust was like wool twine--yet soft--with webs of fibers to run through.

I was thankful that Benny didn't say a thing after Mr. Perez was done. Maybe he didn't catch onto what had happened?

In the months to come, I got good at making my body float away, mentally making myself light and airy like a ghost, able to slip through walls and hover on the ceiling--like I was there but not there.

I was able to push the incidents out of my mind like mistakes. Mr. Perez kept touching me throughout most of that school year. His touches were often disguised under an innocent touch, such as helping me with my coat or my bike seat. This camouflaging made it easier to interpret his finger wanderings as unintended slip-ups, so much that I practically believed it myself. I got good at being able to dismiss my doubt on demand.

    Phone calls with Dad came and went with no mention of Mr. Perez. Why couldn't I tell him? I imagined telling him as I lay on my foam mattress at night. Thoughts of telling Dad always led to scenes of him warning me about ordinary boys, and of his descriptions of getting laid and getting your bones jumped and doing the nasty. I thought of John Travolta, Dave the lifeguard, and future male callers who'd expect me to eat caviar and escargot. How could I ever explain to Dad about this old man touching my privates? He was in his sixties and he preached at a church. Mr. Perez resembled nothing of what Dad carried on about when he went over Men 101.

    Constantly holding in the secret of being touched by Mr. Perez felt much like trying to swallow a lump of steak I hadn't chewed well enough. I was extremely afraid of Mrs. Perez finding out. I imagined her in a rage, yelling that I caused her husband to act this way and that I should be ashamed of myself; I imagined her banning me from her home. She had become like a mother to me. I thought of Victoria back in Centereach––the night she swooped into Dad's apartment yelling, and how I never got to be with her again after that. I didn't want this to happen with Mrs. Perez. I wanted to get back to the mornings when she ran the comb through my hair and it was only that. But as much as I tried to pretend with her, I couldn't keep my shame from my own self. *I like his attention. I keep coming back.*

    I imagined saying no over and over again because I thought that *no* was what I ought to say in order to put an end to what *I* had most certainly invited. I had given up on saying no the way Dad had taught me to say no. In my thoughts of fending off Mr. Perez, I was just yelling "NO!" at the top of my lungs. But I never could get the courage when his hands were on me. I would turn into a wet washcloth then--my legs without bones--with my lips fused together like the skin had been sewn shut.

My longing for my father was not going away, only changing shape so that it was a thick and solid tangible object, with odor and texture. I prayed that he would just *know* to come and get me, that he would show up one day and take me and my brother away with him. This led to several savior fantasies. I imagined a city bus pulling up by our house, alongside San Pablo Avenue, my father getting out and announcing, "Surprise!" I imagined him calling one day to say that he had had enough of this--he was on the very next flight. I imagined waking up one morning to Mother saying that it seemed like the best idea was to send us back to New York--Dad was waiting.

I could not imagine my mother without me, which made wishing for Dad a complicated matter. Mother grew agitated when I let it slip out just how much I missed him. This longing was something that I struggled to keep to myself, which sometimes came out unleashed, like the urge to vomit.

Dad sent a large package that Christmas. Benny and I tore it open to find wrapped presents inside. As if Dad were packed inside the box, the smell of his cologne rose up into the air. Benny shouted at me to get out of the way as I put my whole head in the large cardboard box. I did *not* manage to hold back my crying for the sake of my mother. A sorrowful wail came out with no warning. I cried out loud into that box while Benny removed the presents in a frenzy, elbowing me and calling me stupid. I felt so terrible for Mother, who had gotten up at the crack of dawn to make us hot cocoa on Christmas day. She had tears running down her face.

Fun with Food at the Victorian House

Sometimes you'd never know that our life at the Victorian house could be so tough. Mother still had a way of making fun out of everyday events--eating was one of those events. The consumption of food at the Victorian could be a real adventure. For starters, Mother surprised us with a coconut on rare, special occasions, and we'd have ourselves a coconut splitting ceremony.

"Ok, let's form a circle," she'd announce in the kitchen with a coconut in the crook of her arm.

"Coconut ceremony!" Benny and I cheered, punching the air with our fists, as we each took a spot on the sheet that Mother had placed on the floor. We sat in a little circle as we passed the coconut around, taking turns rotating it in our hands and shaking it back and forth, and guessing how much milk was inside.

The coconut was a little deceptive to me, even though I loved the cracking ceremony. I thought the liquid inside the shell sounded like something good because it was called "milk." It seemed that the coconut milk should have been creamy and sweet. But instead it had an earthy flavor, with floating flecks of brown shell that made me think of dirt. I also thought it odd how unattractive the coconut looked on the outside, considering how much I loved the *inside* of it--the hard shell felt scratchy and coarse in my hands, with the aroma of a heavy petrichor, like mud after rain.

"Are we ready?" Mother asked with a big smile when the coconut was back in her lap. I eyed the hammer beside her, excited about the next part--the cracking ceremony. But first: the prayer.

"Dear coconut," Mother began, lovingly rotating the coconut in her hands, "thank you for growing so beautiful and strong, so that we might enjoy your wonderful bounty. Thank you for letting us crack the shell that kept your milk inside all that time."

After the little prayer was done, Benny and I took turns trying to crack the coconut like a piñata with the hammer. I loved the feeling of bringing the hammer down hard on the thick shell. The trick was to not to make a huge crack in one blow, but rather to make a good-sized *sliver* so that we could drain the milk without spilling it all over the floor (Mother loved to drink the coconut milk).

We enjoyed sampling the sweet, rich coconut after Mother collected all the milk into a mug. She broke it into good-sized pieces and put them in a used plastic bag. For days, Benny and I reached for the bag in the refrigerator whenever we felt the hankering. We walked around the house chewing on the large chunks of raw coconut. and scraping our teeth along the white nutty meat attached to the thick brown shell.

"Hey, I'm tired of this crap!" Mother yelled when she found multiple half-eaten, tooth-indented pieces of coconut on windowsills, bedroom dressers, and even on the bathroom sink.

Pomegranates were my personal favorite. Mother cut the ruby-red pomegranate in half, exposing the beautiful, intricate pattern of seeds encased in the husk. The inside of the pomegranate was like a pod of sweet and tangy kernels, or *seeds*. I loved how the seeds had a membrane that went POP in my mouth when I chewed them. An added bonus––I got to shoot the seeds out of my mouth after eating off all the fruit.

Mother, Benny and I sat on the back stoop plucking the seeds from the spongy white husk with our fingers before popping them in our mouths––making funny faces to match the sweet and sour. We had contests over who could spit their seeds the farthest. For the remainder of that day, my brother and I wore evidence of our pomegranate feast––running around with red-stained mouths and fingers.

Eating couscous at our house was also an event. As with the coconut splitting ceremony, Mother laid out a sheet on the braided rug. We sat in a circle with bowls in front of us, and a warm pot of couscous in the center (I do not recall Tom ever taking part in the couscous dinners—nor the coconut splitting ceremony, for that matter). The rule was that we were not allowed to use any utensils, other than the big wooden spoon to scoop up our serving.

"If you really think about it, forks and spoons are pretty stupid for a lot of foods," Mother declared, sitting cross-legged on the sheet.

We each scooped a large helping of couscous into our bowl, and then proceeded to mash it into balls with our hands. Benny especially loved couscous night. He smiled ear-to-ear as he seemed to take great joy in molding his couscous into as many shapes as he could think of, as if the couscous were a lump of clay or Play-Doh.

"Look! Look!" he yelled, holding out his hand to show off the creation in his palm.

I loved the way the warm couscous felt in my hands, and I enjoyed rolling it into a perfect ball before stuffing it into my mouth. The trick was getting the couscous ball into your mouth before it fell apart. The more you squeezed it down tight in your hand, the more it would stay together. By the time we were through, our faces were covered with little pieces of the yellow grain, and so was the sheet and our clothes.

The best couscous nights were when we'd break out into a full-blown couscous war.

"I declare WAR!" Benny yelled, throwing his fist in the air. Mother and I knew to duck immediately, as the next thing we knew, the couscous was flying through the air. Mother and I threw back at Benny, and then at each other. The kitchen became a war zone of sticky yellow gobs going every which way. When we were through, we had couscous in our hair and all over our clothes. For days, we found little hardened yellow blobs that were missed in the clean-up--on the wall, the refrigerator and the stove.

For a brief chunk of time--when we had our pomegranate seed spitting contests, coconut splitting ceremonies, and our couscous wars--I'd forget about Mr. Perez and about how much I missed Dad. I'd forget about what an oddball I was at the private school. I was glad for Mother's distracting magic--as tough as things were sometimes, I wouldn't have traded her in for a regular kind of mother.

Overnight

All the occasions of molestation by Mr. Perez culminated during one weekend. I believe it was March-- I had turned ten. We were staying for two nights at the Perez home while Mother and Tom went camping. Mother was cheerful and thankful in her cutoff jeans and hiking boots when we met the gracious Mrs. Perez at the door late Saturday morning. I was carrying a brown paper bag crammed to the top and overflowing with my stuffed animals.

"Here's their Cream of Wheat, it's their favorite breakfast," Mother giggled as she leaned over to hand the box to Mrs. Perez, balancing our topsy-turvy unkempt sleeping bags in her arms. The sight of the sleeping bags made my stomach turn, as my mind was already reeling with thoughts of being with Mr. Perez all day and all night. I had already been plotting out ways to avoid being alone with him during the weekend stay, thinking about how I might manage the touching game.

I had been fine-tuning my ability to anticipate his next move. I found his hunt both terrifying and amusing in a competitive kind of way. Sometimes, when I felt safe because other people were in the room, I would inconspicuously strike a pose. I was mimicking the women who flirted with Dave the lifeguard at the pool in Centereach, or my mother serving fruit to a roomful of men––the women in R-rated movies. I enjoyed watching his response, feeling a sense of power in being able to get a reaction. I liked the fact that I was making him want me when he couldn't have me. I was so ashamed of playing the game with him, and later regretted my seducing him, feeling that I had brought on something that might become out of control.

    Mr. Perez drove Benny and I to McDonald's for lunch the first afternoon of our weekend stay, bringing along his five-year-old granddaughter, Maria. We all piled into the front of his old, rusty blue Chevy pick-up. The inside of the truck smelled like Mr. Perez's stained workpants—thick motor oil, train tracks, and the kerosene lamps in Vermont. It was the first time I had ever gone anywhere in public with him, other than to church. For some reason, it was strange to see Mr. Perez doing ordinary things that everyday people do. So many regular-looking things were going on while strange things were happening that no one could see. Was this only happening to me?

    His large belly was crammed against the big steering wheel as we all squeezed into the front cab. The vinyl seats were coming apart so that you could see the rough stuffing and the wiry coils. I was the one to sit beside him, so he and I were skin-to-skin. His white T-shirt was damp, and heat was coming off his armpits, smelling something like skunk-y fermenting sweat and soapy deodorant (as opposed to Dad's deodorant, which smelled more like fancy cologne.). His tough, yet marshmallow-like arm kept bumping the side of my face and shoulder when he made turns.

    Mr. Perez clasped his big, rough hand around my shoulder when I ordered my cheeseburger, fries and Coke at McDonald's. I wondered if the girl behind the counter could tell what he did to me––I felt embarrassed. We chose a booth and he sat next to me real tight like in the truck, only there was plenty of room.

At this point in my life––when lentils, beans and tofu were the main sources of protein––I would have just about *died* for a McDonald's cheeseburger. Benny sure was smiling ear-to-ear, the sides of his mouth covered with ketchup. But my cheeseburger felt like cardboard in my mouth. This hyper-awareness of chewing had become a new thing, whereby the act of eating no longer seemed instinctual or even pleasurable. I seemed to lack saliva, so the food felt awkward and stuck in my mouth––sometimes I wanted to just spit it out.

Later that afternoon, Benny and I were playing in the yard. We had been chasing each other and I was out of breath when I had to go inside to use the bathroom to pee. The bathroom was through the kitchen and off the dining room. The house seemed empty when I entered through the back screen door because there was no noise coming from anywhere. I ran as quickly as I could to the bathroom and locked the door behind me.

Mr. Perez's white underwear hung damp on the towel rack, as usual. I wondered why his underwear were always hanging up in there. Dad or Tom or Benny didn't have *their* underpants on display in the bathroom. Mr. Perez's underwear scared me—they were so large and made me think of his grown-man privates. On this day, also hanging in the bathroom, were his black Ben Davis work pants. I stared at the Ben Davis emblem while I peed, my eyes avoiding the underwear. When I first met Mr. Perez, I thought that the smiling monkey on the Ben Davis tag meant that he was fun, like a symbol to indicate his trustworthiness. I had liked the cartoonish smiling monkey.

I dreaded opening the bathroom door. *Make a quick run for it.* I tentatively unlocked the door and bolted, making a beeline for the back screen door. But, in order to get to the back door, I had to pass through the dining room and that's where he grabbed me. He took me by the arm as I ran past, my body snapping back into him like a rubber band. My eyes shot to the living room window that looked out onto the driveway--Mrs. Perez's station wagon was gone, we were alone. My stomach dropped and my mouth went dry as he pulled me closer. He got in back of me and wrapped his left arm across my chest and belly, clasping my shoulder tightly in place. I could feel that I was in a lock. He put his other hand between my legs and started moving it back and forth. I could smell the smell that I had come to associate with the touching episodes—his mildew-y, skunk-y sweat mixed with motor oil and soap. I immediately froze as I felt the pressure of his big belly against the back of my shoulders.

"Do you like it when I do this to you?" he asked with a winded deep, old-man whisper.

It was the first time that Mr. Perez ever addressed his touches. For some reason, I felt like I was going to faint because of his question--my knees weak and giving out. The feeling was kind of like when the lifeguard in Centereach told me I was a pretty girl during our hand-wrestle, only so much worse. Did Mr. Perez want to have sex? Was he about to ask me to do it? I had thought of this bone jumping, getting laid business several times over the past few months, remembering Dad's posturing in the living room. It had seemed funny, like a joke or a game. Dad's explanation of getting laid had sounded matter-of-fact and lifeless--easy, even. What Mr. Perez was doing seemed to be so far off the mark from anything Dad ever explained...it was scary and confusing, and he was so old. Oh, how I wanted Dad.

My mind spun with what might be the right answer. If I said "No, I don't like it when you do this to me," then I might upset him and *then what*? If I said, "Yes, I do like it," then I would be inviting more and probably worse. Having to decide gave me a spinning sensation--a feeling of weightlessness with butterflies in my stomach-

–like I was flying. I felt my body going more and more limp in his sturdy arm. His hand on my privates was getting more forceful so that it started to hurt.

    I surveyed the room. In front of me hung a gold-colored plastic cross with Jesus in the crucifixion pose. I thought about the fact that Jesus was probably watching me and Mr. Perez at that very moment, and this made me really embarrassed. My eyes fastened to a dusty framed black-and-white wedding photo on the table just a few feet away. The bride wore a beautiful white dress. Looking at the eyes, I could see that the couple was Mr. and Mrs. Perez many years ago. Their mouths started to move the more I stared without blinking. Details in the photo were coming to life––Mrs. Perez's curled hair began to bounce. I was floating off the floor and into the photo, yet unafraid. I heard low, indiscernible conversation and far away laughter over live music. Silverware and glasses clanged.

    "Do you like it when I do this to you?" he repeated impatiently, jerking his arm and crouching so that his face was closer to the top of my head. I gasped and the photo went still. I felt his hot breath on the back of my neck as he bent down close to my ear.

    Without planning it, I next found myself spinning around in a quick jerk with all my might, scooping my head under his arm. Mr. Perez didn't stop me; he let me go. I ran through the narrow doorway that connected the dining room to the kitchen. I felt like I was wearing big moon boots for the seven to ten feet I had to pass to reach the back screen door.

    The bright sunlight hit my face as I burst through the door. It had only been a matter of moments. This was the same backyard, but the colors were all changed, like when Dorothy landed in The Land of Oz. I felt a wave of nausea as I approached Benny. He ran up to me, his straggly long hair messy with sweat, and his knees covered in dusty dirt. He was ready to continue our game.

    "Let's see the bunnies," I said.

At the bunny cage, I crouched down in the dry dirt and put my fingers through the chicken wire and let the rabbits put their wet pink noses on my fingertips. I liked to visit the rabbit cage after Mr. Perez touched me. The rabbit's movements were brisk and timid and seemingly without purpose. Benny stood over me impatiently, kicking the dirt and causing dust to rise. *"Come on,"* he whined. I ignored him while I tried to get as much of my hand in the rabbit cage as possible. I imagined putting my whole body into the cage and becoming a rabbit person. My existence would be simple and undeveloped––almost unicellular––so that all parts of me were the same. I would be safe in my little cage, snuggling with the other furry simpletons.

I felt a stealthy presence, and glanced up to see Mr. Perez watching me from the kitchen window. I felt caught in the act of being a child, of seeking comfort and getting it.

Mr. Perez was unusually quiet and subdued for the rest of that day and on into the evening. He had a smirk on his face like a magician. Was he angry with me for not answering his question? I kept feeling his eyes on me. The air seemed thick, like when a storm is about to happen and the leaves turn over, and the pavement smells hot with electricity in the air.

Night Visitor

Mrs. Perez opened up the sofa bed in her living room, gave us some pillows and laid out our sleeping bags. I surrounded myself with my stuffed animals. Benny had brought his ratty and well-loved Curious George. We fell asleep quickly.

Sometime long after we had gone to sleep, when the house was dark and quiet, I awoke to the sound of heavy footsteps skulking down the stairs right next to our bed. I put my hand on Benny, who was asleep on his side, facing away from me. My stomach sank as I watched the dark figure of Mr. Perez approach. I could hear his shuffling limp as he made his way to my side of the bed. I kept my body perfectly still. I tried to control the pace of my breathing, focusing on Benny's calm easy breaths under my hand, and I tried my best to match my breathing with his. My heart beat so hard and fast, I was afraid Mr. Perez might hear it.

Mr. Perez he just stood over me motionless and in silence when he finally reached my side of the bed. I could hear his wheezing, labored breath a few feet above my head. I thought of his voice earlier that day. *Do you like it when I do this to you?*

I flashed to his underwear in the bathroom, and wondered if he planned to bring me in there and lock the door. Or maybe he would take my clothes off right there, in front of Benny. I knew that sex was a man putting his penis in a woman's vagina, and I was so terrified that Mr. Perez would do this to me. How would it fit? Would it hurt?

My body would not stay calm while my mind raced. I thought my only hope was to appear asleep, so I *had* to stay still. Soon, my stuffed animals were becoming real, like in *The Velveteen Rabbit*. My bear was fierce and protective, ready to attack. I thought of my mother telling me that there are angels everywhere to protect us and I imagined one hovering just above our bed. I could see her big golden wings in my mind--her sweet forgiving face.

While I was forcing my sprinting body to be motionless, Mr. Perez continued to stand still--he did not budge. Was he deciding what to do with me? Time seemed endless. *Why* would he want to stare at me sleeping?

Finally, after quite some time, Mr. Perez turned and made his way back to the staircase. Relief washed over me. I kept my hand on Benny, not moving a muscle, until I was sure that Mr. Perez was at the top of the stairs. I let out a long breath and then the uncontrollable shaking began. I was frightened by my inability to manage my own body--I thought I might pee. I tried to take deep breaths, but felt like I was choking. My skin turned freezing cold. If I could become one with Benny, then his body would take over the functions of mine, so I spooned him as closely as I could, our bodies practically one. I tried to match his breathing again. Soon, the shaking stopped, but I was unable to fall back asleep. I resolved to keep watch, afraid that Mr. Perez might come back.

The next morning, I had a metallic taste in my mouth and a sour pit in my stomach that burned. Mr. Perez came down the stairs to join his wife and smiled at me as if there had never been a late night visit.

I sat at the breakfast table feeling as though I had a fever. It was Sunday and the preacher was blaring on the scratchy transistor radio. Before, the Spanish sounded fascinating and exotic, and I'd try to guess the words off the inflection. On this day, the words curled in the wrong way--the tone too loud--the radio static too much. *What if, all along, the preacher was telling men how to get young girls?*

Mrs. Perez set down bowls of Cream of Wheat. I held back tears as it made me miss my mother. I tried to take a bite, but my tongue felt like a potato chip in my mouth. She didn't cook it right; it wasn't runny enough. She had made it with water, not milk. Benny looked at me across the table in silent recognition of the not-so-creamy thick and lumpy and Cream of Wheat. I envied him for having *that* be his only dilemma.

I stared at the gold flecks that laced the off-white stained plastic table. These looked like constellations to me and I was always searching the tabletop for the Big Dipper and Orion's Belt. I forced the appearance of being normal and interested in food. I wondered if Mrs. Perez possibly knew what was going on. I analyzed her face for evidence. She stood over her stove with the side of her face to me. Did she stay asleep while he crept out of bed?

One part of me walked mechanically up the church steps and through the aisle, while another part of me lagged behind--slow and oozing like molasses. I sat on the pew--beside my wiggling brother full of ordinary thoughts--while I tried to connect the pieces of me. *Does it show on my face? My dress? Can you hear it in my shoes?* I wondered if Jesus was a savior only for some, but not for others. My thoughts of the devil were basic and cartoonish--I pictured the red face and horns, the pitchfork and flames of hell. Did I belong to the devil's club, instead of Jesus' club with the clouds, harps, and flowing gowns? Why? What did I do so wrong?

I played with the hem of my green dress while I tried to drown out the preacher man's voice. He was speaking English, so I could understand the Jesus this and The Lord that. I was using a trick I did while sitting at my desk at the private school--I found a loose thread on my dress and wrapped it around my left pointer finger over and over until it started turning purple. There was panic in not being sure if I would get it loose before the circulation cut off entirely. I imagined my finger falling off; I imagined yelling for help. I frantically struggled to unwrap the thread, until my finger was free. I shook it until the pink returned, and then repeated this on another finger.

Mr. Perez stood up from his seat on the pew when the English preacher was finished, and limped up the aisle to the podium, where he faced the many worshipers. His slow dragging limp seemed magnified, trumping the sounds of people shifting in their seats, babies crying, women whispering. These were the same footsteps I'd heard in the dark only hours before.

His intoxicating Spanish supplication to God made me feel frozen while wanting to run at the same time. His mouth ran continuously--accentuating the syllables by shifting and gesturing with his hands--obvious passion in his words that I could not understand. My hands were sweating; my heart was racing. I imagined that he was telling everyone there that he touches me--that he watches me sleep, that he loves me, and that I love him. *This is my own fault; I made this happen.* I could feel his eyes directed at me, so I stared at my knees. *Why does he have to pick me out? He is telling everyone. Going, going, going, gone.*

At lunchtime, we sat again at the plastic table with gold flecks. The day was blending from one moment to the next--all parts of a dream--which would end when my mother came to the door to pick me up.

"It's called tripe," Mr. Perez said with a smirk in my direction. "It's cow stomach."

My mouth froze, as I had been attempting to negotiate the lumps of unfamiliar rubbery goo with my teeth. Our eyes met. I looked down at my bowl, but he did not take his eyes off me. *Act like you like it.* Mrs. Perez stood over her stove unaware, steam from her witch's pot fogging the window where I sat so that I could not see out.

"Gross!" Benny blurted out.

We sat stirring the soup, scooping the gummy clusters onto our spoons just to look before putting them back into the broth. I thought of cows grazing, eating grass, and sleeping; I thought of manure and the warm sweet smell of hay.

House Hunting

Mother got an itch to switch houses shortly after the weekend stay at the Perez home. Could it be that I'd be moving away from Mr. Perez? Perhaps to a place where he couldn't find me?

I lay lazily spread out on my floor bed one Sunday morning, listening to my *Grease* album, when I heard Mother calling out from the kitchen, "This one!" and "Oh yes, *that*!" and "Ohhh my dream house––" I got up and shot through the open bedroom door to see what she was so excited about. I found her sitting at the orange table, the morning sun shining through the window, and casting a warm yellow light across her face. She was drinking Peet's coffee in her blue terrycloth robe, her multi-colored psychedelic silk scarf tied tightly around her head, with untamed frizz sticking out the sides.
    "Our next house is going to be *the* house," she pledged, looking up from the Sunday newspaper with one eyebrow raised, and pointing at me with her ballpoint pen.
    I knew it right away: Mother was in a house-hunting frenzy. I remembered her fevered thrill in picking out a house when we moved from San Francisco to Berkeley. I didn't know much about gambling, but Mother's house-hunting mode seemed like a gambler's mode––she was omnivorous and hoping each listing would be better than the last.
    "This one has a useable attic!" she gasped, making a circle around the ad with her pen. "I could use it as an art studio!"
    "Which other ones did you pick?" I asked eagerly, taking a seat next to her. I was picturing Mr. Perez sadly watching us haul our boxes into the van from his window.
    "Look, look!" she said as she scooted the paper in front of me and pointed to the section entitled "HOMES FOR RENT." I scanned the ten or so listings that Mother had circled, her fervent house-hunting mode rubbing off on me. I loved hungrily surveying the details of the listings with my own secret selfish agenda, even though I had to ask Mother to read a lot of the bigger words. Would we go looking right away? When would we move in? My heart was racing as I imagined myself in each of the homes––would I get my own bedroom? How big was

the yard? I imagined an actual, bona-fide living room adorned with things like a couch with matching pillows, and maybe even an ottoman. I would invite friends over, and they would be envious of my amazing living room—— so normal and civilized.

"Which house?" Benny shouted, running from the back sunroom in his underwear and plopping hard on Mother's lap with his bony butt so that she winced and adjusted her hips and legs.

"We're looking at new houses to rent," Mother said, kissing the top of his head.

"I want my own room!" Benny cheered, rocking the chair as he bounced up and down in her lap.

"OUCH, Benny, watch it!"

"And a pool and tennis court, *please, please*," he chirped. It was obvious that Benny also deferred to the memory of Centereach when being presented with the prospect of a new home.

"Cool your jets," Mother warned, "I'm not a millionaire."

We went looking at the houses that week, when Mother and Tom got off work. After fixing a quick and easy dinner——like noodles and a can of cheap spaghetti sauce or rice and beans——Mother put her hair back in barrettes and applied her stale lipstick and eye shadow. She then ushered Benny and I to Tom's van, sliding the heavy side door open as we made a dash for the plywood slab in the back. Mother immediately grabbed the rearview mirror when she jumped into the passenger seat, adjusting it in her direction to check on her done-up look while Tom started the engine. She had the Sunday paper on her lap, and read out loud to Tom the addresses of the homes she had circled.

"Remember," she instructed, craning her neck as she turned around to look at us, "Tom and I are married and he's your dad. *Got it?*"

Mother had been having us rehearse pretending that Tom was our dad all week, saying, "Now, *what* will you call Tom when we go looking at houses?"

"Dad! We'll call him Dad!" we cheered, excited to be part of putting one over the landlords.

Even though I had come to dislike Tom, I secretly loved the thought of people thinking we were a happy, intact nuclear family. I imagined the landlords thinking things like, *Wow, just look at them. They look so damn happy and normal.*

One home sticks out--a generously-sized Victorian north of our current house, that was close to a big public school, off San Pablo Avenue. This house was my favorite because there was an actual bathtub in the backyard. I recognized that this was the closest I might get to having a swimming pool in California. I envisioned myself taking long outdoor baths in the sun in my Wonder Woman bathing suit.

"I'm very sorry about this tub. We have been meaning to take care of it," the landlord said during the tour of the backyard, frowning and shaking her head. "It's such a pain, I need to hire someone to haul it out," I couldn't believe she was apologizing for the fabulous bathtub.

"You can leave it here--" I blurted out, not being able to help myself. Tom chuckled and put his hand on my shoulder. This tiny gesture--his steady, warm hand on my shoulder--said *father* to me in a way that made the sham of Tom as the father and husband seem like real life. Would he still be fatherly after touring the homes? I imagined him having the epiphany that he enjoyed the role--our lives forever changed by pretending to be a regular family while house hunting.

For one reason or another, Mother and Tom never did pick a house that week-- they seemed to have put the house hunting on hold. I wouldn't be moving away from Mr. Perez after all; I'd have to stay put for the time being.

Rabbit Hole

Following the weekend at the Perez home, if I wasn't distracted by something engrossing like house hunting or couscous wars, I was pretty quiet and keeping to myself. I lay on my foam mattress in the fetal position with the covers over my head. I lay at night, spooned with Benny, my hand wrapped around the rough skin of his bony arm or his tummy, staring at shadows on the walls, my heart beating fast. I tried to eat, but my throat could not swallow and my teeth didn't know how to chew. At school, I advanced from the suffocating thread around my finger to putting my middle finger in hinge of my desk and closing it slowly, over and over again, making deep indentations, my eyes watering from the pain. I threaded needles from Mother's sewing kit through the fine layer of dead skin on my hands.

One evening during this time, Mother set down bowls of her vegetables, barley and lentil soup. The steam made condensation on my face as I sat motionless, not eating. For some reason, mealtime brought on the deepest yearning for my dad. It was as if my grief was most accessed by this primal nurturing thing: eating. I could feel my mouth trembling, a lump rising from my stomach and making its way to my mouth, like a bubble rising due to physics. I struggled with the muscles of my throat to abate the inevitable swell. *Why can't I be normal?*

"Eat--" Mother barked. She was getting impatient with my morose behavior and my lack of eating. She had warned that she would have to take me to the doctor for a shot--my worst fear before I met Mr. Perez.

The tears started despite my pleading with them to wait for my mother's sake. The table grew silent, my hot tears dripping off my chin. Mother whipped out of her chair in one jerking motion and stood behind me, placing her hands on my shoulders and squeezing hard.

"Fine. You can have what you want. I'll send you back to your father," she cried, shaking my whole upper body with every word. She stormed out of the room and ran down the hall to the orange bedroom, slamming the door behind her. I heard her muffled sobs through the walls.

"You're a fucking brat," Tom spat, throwing down his spoon.

Through my shame and guilt, I felt something much more powerful––a wave of relief ran through me with such strength that I felt that I had turned a different color. After all this time, Mother finally *got it*, and I didn't even have to ask. *I'm going to Dad's. I'm leaving.* The relief was so strong that my tears flowed faster, and I had to leave the table. Benny burst into our bedroom.

"Will I go too?" he asked, smiling and dancing on tippy-toes.

The days following, I did not mention my mother's plan for me to return to Dad, waiting for her to bring it up in attempts to not hurt her feelings by seeming too eager. But she never did bring it up again, and I never got shipped back to Dad.

I avoided the Perez home after the overnight weekend, feeling as though I had played with something that got out of control. I felt guilt over my absence and wondered how I would pay for it.

I was out in the yard playing on the avocado tree when Mr. Perez came out of his house holding a shotgun. I stopped like a chameleon lizard, but he saw me. He locked his eyes on me.

"It's time to kill the rabbits, do you want to watch?"

It knocked the wind out of me. The blow to my middle was so strong, it was as though I was hit with a basketball. My mind raced with words to stop him, but my mouth wouldn't move. I felt myself silently pleading with him not to do it, and he met my eyes with the same cunning look he had given me throughout that weekend at his house. *Got you.* Out of nowhere, I sprung into action and jumped off the tree, hitting the ground with a thud. He just stayed put with the gun.

When I turned to run, I found myself scurrying to the narrow dark crawl space under the house, instead of taking the long flight of stairs to the back door. I crouched into a ball in the moldy damp dirt, where there was a ray of sun coming in through an opening. I wrapped my arms around my knees and the uncontrollable crying started. I tried not to make a sound, covering my mouth with my knee and rocking back and forth. *Not my rabbits, not my rabbits, not my rabbits.*

I thought of the days when the rabbits had saved me, when I had drawn myself into their world and disappeared into them. I was still connected to their little fluffy bodies––their noses, their tails. I thought of how, when I would put my hand into their cage and feel their soft underside, I could feel their hearts race.

My heart was racing, too––my heart was connected to the rabbit hearts and my eyes connected to their eyes. I could see Mr. Perez's chubby rough hands wrapped around the gun––the same hands that had been on me––shaking and sweaty with hair on the knuckles. With bunny rabbit ears, I could hear his limp approach the cage. There was nowhere to run––wire and wood on all sides––no way out. Mr. Perez would block the only exit, with the gun pointed. *If I hear the shot, I will feel it too.* I covered my ears with my hands.

The shots came and went so fast. The rabbits were gone. Gone because of me––they were sacrificed for me, instead of me. *Am I still here?* I lay curled on the dirt, the earthy dust in my nostrils and the back of my throat. I imagined my innocent friends now limp in his hands. I lay there for what felt like a long time––I wanted to be sure that Mr. Perez was gone before I came out.

It had been a few hours since the shots were fired. I happened to be standing by my bedroom window, which looked into the Perez yard. The sun was setting and the sky was orange and pink when Mr. Perez appeared from behind the long rough wooden table in back of the bunny house. I quickly receded behind the windowsill, and peeked out inconspicuously. In one of his hands were the rabbits, swinging with his step, their bodies raw and pink. He had skinned them. He held them by their ears--their once warm and twitching bodies now loose and limp. I instantly felt that *I* was going limp--a numbness washing over--as I tried to take my eyes off the sight. I was unable to move. Not moving was part of becoming invisible, something those rabbits with fast hearts had been unable to do. In his other fist he carried the gun and a large knife.

He stopped for a moment in the middle of his grassless yard--his posture bent and uneven--and turned his face to scan my yard. *He wants to skin me, too.* I held my breath, with the familiar sense that--if I don't breathe--I'm not really there. Could he somehow see me in the window? He continued walking toward his house with the sunset in back of him, the flaccid rabbits swinging with his steps. One of the rabbits hit the screen door as he grabbed the latch. I caught a glimpse of the pink nose, just before they disappeared into the kitchen with foggy windows. I imagined my rabbit friends thrown into the witch's kettle, to be segmented into lifeless, anonymous pieces like tripe, tongue, and ham hocks.

Benny Blows the Whistle

"Mr. Perez touches Astrid's vagina!" seven-year-old Benny randomly called out.

All the blood drained from my face; I thought I might throw up. We had been being silly in the kitchen.

Benny was on the floor, rolling around and Mother and I were on the couch, laughing––the Saturday afternoon sun shining through the windows.

Mother seemed to be choking, bringing her hand to her mouth, the crimson of her cheeks giving way to white, and then––silence. It was probably no more than thirty seconds––one-minute tops––when the room stopped, but it felt like forever.

"*What?*" she shrilled, grabbing my arm. "Is this true?"

Mother's expression had morphed into a howling ghost. I darted my eyes away from her––to my feet––unable to look at her.

"Yeah, he does it a lot," Benny added in a plain-and-ordinary voice, wrapping his shoelace around his finger over and over. Who would've guessed *Benny* would be the one to blow the whistle on Mr. Perez?

Over the next several days we behaved much like a family preparing for a funeral. There were procedures to follow; smiles or laughs seemed fake. Did Mr. Perez's touching cause some kind of permanent physical damage? Mother treated me as if I were ill or had been in an accident. Tom was extra quiet and left the house a lot. Both Benny and I stayed home from school the following week, in order to do this stuff Mother called grieving and processing. She made attempts to pull my feelings out of me.

"*Please* talk to me. How can I help you if you won't talk?" she begged with tears running down her face.

My mouth wouldn't move. I just couldn't bear to talk about what happened. What would I say? I know it was hurting Mother––at night, she retreated to her room, and we'd hear her sobbing from behind the door. *My fault.*

"Honey, if it makes you feel any better, I wanted to tell you that he was really after *me*," Mother confessed to me one afternoon that week, when we were sitting at the orange table. She said that his infatuation with her had started on Halloween, when we went to the Perez home in our costumes. She had gone trick or treating with us dressed up in a pink long and slinky tight-fitting satin dress, calling herself "a lady of the night."

"He was always looking at me after that night," she was shaking her head and looking at the floor. "He probably figured that he couldn't get me, so he went for you. I'm so sorry."

I was furious, though I could not tell exactly why. I stared for a long time at our Halloween photo taken in the Perez home that was hanging on the refrigerator. Benny had gone as a mummy and Mother and I had had a good laugh, having used about three rolls of toilet paper to wrap around his whole body. I had dressed up that night as a princess, with a handmade crown I made out of construction paper, wearing one of Mother's full skirts pulled all the way to my chest. I looked like a peasant next to my mother in her shiny pink satin that clung to her body. I had loved seeing her in that dress. She almost looked like a High Heeled Woman. She even wore makeup. I had thought *This is what she would look like.*

We went to the courthouse to file a report on Thursday or Friday. Mother seemed to take pride in the fact that she had arranged specifically for a female officer.

"Don't worry, honey. She'll be wearing regular clothes," she said with unambiguous reassurance. "She won't have a gun or anything, she'll look just like a regular person."

It was amusing that Mother thought the police uniform would be traumatizing to me, and that regular clothes would be comforting somehow. I played along that she was right. I wasn't sure if the uniform would bother me or not; I wasn't sure if the gun would be distressing. I couldn't tell.

I couldn't sleep the night before we were to go to the police. I was imagining every scenario and going round and round in my mind with just *how* I'd explain what had happened. Thoughts of bravery were overridden by an unexplainable paralysis that made taking a leap and spitting it out seem impossible. Would Mr. Perez go *straight* to jail, or would it take a while? I imagined staring frozenly out the front window, armed officers pouring out of their squad cars and surrounding his house. I imagined Mrs. Perez dropping to her knees on the sidewalk and sobbing out loud as they hauled him off in handcuffs--all because of me.

 The Bug slid into reverse as Mother parallel parked in front of the enormous courthouse on Martin Luther King Jr. Way. (The building, in fact, was *not* enormous. It just seemed enormous that day.)

 "Come on, honey," Mother coaxed apologetically, standing beside the open passenger door in the cold. I knew my procrastination could not last more than a minute or two.

 "Get out!" Benny ordered, pounding his fists on the back of my seat.

 The morning was brisk and gray. I kept my eyes on the sidewalk with my chin tucked into my coat as I straggled a few feet behind Benny and Mother. As we began our ascent of the layers of brick steps, I wanted so badly to call out, "let's forget it!" and turn around. But I made my way up anyway--one foot in front of the other--up, up, up.

 "Hi sweetheart, take a seat," the heavyset, curvy black female officer said as she gestured for me to take one of the large comfy chairs in her second floor office.

 The officer had a big, toothy smile and a voice that sounded like Mother's storytelling voice--round and curly, with rich inflection. I liked her immediately. She was indeed *not* wearing a uniform, as Mother promised, though she was wearing a very wrinkle-free dark blue matching polyester skirt and blazer, which might as well have been a uniform.

 I wanted to say hello back, but I couldn't. My tongue was all big and dry in my mouth. There were waves of dizziness, and a moist condensation on my hands––maybe I was suddenly sick?

"Come on, honey," Mother nudged, gently pushing me from behind, toward the chairs, as the officer closed the door behind us.

As usual, Benny was looking as though he were trying to contain something inside him that was about to go off any minute––his quick and bony legs on *GO*. His eyes darted around the room, craning his neck and crouching to peek under the officer's desk––I figured he was probably thinking, *where's the gun?*

The officer lady first asked me about my school, about my cat, and what things I liked to do. I warmed up to her a little, but I still dreaded what was coming.

I dug my nails into the vinyl arms of the chair as she tried her best to pull a report out of the silent, paralyzed me. I couldn't get past the simple fact that she even *knew* about Mr. Perez––it felt so embarrassing to have anyone know about him, much less ask about him.

"Let's try this another way," the officer said as she got up from her chair and retrieved a basket from the little closet behind her desk.

"Pick a doll, sweetie," she said as she walked over and placed the basket on my lap.

I liked the floppy cloth dolls, and wished it was *only* the dolls, and nothing else. I poked my fingers around at the three or four of them, each with a different color of yarn hair. Benny shot up and walked over to check it out.

"I want this one!" he chirped, grabbing the only boy doll.

"Very well, Benny," the officer giggled.

I liked the one with orange braids and freckles. I held the doll, moving the arms and legs and touching the fabric of the little hand-sewn red dress. I was glad to have something to do with my hands.

"A lot of kids find it easier to show me where they were touched using the doll," the officer explained, leaning in and balancing a yellow pad of paper on her knee. "You can just point to the parts on the doll. Do you think you can do that, Astrid?"

I nodded *yes*.

"The very first time Mr. Perez touched you. Where were you? Can you tell me that?"

I picked at the doll's yarn eyes and her thick orange braids––my heart racing––as my mind went to Shirley Temple and Mr. Perez's special chair. I recalled the smell and the feel of the smooth worn-down leather of the La-Z-Boy chair.

"His chair. In front of the TV––" I managed to blurt out. Mother let out a long sigh. My face was burning hot; I knew my cheeks had to be bright red.

"Good, ok," she nodded, not looking at me as she moved her pen across the pad of paper. *What is she writing?* "Now can you tell me *where* he touched you on your body that time?" she looked up from her lap, "You can use the doll if you like."

The humid silence hung thick before I finally lifted the little red dress and opened the loose cloth legs––even Benny was uncomfortably quiet. In one quick darting motion––as if I were daring to touch a hot burner––I placed my pointer finger in between the dolls legs, and then immediately withdrew my hand behind my back.

We went round and round with this doll routine several times, where in the officer lady managed to uncover each incident with Mr. Perez. It got easier and easier to point to the doll's privates––I never did say it out loud, not even once.

"Benjamin, I'd like to ask *you* some questions now," she announced. My stomach dropped. *Why Benny?*

"Oh? Ok," Mother said like she was thinking out loud.

Benny appeared excited to be included. He started bouncing his boy doll on his knee, like he was getting ready.

I watched in shock as my little brother pointed to his doll's private parts (it was plainly obvious to me that he was not exactly uncomfortable to say the words, he was just wanting to play the doll game, too). I knew Benny *knew* about Mr. Perez touching me--after all, it was Benny who told--but somehow this made it so real. Benny was often present during the incidents, but we didn't talk about it--not even once. I always hoped he wouldn't bring it up; I even hoped that somehow he didn't notice. *Benny saw it, so it really happened.*

It was time to go back to school the following Monday morning. The kids immediately stopped talking and stared at me the second I walked into the busy, chatty pre-eight o'clock classroom. I felt all eyes on me as I agonizingly made my way from the door to my desk with my head held low.

"Mr. Schwartz told us about the man touching you in the privates and you going to the police," the girl next to me whispered, leaning in toward my desk.

Her lips moved as she continued whispering--asking questions--but it was as if her voice no longer had a sound. A hot swell swept over my body like I had just ingested something poisonous--my ears ringing and my cheeks pulsing. I don't remember the rest of that day.

"Astrid, I got a call from the woman officer," Mother started in after asking me to sit at the orange table a week or so later. She had a very serious, piercing look spread across her face. "She said that Mr. Perez was questioned and he denied ever touching you. He said he never did it."

"*What?*"

My stomach lurched. This possibility had never occurred to me. Did Benny and I get the story wrong?

"Yeah, it's true. I'm sorry honey," she said apologetically and angrily, shaking her head and looking away, before bringing her teacup down forcibly and spilling her tea on the table. "Disgusting asshole."

Surprisingly, my instantaneous urge to defend Mr. Perez had not faded at all. Why did I immediately want to shut someone up when they cursed him? Why did it feel like they were cursing *me*?

"The next step is that we would have to go to court," Mother started to explain, turning to face me and letting out a sigh. "You would have to get up in front of lots of people and talk about what Mr. Perez did. They probably wouldn't allow the dolls."

I knew immediately that I definitely did *not* want to do this.

"I've been giving this lots of thought, Astrid," she continued. I wanted to shut her up--I didn't want to hear her thoughts.

"I really don't want to put you through getting up in front of strangers to talk about this. And if we won, Mr. Perez would be sent to jail." She paused and took my hand in hers. "People that go to jail for doing what he did get beat up by other prisoners. He's old and weak. He'd be *killed*, I'm sure of it. It's terrible what he did, but I wouldn't really want *that* to happen to him. Would *you*?"

We dropped the case.

Home School

Little did I know, we'd be leaving that rich kid private school pretty soon. It seems that it was right after the molestation, but maybe it was a little longer-- Mother stopped teaching there and so we stopped going.

I related our withdrawal from the school with Mother's black widow save. One afternoon, when we were waiting for Mother to finish tidying up her classroom after the other kids had all gone home, one of the teachers at the private school noticed a black widow spider in a closet. The adults began fretting and gathering what they needed to kill the deadly spider. Mother got wind of this and went stomping down the hall with a fast stride, me and Benny running to keep up.

"I hope I'm not too late," she muttered worriedly.

With bewildered adults standing by--shaking their heads and wincing--Mother gently cupped a dusting cloth around the black widow and slid her into a Mason canning jar.

"It's all right sweetheart. I'm sorry. You can't be here anymore. You'll have to come home with us," she said in the soft voice she reserved for bugs and animals and small children.

I felt proud of my mom, seeing as how all the other adults were such scaredy-cats compared to her.

Shortly after we drove off in the VW Bug with that black widow in a jar, Mother announced that the people at the private school were pigs and assholes and that we weren't going back. So, one day, we just didn't show up. The three of us sat at the orange table together, enjoying tea and buttered toast in the afternoon, laughing and making fun of the teachers and the administrators of the uppity private school. Had they fired Mother for liking spiders so much?

Incidentally, we did keep that black widow for some time, offering her bugs like ants and small beetles and refilling her jar with fresh leaves. However, the day came when there were two plump yellow eggs in her web.

"It's time for you to go, sweetheart," Mother said tenderly as she held the jar at her eye level.

We drove the black widow and her eggs out to Tilden Park that very day. The three of us walked single-file through an unpopulated area of the large park, trying to choose what Mother referred to as "the perfect spot."

"I think this will do," she said after we'd been walking for ten minutes or so.

Mother got on her knees and placed the Mason jar on the ground next to a large tree before carefully unscrewing the lid.

"Be free, beautiful girl," Mother said as she stood up and brushed her knees off. "Say goodbye, guys."

"Goodbye, Black Widow!" I called out.

"Have fun with your babies! Enjoy the forest!" Benny added.

I thought she would immediately run free––like an animal that had been held captive at the zoo––but instead she stayed put in her Mason jar.

"She'll get out explore soon enough," Mother assured, after we watched the black widow for several minutes, trying to coax her to leave the jar. I kept turning my head to peek at her as we headed back toward the Bug, until the jar was out of view.

Mother had decided to do this thing she called *home school*. I liked the sound of it because it had "home" in the name. We loved the home school life because it meant lessons when we pleased, lessons ending when we pleased. The school day usually started with some form of direction, but would quickly turn into goofiness or fighting, where books were tossed.

"Screw it, just do what you want," Mother would snap before storming out of the room.

The school year was more than half over, anyway. Mother had enrolled at San Francisco State to get her masters in early childhood education, so it was easier to have our school on her schedule. Soon it would be time to go to New York, so we just stayed at home, biding our time with occasional home school lessons.

Benny and I kept ourselves busy. We took the Berkeley city bus by ourselves, up University Avenue to Shattuck, to our favorite store––a huge five-and-dime called Kress's. Sometimes we only had loose change, other times a few dollars saved up. We'd browse the aisles for hours and stopped at the store diner to order Cokes and fries and sit on the stools at the counter, talking to the waitress.

We got bored of never being able to buy much and so we established, what we called, "riding the freeway." We became shoplifters, savvy at slyly taking items off of shelves and stashing them in our bags.

"Let's ride the freeway!" we said in unison, giving each other *the look.* Mother often took us along to San Francisco State campus when she attended her classes. She'd give us a couple bucks and tell us to meet her at such and such a time, usually several hours later. We frequented the college bookstore off and on throughout the day. On the first visit to the bookstore, we each bought something small, like a pencil or a sharpener. We then used those practically empty bags to stash stolen items for the rest of the day—stencils, erasers, stickers, fancy pens. One time, Benny somehow managed to steal an actual poster, walking right past the clerks at the registers with it sticking out of the bag.

"You are *gooood,*" I swanked.

We weren't always derelicts at S.F. State. There was a very tall set of stairs on campus. (In my mind, they were like the kind one might see in Egypt, though I'm not sure if they were really so.) We climbed high up to the top of the stairs where we pretended to be tomb hunters, able to see for miles.

We toted our art supplies in backpacks and did sketches of the students who sat on big cushioned chairs as they did their homework in the common area; we bought Cokes and chips at the cafeteria.

One time, we even caught a viewing of *The Yellow Submarine,* squeezing past the crowded line of film students ushering into the small theater-style classroom.

That year, we had a little mishap pulling into the big parking garage at San Francisco State. For some reason, Mother had borrowed her friend's pickup truck that had a camper shell on it. Benny and I loved how the camper was like a bona fide living space––with a real sink and stove and bed––seemingly made for midgets. I liked the shelves and cupboards full of cups and knives, plates and pans.

    Mother let us ride in the camper while she drove. I liked the autonomy of it, how we could be cruising along the freeway completely separated from the driver, in our own little compartment. We liked to lay on the mattress bed that was way up top, looking out the tiny window at the road and all the other cars down below. It was especially fun to go across the Bay Bridge. We could see the suspensions of the bridge all the better; we could see the water down below. We liked to look into other people's cars to see what they were doing, and what they had on their seats and in their laps—if the car was clean or a mess, if they had a dog or kids.

    We were pulling into the covered area of the parking garage when the camper shell didn't make the clearance and hit smack into the cement ceiling. In an instant, my head went thwack against the window. Benny's face went thud and he started crying, putting his hands over his face, with blood pouring out of his nose.

    Mother opened the driver's side door and jumped out, frantically running for the entrance to the camper. Frantic, she swung open the camper door and crawled to Benny. He was crying and crying and holding his nose, blood coming down his lips. People behind us were honking their horns, probably pissed off to be late for class.

    I have no recollection of how we ever got the camper out of that spot. I do remember that the incident led into a lengthy dispute between my mother and her friend, with her friend trying to get money for her broken camper. Mother said the friend was an uptight bitch. They stopped being friends.

Channeling for Benny

Mother started really fretting about Benny around the same time that we were doing the home school thing. She said he had what she called a breathing problem, which would crop up out of the blue. He walked around smelling like a eucalyptus tree from all the vapor rub and Tiger Balm she smeared all over his chest and back. She also put eucalyptus leaves in the vaporizer, before running it full blast on the floor in our room--causing a thick and humid eucalyptus haze-- with condensation all over the windows. Benny had to endure strict diet regimens due to her preoccupation with his breathing problem—no dairy, no wheat and nuts, no eggs, and so forth.

"Look at his skin, it's all connected," she said fretfully as she dipped her fingers into the small jar of the oily green and gritty calendula salve and rubbed it all over his body. Sometimes, she even covered him with clear Saran Wrap after applying the calendula salve.

"I've got to seal it in," she muttered as she frantically pulled at the thin plastic wrap with her slippery, greasy hands, cursing as it clung to her arms and balled up at the sharp edge of the dispenser.

Benny walked around the house looking pissed off in his underpants--all bowlegged, stiff and awkward-- with Saran Wrap covering everything but his head and neck.

During a particularly bad spell, I'd find Mother kneeling over Benny with tears running down her flushed face, as he lay face down on the old braided rug while she repeatedly whacked his back and pushed on his lungs in quick successive thrusts.

"Cough, cough, come on, get it out--" she urged anxiously with big locks of her hair stuck to her wet cheeks.

"What if he stops breathing, *what am I gonna do?*" she wailed, and I wondered if I was supposed to answer. How come Benny never had a breathing problem in the muggy and pollution-infested New York? He ate whatever he wanted in New York––Lucky Charms, soda pop and red meat galore––with no anaphylaxis, no hives, no worsening of dry skin.

Aside from his apparent breathing problem, Benny continued to have his fits. He thrashed and gyrated when something set him off, his face twisted and scarlet with the big purple vein on his forehead popping out.

"He's just so uncomfortable in his body," Mother explained, shaking her head, "he's such an old soul, he's already done all this shit."

She scared me when she went on to point out that life was remedial, tiresome and boring for Benny. My brother was the only thing that stayed the same. Why was she talking like he wanted off this planet?

"He's gotta let it out, " she sighed during his fits, shutting him in our yellow and green bedroom or the front room, crossing her arms and leaning her back against the outside of the door with all her weight so he couldn't get out. The doorknob rattled and the door bowed in with his attempts to set himself free.

Sounds of smashing, crashing and thrashing came from behind the door with Benny sounding like some kind of ape creature. Once he quieted down, we'd find something else broken—a lamp, a plate, a toy. She encouraged him to use pillows, but he seemed to prefer the feel and the sound of a shattering object.

Mother put Benny in a lock when he was extra wild, using all her strength to curl him into a ball on the floor or the bed. She put her whole body over his back, pinning his hands under hers. The two of them grew sweaty and out of breath as they tossed and struggled, with Benny screaming and yelling, "Fuck you!" and "I hate you!"

Sometimes, when it was all over, I'd find them in the orange bedroom, with Benny curled up in the fetal position in Mother's lap. She'd be quietly singing him a song as they rocked back-and-forth with her cheek resting tenderly against the top of his head, Benny limp and infantile like a baby in her arms.

Mother said that Benny needed to do this thing she called "channeling his energy."

"Benny really has a way with fire," she commended proudly at the table one morning while we were having breakfast.

He had been the first one to notice when her blue terrycloth robe had gone aflame by the stove in the kitchen. She had marveled about that for days.

Mother came up with a way for us to play with fire, and––even though I was the oldest––Benny was in charge of the fire games. She handed Benny a stack of newspaper and a book of matches before filling a large aluminum washing basin with water. The two of us kneeled on the hardwood floor of the washroom in back of the house and hovered over the basin, impatiently balling up the newspaper, one sheet at a time. We set the balls of newspaper in the water to float and then Benny struck a match and lit them on fire, one at a time.

The heat danced on my face as I got real close to the flames. I liked to watch the fire turn different colors, especially blue. The flames curled under and spread, the tiny letters in the newspaper articles and the ads disappearing as the fire quickly swept across and engulfed the paper. Benny liked to time how long the fire would last, but––to our disappointment––it went out so fast, the paper turning to ash quickly before sinking to the bottom of the basin. We did this over and over again until we ran out of paper to burn.

Dad's Big Apple

The time finally came to be with Dad again. It was June of 1979—I was ten and Benny was seven. I was a different girl, changed from the girl I'd been in Centereach not even one year before. I was sure that Dad saw it in my eyes, my step, my clothes. I hoped he would love me just the same as always, despite all that had gone on those months at the Victorian.

We flew in on a redeye flight from San Francisco, arriving at JFK airport early in the morning. The stewardess walked us off the plane to Dad, who was waiting at the gate with a beaming smile and tears in his eyes. I was drunk with jetlag and fatigue, my knees weak at seeing Dad—a surreal moment that I had spent hours and days dreaming about.

Everything seemed to be sparkling the moment we stepped off the plane. Dad's world—New York—was a magnificent place where everything was new, including me. Yet, it seemed that the *time gone by* was a pesky and painful solid object that I was dragging through the terminal by my ankle—I had to shake it off and gown-up in the clean slate that magically appeared the moment the plane landed.

I was relieved that Dad seemed just the same as always when he pulled us into his arms at the JFK airport, as if no time had passed at all. He looked so polished in his collared dress shirt and designer jeans, his thin hair combed––his gold bracelet. My arms clasped tightly around his neck as he swept me up off the ground.

"My princess" he said into my ear over and over as we spun in circles, his familiar cologne sticking my skin and clothes. He swept Benny up in his other arm, calling him "Pooh" and talking French like he always did, before all three if us collapsed onto an airport bench—pawing, kissing and staring at each other. I was limp and weak in my relief.

The sweltering, sticky humidity hit our faces the second we stepped out of the airport and onto the sidewalk.

"People, the air is so fucking thick, you could cut it with a knife," Dad groaned as he stepped to the curb to get a taxi. It would be a phrase he'd use all summer.

Dad had sold the Fury and left Centereach for Manhattan. The muggy heat, the shorts and the tank tops, and the millions of comingling odors were Dad's new New York—his *New York City*. He now only traveled by taxi and subway, so we left the airport by taxi, and whizzed through the traffic. Dad sat in the middle of the backseat, each of us wrapped in either arm. I rolled down my window, letting out the cool air conditioning, and stared at the skyscrapers that reached the clouds. New York City was a busy, busy place full of hustle and action. People of every nationality, age and shape were like worker ants, walking fast and stepping right out in front of cars as they swarmed the filthy streets. I felt disoriented by the noise, the crowds, the heat, and the smells, after having left the calm night sky of California only hours before.

"People, this is going to be one fine summer, one *very* fine summer," Dad announced, kissing the top of my head then Benny's. Minute by minute, my life in California was disappearing.

Dad excitedly showed us his one-bedroom Manhattan apartment. The small kitchen was connected to the dining area, with a chandelier hanging over the old Centereach table for four. On the table was an unopened box of Entenmann's powdered sugar donuts and a bowl of strawberries with whipped cream that he had bought for our arrival. Dad *always* had to get strawberries for Benny.

"Look Pooh, your favorite," he said, scooping Benny up and landing him in a chair right in front of the strawberries. Benny squatted like a monkey, his bare feet on the ass of the chair and his knees against the top of the table, dipping one strawberry after the other in whipped cream until he ate them all, leaving a small plate of green stems. His face and fingers were dyed red for the rest of the day. I myself enjoyed two donuts, licking the sugar off my fingers. Life was good. Even my tabby, Henry, was there.

Right away, Dad took us to Macy's and Bloomingdale's, replacing our secondhand finds with brand new fashion-labeled clothes. I zipped through every girl aisle and tried on *everything*--including the panties--while Dad waited patiently by. We got shirts with glittery and shiny bubble-letter decals and sets of action hero Underoos.

    The shopping spree climaxed with my acquisition of the chunky wooden platform sandals that I had been pining for. I could barely walk in them, but I never took them off, clomping around the apartment while Dad complained, "The people below us are gonna *murder me.*"

    That summer, Dad taught us all about what he called "The Big Apple," including how to walk down the busy street.

    "People are less likely to bump into you if they're gonna get jabbed by a pointy elbow," he explained on the sidewalk in front of his apartment, while demonstrating the technique of walking with your hands on your hips and your elbows out.

    The elbow walk was especially useful at Grand Central Station, where we held onto Dad's designer jeans by the belt loops, running to keep up—one of us on either side. "Stick your elbows out people, we have a train to catch," he'd announce as we leapt off one subway to catch another, his stride part Broadway dancer and part rushing New Yorker.

    Trapped heat rose from the subway tracks and hung stagnant in the dirty underground stations while crowds of people waited for their train—the men in fancy business suits looking just as much like wilted overcooked vegetables as the homeless women carrying trash bags that Dad called "bag ladies." The smell of piss was thick. I grabbed hold of Dad's hand when the train approached at high speed—afraid of getting sucked into the tracks somehow—a rotten egg cyclone hitting my face and blowing my hair in front of my eyes. People bulldozed their way toward the automatic doors when the train slowed to a stop, the brakes painfully metal-on-metal. People rushed inside the graffiti-marked cars, stepping on cigarettes, gathering bags and bumping into exiting passengers—their cologne and perfume, tobacco, hotdogs and sweat mingling with the sulfur.

Inside Grand Central Station was the constant buzzing echo of imperceptible voices and hundreds of hard shoes on rock crystal. Dad was the leading goose as we ran to keep up with our fingers fixed to his belt loops. Clocks were everywhere. It seemed everyone was late for something—people checking their watches and lining up impatiently to make a call at the long row of phone booths.

Dad often spoke to us via sign language on the subway train. His gestures were overly exaggerated and dramatic, and he seemed oblivious to the other passengers gawking at him. I was sure no one else could understand our secret code. It was as if Dad, Benny and I were in our own impenetrable little bubble—no one else.

All senses were ignited in New York City. The streets were lined with vendors and––aside from the blend of hundreds of smells––there were tastes of every kind. Young Italian men with strong accents sold ice shaved as fine as fresh powdered snow. The flavor choices were not limited to the usual grape, cherry, and lime, but included coconut, Coca-Cola, piña-colada, coffee, and passion fruit. Competing for business were the hotdog vendors with their steamy carts covered by umbrellas––the best hotdogs in the world. We smothered our dogs in sauerkraut and mustard, and ate the messy bundles on the go as we walked the streets.

Dad took us to Jewish delicatessens, where he introduced us to hot pastrami on rye and colossal pickles, and pizza parlors where we'd order up a slice from the counter window right on the street. We watched the loud Italian men tossing the dough way up high in the air, spinning it and catching it with one hand.

We went to Beef Steak Charlie's on Friday nights when he got off work, where they served Dad unlimited sangria and all-you-can-eat shrimp with the steaks. On the subway to Charlie's, we sang their commercial, happy and arm-and-arm:

You're gonna get spoiled…
At Beef Steak Charlie's Tonight
Cha, cha, cha!

Dad became more and more fun with each carafe of sangria he finished. He liked to comment on the waiters and busboys, his eyes always scanning the place.

"Holy mother of god would you look at the ass on that one," he mumbled, craning his neck.

"Dad! Knock it off!" I snapped, but not real serious because I found his gawking halfway amusing.

I never ate any of the shrimp on account of my non-seafood eating ways, but Dad bragged about how many plates of all-you-can-eat shrimp *Benny* could put down. He seemed proud of Benny when the waitress exaggerated her amazement over the empty plates, putting her hand to her mouth and praising, "Oh my! you sure like your shrimp, there!"

Benny and I could finish our whole steaks. We seemed to have a bottomless hunger for meat in New York, as if we were having our fill and storing it up for the coming months in California, when we hardly got any meat at all. Ordering the steaks was almost as delightful as eating them. Dad always said that a steak must be prepared *exactly* as the customer orders it, and once sent Benny's back because it was medium instead of medium-rare.

"Watch kids, this is how it's done," he announced—showing off—before calling over the waitress and showing her the not-so-pink center.

Normal in NYC

"Princess, *why* didn't you tell me?" Dad asked with tears in his eyes, as we sat together at the table one afternoon.

The big electric fan was barely making a dent in the heat—placed right in front of our faces on the table, and blowing full throttle. Dad's voice sounded a little like a robot in the reverberation of the fan. He was pleading with me, gently holding my chin between his thumb and pointer finger and gently placing a big strand of hair behind my ear. I wanted to turn my head away to hide my eyes but I didn't want to hurt his feelings.

It was the talk I was dreading. I had been anxious that Dad might ask about what happened with Mr. Perez, and about how I felt. I had hoped he'd just sweep it under the rug as I thought I'd done. I liked to keep California compartmentalized—contained, separate. Where would I start if he asked? If I had to describe my perils in Berkeley that year, I'd have to explain Mother first. I'd have to put to words how Mother was both magnetizing and calamitous, and how I felt protective of her. This was a notion—a something—that I didn't know how to explain.

"I wish you had called me. I would have come to get you. I would have done *anything*."

My heart sank. It was unbearable that the end to my ordeal in Berkeley might have just been a phone call away, but I hadn't been able to pick up the phone. It had been my mother who told Dad about Mr. Perez touching me, after the ordeal was over. Dad had called to talk to me after he found out—my hand slippery and shaky on the receiver, my heart racing.

"My princess," he was crying that day on the phone, his voice so small, "I can't believe this has happened."

I recall very little of that phone conversation, other than feeling so ashamed that all I wanted to do was to hang up.

What if I had been the first one to call and tell Dad? Would he *really* have caught the next flight to get me? I remembered my mother sobbing in her bedroom when I couldn't eat her lentil soup; she had said she'd send me back to Dad like I wanted. Mother needed me. How could I come out and ask for Dad? How could I break her heart? I felt on the spot to defend this, and guilty that Dad was so sad over why I didn't tell him first.

I was glad for the loud fan that was blowing my hair in my face. I said nothing back. I kept feeling like I might talk, my voice bubbling up, but stopping just at the top of my throat. The seconds ticked by so slowly. I hated my silence. *Why am I like this?* I would have liked to say that I had wished for him so many times while I was in California, that I missed him so much I felt sick. I almost told him; I almost did. And here he was telling me that he was only a phone call away. It sounded so simple there in that tiny Manhattan apartment. I just wanted Dad to change the subject, change the scene. I was in New York—I was somewhere else, *it* was far away.

"Come here, princess," he said, pulling me onto his lap and wrapping his big arms around me. I buried my face in his damp white T-shirt and felt the tears falling. I hoped the tears would make Dad stop talking…and they did.

Dad still worked as a social worker at the agency for troubled youth on Long Island, and had planned a bunch of time off for our visit. When he did have to work, he left us with a woman named Sonia, who lived in a small duplex in a suburban neighborhood of Queens. Sonia had a chubby infant son with lots of dark hair, who was almost crawling. I was very excited about getting to play with a baby.

We took two subways to Sonia's at the crack of dawn (or so it felt like it). Benny and I never seemed to transition from the jetlag, so the wake-up call was rough. However, Dad never called out the typical jarring "Rise and shine!" or "Time to get up." Instead, I woke to the tickle of his mustache against my cheek and the comforting bouquet of his coffee, cigarettes and cologne as he leaned down to gently give me a kiss.

"Good morning princess," he whispered in my ear, before walking over to Benny to kiss him too. "It's morning, Pooh."

I liked being at Sonia's. She did all the things that regular mothers do, like making snack trays on plastic plates with little dividers that separated the foods. From her refrigerator, she pulled out Tupperware containers full of items like celery sticks and perfectly cut slices of cheese and what she called cold cuts. I liked to watch her in the kitchen at lunchtime--in her pleated sensible shorts and tucked-in striped shirt--as she made bologna and American cheese or peanut butter and jelly, with chips and sugary yogurts or cookies to go on the side.

Sonia had a rule that we must always eat at the table, the only exception being when we were outside in her little yard. She had to remind me to take my food to the table on several occasions--sounding more annoyed each time. Aside from not eating in her living room, there was also no swearing allowed at Sonia's, which was a little tough to follow. There was a part of me that liked her rules, and enjoyed watching her carry them out in a kind, yet stern way.

Sonia had a little plastic kiddy pool in her backyard that she filled with a hose. She'd sit beside us in one of her folding lawn chairs and stick her toes in the water while we played in the pool with her baby son. I loved holding the baby on my knee and making him giggle.

We took walks to the neighborhood park, Sonia letting me push the stroller. She laid out a blanket on the grass and set out the tidy lunch that she packed. Coming to plop down on Sonia's blanket all sweaty and thirsty felt rewarding and comforting. She'd pour cold apple juice into plastic cups and arrange the snacks that she packed in little sandwich bags. We'd eat together while we watched the other kids play. I wondered if everyone at the park was noticing us and assuming that we were Sonia's kids. They'd be thinking things like, *Look at their perfect lunch, aren't they lucky.* They'd be imagining that we have a nice house and a father who walks in the door every evening at 5:30 p.m.

Sonia really treated me like a kid—she'd ask me to wash my hands or take my plates to the sink in a voice that was different from the voice she used for my dad or her husband. She sweetly offered games and puzzles and asked about school and my favorite color. I always had this peculiar notion that I was putting one over on Sonia by playing along like I really *was* a kid. It seemed like I was a phony and she was going to find me out. Sometimes, I pictured her seeing me in California, shoplifting with Benny or standing next to the cocaine tray at one of Tom's parties--how she would gasp.

Some days, Dad brought us to his work on Long Island. We had to take a few subways and then a train to get there. He'd buy us donuts and chocolate milk on the way, rushing and saying, "Hustle people, hustle!" while we ran to keep up.

I loved going to Dad's office. Everyone had their own cubicle, including Dad. His was very tidy--even his ashtray was clean--with a nice framed photo of Benny and I on his desk. I imagined him looking at the photo throughout the nine months that we were without him, when we were in California. I liked to go through the drawers of his desk, pulling out the stapler, the paperclips and the mints (which I ate).

His co-workers lit up when we walked through the door, especially the secretary named Cynthia. I loved seeing Cynthia, who had been there as long as I could remember--since Carle Place days. Also, she always gave us candy.

"Look how you've grown!" she gasped in amazement at our first visit to the office that summer, putting her hand to her mouth.

Cynthia was in her fifties, with short graying and frosted hair; she was always done up with a matching outfit, heels, and lots of makeup. She seemed to adore Dad. He considered her a good friend, telling us that the two of them would have dinner or lunch sometimes when we were in California.

"Your father talks about you non-stop, you know," she reassured.

Dad still talked about "making a difference" at work, and how he was helping troubled teens get jobs and the help they needed at school. I thought he was like a superhero for older kids; I felt so proud to walk into the office with him.

"Some of these kids––" he said at the apartment, shaking his head and looking out the window, "Some of them. It just kills me. Their lives are just a living hell."

He told us about kids that were abandoned, their parents just dumping them off with a relative or a friend; he told us about kids whose parents died or went to jail, or kids who had gone to juvenile hall. In my mind, these kids were so mature––so intimidating––probably with pubic hair and smoking joints and cigarettes.

Ones Disco

The Donna Summer record *Bad Girls* was out that summer, and her songs were everywhere—blasting out of passing cars, open storefronts and from people carrying giant portable radios on their shoulders. Dad and I danced and sang along to "Bad Girls" and "Hot Stuff" in his apartment living room, shaking our hips and clapping our hands above our heads. Dad bragged about being a real superstar at his favorite disco, and showed off about how good he was on the dance floor when they played Donna Summer.

"If you could only see your father, he is on fire," he boasted, not looking at me.

I *did* end up getting to see Dad at his favorite disco, which was called One's Discotheque, located at 111 Hudson Street. They'd let kids in sometimes and I repeatedly begged Dad to take me. He talked about going there often when Benny and I were in California, and that he knew some of the people who worked there.

I loved to watch Dad getting ready for Ones. He always let his chest hairs show by undoing a few extra shirt buttons for the occasion. He'd comb his hair in front of the mirror and say out loud that the club just couldn't get enough of him as he threaded his leather belt through the belt loops of his Calvin Klein jeans.

"This tushie can move, move, move," he'd hiss, stepping into the living room from the bathroom, and shaking his butt side-to-side while giving a loud clap above his head.

I loved watching Dad in his element at Ones. Right before we'd walk in, he'd stop and say, "OK folks, let's make an appearance, shall we?" He was so handsome and flashy in his heavy cologne, and always having something exciting to say at the bar to make people laugh or gasp. I was drunk with him and I was sure that everyone at Ones was drunk with him, too.

Dad and I spent hours on the dimly lit dance floor, our bodies illuminated by the blue and red and yellow rotating dots that were coming off the spinning disco ball. I was in heaven with the loud music and the dancing, and I thought that Ones Discotheque was positively the best spot in the entire universe.

We couldn't go every weekend, though––partly because Benny hated it. He sat at the bar all afternoon, drinking Coke after Coke and eating about a dozen hotdogs from the little hotdog cart inside the disco. He whined about leaving and teased me about how stupid I looked during breaks.

"Princess, let's go find the best disco dress out there," Dad said one afternoon when we were passing a decent second hand store. My heart raced as we dashed inside and started browsing for *the* dress.

"Oh mother of God, have I found it," I heard him say from two aisles up. It was firecracker red with big dark red flowers all over it, with a low-cut halter-top that tied at the back of the neck. The dress was too long, and a little too big.

"I'm going to have this done," Dad decided, instead of fixing it himself.

In preparation for the seamstress, Dad had me stand on a kitchen chair and stay still while he crouched on the floor below me and pinned it to the right height and waist size. This time, instead of holding them in between his teeth, he pulled the pushpins one-by-one from a little gold-colored pincushion that looked like a miniature crown.

"Let's make a slit," he whispered, looking up at me with a twinkle in his eye.

I could hardly stand still. I was picturing looking just like those dancers in *Saturday Night Fever.* With the shiny sharp scissors from his sewing box, Dad cut a slit up the side of the dress that went all the way to the top of my thigh while I begged, "Higher, higher!"

We took the dress to the drycleaners the very next day to have this thing done that Dad called *altered.* The seamstress was to sew the edges of the slit, take in the waist and hem the bottom to ankle-length.

About a week later, I was eating my Lucky Charms and Dad was drinking his coffee and smoking a Kool when he raised his eyebrows and declared like he was up to something, "Princess, it's *the dayyy...*" I dropped my spoon with a splash.

"My disco dress! Let's go *now!*"

Just as soon as Dad was done with his coffee, we were out the door and down the elevator and off to the drycleaners. We walked fast and hand-in-hand down the busy street, Benny running to keep up as he held onto Dad's other hand, probably pretty annoyed.

Dad started singing a made-up song, doing a little skip: "We're gettin' the dress, we're gettin' the dress folks, we're gettin' the dress...."

Dad pulled the little white ticket out with our name on it out of his wallet when we walked into the small, humid drycleaners, and had me hand it to the older lady behind the counter.

"It's an *alteration,*" he reminded her, winking at me. Dad was the only person who had ever used the term "alteration." He made it sound so upscale and extravagant.

I loved the smell of the drycleaners because it smelled like Dad––he brought all his best dress shirts there. The smell was dryers and fabric softener, hot irons and starchy steam. His shirts came home covered in a plastic film, which he removed when he took them off the hanger to wear them, before spraying himself with cologne.

The lady behind the counter––who was no taller than me––did not seem to notice the giddiness going on. She turned to her right and pressed a button that made all the hanging plastic-covered clothes start with a jerk before chugging loudly along a track way up high. I was so excited, I could hardly stand it, as I anxiously watched the clothes whip by, looking for the color red. She seemed to know exactly where to locate my disco dress on that moving rack. Dad saw it first and squeezed my hand.

"I see it princess!"

The red dress was nicely pressed and covered with the clear plastic, just like Dad's shirts. I stuck my nose past the wire hanger and inside the wrap, taking in that drycleaners smell.

I proudly walked with the dress draped across my arms the three or four blocks back to the apartment, the thin plastic sticking to my chin and neck. I couldn't wait to try it on with my chunky-heeled sandals.

I stood in front of the mirror in my red disco dress for a long time as soon as we got back to the apartment. It fit me perfectly. I stuck my leg out of the slit at various angles and tied the halter strap different ways, experimenting with the visual effects of my barely-there boobs. I practiced dancing in it.

My mind flashed to Mr. Perez and what he might think of me in the dress, imagining what he might do if he saw me in it. The thought caused an instant pang of unease, as I pictured him so excited and approving, reaching out to grab hold of me with his stubby fingers. I recoiled and looked away from the mirror, but only for a few seconds. Being in New York--and under Dad's influence--I was able to quickly push Mr. Perez out of my mind.

The following weekend was a dream come true at One's Disco. I was a superstar. I basked in the envy of other girls, noticing that all the other females were looking at my dress. Dad and I danced all afternoon; he was always up for more dancing, and never seemed to tire out. I thought that he was the best dancer there--the most handsome--and he probably was.

Dad was keeping up with the new moves that went with the changing sound of disco, boasting to an imaginary audience, "People, I am on fire, watch me go." I thought he looked like one of the dancers on the new TV show, *Dance Fever.* The end of the 1970s was right around the corner--a new decade of sound and fashion on the horizon. You could feel it. Songs like "Last Dance" and "Night Fever" were a thing of the past. By July, "Good Times" was out, a song off Chic's new record *Risque.* The song had a celebratory, happy ring to it that went with the roller-skates and the glittery, gold shorts that had become so popular.

The old wooden bar at One's seemed to stretch a mile long. We sat there on the barstools when we took breaks, Dad ordering one vodka martini after another-- the kind with the skinny plastic stirrer and the green olives. It was obvious that he felt at home and in his element on a barstool. He took pride in making sure that Benny and I got bright red maraschino cherries in *all* our Cokes and Shirley Temples.

I tried to imitate the elegant way Dad held his martini glass at the stem with two fingers, his pinky and ring fingers sticking out to the side. He brought the glass to his lips slowly and sipped like he was an expert in class, his mouth barely moving. I was always happy to see Dad put down another martini because the more he consumed, the looser he got, and the longer he stayed on the dance floor.

"Work it, work it, work it, girl!" Dad cheered as he taught me how to sit on a barstool. He demonstrated how sitting on the edge of the seat with my legs crossed would allow the slit in my disco dress to fall open naturally. It was a challenge to sit this way, as my foot hardly reached the middle of the stool, my shoe slipping over and over on the wooden bar.

"A woman's got to take advantage of everything she's got," Dad advised. I watched the crowd from this pose with my drink in my hand, the slit in my dress open and revealing my full leg. Did people think I was a grown-up?

"Have I told you you're the prettiest girl in here?" Dad asked at the bar, bending over to kiss the top of my head. I believed it because *he* said it. He told me that, at any point, there could be modeling and acting agents looking for new faces, so I should always look my best at the disco. I fantasized about getting discovered, and scanned the crowd for possible agents—not just at Ones, but also at restaurants, Macy's, or on the street. I knew that Dad had been giving me these tips for some time at this point, but I continued to hold the hope of finally being what he called *discovered*.

Dad bragged about people discovering *him,* saying, "Look out world" and panting, "I am so hot, hot, hot," thrusting his pelvis with each repetition of hot.

The Price of Beauty

Occasionally, we took the train to visit Aunt Annette––our mother's sister––who lived in a lovely home in a well-to-do part of Connecticut. Aunt Annette was my favorite aunt––luckily, Dad remained her close friend after he and Mother separated.

Aunt Annette and Dad sat on the white couch in her large living room drinking martinis and wine and smoking Kools and Salems while singing along to Judy Collins. Dad went into his own world with "Send in the Clowns." He'd stare past everyone in the room while singing the lyrics with a far away, tragic look in his eyes. Sometimes, he sang the song in his Broadway mode by standing to face the fireplace with his chin held high and tears in his eyes, while gracefully raising his arms to his sides like a ballet dancer.

"'Send in the Clowns' is the soundtrack to my childhood," Dad said, which made me listen to the sad lyrics extra closely, feeling sorry for him.

Aunt Annette and Dad talked for hours and hours, through the evening and then long after we went to bed. As I fell asleep to the sound of their faint laughter through the walls, I imagined all the times they probably got together through the year, when Benny and I were in California. I didn't like the thought of them getting together without me––it seemed unfair. How could my father and my mother's sister could get along so well, and not my father and mother? If the two sisters were from the same litter, then how come they couldn't be more alike?

Aunt Annette's quaint Connecticut was green and lush with many swim holes and a beach not far away. I loved my time with her. I regarded her as being so much like my mother, only more regular.

Aunt Annette had a large bathroom connected to her master bedroom, where she'd let me talk to her and watch her get ready for the day. Sometimes, she put steamy rollers in her hair. She said that she and my mother's hair was "a curse," and explained that by curse, she meant that their hair was so kinky and full and unmanageable. I wondered why Aunt Annette tried so hard to smooth out her frizzy curls with rollers and the blow dryer and the flat iron, while my mother just happily let hers be as wild as ever.

Aunt Annette's vast bathroom counter was covered with dirty partially full mugs of old coffee, some with green mold floating on the top. I wondered why she never removed them for cleaning, but I secretly was glad that she didn't. I liked that she had this one little element of slobbiness--I thought it made her more like me.

My aunt let me try on her makeup and hair clips. I marveled at her many makeup brushes and applicators, and her mirrors of various sizes and magnifications. These instruments to construct and hold up femininity were fascinating to me, as they were *not* utilized by my aunt's sister--my mother.

Aunt Annette took me to Macy's and, after an afternoon of shopping, we went to the restaurant in the middle of the store to have lunch together. I imagined everyone assuming that she was my mother as we walked through the aisles. I felt proud to stand next to her--with her makeup, slacks and hair spray.

That summer Dad had a hairdresser come right to the apartment just to do my hair. He was a friend of Dad's; they kept touching forearms and putting their faces close to each other. I wondered if he was Dad's boyfriend the way Tweety Bird Man was Dad's boyfriend. The hairdresser friend was very flamboyant, using his hands excessively to illustrate what he planned to do with my hair.

Me, Dad, and his friend the hairdresser were crammed into our tiny muggy bathroom, all squeezed in front of the small vanity mirror. I sat on a bar stool in between them, eyeing the expressions in their half-face reflections. They didn't meet my eyes, but rather scanned my head as if it were an inanimate object, their hands pulling at my dirty-blonde strands--experimenting with lengths and volume--and chatting up ideas for style.

While all this was going on, Benny sat on the floor of the living room watching TV, next in line for a bathroom haircut. Dad had asked him what kind of style he wanted, and Benny had replied, "Like a boy," which sent Dad into fits of laughter.

"She's got these cheekbones——" the friend said, pulling up a chunk of my hair to the level of my jaw while cocking his head to the side, and saying my cheekbones ought to be what he called *accentuated*.

"That short, you think?" Dad said skeptically.

"Perfectly European" was how Dad liked to put my cheekbones, moving my head to the side by my chin in a quick motion, or asking me to suck in my cheeks to make a duck face.

The hairdresser pulled a pair of shiny sharp scissors from a little leather pouch that he brought, and began cutting my hair——clumps of wet strands falling into the small round sink. I kept tabs on my reflection, half scared to look. *Not too short.*

Dad often talked about "the price of beauty," and "the sacrifice of beauty," saying, "Princess, it ain't enough if it ain't painful." These phrases kept popping into my mind that evening.

The hairdresser didn't say much as he snip-snipped, but it was obvious he knew what he was doing. The current of his cologne said *style* as his arm swept past my face over and over.

A Fairytale Stewardess

The summer in Manhattan was over too quickly; I would be threaded back to the land of my mother. I grew more and more anxious in the days our airport departure approached.

The divided worlds of my parents did not touch at all. It was as if they were on separate continents with a climate, language, and culture unique to each one, joined only by airplanes and airports. The airports were cold, echoing and sterile holding tanks——seemingly without time zones--with both unmatched hurriedness and unmatched waiting, and a constant edgy anticipation of tearful hello's and goodbye's. It was where Benny and I stood by to either be teleported or received.

  I woke up crying the day Dad was to take us by taxi to the airport. I cried so much at breakfast that I couldn't eat my cereal. I tried to keep my whimpering silent, but it came out in long squeaky sighs that I couldn't hold back. Benny sat silently eating his Lucky Charms, not looking at anyone.

  I knew there was some kind of custody arrangement that stated we were to stay with our mother during the school year and Dad in the summer. I don't recall if it was Mother or Dad who said it was a judge that dictated this arrangement. I pictured a frowning, staid man that looked just like Abraham Lincoln sitting in a kingly chair, sternly barking "Summers only" to Dad as he brought down his wooden gavel against his colossal desk. The thought made me mad.

  "The judge doesn't want to let a gay man have kids," Dad said more than once. It seemed so unfair.

  "Come on, princess, let's try to get through this," Dad said low through his teeth and tight jaw, not looking at my face. His posture was bent as he mechanically gathered up our luggage and stacked it beside the front door. I felt that Benny and I were vanishing from Dad's apartment--from New York--all pieces of us being removed one-by-one so that nothing was left. How would Dad get by without us? I imagined him returning from the airport to a quiet, empty apartment, and crying while he played "Send in the Clowns" on the record player.

  I cried in the taxi the whole way to JFK. I would later associate Elton John's "Little Jeannie" with leaving Dad because it played on the radio in the taxi that morning. I sat to the left of Dad, mashed up to him as close as possible and burrowing my head into his chest. By the time we got to the airport, there was a wet stain the size of a cantaloupe on his light pink dress shirt from all the tears I cried––the image of Dad walking through JFK airport with a sad look and a giant wet stain on his pink dress shirt forever stamped in my mind.

We had to wait an agonizingly long time to board at our gate. Dad sat on a firm and unyielding seat with me on his lap, straddling him face-to-face, with my arms and legs wrapped tightly around him. Our skin stuck together with sweat, tears, snot, and cologne as I rested my head in the crook of his soft neck. I kept gagging with my sobs, occasionally heaving, but bringing up nothing on account of my empty stomach. I could feel everyone staring at us, and was vaguely aware of a sense of embarrassment, but was more overcome by my inability to do anything different. It seemed that physical manifestations were magnified at the airport—crying, peeing, vomiting, shaking, hiccupping, et cetera.

Benny sat in the heavy-duty plastic seat to the right of my soggy display, his arms crossed in front of him, staring straight ahead expressionless. I could only imagine that he wanted to run away, and felt trapped in a world where the females who took up all the space.

When the smiling stewardess came to fetch us first, I was a mess of wet hair, drool, and uncontrollable hiccup-like surges. Benny walked a few feet ahead of me, probably hoping that people would think we weren't together. I slowly stumbled backwards so that I could watch Dad as I made my way through the connecting terminal. I caught one last look at his pale and tearful face just before I turned the sharp corner to enter the airplane.

The stewardess that day was like some kind of flawless angel sent just for me. She immediately took it upon herself to abolish my sadness, putting a small starchy pillow in back of my head and tucking a scratchy wool blanket around my sides. She brought me a Coke right away, which took away some of the ache in my belly. That stewardess smiled at everybody with her bright red lipstick and her white teeth, but––for me––she stopped every time she passed, offering kindness through treats, nudges, gentle pinches and winks. She lowered herself to my height a few times, and I got a close up of her thick mascara and blue eye shadow.

"Sweetheart, how about some playing cards?"
"Honey, another Coke?"
"Let me see that pretty smile!"

I watched her every move whenever she was in my sight--the way she glided through the blue carpeted aisle in her high heels and stockings--stopping to attend to passengers with a swift turning gesture, and talking quietly to show attentiveness. Her perfectly straight shoulder-length blonde hair seemed to move in uniform with her hips--a trick I thought she must have learned at some kind of flight attendant training school. She wore a navy blue polyester knee-length skirt, a white button-up shirt with a starchy collar, and a little red tie around her neck. Her airplane getup was completely free of wrinkles--I wanted one just like it.

Somewhere about a third of the way through the flight, I realized that I was no longer gagging and tearing. Though my throat was hoarse and my eyes were swollen and stinging, I felt fuzzy and almost drunk, basking in the doting this flight attendant. I made a very conscious effort to push away thoughts of my father whenever he popped into my mind, which wasn't easy because I was exhausted by the throws of emotions that morning. The guilt over this was tremendous, so much that I thought that Dad might suffer some ill fate on account of it. I would be punished for pushing him out of my mind. I looked out the little round window on Benny's side, focusing on the clouds below. I homed in on the coloring books, the Colorforms, the magazines--whatever I could find. I could do nothing about the miles that were ticking by every minute; I had no choice but to look forward.

I was dreading letting go of the stewardess when we were first to exit the plane. What would she think of

Mother? I walked behind her, with my heavy and bulky carry-on over my shoulder, thudding my hip and thigh with every step. Benny was a few feet behind me with his bulging backpack over both shoulders. I kept my eyes on the stewardess's brown high heels as she walked without sound like a fashion model through the carpeted terminal. She kept looking over her shoulder at me and my brother with a smile and a nod as she glided with fine-tuned buoyancy, not slowing her pace a notch. I thought she was the perfect representative of *female*––surely one Dad would approve of. I imagined that there was no amount of guesswork for this kind of woman.

Take me with you.

My stomach lurched when we reached the gate and there was no sign of our mother. I scanned the crowd for the wild dark fro, but she was not to be seen. I was mortified.

"Sweethearts, do you see your mother?"

"She'll be here any second," I said not looking the stewardess in the eye.

"*Great,*" Benny groaned sarcastically before he whipped out his comb and started incessantly slicking his hair down.

The stewardess said that she could wait with us for a few minutes. We awkwardly stood together as people from our plane walked hurriedly past, wrapping their arms around welcoming loved ones, slapping each other on the backs and shouting out congenial hello's. I caught a sideways glance of the stewardess biting her half-frowning lip.

"Sweetheart, what's your mother's name?"

I almost couldn't answer, fumbling to cough up the words. I wanted to disappear when she made her way to a desk a few feet away, and asked someone to page our mother. *Everyone is looking.* I tried to catch Benny's stone face for a commiserating look, but he continued to stare straight ahead, his lips tight like he wanted to punch somebody's lights out.

"Katherine Arlen to gate 29. Katherine Arlen to gate 29, please--"

The robotic female voice echoed off the concrete walls, to the ceiling and then to the hard floor, where it was kicked around by hard-bottomed shoes. Our mother's name was scattered throughout the SFO airport like confetti--raining on people's hair, on their jackets, and falling on open magazines and into coffee cups...*Katherine. Katherine.*

When Mother did not show up at the gate, the sweet stewardess said that she would have to bring us to another spot—a place for lost kids to wait—since she had to prepare the plane for the next departure. In my memory, this place was actually called lost-and-found, though it may just be that it *felt* like a lost-and-found.

Benny and I straggled behind her through the airport. I was sure that everyone passing knew exactly what was going on—that we were stranded, unwanted, forgotten. *Lost and found.* I continued to keep my eyes on the flight attendant's high heels as I imagined a large dusty box full of items left behind—old jackets, reading glasses, watches, weathered paperbacks and backpacks.

I managed to shut out the busy people, the shops and the echoing intercom voices of the airport as I imagined a life with the stewardess, who would *surely* take me home with her when my mother did not show up. I saw us in front of the mirror in her large bathroom, braiding my hair. I imagined her touching a large makeup brush to my nose in a quick gesture--a cloud of powder dancing in the air--the two of us laughing, our faces almost touching. I fantasized about the two of us sipping tea out of little cups and eating a plate of cookies coated with powdered sugar, her listening intently to my daily woes. She'd walk me to a classroom, holding my hand as we entered a school, her heels sounding like music through the halls, turning admiring heads our way. I'd be her helper on the plane, passing out Cokes and blankets in my pressed red, white, and blue polyester suit. I imagined her taking me to Dad.

Finally, though--with her smile weighted by apology--the stewardess led us to the waiting area. In my memory, there was baggage everywhere. The baggage spilled out from the tables and onto the floor and into the corners. There was a large man in the midst of the cardboard boxes, the Samsonite, the duffle bags and the briefcases--he was sitting at a desk. He slowly lifted his head from some paperwork, and lowered his glasses to the tip of his nose to squint at the three of us. The stewardess spoke first.

"Their mother didn't show up. I'm sure she's just having difficulty finding the correct gate," she said while looking down at me with a wink.

Benny let out a long sigh and sat down on the hard floor, unzipping the front pouch of his backpack, and removing his baseball cards one-by-one.

Don't leave, don't leave, don't leave.

"Her name is Katherine Arlen. If you could please continue to have her paged overhead, there is a message for her at twenty-nine."

I stood frozen as she bent down to my level one last time. Everything looked the same about her as when she somehow managed to connect the dots between our parents--except for her eyes. Her eyes said "I'm so sorry," even though she was smiling.

On the plane, she had multitudes of tricks under her sleeve to cheer up and pamper, like Mary Poppins pulling furniture out of her small handbag. Now she didn't try *any* tricks or say anything catchy or comforting. She just squeezed my shoulders with her hands and kissed my forehead.

I Know.

I could tell that she knew I didn't want her to leave--this seemed to delay her departure, luckily. She stood in between me and Benny for a few minutes, looking around the room and straightening her skirt.

"Busy day?" she asked the man behind the desk.

"About the usual here," he answered, a bit uninterested.

"Nice card collection, who's your favorite player?" she asked Benny, his cards spread out by her feet.

"Hank Aaron, I guess," Benny mumbled about his go-to player who had already retired, but was the icon of one of the older kids he admired at the Centereach apartments.

"Good choice!" she patted Benny on the top of the head and then checked her watch before smiling at me. It was obvious that she simply *had* to go.

The reverberation of the airport filled the room when she opened the door, like the sucking force of helicopter rotors cleaving through the air. In that flood of noise swished the winded, colorful figure of our mother. She bumped hard into the back of the stewardess, who had turned her blonde head one last time to wave goodbye. For a second or two, the two women stood side-by-side, stunned. I let out a gasp and Benny called out "Mommy!" dropping his cards and running over to grab her. Before it was over, I caught a still mental image of Mother and the stewardess together--to keep in my mind--before Mother swooped up Benny in her arms and they awkwardly composed themselves and giggled "excuse me." It seemed as though the stewardess had belonged to a pretend world, while Mother was real life--I had caught Santa Claus or the Easter Bunny in the act. I had somehow summoned the stewardess by wishing for her, and now she was disappearing like a genie. *Poof!*

The Educational Slaughter House

While we were in Manhattan with Dad that summer, Mother and Tom had moved us out of the old Victorian and into a two bedroom house on a nice street in North Berkeley. I was disappointed that the new house did not have a bathtub in the backyard, and disappointed that I didn't get to help choose the house, like I almost did that week when Mother went searching for rentals in the Sunday paper. Still, I was glad to finally be away from Mr. Perez for good.

Mother told a story of how, while she and Tom were away camping, the Victorian house was burglarized and vandalized with spray paint. She said that it had been the Perezes--their son Ricky in particular--getting back at us for the accusations we had made in the previous year. She said that they had also reported Tom to the police for his pot plants.

"It was time to go," she declared, "who *knows* what they'd do next."

Mother never did share with me what had been spray-painted on our walls. Through the years, my imagination etched the words of the Victorian house vandals.

Slut
Whore
Cunt
Bitch
Liar
Tease

The house had two bedrooms—Benny and I shared a room, and Tom got one to himself, which he called his "study." Gone were the foam mattresses--Mother got us a bona fide bunk bed while we were in New York (I slept on the top). Large windows overlooked the busy street in the front room, which was sort of like Mother's bedroom, even though it was also the living room.

Tom built Mother a way up high loft in the living room/ Mother's bedroom, with a splintery plywood ladder nailed to the side. The top of the loft was no more than 20 inches from the ceiling, so I had to crouch to avoid hitting my head when I was up there. On the other side of the wall was my and Benny's room. Our bunk bed shook and the whole house rumbled when Mother and Tom were jumping each other's bones up in the loft.

It was understood that the area underneath the loft was Mother's personal space––it was where she kept all her special belongings. The room was homey and cozy, with the old braided rug, and multitudes of pillows on the floor.

Right off the front room that was also Mother's room was the combined kitchen and dining area, and the home of the old orange table. Mother nailed a bed sheet over the large open doorway that connected the dining area to the front room. We were always getting tangled up in the old off-white, floral-print bed sheet as we made our way through the doorway. The nails popped out of the wall and fell to the floor if we swatted the sheet too vigorously.

"Come on, give me a break," Mother huffed as she grabbed the hammer from the kitchen junk drawer to nail it back into the doorway.

Overall, our new house was much more modern––and in a nicer neighborhood––compared to that of the old Victorian.

I was glad to get away from the Perez's. Even though we were in a new house and a new neighborhood, I fearfully imagined Mr. Perez finding me somehow.

For one reason or another, we registered late for school that fall of 1979. Mother said we were going to have to go to public school, but not to worry too much because it was just temporary. Even though we were ten and seven years old, Franklin Elementary would be the largest school we ever attended. We spilled into the busy office on an afternoon sometime in September, our mother pulling out loose papers from the crook of her arm. She had plowed through the school parking lot, a few steps ahead of us with those papers flapping in the wind, muttering to herself something about this thing she called bureaucratic bullshit.

Mother stood winded in the school office, talking in a way that seemed to express that the school secretary was a pain in *her* ass, instead of the other way around. She was tossing through those papers like she was looking for something, and flippantly answering questions. These were the times that I would have given anything to be able to slap a pair of high heels on her and do her up with some cosmetics.

"...yes, but you see, their father has their records from New York. He just *won't* mail them to me--"

"...yes, that's correct, they attended the private school until March last year. I am a certified teacher, *I* finished out their school year."

"...well, again, I can't get their father to send me those birth certificates. Those are back East, I've had to order more copies--"

"...no, there were no formal grades at the school in New York. It was an *alternative school*."

The secretary looked up from our small pile of miscellaneous papers on her desk, removing her reading glasses and letting out a sigh as she rubbed her wrinkled forehead.

"Ms. Arlen, you know she will have to be tested for placement--" (There was some argument about Benny repeating kindergarten, which ended in him being able to join the first grade.)

That woman sent me down the hall for testing right then and there, and had me take a seat at a long table. The big room resembled a grown-up library; I didn't see any kid books around at all. I sat in the hard plastic seat with my stomach in my throat, shocked that I was *already* doing schoolwork, as I had thought that we were only registering on this day. What would I have to do next?

The fear of not being able to answer the questions made me extra fidgety. I made indents on the pencil with my teeth while I read and then reread the typed questions on the test booklet. I shifted in the hard seat, scooting the chair back and then pulling it forward, crossing and uncrossing my legs. I bit my lip.

I stared at the large clock on the wall, which was hard to ignore, ticking loudly with every second, the large hand jerking with a click every time the second hand spun to the twelve. There were bookshelves lined up against the walls of the room. The books were large and intimidating—encyclopedias and dictionaries, world atlases and scholastic references. I recalled the things that Mother referred to as bureaucratic bullshit and thought *this sure is bona fide bureaucratic bullshit*. Mother's offhand words popped into my head—sheep, pigs, Republican Nazi's. I contemplated ways to shape myself into the form of a girl who would know the answers to the questions.

The Constitution of the United States

Pronouns

Continents

Word problems

My head spun. I felt heavy under the weight of my botched patchwork education. My mind went to my last school experience––to Mr. Schwartz and his classroom of rich kids––to Mr. Perez and my frequent absences, to clapping my hands and marching to the times tables. Now, those I remembered.

Two times seven is fourteen

Three times seven is twenty-one

Four times seven is twenty-eight...

My feet tapped to the rhythm of the sing-song times tables and I banged my pencil against the table to the beat.

There were no questions about Greek mythology, there was not a section on how to blend watercolors or pencil shavings or knit a scarf or how to catch a lizard with a homemade noose made of grass. If there had been such questions, I might have aced that test booklet.

"She'll need to repeat fourth grade," were the only words I heard when we were called into an office some time after I turned in my test booklet.

I was placed in Mrs. Tang's bilingual fourth grade class where--aside from learning how to find a book from the catalogue in the library, and how to calculate fractions from a word problem--we learned about the Chinese New Year (Kung hei fat choi), and how to make Chinese lanterns out of colored paper.

I struggled to keep up in that classroom. I kept quiet and panicked at the possibility of Mrs. Tang calling on me to answer a question. One time, when she called on me and I just hung my head, biting my lip and digging my nails into my leg, she sharply announced to the class that I went to a school where there were no grades.

"They hardly taught her anything--that's why she never knows the answers."

But I *did* understand that--according to the Chinese calendar--it was the year of the sheep. On the day that Mrs. Tang announced this fact, I imagined Mother and Tom smoking pot and laughing it up in the kitchen, talking this and that about "sheep" in reference to people who are just blind followers. I thought, *This is the year of the sheep, all right. You fucking got that right.*

Stinson Beach

We spent many warm days at Stinson Beach that fall, before it got too cold, when the 70s was about to roll into the 80s. Stinson Beach was in Marin County, close to Point Reyes. It took a little over an hour to get there from our Berkeley house. Mother and Tom packed us up in the Dodge van and we'd head down the windy, scenic Highway 1. They preferred the hidden nude beach that was off a steep hiking trail, rather than the crowded, busy beach with suited people on towels with radios and ice cream.

Benny and I looked forward to pulling into the little town at Stinson because we were always promised a trip to the Stinson Beach Market. The market looked almost like a big wooden house––funky and welcoming––with two levels and big windows. There were always several people standing around the porch entrance, soaking up the sun and drinking coffee or juice. People were in wetsuits and bikini tops, wrapped in towels; some were parking their surfboards and boogie boards and bicycles.

Inside the store, Benny and I wandered through the narrow aisles, salivating over treats. Mother always let us each pick out a small glass jar of Knudsen juice. There were so many flavors to choose from, like raspberry-apple, pineapple-coconut and hibiscus-cooler. She cautioned that we couldn't afford much, but we usually got a bag of chips, too.

We parked along a road that overlooked the beach from a high-up cliff, and carried our backpacks the long walk down the narrow dirt trail lined with dry weeds, thorn bushes, and wild licorice. We walked single file with Tom leading the way, stepping to the side and saying hello to the occasional sweaty and winded passer-by. I was always glad to be going downhill, knowing the walk back would be treacherous. We took turns drinking from a soft leather kidney-shaped pouch along the way, which hung at Mother's hip, and strapped across her body with thick red twine. When it was my turn, I squeezed it in both hands above my head, squirting the lukewarm, leather-tasting water into my mouth.

"Not too much!" Mother warned, saying we had to make it last amongst us all.

We were usually quite hot and thirsty when the path finally leveled and opened to the beach––I wanted to plop down immediately. But Mother liked to pick the best spot, often walking back and forth across the hot sand in her cut-off jeans and tank top, using her hand as a visor to shield the sun from her eyes.

I was uncomfortably conscious of the glaring naked bodies upon arrival. My awareness of the overbearing presence of pubic hair and boobs and flapping penises would recede by the end of the day, but––when we first arrived––I couldn't help but look with quick, side-glances. I took note of the shapes that were there that day—the extra fat ones, the long saggy boobs, the hard oiled bodies, the ones with extra full pubic hair or the extra big penises (and the extra shriveled ones).

I thought of Dad, remembering Stonybrook Beach by Centereach, and Jones Beach in New Jersey. At Dad's beach, I'd always hoped to sit right by the biggest radio, and closest to the snack bar. There was Coppertone and popsicles and crowds of suited people. How could two places be so similar and so not the same?

We set down a big blanket and opened our backpacks when Mother finally found the perfect spot and shouted "Here!"

We pulled out the big glass bottle of half-full Co-op unfiltered apple juice. We ate whole wheat fig bars––flattened and gummy from the travel––raw unsalted nuts, chunks of heavy grain bread, sweaty cheese and bruised, ripe fruit. Tom and Mother drank Dos Equis and Ranier.

Mother shucked immediately as if she had been painfully storing up the desire to do so. She seemed extra fancy-free––she ate, sat cross-legged, bent over, and played Frisbee––running with breasts a flappin,'––her soft body jiggling when she moved. I hated it. I felt as though people were seeing *my* nakedness because she was my mother. It seemed that—if strangers were viewing her plain-sight privates—they were also viewing mine just because I came from her. I wanted to cover her up.

Rather than dissipating with age, my hesitancy to take off all my clothing only grew with time. I felt shy and uncomfortable even taking off my shorts and T-shirt to reveal my Wonder Woman bathing suit underneath--which I wore at eight, nine and even ten-years-old, until it grew too tight. People stared at the suited me as if *I* were the oddity. I felt an underlying pressure to peel away Wonder Woman, as if all were simply waiting on me to do so.

Benny didn't get naked, either. He wore his suit—and often all his clothes—the whole day. He kept his shoes on because he hated the feel of sand between his toes.

There was a big commotion at the nude beach one Saturday. I was sitting at our blanket when I noticed a group of naked people in the distance. They were standing around something on the shore—I could tell by their body language and their faces that it was something bad. Was there a shark attack? Did someone get hurt?

"What's going on over there, do you think?" I asked Mother, who seemed not to have noticed. She looked at the small crowd for a minute, shielding her eyes from the sun.

"I have no idea, why don't you go check it out."

"Benny, let's go," I said as I shot up off the blanket and grabbed Benny by the elbow.

As we got closer, making our way across the sand, I could see that the people were surrounding a man who was lying face up on the shore. I stopped for a few seconds.

"What's wrong with that man?" Benny asked.

Just as I was about to answer that I didn't know, I noticed the color of the man's skin, which was basically a yellowish-white-gray, and not that of any skin color I'd ever seen. In my gut, I *knew* what I was about to see, but I couldn't let myself believe it, nor could I stop stepping forward toward the man and the naked onlookers—I kept going at a slow pace, Benny quietly walked beside me.

When we reached the small crowd, we poked our heads between two people to get a closer look at the strangely colored man. I gasped and my stomach dropped—he was clearly dead. He was wearing blue plaid swim trunks, and lay face up with his abdomen huge and unnaturally full, like a taut balloon.

"Ouch!" Benny spat as I grabbed his shoulder and looked at his face. He was staring expressionless at the dead man, biting his bottom lip.

Ten or more naked adults were standing around him—with bushy pubic hair and hanging genitals, some more fretful than others—talking about what might have happened to the suited dead man, scratching their beards and their heads. That's when I heard a woman talking about how something had bumped her leg under water, and that she had discovered in horror that it was the drowned man.

Seeing a dead man was shocking—his skin, his toenails, his eyes slightly open. However, what struck me the most was that the dead man—who had washed up on the nude beach—was wearing a *bathing suit*. I do not recall anything from that scene beyond the blue plaid swim trunks.

Often times we met friends Chuck and Sara at the nude beach. Just like Mother and Tom, they immediately disrobed upon parking on the hot sand. One Saturday, I was lying on the blanket working on a drawing with my colored pencils with Sara sitting beside me. She was cross-legged with her legs open, carrying on a conversation while she pulled at her labia, just the same way one would mindlessly pull at a strand of hair.

I loved to ride Chuck's boogie board. I pulled it along the sand by the attached string, from the shore to where the water met my waist, and waited for the second the wave reached its peak and started to curl under. Quickly, I jumped on top the boogie board--straddling it with a leg at either side--and tried to ride the wave to the shore. It took many attempts to master the maneuver just right, so I could get a perfect, balanced ride. I felt freer that ever. I imagined I was an ocean princess or a beautiful mermaid, riding dolphins with jewels on my head--my posture elegantly straight, with my wet hair stuck to my back, and my face tilted to the sun as I rode to the sand over and over.

Back at the blanket, I'd find my brother--fully clothed *and* wearing a hat. We'd take off for one of our ocean side adventures, around the corner and away from the naked people.

Unlike Dad's calm and manageable beach in New York, Mother's Northern California beach was frigid and angry, with an element of danger--imposing and forceful waves that gained height and momentum as they came to shore, with white tails that spewed into the air and whipped against giant angular rocks.

Benny and I walked along the shore, picking up sargassum seaweed and searching for long strands of washed-up bull kelp. We thought the bull kelp looked like something from another planet, and would pretend it was an alien, wrapping ourselves up in the slimy tangled blades and yelling "HELP!" The alien games were fun, but the *best* part of finding the bull kelp was trying to pop the giant bulb-shaped pods.

We played in gentle pools created by large rocks, searching for critters (the California beach did *not* include the horseshoe crabs I so loved and understood, and rarely did I ever see the familiar hermit crabs that were so abundant in New York). We grabbed onto jagged crevices--climbing on top of rocks--laughing and sliding down the side as we banged and scraped our knees, shins and elbows. Benny and I were one on the shore, away from the naked grown-ups--the bottoms of my feet covered with sand and burning; Benny's sneakers soaking wet. I sure was glad for my brother.

"STOP!!" Mother shrieked one early evening when we were driving homeward along Highway 1 from Stinson Beach.

I gasped and my stomach dropped. *What happened? An accident?* Tom screeched the van to a halt on the side of the road, also seemingly in a panic. "What the fuck?" he said--sounding scared--and looking in the rearview, then the side view mirrors.

"A gnome! I saw it!" Mother half-whispered, hanging her body out of her passenger side window, pointing, "Right there, through the trees!"

Mother always insisted that gnomes were everywhere. She said that one must be very, very observant and very quiet in order to spot one. She got very slow and quiet in her voice when she talked about gnome people. I hung on her words, seeing the little forest people so clearly in my mind. For Christmas, she bought us the large, colorful book *Gnomes* by Will Huygen. I marveled for hours at the many detailed illustrations. I was never sure if she was trying to entertain us, or if she truly believed in gnomes. She sure seemed genuine.

Benny and I jumped up and stood behind Mother's seat to look out her window, which was partially obstructed by her bushy hair. We were bumping our heads together and elbow-jabbing, craning to get a look at the gnome.

"Sshhh," Mother whispered, intently keeping her eyes on the trees while reaching around to blindly put her hand over our mouths to keep us quiet, "we don't want him to know we saw him. Be very quiet."

She pointed out the tree in which she had spotted the flash of a gnome––a round little fellow with a beard and a red coat. My eyes scanned the area. *Please, please, please let me see him.* But the gnome had vanished, as gnomes do.

The Berkeley Marina

Saltwater made me miss Dad. The smell reminded me of him—wet shells, dry and salty warm rocks, clammy slime and sea foam, seaweed, hot sand. The smells were so similar on both sides of the country, only Dad's saltwater smells included Coppertone and Jolly Ranchers, Fun Dip candy and Charleston Chews. The smell and feel of saltwater in the air brought on the transistor radios and colorful towels; the Barry Manilow and the slick coconut tanning oil.

Mother's saltwater was backpacks and sweatshirts and hunks of Co-op bread--blankets instead of towels. Her saltwater was unpredictable—jagged rocks and water too dark to see beneath. What mysteries laid beneath Mother's saltwater?

Most things unknown made me think of Dad. The thoughts came unbidden to my mind, when I'd try to match up an experience with a smell or a taste or a feeling. Triggered memories were visceral and disorienting, kind of like déjà vu. I was disoriented and melancholy, but it was hard to tell why.

Mother was making *new* saltwater associations and memories. Crabbing at the Berkeley Marina was another thing she initiated early that year, and probably the best thing we did during those months at the North Berkeley house. She bought a crab net and taught us how to tie on bait and carefully lower the small square net over the edge of the pier, into the water. We hung our heads over the side of the wooden railing and let the rope slide through our cold palms little by little until the net disappeared into the dark bay.

She brought along a thermos full of hot chocolate on our first crabbing day. This was a rare treat so we sipped the steamy plastic cups slowly while sitting on a wooden bench covered by a small roof. That little shelter gave me the idea that we were doing something sneaky in there--or at least extra fun--being that we were hidden from the other crabbers, fishermen and people walking on the pier. I sat close to Mother, looking out at the foggy bay and the seagulls that dipped into view, smelling the lavender and coconut on her hair.

She sat sandwiched between Benny and I, and told us about fishing with her father in the state of Delaware when she was a little girl. She said they would get up before the rest of the family and watch the sun come up from the small fishing boat. I liked to imagine Mother small, with a head full of curly brown hair-- jeans rolled up to her knees--reeling in a fish with her dad helping her hold onto the rod.

Mother took us to the grocery store for what she called bait, abandoning her non-meat-buying ways by confidently purchasing a turkey leg to lure in the unsuspecting crabs.

I salivated over the sausages, steaks, pork chops and bacon--all displayed so orderly behind the glass at the meat counter.

"Pick out a good one," Mother told Benny with her hand on the top of his head.

I loved watching her point to the turkey leg, saying to the man behind the counter, "that one, please." I imagined him thinking it was for us and that Mother was going to cook us a regular meaty meal that night, with something on the side like mashed potatoes or rice pilaf.

I squatted on the soggy planks of the marina pier and carefully unwrapped the thick white butcher paper. The turkey leg was cold and moist in my hands. There was nothing to compare it with—the cold meaty muscle, and the waxy surface covered with prickly spots where feathers once sprouted. I was timid at first when Mother taught me how to tie the turkey leg to the bottom of the net with twine.

"Just pick it up with two hands," she said half-annoyed, "don't think about it."

The three of us pulled the rope together after waiting some time with the crab net over the pier. There were five or six crabs scurrying on the bottom of the net every time--all about the size of Mother's hand, and fighting over the turkey leg. Mother unlatched the top, and the triangle-shaped sides flapped open. We squatted on the planks to get close to the crabs, cheering as we watched them shuffle to the edges of the cage in their sideways walk.

"This is how you grab them," Mother said matter-of-fact as she casually lifted a crab by the back end of his shell, and held him tightly between her fingers. He frantically snapped his claws at the air, the largest claw drawn like a fencer, ready to strike. I loved grabbing the crabs this way and took every opportunity to do so, feeling like a daredevil or an animal tamer.

Mother let us play with the crabs a bit on the damp pier. She placed them in front of us so we could watch them scurry, scooping them up before they dropped off the edge.

We talked about sea life on the floor of the ocean and how crabs were like spiders of the sea, crawling around down there. This did not make them appealing to me as food.

We ate them only once, and that was our first time crabbing. (Mother said eating seafood was an exception to her vegetarian ways). Benny absolutely loved the crabmeat dipped in butter, but I was upset by the cruel boiling process. Mother decided we would just let them go from then on.

"You're just a fish person, honey," she said to me lovingly as we loaded our dripping net into the back of the Bug. After all, she was an animal person; she had cried at the sight of a dead buck, and she even saved a black widow.

Within a few months, just after I turned eleven and Benny turned eight, Mother stopped staying with us for crabbing. She dropped us off at the Berkeley Marina with the plan to pick us up at the giant cement sundial by the parking lot at the end of the day. Benny and I spent the afternoon––just the two of us––waiting on crabs and eating our sack lunches.

Engraved in my mind was the smell of sea spray in Benny's shoulder-length hair, and the image of him on the Berkeley Marina pier––his skinny and scrappy silhouette in the sun, standing on the planks in his worn high-water pants with rips in the knees. At no other location did I get more of a sense that Benny--and *Benny* alone--was my constant beacon. He was my buoy in the water, and I his.

Public School Woes

If we weren't crabbing or going to the beach or playing hooky, we were facing the day at the big public school. Girls sat in clusters at recess and at lunch showing off their realistic plastic model horses, making corrals for them, and cooing over each other's horse collecting accessories. These girls attended gymnastics and ballet lessons; they wore Famolari shoes and Bon Jour jeans. I wore the summer clothes Dad got me in New York for as long as I could, before it got too cold. When it rained, my only raincoat had Sesame Street characters on it. That jacket--along with my too-small polyester green dress and matching green tights--sealed my reputation among the public school girls for good.

"Look! It's the Jolly Green Giant!" Tara Stack sang out as I got on the bus in my green dress, a wave of pre-pubescent laughter filling all five rows of seats in her vicinity--Benny desperately trying to find a separate seat. Tara, my age but a grade or two ahead of me, made sure nobody wanted to be my friend. But, I can't say that I didn't help her along with my social faux pas.

On Valentine's Day, when classmates exchanged those little cheap punch-out cards, there was one card in my little sticker-laden brown bag that was my favorite. One of the popular girls had given me a card that read *Disco!* in purple bubble letters on the front with yellow stars. Jeans with designs on the pockets were in style and I didn't have one pair. I cursed myself for being in the moment and only buying shorts and tank tops when I was in New York, and not thinking ahead to stock up on designer jeans.

I figured that I would sew that disco Valentine's card right onto the ass of my Salvation Army jeans. When I got home from school that day, I carefully took a needle and thread to the stiff card, sewing it to my back pocket, making sure that the stitches were unnoticeably small.

I strutted into school wearing the pants the very next day. I was proud of my needlework, which was holding tight through P.E. and even when pressed against the seat of my desk. I was sure that everyone figured I finally had a break in fashion, until I heard a voice from behind me in the hall.

"Oh my God, she sewed the Valentine card I gave her to her pants!"

Squealing, unrelenting laughter echoed through the hallway as the pack of girls rushed to me at all sides, blinding me with their teasing like a cloud of locusts. I took off like a shot to the girl's bathroom where I locked myself in a stall. I frantically pulled at my fancy stitching while I cried silently, tearing the Valentine's card from my jeans. I slinked around until the end of the day, trying to avoid the mean girls.

I took a liking to the school nurse—a stout woman who seemed to know how to fix anything. I was referred to her one afternoon when the clasp broke on my black China flat shoe. I had gone to the office in hopes of finding something to fix the strap so that my shoe wouldn't keep falling off. The secretary gave me a look that had become familiar when directed at me--a look that said "Well, this is odd." She led me through the busy office and into a little room, introducing me to the school nurse.

"A broken shoe--" the secretary muttered. The little room was more like a cubby, with two chairs and a cot (later, in my classroom, I fantasized about laying on that cot underneath the scratchy wool blanket and getting the school nurse all to myself.)

"Ah, well," she said, her eyes at my feet, "let's take a look."

The nurse's approach was efficient yet kind. If I had felt embarrassed about going to the office for my broken shoe, I wasn't anymore. The nurse had me sit down as she turned around in her swivel chair and opened a big drawer as if it were labeled "Broken Shoes." She pulled out a big safety pin.

"Let me see, sweetheart," she said, placing my foot on top of her pudgy knee. She pinned the strap to the shoe lickety-split.

"All fixed!" she said, tapping my foot and gently placing it on the floor before sending me back to class.

I went back to see the school nurse more than once. Not for colds or a sour stomach, but rather for my ailing China flat shoe, which she gladly cured each time.

I cried many mornings, begging to stay home from school. A good number of times Mother said yes, partially because of my hysteria and partially because of my horrible headaches. That year, I was plagued with throbbing, temple-searing pain in my head that had me vomiting and laying in my bed with the lights off.

"Look at your forehead!" Mother gasped one morning as the two of us stood in front of the bathroom mirror brushing our teeth. "Oh no––" she went on fretfully, "You are growing a *lump*, can't you see it?"

I shifted my head to various angles, craning my neck. She grabbed my head, locking it in a sideways position.

"Here!" she spat like she finally found something that was lost, drawing a circle on my forehead with her finger. I thought that maybe I could make out a lump, but I wasn't sure on account of my already-big forehead.

"Your headaches are causing an actual *lump* on your head," she agonized, shaking her head.

She was in her vexing mode––just like when she fretted over Benny's breathing problem––wringing her hands and talking in a trembling way toward the floor, as if someone had gone missing.

"It's that bullshit school. It's too hard, look at what it's doing to you."

A *lump*. My misery had an actual bona fide physical manifestation. I was happy to get to stay home that day, though I worried about the lump on my head. How many other people had noticed it? I wondered what was inside of it. Pus? Blood? A big tumor? According to my mother, the lump *grew*. It grew as my stress at the public school grew. I agonized that my dread of going to school and the stress over my misfit status would only make my forehead lump grow bigger, the way that lies made Pinocchio's nose grow bigger. This would surely cause me to be an even more awe-inspiring oddity.

"Oh no, look at it now!" Mother fussed, seeming to panic more and more over my lump and over having to send me to what she called "the educational slaughterhouse."

I was pretty sure the school was sending her warnings about my and Benny's repeated absences. She went on about how she was going to figure out what to do about my forehead, and about how she was going to find us another school--she *promised*.

She took me to the Hahnemann Homeopathic Clinic on Bonita Avenue to investigate--among other things--the lump on my head. The practitioner there asked questions that didn't seem to have much to do with a headache.

"Do you feel cold at night?"

"Do you like spicy food?"

"Do you bite your nails?"

After asking so many questions, she ran her finger down the column of a big fat book, closing it with a clap that rang *certainty*!

"I've got it," she said with confidence, before sending us downstairs to the homeopathic clinic pharmacy, where we'd pick up the prescribed "remedy," often a concoction that would give you some of what you've got, like giving snake venom for a snake bite.

The remedies were little sweet-tasting white pellets that came in blue plastic vials with names like Pulsatilla, Belladonna and Nux Vomica. I was not to swallow the remedies with a glass of water like most medicines, rather I was to hold the pellets under my tongue for a certain number of seconds, letting them dissolve.

Mother placed the pellets under my tongue before I headed out to the bus stop in the morning, along with an herbal salve that she applied to my back and neck. She also started giving me Rescue Remedy--a potion in an alcohol base that was supposed to help with emotional upset and what she called trauma--that she usually gave to Benny when he had his fits.

"Stick out your tongue, honey," Mother instructed, drawing up the Rescue Remedy in a little glass dropper and counting out loud as she placed an exact number of drops on my tongue. Benny knew he was next in line, and stood beside me with his tongue out. Sometimes, she placed the drops of Rescue Remedy right on our necks or foreheads.

I sat on the school bus tasting the leftover gritty sweet powder of my remedy under my tongue. I hoped it was going to do the job, and help me with the lump on my head, and help me to feel less upset about going to school. The smell of the herbs on the back of my neck made me feel a little sick, and I was terribly afraid that other kids could smell it, too. I sure could smell Benny's calendula oil through his clothes. Did other kids have remedies and herbal salve and Rescue Remedy? I liked to think that they did, and they just didn't want people to know, like *I* didn't want people to know.

Pretending To Leave

It seemed that, with each move to a different house, the fights between Mother and Tom escalated to a new level. At the North Berkeley house, we learned the power in *pretending to leave*. Again.

One sunny weekend afternoon, the arguing escalated to screaming, Mother's voice fierce and guttural, as she sprayed spit trying to get Tom to see her side, which was being distorted by half-sentences and cuss words. An argument that had started out about something ordinary had quickly turned to accusations that seemed to have nothing to do with the original matter at hand.

It started in the kitchen shortly after they had their coffee, and it had been ramping up ever since. If they were trying to get away from each other, they'd only made it about five feet––they were standing by the entrance of the short hallway towards the bedrooms. I was shamefully aware that I had been inching closer to them from my spot in the front room. I was inconspicuously slinking against the wall by the doorway, and pulling back a sliver of the sheet to watch them. Benny sat quietly on the rug, his arms wrapped around his knees.

"I know what you do!" Mother accused with her finger pointed at his face.

"What the fuck do you know?"

There was a long pause.

"I know what's in your journal," she confessed quietly, seemingly satisfied with herself. I could tell by her voice that she was smirking.

"*What?*" Tom gasped, audibly drawing in a large volume of air.

I cringed. Did she peek at *my* diary?

"She sticks her tits in your face!" she blurted out like she had been waiting to say it, still aiming her finger at him.

Silence.

"How could you do that to me? My privacy--" he sulked as he turned his back to her and quietly walked through the short hall.

I craned my neck around the corner to get a better look. Tom entered his room in the back of the house, bracing his middle like he'd been kicked in the groin. His lock went *click* after he closed his door. Mother stood outside the locked door with her hands at her hips and her head down, shifting her weight from one foot to the other like she had to pee.

"I read it! I have proof!" she shouted into Tom's door through cupped hands.

She was breathing fast and pumping up in a way that indicated an impending explosion. She reminded me of a can of soda that's been shaken, and ought to be let alone to sit for a while before it gets cracked open. I inched into the kitchen and watched her sideways, and realized I was holding my breath. I poked my head through the sheet to shoot Benny a look to express *Let's make a plan.* He didn't look at me though--he was looking at the wall with a blank stare, hugging his bony knees with his bottom lip sticking out. I popped my head back through the sheet when Mother began pounding on Tom's door hard with her fists.

"That's it! Go ahead and hide!" she yelled. She was putting her kinky hair behind hers ears over and over, and wiping at her forehead with the back of her shaky hand.

"You fucking coward! A coward!" she paused, putting her ear to the door, but there was no response. "I think you did it! You really *did* fuck her, didn't you?!"

She started pounding her fists something awful on the door so that it bowed in and I wondered if it might break.

"Come on out and say it to my face!" she yelled. There was still no reply from the other side.

I grew more and more aware and ashamed of my own satisfaction in the whole drama--of my hate for the silent, aloof and pot-smoking Tom--and of my hope that this might be *the one* that finally ejects him for good. I was a supplicant, clutching my precious pathetic and edgy hope that things might finally change.

Mother gave one last hard punch on the door with her bare hand before she staggered into the kitchen to face me and Benny in the front room, her bloodshot eyes bulging out of her head and her hair all wild like Medusa. She was shaking and holding her punching arm in her opposite hand.

"Okay kids, this is it," she announced, tossing her arms in the air like *I surrender*, "we're leaving. You can see what's happening here--"

She walked past us to where she kept her things under the loft, continuing, "Pick out a few things that you absolutely need. We're not coming back."

I heard the zipper of her backpack peeling down and watched her gathering items while mumbling under her breath. Frozen against the doorway, I clenched the wad of bed sheet in my fist, and Benny was still staring blank-faced. I quickly unglued myself and grabbed Benny by the elbow, my heart racing.

"Come on! This is *it*!" I said as I pulled his loose, slack body into our room.

I was shaking as I tried to decide what belongings I would take, weighing sentimentality against necessity. Our room was a blur of things strewn about-- belongings that had been taken for granted--each shabby old item suddenly a precious commodity. While I moved quickly, Benny was slow. He had started to cry, cemented to the middle of the room. He had only grabbed up his Curious George, which he held to his chest with both arms in a bear hug, crying into the ratty brown fibers.

"We'll need clothes--" I listed, grabbing shirts, pants and underwear for the both of us--mostly off the floor--and throwing them into my backpack.

I dragged my soggy ball of a little brother by his flaccid arm, past the hall and into the front room, where I found Mother ready to go with her backpack over her shoulder and two big trash bags in her arms, bulging with what looked like bedding.

"Looks like you got everything!" she yelled in the direction of Tom's locked door. "This is it!"

The three of us stood there for a minute, as if waiting for the starter's gun to signal *Go!* We were waiting to take her lead and I got the feeling that she was waiting for Tom to come out and beg her to stay.

I caught a glimpse of his stony figure on the porch out of the corner of my eye when we began loading stuff into the Bug on the curb. Mother had noticed him, too.

"Just don't say anything," she whispered under her breath in my direction with a satisfied half-smile.

Then she was loud again: "I'm sorry that we have to do this, kids! You heard what he did. I can't live like this."

I felt terribly embarrassed at how glaringly obvious she was being. Were the neighbors were watching? They *had* to hear the ruckus, though I didn't see anyone watching when I scanned the street.

We started haphazardly shoving everything into the backseat as if a tsunami were headed our way. Mother was grabbing up each belonging from the pile by my feet and hurling it into the car, one item on top of another—my pillow, my doll Sharon, my records, my diary, my backpack.

I glanced up at Tom standing by the front door on the porch. He was in some kind of security guard pose, with his arms crossed, giving us a piercing, cocky sneer. Our eyes met and he stared me down something awful, so that I had to look away.

"Say goodbye to this house!" Mother yelled without looking at the house.

She continued to hide her face from Tom, and he still wasn't trying to stop us, though I imagined that he must have wanted to. I wanted to pull out of there before he found the humbleness to open his mouth.

Mother put the keys in the ignition and started the Bug, revving the engine before she popped the clutch. We tore away from the curb, leaving Tom a speck at the top of the steps. And then I asked the eternal question: "Where will we go?"

"I haven't gotten that far. We'll be fine," Mother said, not looking at me, "We just needed to get out of there."

Her resolve was already wavering without that icy figure on the porch. She was driving with only one hand--her non-dominant hand--and the Bug was swerving a little. Benny and I crouched in our seats--me in the front and him in the back. Mother had loaded up the sleeping bags and they were on our laps. *Will we camp?* I imagined us going to check out rentals that very day, driving from one vacant house to the next in our Bug full of belongings.

I loved the idea of an empty house, a house that could be filled with anything. I longed to fill it with my things. I imagined a large house full of bare walls that echoed my voice when I talked--with long, stretching, slippery floors and empty cupboards. Though we moved a lot on both sides of the country, the shifting of one home to the next always occurred when I was away--the rooms filled in my absence, so that I came to it already equipped with my things. An empty house might mean a new life with a clean slate and a chance to mold who we were and how we lived.

I saw myself helping Mother to select the *right* house, one with a nice yard and a sunny kitchen, where she could finally have her own bedroom. Is it possible this time that she has chosen us first? I imagined the many ways that I would show my mother that I was enough for her. I would make her tea and we'd have long conversations together at the orange table; I would help her with laundry and cooking. She'd see how life would be better without cupboards and a refrigerator full of labeled items that we can't touch, without a bedroom that is off limits, without handfuls of stoned men lying around the front yard and living room--without the fights. She'd be a new mom without these distractions that had swayed her off course. Perhaps she'd even take to wearing high heels--like a stewardess or a businesswoman--that would clack on our new floors with the celebration of certainty.

    Mother parked the Bug at the Berkeley Marina in a spot that overlooked the bay, the long pier visible to our right. The three of us sat completely still after she cut the engine, the Bug making clickity-click sounds as it cooled down. The wind rocked our little car every few seconds, but the air inside was so sucked up and still--I could hear our breathing. I turned the little silver window crank, and the wind immediately caught my hair, filling the Bug with the smells of the marina--fish slime, sea spray and the oil on the wooden posts of the pier. The sound of water against rock also rushed in, but Mother didn't seem to notice any of it. She was looking straight ahead and blank-faced at the bay. I felt an immediate urgency to hold her up.
    "It's going to be okay, Mom. Remember what he did, he's terrible."
    But it's as if wasn't there. She kept her eyes to the bay, holding that limp hand of hers, and that's when I noticed that it had started to swell something awful.
    "Mom, your hand--"
    She slowly and mechanically brought her puffy, shaking hand to her eye level. She turned it side-to-side, examining it like it was not attached to her at all.
    "Oh..." she mumbled slowly, "I can't go anywhere with this hand."
    My heart sank. *Think quick.* I began trying to convince her that we *could* do it, that she wasn't driving so bad. I'd tell her we'll get some ice for her hand and

we'll wait a while and then go get a paper and look for houses to rent.

She turned to me slowly, squinting with a stupefied expression for a few long seconds.

"*Houses?*"

It was if the idea to leave was a total surprise, like it was never *her* idea. I got the sense that she was at the bottom of a muddy well and that I was trying to get her to grab onto a rope. I needed to pull her back.

"You said we weren't going back," I reminded her, my voice shaking, "we need to figure out where to go."

I tried to keep my voice steady and calm, afraid that she'd sniff out my worried uncertainty, sealing her desire to forget it and head back to the house. Keeping my mother on track was a very delicate operation--I needed to convince her in a way that both boosted her confidence and made her feel like breaking free was *her* idea, not mine. This was the part where she often turned on me. From under the rubble in the backseat came my little brother's voice.

"We're just going home, stupid," Benny snapped in a condescending, snotty way. I shot him a look that said *I'm gonna beat your face in if you don't shut up.*

Mother kept her eyes on me. She was deflated and small there behind the wheel, holding her gimpy hand. She began pleading with me, big tears rolling down her face, shaking her head.

"Honey, I can't expect you to understand. You've never been in love. I had to teach him a lesson," she turned her head to look at the water. "We'll wait here awhile and when we go back, he'll be so sorry that he'll be better."

"No, Mom, he *won't* learn. It'll just happen again. This is our chance--"

But I already know it's too late.

"I'm not strong like you, okay?" she snapped, talking to the window with her tears falling in fat rivulets, dripping off her chin and down her neck.

"Yes you are Mom, you *are* strong."

"No, I'm weak," she cried, not looking at me and wiping her snot and tears with the cuff of her shirt. *I've lost her. We're going back to Tom.*

"I can't leave, I just can't. I can't," she surrendered with her chin quivering, "And my hand--" She continued rubbing the swollen hand with her good hand. I sensed that Mother was picking up on my fret by the way that she kept looking away from me. I would always be the hopeful seeker to my mother, a hovering fruit fly to her peachy champagne. She was the sought one—agitated, swatting, slipping away.

I thought of all the times I tried to convince her to leave during the fights, all my urging blending into one futile mess. I recalled one incident when she locked us both in the bathroom. She cried into my lap as I sat on the side of the bathtub with her kneeling at my feet. Her tears made two big wet spots on the oversized T-shirt that covered my knees as I ran my fingers through her thick dark curls. I promised her that everything would be okay, that we'd work it all out. But she just cried, "I can't, I can't, I can't..."

"I'm not strong like you," she said to me that day in the bathroom, just like she was saying in the Bug, her face all wet and puffy.

Where on earth did my mother get the idea that I was so strong? Was I strong just from her saying I was strong? Maybe I was strong because I saw what ought to be in sharp detail, while her focus was all fuzzy. Whatever the reason, I had the feeling that my apparent strength just kept her with him. My being "strong" let her off the hook. How safe was a world in which I was braver than my own mother?

"Told you," Benny shot from the backseat, and I immediately turned around to slug him one. His flesh felt satisfying against my hand. In an instant, he was on top of me and we were a blazing ball of sibling fisticuffs--

Mother an innocent bystander in the way. She grabbed her door handle at once, and ejected herself from the car.

"Can you guys *ever* give me a fucking break?!" she shouted into the car as she slammed the door.

Mother walked away with her back turned to us, looking like a child in her running sneakers and rolled up Levi's and oversized wool sweater, bowing her head against the wind with her arms crossed. I opened my door to get out in an impulse to follow her, but I just stood by the Bug––my legs wouldn't move. I watched her get smaller and smaller until she stopped and turned toward the bay. She stood there staring at the water before carefully stepping out onto a large rock about twenty feet above the edge, looking like the prow of a ship––alone against the vast openness. I watched her intently, holding my breath, the wind whipping my hair over my eyes. *Don't fall, don't jump.* Benny sat in the backseat with his arms crossed, half-panting from our scuffle. He looked so foolish with all the belongings cluttered around him. I hated him for it. I hated myself for being terrified *again* that maybe my mother didn't want to be alive. I hated that the trick abandonment meant for Tom had played out on my brother and me instead.

Back at the house, Benny and I kept to our room. It had been nearly unbearable to walk up the front steps and past Tom with our arms full of our possessions like a couple of sorry losers.

"Oh, I see you're back––" he had sneered, smiling.

Soon we heard laughing and gregarious teasing through the walls––tickling and wrestling––and then the sounds of sex.

Benny immediately began categorizing his magazines and comic books for the hundredth time. Unlike me—sloppy to the core—Benny was meticulously organized and clean. Especially in times of stress, I could find him on the floor sitting next to his milk crate shelves with stacks of paper things—papers with cryptic scribbles that only he understood, comic books, lists. Next to the stack of paper things was his stack of memorabilia items—baseball and Star Wars collecting cards, little pins from airplane rides, bright toothpicks with frilly ends, a ticket stub from Shea Stadium. Benny always found new ways to sort his things, sometimes discarding one strategy only to return to it after a few other systems had been tried. At eight-years-old, items were alphabetized and organized by genre, color, and number. He went ballistic if an item were taken out and not put back to the proper place.

    As for myself, on the day that we returned from the marina with our tails between our legs, I tried Benny's emotionless mask on my own face. I stared at the wall from my bed with my arms crossed while I played Cheap Trick loud on my record player, drowning out those moans from the other room.

    I wondered if my little brother was onto something—some kind of intuitive resolve that he couldn't change a thing. Why couldn't I be more like him?

Dance Jam

    Around the same time that Mother tried to make Tom think she was leaving, she started going to "Dance Jam" on Saturday nights. I loved to come with her, and sometimes got to bring a friend or two along. Dance Jam was held at a gigantic old warehouse in lower South Berkeley that had been converted into a dance studio with an epic hardwood floor and great big mirrors that lined the walls. Lessons and rehearsals were held there during the week, but on Saturday nights, the warehouse was used for Dance Jam, where all ages were welcome. Dozens of people poured in, paying the admission fee of a dollar or two to dance the night away.

    While Dance Jam was no One's Discotheque, I loved the dimmed lighting and the booming volume of the music. There was also a snack bar where Mother treated us to Dixie cups of unfiltered apple juice for a quarter.

The best part for most of the kids was the loft (not *me*, my favorite part was the dance floor). We'd climb the ten or fifteen foot wooden ladder to the tall *fort* of giant pillows, where we played and spied on the grown-ups down below. The loft also offered a place for kids to sleep when it got really late (Benny was one of those). By the end of the evening, there were always several smaller kids crashed out on the pillows, parents struggling to carry their floppy, slack bodies down the ladder. Sometimes, a pair of adults would come up there to make-out, which was always a bit awkward. I tried to not stare, but couldn't stop myself from peeking at them as they kissed passionately and clawed at each other on the pillows.

I danced all evening, so I didn't spend very much time in the loft. I wore my maroon-colored leotard and matching tights every time––no skirt or dress. There was a lot of Santana and Grateful Dead and other music that I didn't like very much. I waited all evening for "My Sharona" to come on, which they played every single time, but only once.

Tom never came to Dance Jam, so Mother often danced with whomever and however she pleased. She seemed truly herself there––she never stopped moving. She twirled and gyrated; every single part of her body was involved in her dancing, even her hair. She was easy to spot amongst the crowd, with her bouncing massive dark fro, and her purple-blue sleeveless top covered in specs of glitter. Her chest, neck and face were covered with sweat early in the evening, strands of ringlet curls glued to her face. I loved dancing with her––we formed a little circle, our hands held tightly together, and spun wildly over and over, laughing and falling over each other and bumping into people.

Most of the women wore unitards or leotards with tights––or form-fitting thin tops and flowing skirts––

while most of the men wore loose draw-string cotton pants and sleeveless tops. The adults did a lot of what was called "contact dance" at Dance Jam, which was the new craze amongst the Berkeley hippies at the time, wherein people moved their bodies in unison, always touching and never separating. I hated it when I spotted her doing this with a stranger, her sweaty body enmeshed with his sweaty body.

One time, when it was getting very late and I happened to be up in the loft, I saw a woman down below remove her shirt while she was dancing, letting her bare breasts flap about. This encouraged another woman to remove her top, and then another. The men were eyeing the topless women, moving in closer. My stomach dropped. Would my mother take off her top, too? Being *sure* that Mother was about to go topless, I ran down the ladder as fast as I could. Panic-stricken, I weaved though the adults on the dance floor to get to her, grabbing hold of her arm.

"What?!" she yelled over the music, stopping her dancing and eyeballing me, annoyed.

"Don't take off your shirt like those ladies!" I ordered her, suddenly feeling a little embarrassed about my desperation that was probably pretty obvious.

"What's your trip, Astrid?!"

"Just *don't*––" I wasn't sure just *why* I was so terrified at the thought of my mother going topless at Dance Jam––I just was.

"I'm not going to, *Jesus Christ*," she snapped, yanking her arm out of my grasp and going back to her dancing, turning her back on me.

On a few occasions, a man would try to dance with me on the dance floor. He'd inch his way over and get into my personal space and stay there, trying to meet my eyes as he did his best to mimic my movements. My insides churned, as I tried to inconspicuously move away from him. I could hear Dad teasing that the man wanted to do the nasty. Did he know I was eleven?

We stopped going to Dance Jam by the time I was twelve or thirteen. Maybe it closed, or maybe Mother and I had just had enough of it. We continued to have our own Dance Jam's in our living room, playing Chris Williamson and Van Morrison on the stereo, spinning around in circles––we didn't much miss the original Dance Jam.

Mother's Loft

I entered the front room through the hanging bed sheet in the doorway one morning to ask a question, when Mother and Tom lay in the loft. I had heard Mother whispering and giggling, so I assumed it was safe to go in.

"Oh, fuckkk," Tom groaned.

The smell of the front room that morning was grown-up breath and stinky armpits. I quickly darted back through the sheet and into the kitchen, where Benny was pouring his cereal.

In a minute or so, I heard Mother's feet coming down the rickety ladder of the loft. She got caught up in the sheet as she blew through the front room doorway and began swatting at it as if it were a pesky thing. She stood for a moment looking disheveled with her eyes swollen and her hair all wiry like she had touched an electric socket.

"Let me tell you what you've done," she said as she approached me in her loose blue robe, half-second flashes of her bare breasts peeping out with her accentuating gestures.

"When adults get ready to make love, there is a warming up period that is very sensitive." She was half-whispering, half-hissing with that rank grown-up morning breath. I felt myself trying to pull away from her.

"If this time gets interrupted, the whole experience of making love is ruined."

She stared me down with a piercing look for a minute, shaking her head, her hands on her hips. I didn't know what to say.

"So, thanks a lot, Astrid. I don't ask for that much, you know."

My face went hot with embarrassment, feeling that I'd been included in their act––this *lovemaking*––by ruining it. I thought of Tom's hands on her just moments before, *warming up*. Was the warming up like an engine? or was it more like stretches before a race?

She turned her back and went through the sheet again and I heard the loft go squeak-squeak-squeak as she climbed back up.

"Making love" was an odd term to me, especially when I tried to pin it on the bucking, wall slamming, and primal groaning that seemed to go along with it. Did more love get created when people did the nasty? Then why was it called "nasty"? I kind of preferred my father's term, *Getting laid*––somehow, it seemed less embarrassing.

My mother's love nest was a funny place. She had created a den underneath her loft bed—a place to keep the gigantic aging cloud pillows, along with about a million other pillows. Amongst all the pillows lay what Mother called *The Pals*.

The Pals were a gang of stuffed animals that she had to have around her bed wherever we lived. There were several of them, but the *most* loved were Richie (an orange droopy dog), Oinker (a pink pig), and Zig-Zag (a brown monkey). These adorned Pals were often in her bed, but sometimes in the Pal pile, mixed in with the others, though bearing their high status. They were obviously well loved, with their fur half-gone and their material slack.

Tom had given Mother the three Pals before San Francisco, because they were in her bed way back then. I had become attached to them myself, snuggling Richie or Oinker while Mother read to me. Her favorite stuffed animals smelled like her and I sometimes grabbed one if I were particularly sad, brushing their tatty fur against the bottom of my nose.

One morning, I awoke to find Mother crouched low in that pillow den under her loft. She didn't lift her head when I walked through the sheet in the doorway. She was doing something with her hands, though I couldn't tell what because her back was half-turned to me.

I had fallen asleep the previous night to thunderous fighting—screaming, body slamming, and crying. Tom had forgotten her birthday. I saw her tears and then her pure focus with a thread and needle as I approached.

"I didn't mean to hurt them," she whimpered softly, still not looking at me.

It was then that I saw Oinker in her lap. Mother was suturing a large stab wound to his abdomen. Some of his little white stuffing pellets lay scattered on her nightgown. Her hand shook as she passed the needle and then pulled the thread through his tough fibers.

"I was just so mad at him--"

Beside her, ready for their repair, lay Richie and Zig-Zag, slashed and maimed. I knew that she wanted my support; she wanted me to stand by her and absolve her guilt. But I couldn't speak. How she could have hurt something that she loved so much? It was as though my mother had committed a real murder-- *three*--and *I* could very well be next. I don't recall what I said to her or how I left that room. Mother kept those three scarred Pals with her for years after that. They stayed as well-loved as ever, bearing the old wounds that Mother had sewn.

Mother Nature

Mother may have had her share of unpleasant moods, but she sure had a way with the outdoors. If we were raised with some kind of religion, I'd have to pin it on her appreciation for nature. She had a way of pointing out the kinds of miracles that are right in front of people all the time--they just couldn't see. She could.

One of my favorite places was Yosemite National Park, where I stood in wonder in front of the miraculous Half Dome. I was eight and Benny five the first time we visited Yosemite. Mother took us one or two more times before we were teenagers. However, she and Tom went more often, when we were in New York.

"Giant ice did this," Mother said as she stared out over the canyons. I thought of what a freezing winter that must have been. But then she explained *glaciers,* and that the cliffs and valleys were formed hundreds of years ago.

Mother huffed about Yosemite being "so exploited" when we'd walk past all the camera-clicking tourists and the informational plaques surrounded by small, awestruck crowds.

"Ha, they'll never know *all* her secrets," Mother scoffed about the tourists. "No one person could see every single nook and cranny."

That year--after I turned eleven--we took a trip to Big Bear, pitching our tents at a campground in the San Bernardino National Forest. The sites were spaced well apart without the noise of other campers but also without hot showers. I felt that my fantasy prairie girl experience was more authentic, what with the tall pines and the nearby running stream and our crude fire pit.

Sometime in the beginning of this trip, we hiked on trails that led up to high places, some overlooking the smoggy San Bernardino Valley. The mountain air was clean and crisp at these elevated spots. At the peak of a trail, or at the top of a hill, Mother liked to stand with her back arched, her eyes closed and her arms stretched above her head. In this stance, she took in a long, slow deep breath through her nose and then let it out with a washing sigh.

"Can't you feel it?" she'd say with the sun in her face, the auburn in her hair coming out like honey warmed up.

I closed my eyes and tried to pin down what *it* was that she was feeling. I could better hear a woodpecker or a stream ripple; I could smell the bark of pine, and the petrichor scent of the earthy, musky ground. The sunshine on my face gave me the feeling that life was good.

She brought us to an old pine tree. "Press your hands on it," she said, placing her palms over the backs of my hands, "Think of everything that this tree has seen. You might be able to feel it." I saw Native Americans running past, bear and deer and wild hailstorms.

Mother said that it was no accident that a stream would show up just when we were most tired or hot, and that a large cliff might be stumbled upon right when she was feeling too proud or high and mighty, just to show her how small and insignificant she really was.

Mother, Benny and I (and even Tom) called out shapes seen in clouds when we were high up. In the clouds, we saw rabbits, cars, frogs, faces––the possibilities were endless. Sometimes, Mother and Tom made horns with their hands and yelled like Tarzan so that the forest, valley, or river below echoed their call.

During the camping trip to Big Bear, a snake slithered right out in front of us while we walked along a very hot and dusty trail.

"Stop!" Mother shrieked at the outer limits of whispering, grinding to a halt. She threw her arms out to her sides to stop us, the way she did when she slammed on the brakes in the Bug when I was in the front passenger seat. We tripped forward for a second as we hit her arms––head over knees––before catching our footing. I caught my breath and stood stock-still, staring at the snake–– as did Tom, who had also stopped in his tracks.

"Sshhh," Mother whispered, "stay still and be quiet, I want to talk to her."

I watched in fear as Mother gracefully slithered to the ground in one swift and smooth uniform motion. She laid her face in the dirt with her butt in the air. Amazingly, that snake stayed put on the path, and met Mother eye-to-eye, as if they were in a staring contest.

"Mom stop, come on, *please* get away from it," I pleaded, my voice trembling.

"Yeah Mommy, get up. It's gonna bite you," Benny added.

"Yeah, that's enough--" Tom warned.

Mother's stare-down with the snake was probably only twenty or thirty seconds, but it felt like much longer than that. When the snake slithered away, she got up and dusted off her hair and her clothes.

"You have to become a snake to talk to one," she said matter-of-factly.

I always wondered what it was that she and the snake said to each other that day. She said it was a rattler—this I don't know to be true or false, but I'll never forget the sight of our mother being a snake person there somewhere in the San Bernardino National Forest.

We were in the middle of reading *The Phantom Tollbooth* by Norton Juster on this camping trip. We sipped on Celestial Seasonings Sleepytime tea with honey by the fire--once the stars were out, and it was closing in on bedtime--while Mother and Tom shared a doobie. Tom sat alone and drank beer while Mother crawled into the tent with us to read. Benny was a little fidgety, zipping and unzipping his sleeping bag as she tried to keep the flashlight steady. I intently watched Mother's sweet sun-kissed face in the yellow glow of the flashlight, hanging onto her magical storytelling voice as she warmed up the army green tent.

One of the mornings, after Mother finished reading us a chapter by the breakfast fire, she and Tom announced that they were going on what they called an adult hike.

"We'll be walking fast and there'll be some steep trails," Mother explained. I knew that meant *Tom* would be walking fast. I could tell he was annoyed when Benny and I were along on hikes--he was always charging ahead with his long legs, even Mother hardly able to keep up.

I watched their figures disappear through the tall trees with the morning sun on their backpacks. I tried to keep the familiar pesky anxiety at bay.

Benny and I ate handfuls of nuts and poured water into our little tin cups from the big plastic jug that sat on the picnic table. We drew on the sketchpads with our colored pencils. The quiet, still campsite seemed so vacant and vulnerable without the adults--I kept imagining leopards and bears out of the corners of my eyes. That got me to thinking about the Native American people Mother talked about by the fire, how they must have been such planners, always prepared and probably always calm.

I gathered up Benny and we set off down the pike to scout out our neighbors and to look for much needed survival items. Such an adventure took us away from the empty campsite and distracted me from worrying about my mother (she could have fallen off of one of those cliffs, been bitten by a snake, gotten lost...anything).

We were looking for sticks to make a shelter when we stumbled on a campsite with a couple finishing up their breakfast. I pulled Benny behind a tree by his T-shirt, putting my finger to my lips to shush him to stay quiet.

"*Why* do we have to watch them? I wanna go," Benny complained as we stood quietly behind the tree watching the couple drinking out of their tin mugs, their morning fire almost out.

"Just shut up," I snapped.

The longer I watched them, the less anxious I felt about being alone.

"Let's stay on this trail," I whispered to Benny, motioning to the little trail next to the couple's campsite.

Benny was happy to walk along the trail. I kept a mental record of where we were going so we could get back to our campsite. The last thing I wanted was to get lost.

"We should look for food in case Mom doesn't come back," I said to Benny, who was walking a few feet behind me. I knew it wasn't very nice to scare him like that. It was *me* who was scared, and I wanted someone to share the hot potato of worry. His footsteps stopped.

"What do you mean?"

I just kept walking, not answering. I swooped down to grab an acorn and took it over to him.

"This." I said, putting it in his face, "This is an acorn. We can crush these like Mom said. Start putting them in your pockets."

We quietly searched for acorns along the path, stuffing our pockets. After some time passed, we headed back to the campsite to begin the process of crushing the acorns.

My heart sank when Mother was still gone. But it seemed that those acorns offered some kind of order, so we took to breaking the shells with the hatchet, an understatement of overkill.

"Blaaach!" we spat with sour faces at the bitter taste. I wondered how people ever ate them. Somehow, I had imagined they would taste buttery--perhaps an association with acorn squash.

We spent the rest of that day performing ceremonies in our "teepee." I can still see Benny's face across from me, sweaty in that humid tent, trying to follow me in some kind of yelping chant as we clapped wooden sticks together. Mother and Tom *did* make it back sometime that evening, though I have forgotten that part of the story.

Kim

The school year was half over, and I still hated going to Franklin School. I also still hated the school bus. It was too large for the road--so awkward and loud--and full of mean, bullying kids. One *good* thing about the bus: it led me to Kim Tanner. Kim waited at the same bus stop, though it sure took us long enough to meet. She would be the one to get me through the remainder of my time at that huge, godforsaken public school. I think I saved her as much as she saved me.

Kim lived around the corner and we hit it off right away once we finally connected. We spent many, many afternoons drinking Twinings Constant Comment tea with cream and sugar at her house, and English Breakfast tea with milk and honey at my house.

I dreaded the school hours without Kim. We were in different classrooms, so we met up at the cafeteria at lunchtime, where she would eat her tray of fish sticks and tater tots while I pulled out my sandwich of one thousand grain bread (cut with a chain saw), greased with peanut butter (with oil separated, no salt) and raw honey.

Kim was pretty like her mother, with long blonde hair and bright blue eyes. She had a big gap in between her two front teeth that added to her spunky personality. I loved the gap and wished I could have one, too.

Though she was beautiful, for some reason, Kim's mother kept to her bedroom pretty much twenty-four-seven. It was a shock to see her *out* of bed, like a corpse rising from the grave. Every now and again, we heard her high-pitched southern drawl yelp from her bed upstairs, "Kimmm-eeeeeee!" This was Kim's cue to bring her mother something to eat or drink, or to be prepared to take the order for a shopping errand or a chore. If I dared to join Kim up the stairs to respond to her mother's call, I caught a glimpse of a grown woman curled up in her covers. Dirty dishes and clothes scattered around the entire periphery of her bed, the thick stench of mold and soiled laundry filling the room.

Now, seeing a depressed mother was nothing new to me, nor was seeing a drunk mother, or seeing a mother so deep in her funk that she didn't even seem alive. These aspects of Kim's mother didn't surprise me as much as the fact that her mother never seemed to leave this state. Her mother's funk wasn't a pause in an otherwise productive life––her funk was a permanent way of being.

Kim's mother had been born and raised in Texas, which accounted for her slight southern accent, Kim explained. Kim bubbled over her mother's history—that she had been a real beauty, winning awards and accolades, with a long following of boys who vied for her attention. I waited for the part in the story that explained the fork in the road that led her mother to this place, but Kim skipped that part, as if her mother's life did indeed end before Kim was even born. Seeing her body loose on that mattress, I caught a shade of the prom queen beauty, her eyes still bright blue and her hair still long and blonde.

I asked Kim once if her mother had any boyfriends, when the two of us lay in the dark under the covers at my house, listening to the sounds of my mother having sex with Tom in the loft on the other side of the wall. She said that her mother's old high school sweetheart came once. She said he wore a cowboy hat and talked southern like her mother, and that she heard them making the sex sounds.

"Did he move in with you?"

"No. He only stayed a couple days."

Kim and I were *latchkey kids*, except for her, there happened to be a mother in a bedroom who sort of didn't count because it was like she wasn't really home. My mother was usually gone when I got home from school–– in class at S.F. State or working at a daycare center. We had free range at either house and spent our days after school drinking Constant Comment and English Breakfast and listening to music.

Kim was into punk before it was popular to be into punk. She introduced me to Sid Vicious and The Sex Pistols and The Dead Kennedys, and she loved Cheap Trick like me. We'd lie in her bed late at night during sleepovers with her portable radio by our heads, listening to a program about punk rock music that aired on a Bay Area radio station. She'd hang onto the words of the people being interviewed and the commentaries of the DJ. I sometimes lost interest or started goofing off, but Kim was fixed to that program.

When Blondie's *Parallel Lines* came out, we were engrossed in the album, dancing for hours in the living room with pretend microphones. We knew every line to every song on that record.

Kim's house was piled high with trash and clutter. Dishes and rotting food lay all over the kitchen. We fixed our own meals when hungry, washing a grimy pot for mac and cheese or Rice-A-Roni. Some days, we scrubbed that house clean because her mother was barking from upstairs, and writing out long chore lists for Kim to complete. The cleaning gave us something to do and seemed to calm that bear upstairs, allowing us more time together. Some days, I wished that Kim could come out and play but she had to stay in and clean, and I wasn't even allowed over there until the cleaning was done.

I enjoyed being her partner and cohort in this difficult and seemingly lonely life of hers. We were two peas in a pod. Our hardships and heartache might have been for different reasons, but I think we ultimately felt so very much the same. My life seemed just a little easier with Kim in it.

Kim had an older brother who was awfully cruel to her. He tortured her in ways that made me wince—pushing her to the floor and spreading her legs into a split so far that I thought they might snap, or punching her right in the face.

She and her older brother were always on dog shit duty; it was one of the chores on their mother's list. I recall her brother covering his hand with a plastic bag before picking up a giant pile of dog shit and chucking it right in Kim's face. She cried and cried with her blonde hair stuck to her cheek with thick, fresh brown crap, yelling, "Fuck you!"

Their large dog "Ape" seemed to love the dog shit clean up and the dog shit wars, loping around enthusiastically and trying to hump our legs.

In my memory of him at this time, little eight-year-old Benny was a feisty, scrappy tag-along. He was still far too small for his age. His hair was long. To add to his awkwardness, most of his pants were too short. However, he mostly wore shorts––his knobby knees sticking out on his spaghetti legs.

Benny was like the Tasmanian Devil when he was pissed off. The fits he pitched had a different edge at this point, with threats and insults and cursing that had grown more sophisticated or elaborate, such as "You're a mother-fucker-titty-sucker-two-ball-bitch."

He liked to try out his pseudo-karate moves, but he wasn't much of a threat due to his size, so he often resorted to objects like rocks and scissors as weapons. He might not have been such a terror if it weren't for the fact that I was often picking on him. I liked to meanly remind him that his head was too big for his body and that he looked like a girl.

Benny attempted to join in on whatever I was doing with my few neighborhood friends. One time, we were playing a game outside that involved a broom and jumping over it. I told him sure, come on and join in. I coaxed my friend to get on the other end of the broom and we lifted Benny up off the ground from between his legs. He screamed in pain from his balls being squashed, begging for us to let him down.

Perhaps this meanness was general brother/sister cruelty or perhaps it was me taking out the school bullying on my little brother––maybe it was a mix of both. The funny thing was, I loved him so very ferociously.

One Saturday morning, Kim came rushing in to our house, informing me that the kids around the corner had surrounded Benny, calling him "small" and slapping him around. I was still in the over-sized shirt I wore as a nightgown, watching TV. I bolted out the door and ran to the scene without getting dressed furious and scared for my brother. I found Benny outnumbered and quietly failing at trying not to cry. I saw red and went hot with adrenaline as I usually did when I caught someone picking on Benny. I proceeded to take on all four or five kids, threatening to kick their asses, and swinging my fists at them. I had a distant awareness that I was far outnumbered but I didn't care (and they were all a year or two younger than me, anyway).

Just as soon as I threatened, "Don't you ever let me catch you fuckers picking on my brother again!" one of the boys got behind me and lifted my nightshirt up to my armpits. To my horror, I had forgotten that I was not wearing any underwear. In an instant, the kids were laughing hysterically, putting their hands to their mouths and pointing their fingers at me.

"Naayy-keee!" one of them yelled after me as I high-tailed it back home, right behind Benny, who had already taken off, Kim following us both.

Benny had begun showing an interest in sports for the first time. He joined a soccer team, and seemed excited about it, wearing the uniform twenty-four-seven. It was the first sport he had ever played. But the practice regime involved a schedule with pickups and drop off's. Mother kept up for a little while, even baking the team a bona fide tray of brownies once (ganja not included). But Benny started missing a lot of practices, and was being teased. Early in, he got into a scuff with one of his teammates, going after him with punches and kicks and yelling out motherfucker or something like that. He was kicked off the team.

He had taken to wearing those tight terry cloth bands around both his wrists, and continued wearing them even after he was no longer on the team. He wore those absorbent athletic wristbands day in and day out—-even while he slept.

To me, those ridiculous terry cloth wristbands resembled the Benny that was still impressionable, the Benny that had not yet reached his full capacity for cynicism. That cynicism eventually hit my brother like a final call, an all bets are off, and an it's too late. But in 1980, Benny eagerly and whole-heartedly rubbed the sweat off his forehead with those dirt-stained things, and proudly wore shiny shorts for any and all occasions.

Welcome to Rainbow Diner

That spring at the North Berkeley house, we transformed our backyard into a quaint little one-table outdoor restaurant.

"Our sign has to be perfect," I kept cautioning Benny, thinking about his sloppy writing. Benny, Kim and I were on our stomachs in the front room—-a big piece of newsprint spread out in front of us—-crayons and colored pens and pastels scattered all around our periphery.

We had picked out a name the night before—-Kim was spending the night—-when we came up with the brilliant idea to make a restaurant.

"I want to call it Rainbow Diner," I had said, very certain on the name.

Kim and I excitedly talked about being waitresses, and about all the money we'd make.

Kim was bouncing up and down on a big light blue cloud pillow, unable to sit still and spouting out, "What if it gets really popular?!"

"We'll have to get more tables!"

Benny butted in--worrying about his fair share of participation--interjecting that he gets a turn at being a waiter and he gets to help make the menu.

Our sign had a huge colorful rainbow when we were finished, with each letter in a different color: "Welcome to Rainbow Diner! Come on in!"

We hung it on the porch--using nearly an entire roll of scotch tape--with arrows pointing to the right side of the house, leading to the yard.

We only had a few dollars to shop for supplies, so we had to be choosy with the menu. Some items were included simply because we already had them in the kitchen:

- Green Salad
- Fruit salad
- Hardboiled eggs
- Crackers and cheese
- Lemonade
- Water

We created menus out of construction paper folded in half with choices listed on the inside in colored felt pen. We even came up with combo items, like crackers and cheese with salad.

Next, Mother gave us a few dollars, and the three of us excitedly walked to the grocery store, talking up Rainbow Diner.

"My, you really know how to pick a cucumber. Aren't you a grown up girl!" a woman remarked in the produce aisle.

"I'm shopping for my restaurant," I announced with my nose in the air, feeling like I was about to get famous.

"Oh, your *restaurant*?"

"Yeah, it's called Rainbow Diner," Benny chimed in.

I loved that she appeared so interested--her reaction a good indication of how *everyone* was going to receive our diner. I looked around at who might be watching and listening, glad to get the chance to rustle up some customers.

I took every opportunity at the grocery store to tell strangers about Rainbow Diner, giving them our address. Aside from the lady in the produce aisle, we also informed the checkout man, who promised to come. We advertised on the street as we happily took turns carrying our brown bag on the way home, yelling, "COME TO RAINBOW DINER!"

We were busy in the kitchen as soon as we got home. I stood in front of the cutting board with Benny beside me, chopping up apples and oranges. We used the lettuce that was already in the crisper, which was browning at the edges. I boiled the eggs myself––the big pot at my eye level, so I had to get on tippy-toes to look inside––watching intently as they bobbed and spun in the boiling water. I wasn't sure how long they needed to boil.

"Mom! How long do I boil the eggs?!" I shouted over my shoulder to Mother, who was in the back of the house with Tom, in his study.

"Ohhh..." her voice was far away and hard to hear, "I don't know. Five minutes?! Just a few minutes should be about right!"

I scooped those eggs out of the hot bubbling pot one by one with a spoon after a few minutes passed, and set them out to cool.

I stared at the old outdoor picnic table in our yard. It had come with the house and was very weathered––without finish––a sure splinter-inflictor. Benny had picked up a stick and was banging it on the patch of dry dirt in the yard.

"I think we need a tablecloth or something," Kim said. I knew we didn't have a tablecloth. I ran inside and grabbed an old bed sheet with a faded yellow floral pattern, and we spread it across the table. We stood back and looked at it quietly, satisfied.

"Here! Let's pick these flowers," I added, heading for an overgrown corner in the yard that was covered with dandelions. Benny dropped his stick and began enthusiastically plucking several. We placed the dandelions in a jar full of water on the table.

"It looks like a real restaurant!" Kim announced, clapping.

I thought of Dad when I looked at our restaurant table all done up for the first time. I thought of him showing me a cloth napkin at a fancy steak restaurant in New York City, saying, "On your lap, princess, on your lap."

"You should be able to see your reflection in your spoon," he had said, holding his spoon to his face with one eye squinting. I loved watching Dad carry on about elegance and etiquette––the way he sounded like such a bragger. What would he say of *my* restaurant? I tried to imagine him entering my yard, saying, "People! Let's make this sparkle!" Funny thing was, I just couldn't picture him there.

We did get a few customers on our opening day. Our mother's friend Lauren came to the diner, full of exaggerated enthusiasm over her wilted greens. We stopped her on the porch when she arrived, as she was making her way to the front door.

"Nope, nope, come this way!" I ordered, running up the steps and grabbing her hand to drag her to the side of the house, "You have to go under the sign. See?" I pointed to the Rainbow Diner sign, still pulling her hand.

"Oh yes, of course! *To the restaurant!*" she affirmed with a nod.

"Yep! to the restaurant. Welcome to Rainbow Diner," Kim announced, grabbing her other hand.

"Welcome to Rainbow Diner!" Benny dittoed, running in front of her and waving his arms.

"Wow, guys, this is really great," Lauren praised as she sipped her ice water at the backyard table, going over the menu.

A few hours had gone by since Lauren's visit and there had not been another customer. We had removed our Rainbow Diner sign from the porch and the three of us stood on the street corner waving it in hopes to reel people in. Kim held one end of the sign, and I the other, as we danced while franticly yelling at passing cars and people on foot. Benny was extra loud and animated, running around us in a circle and screaming, "COME TO RAINBOW DINER!"

A plump, friendly older woman saw us from her car. Perhaps thinking we were in distress, she pulled over. We were completely thrilled, jumping up and down as we approached the passenger window.

"What is *this*?" she asked, smiling and leaning over her center console.

"It's our diner!" Benny announced first.

"Just drive this way," I said pointing in the direction of our house down the street, "We'll lead you!"

This kind lady drove slowly as we clapped and squealed the half a block to our house, waving our arms at her to *come, come this way*. When she stepped out of her car, I scrambled to try to put the sign back up, but couldn't, so I just held it in front of the house for her, saying, "See?! See?!" She giggled and blushed and then behaved as though Rainbow Diner were a five star hole in the wall.

"I am very excited to try out this new restaurant of yours. Won't you please show me to a table?"

The three of us escorted the lady through the side, Benny and I already jabbing each other in the sides to compete for first-line host. He had a running start because I had gotten myself hung up with the sign.

"Please do have a seat," Kim said cheerfully, fanning her arm to the picnic table bench.

Much to my dismay, Benny was first to get a hold of the menu after the lady sat down. I was not about to let him be the waiter. That sweet Rainbow Diner customer sat jaw-slacked as I ran after my brother, grabbing his scrappy little body and bending his arm back while he fought like hell. He kicked and hurled himself, folding in his arm at his chest to hold onto the menu, which was crumpling in his grasp. I was remotely aware of our bewilderment guest, but my desire to be the waitress was shamefully overpowering.

"You *guyyys*! Stop it!" Kim started yelling. Then she started laughing.

"Give it to me, you stupid asshole," I ordered through my teeth, pulling Benny's long hair so that his head snapped back. I dragged him to the ground and sat on him, peeling his arm open. There was no grass in this particular area of the yard--we were stirring up a cloud of dusty dirt, with Benny becoming covered in brown soot. He hissed and spat at me, pumping his hips up and down in an effort to flip me off of him, but I had him good. Pinning him with my knees on the insides of his elbows, I peeled that menu out of his fingers, ripping it in the struggle.

"I hate you fucker!" he cried as I sprung off him, smiling and waving the weathered construction paper menu high above my head. Benny stormed off, crying up the back steps. It was only then that I tended to our flabbergasted customer, dusting off my knees and adjusting my tossed hair before I approached her, stating very politely that line that I had so desired to say: "Welcome to Rainbow Diner. Here is your menu. I'll be your waitress today."

By the following day, Rainbow Diner had morphed into some kind of garage sale/food stop. We had moved out to the curb, where we placed milk crates to display merchandise. We gathered up unwanted items, such as old toys and clothes, which we organized inside and on top of the crates--price tags attached with scotch tape. We kept the Rainbow Diner sign up, but had moved its location so that the arrow pointed to our sale. The wrinkled and ripped menu lay on top of one of the crates--just in case a customer was hungry--with a rock on top to keep it from blowing away.

Kim was back to help. She brought over about one hundred of her old stuffed animals--the cheap kind that you might win at a traveling carnival, with matted bright pink or blue polyester fur and plastic googily plastic eyes that were falling off with the glue coming loose.

I brought out the newsprint paper and the art supplies and we lay sprawled on the sidewalk, creating art to sell. Soon Rainbow Diner was not only a garage sale and a restaurant--it was also an artist's boutique.

We didn't get very many customers that day, though a few people stopped by to check out our sale before giving us a funny look or a giggle and mumbling something like "Cute."

A woman pulled up in her car and we were no less thrilled than we had been the previous day, when we had been graced with such patronage. She browsed the menu and said very decisively, "I would love a hardboiled egg, please."

I didn't have to go far to fetch her egg. Those eggs that I had boiled the day before lay conveniently in a bowl on the ground beside one of the milk crates. I was delighted in *finally* getting to reach for one. The woman paid the quarter or the dime for her egg and then held it out in front of her.

"Mmm, looks good," she said real friendly like.

"Go ahead and crack it!" I coaxed.

"Crack it!" Benny cheered, his face about ten inches from the egg.

I can only imagine that the kind woman had planned to leave the shell intact, smiling all the way to her car for our sake, before she chucked that sun-ripened egg into the garbage. But our encouraging must have hit her soft spot, for she bent down to tap her egg on the hard plastic of the blue milk crate.

"Oh!" she gasped when the warm shell opened easily with one beat, releasing the contents of the less-than-soft-boiled egg, an ooze of runny yoke and gelatinous white running down her hand.

Quite unfortunately, Tara Stack walked by our house that day, witnessing our business endeavors. For the rest of my stint at the public school, every single time she saw me, she yelled out, "Welcome to Rainbow Diner!" in a hillbilly voice. She rallied several other girls in the teasing, so that I heard about Rainbow Diner at seemingly every turn. She knew the fifth graders who volunteered in the lunchroom, and they were particularly brutal. These girls were adorned with puffy white serving bonnets on their heads--a symbol of high social status. On the rare occasion that I ordered a hot lunch, they smirked from behind the metal compartments of peas and mashed potatoes, announcing, "This *isn't* Rainbow Diner, you know." Or, as they aggressively plopped a serving of corn on my tray with their big shiny spoons, "Welcome to Rainbow Diner! Here you go!"

One afternoon after school, Tara Stack and her posse surrounded me in a corner of the schoolyard as I walked to the bus area where I met Benny and Kim. The gang of girls began to hit me in the knees and the shins with their violin and clarinet cases, chanting "Rainbow Diner, Rainbow Diner." Despite trying so hard not to, I started to cry. I managed to run away with the thought of going straight to the principal. They laughed as I ran off, howling, "Cry baby!"

When I reached the principal's office, winded and full of tears, I stopped outside the big door. I realized that the bullying would only get worse if I told. Besides, it was during times like these that I avoided anyone's gaze, grossly aware of the lump on my head, which Mother kept proclaiming grew larger with hardship. I figured it *had* to be enormous right then, though oddly my forehead seemed to feel the same when I checked with my hand.

So, I missed the bus and took the long walk home that day, worrying about whether or not Benny made it to the bus and wishing Kim had been there when Tara and her cronies attacked. I regretted that I ever had the stupid idea to open Rainbow Diner in the first place.

Between the bullying, the growing lump on my forehead, and the bureaucratic bullshit, Mother figured it was high time that she pull me and my brother out of Franklin School. I was all too happy to simply not show up at my desk one day, never returning for goodbyes or to gather papers. I liked to imagine Mrs. Tang astonished at the mysterious vanishing of me.

Mother enrolled us in a little school that was kind of like the free school in New York. This school was held in a house, and was really more like a daycare center, with me being the oldest pupil. Just like the free school in New York, the teachers went by first names, and there were stacks of unfinished artwork everywhere--and costumes and music and a playhouse out back. There was also a scheduled afternoon naptime. This was an awkward time for me, when I'd lie on the small foam mat, counting the cracks on the ceiling.

"Close your eyes, come on," the grown-ups whispered, but I just had no desire to sleep--unlike the little kids, who lay sucking their thumbs and holding soft blankets while they slept soundly on their mats. I was too big for my mat; my legs sprawled on the hardwood floor. Benny was always ready for a nap, as sleep came easily for him. I lay with one eye open, enviously watching his eyelids.

There were brief tutorial sessions, wherein one of the adults went over some math problems with me or helped me with a grammar sheet or two. I was always the only student during these times, though, with neighboring children working on other things.

I missed seeing Kim at school. I imagined her at lunch by herself, and standing at the bus stop by herself. I felt so sorry for her for having to stay at the crappy public school. We still did overnights and saw each other after school. One time, she started to cry when we were sipping our Constant Comment at her house.

"I wish I could go to your school," she said, tears rolling down her face.

I so wished she could come live with me, away from her mom and brother.

Dad Visits California

Dad came to visit us that spring in Berkeley, shortly after we started going to the school that was like a free school. It was the first time he ever visited us in California. Needless to say, we were completely ecstatic.

Mother was actually the one to pick Dad up at the San Francisco airport. It was late—a night flight—but Benny and I came along. We were bouncing off the backseat of the Bug with excitement at the thought of seeing Dad. In the back of my mind was this realization that my parents would soon be standing at close proximity to each other--in the same car, even. How would this go?

At the airport, I felt I was floating in the intoxicating anticipation of seeing my dad. We anxiously waited at the gate, Mother obviously tense in her quiet mood. Tom had stayed home, not wanting to join.

Dad was wearing this incredible garb when he stepped off the plane. He was dressed in tight jeans with a pair of handcuffs attached to one of his belt loops, a leather vest and chaps. (At first I couldn't figure out just what were the chaps. Then I remembered that I had seen them in a cowboy movie.) There was a shiny diamond stud where his right ear had been pierced. His hair was short and slicked back and his mustache fuller with more style to it, with the ends curled up a little. What struck me the most though, were all of his pins. He wore many, many pins on his shirt proclaiming this and that about gay rights and gay pride. This was a totally new look for Dad.

Benny and I rolled with his new style quite well, running into his arms. As with our last airport hello scene, the three of us collapsed into a row of seats, hugging and kissing, Dad's cologne immediately putting me under an amorous spell.

I was vaguely aware of Mother off to the side, giggling awkwardly. Dad stood up and said hello and then I watched my parents share a quick hug.

We walked through the SFO airport with Benny on one side of Dad and I on the other, each holding onto his hand. We were interrupting each other, vying for his attention. I couldn't help but notice that people were giving us dirty looks or craning their necks to catch a glimpse of us, turning around to rubberneck as they passed. I knew it was Dad's outfit; I knew it was the unfair ridicule of gay people that Dad talked about. I searched his face for his reaction, to see how he handled the glaring looks. He seemed to be paying no attention, but rather smiling and laughing and only looking at me and my brother. So I just ignored the gawking people, too.

We got into the Bug after collecting Dad's luggage. It was surreal to see Dad in the Bug--in California--sitting next to our mother. We'd be driving Dad to the place he was staying--a man from Long Island that had taught art at the free school, and had moved to San Francisco.

Our parents started passing a joint back and forth. I had never seen Dad smoke pot before, and it gave me an eerie feeling. What had happened to Dad in such a short time? Why had he changed so much?

I was hoping the drive to the friend's house would keep going and going, afraid a new turn indicated that we were about to park. Even though it was dark, the streets were familiar--San Francisco neighborhoods with rows and rows of two and three story Victorian-style homes and apartments sandwiched together, no space in between. The streets went up and down, and up and down, the Bug chugging along slowly.

I was watching my parents talk. I don't even recall what they were saying. I eyed the backs of their heads intently, paying close attention to Dad--his side-profile, his new mustache, smiling politely as he took a turn with the joint. Mother was shifting the gears, the sleeve of her long shirt draping across the center space and gearshift that separated my parents.

To my delight, they decided to stop at a late-night diner. Benny and I were in a state of euphoria with the burgers and the 7up's, which Mother couldn't say no to on account of Dad being there to buy. It seemed like a dream to be sitting there in that booth—so late at night, Dad's new look, Mother at the same table, marijuana joints, beef. What next?

Dad took the Bay Area transit train called BART to visit us at the North Berkeley house a day or two after his arrival. Dad said he was in San Francisco for some kind of conference for work, so time was limited.

We left on foot to find a place for lunch, Benny hanging on one of Dad's arms, and I on the other--just like in New York. As we strolled toward Shattuck Avenue, we played with the handcuffs and asked about the pins. When Dad explained about the unfair treatment of gay people when we were in New York, he had warned us to be quiet about his being gay, saying that we might get hurt or in trouble if we talked about it in the wrong crowds. Now he seemed to be advertising it. Was he safe now?

"These pins say, 'Hey, I'm not taking your shit anymore. I'm gay, people, get over it,'" he apprised, pointing to the pin that said GAY POWER.

He explained again that gay people are teased and left out and that it isn't fair. I thought of the teasing that I endured at the public school and figured I would be on the gay rights crusade, too--just like when Benny and I had a protest in the parking lot in New York.

"Here, my darlings--for you," Dad said as he stopped right in his tracks on the sidewalk to remove two of his gay rights pins. He placed one on Benny's T-shirt, and one on mine.

"YEAH!" Benny cheered, pulling at his shirt to look at the pin and then pointing it toward the oncoming cars with such enthusiasm that he almost tore his shirt.

We walked a fairly long way before picking out a restaurant. I felt so proud to walk next to Dad--my costumed father--decorated with a message. I couldn't help but notice more of the dirty looks that Dad was getting. I felt righteous to be a rebel for the cause.

Dad visited our school before he left for New York. This was the first time I ever felt embarrassment by him. He walked in wearing his full get-up, no censoring at all—hand cuffs, pins, the whole bit. Everyone's face dropped at the sight of him. The teachers and the kids grew very quiet, staring slack-jawed. I shamefully stood in front of Dad, trying to block the view of his pins, somehow thinking that it would be the *pins* that would give him away. I felt tremendous guilt over being ashamed of him; I was a sell-out, not strong enough to stand up for "the fight." I got the feeling that Benny felt the same way, as I looked over at him to see him biting his lip with his head down. What was it like for Benny to be a boy--to be Dad's *son*? Did he want to be like Dad, or did he want to be more like a regular, stereotypical boy?

Dad's visit felt like a dream or some kind of fantasy, with the way he had so drastically changed his appearance and the way that he was there and then he was gone. I always understood why Mother did not have a place in New York. I found it very disconcerting that—likewise—there seemed to be no receptor for Dad in California. *He* sure seemed to feel at home in California, but I didn't know where to put him there.

Benny and I took to wearing pins of our own in the weeks following Dad's visit. I don't even remember what they said. We went to the Salvation Army on San Pablo Avenue and bought handfuls of gawdy old jewelry, which we hung off of every part of our bodies.

Shortly after Dad's visit to California--even though June was right around the corner, and we were just getting used to our new school, Mother switched our school for the third time that year. Somehow, I put the switch together with Dad visiting the school in his pins and his handcuffs. I pictured the teachers telling Mother that we needed to leave because Dad was just too outrageous. Thankfully, the next school was not a public school, but rather what the grown-ups referred to as an "alternative school."

The little alternative school averaged thirty students and had an actual curriculum, as well as some organization and structure. Students ranged in ages from six to fourteen and were divided into two groups—the older kids and the younger kids. Hence, Benny and I were in different groups, but I got to see a lot more of him at this school.

The alternative school was held in a two-story house close to downtown Berkeley, around the corner from the UC Berkeley campus. Each room was painted differently, with wild and colorful murals covering all of the downstairs and the bathroom.

There was yoga class and a morning circle time, where we got a chance to talk about our feelings. Scheduled classes began and ended with the sound of a large gong, which was struck on the hour by the director of the school--an infectiously warm earthy and motherly woman.

It was another group of kids to get used to, another attempt to fit in. In the back of my mind, I knew that Benny and I would be taking off soon. Maybe we'd even be enrolled in another school by fall. Would we keep these friends?

I longed for Kim during the weekday, and looked forward to seeing her after school and on weekends. Sometimes, she came to school with me for the day, which was a big treat.

Kim and I sat together on the couch in her living room and brainstormed about how to sway her Mother to agree to send her to my school.

"The only way to convince my mom is by saying I'll do a bunch of jobs," Kim said as we finalized our plan.

We got a piece of paper and wrote out a long list of chores.

"I'll come over every day to help you," I promised.

The jobs weren't just the usual "do the dishes" or "sweep the floor." Kim's list included "do all the laundry in the house" and "scrub the bathroom" and "bring breakfast in bed."

When we went to finally present the list to Kim's mother--trying to soften her up--we made a lunch and brought it upstairs. Hopeful and cautious, we walked into her mother's bedroom, Kim holding the plate with a PBJ and chips, and me holding a Tab.

Her mother was in her bed reading a book, her covers covering half her plump body.

"Oh, what have we here?" she said, half-smiling, with a palpable tone of entitlement.

"We made you lunch!" Kim said cheerfully before placing the chore list in her mother's lap.

"If I can go to Astrid's school," she started in nervously, "I promise to do these chores every single day."

Kim's mother studied the list while taking bites of the peanut butter and jelly sandwich. I examined her face for approval. My mother would have been animated, saying things like, "Oh! How wonderful! Look at this beautiful list!" But Kim's mother seemed as though she was making a concerted effort to contain any praise.

"I could get used to *this*," she said, opening the Tab and taking a long swig, "let me think about it."

That afternoon, we cleaned the whole house while blasting Blondie and Cheap Trick on the downstairs record player. We talked about how perhaps we could add living together to the deal.

Kim never did get to go to the alternative school. Like a stab in the back, her mother enrolled her brother instead.

Summer came just as I was getting settled into my new school––it was time to fly to New York to see Dad. Mother would move us again during the summer. This time, we had a chance to see the house before we left—a sunny home with two big front rooms, still in North Berkeley. This gave my mind a picture to carry while we were in New York, imagining my soon-to-be new home.

All is Bright in Sunnyside, Queens

"I moved to Sunnyside, princess," Dad had told me on the phone that June of 1980. "It's in Queens."
Not only was *Sunnyside* in the name of Dad's new home, but so was *Queens*. I was instantly confident that his new place was beautiful and happy and even regal. I pictured flowers everywhere and castles, velvet furniture, and dancing studios. The reality was not quite so.
Dad had moved to a one-room windowless basement apartment in a nice big brick house in Sunnyside, Queens. He rented from Vincent Seller, who lived upstairs. Dad said we were only allowed to go upstairs when invited, which was not very often.
Benny and I didn't mind that Dad's new place wasn't anything even closely resembling a palace. We were in heaven again, back with our dad—we were back to steamy subways and sign language, Ones Disco, shopping at Bloomingdales and Macy's, and back to weekend visits with Aunt Annette in Connecticut. It didn't make much difference to us that Dad had shown up at the airport in his thick garb, just as he had when he visited California a few months prior. Hell, he could have shown

up at the gate in a ballroom gown and I would have adored him publicly just the same.

There was a terrible heat wave in New York that summer, with many old people falling ill and actually dying from the sweltering heat.

Benny and I took turns sleeping alone on a floor mat, alternating nights. The lucky one *not* on the mat got to sleep with Dad on the old pullout sofa. There was no air conditioning in his basement apartment. When it was my turn with the floor mat, I put the sheets in the sink and ran the cold water. After a little wringing, I slept under those wet sheets with the fan blowing full-throttle in front of my head. Some hours later, the sheets were completely dry, with that fan just blowing muggy, sloppy heat on my hair.

Cockroaches—seemingly about the size of a mouse—were scurrying from the back of the stove and out of cracks in the floors and the walls. I could hear their little feet going pitter-patter across the linoleum, close to where I slept. The sound made me think of their reddish shell-like backs, and their strong hairy legs. The sheet was my only protection if it was a floor mat night. On Dad's sofa, they had to travel upwards to get me. In my mind, Dad was warding off cockroaches just by being there next to me.

Queens was full of ethnic pockets that Dad called *boroughs*, Sunnyside being one of Hispanic and Irish residents. The heat drew people out of their apartments and into allies yards, and onto back steps. The ethnic groups hung out in clusters mostly of their own kind, the younger ones playing marbles, spraying hoses, or break dancing on cardboard scraps with boom boxes playing. Old ladies in sleeveless polyester or worn cotton dresses sat on rusty lawn chairs outside of their apartment buildings talking, playing cards and drinking iced tea.

We walked a lot from here to there, pulling on Dad's belt loops as he weaved us through the neighborhoods, each block having a different flavor. With all that diversity, it seemed to me that Dad fit in to every quarter somehow. He strutted through any part of town, whispering this and that about the idiosyncrasies of various groups.

It seemed that Vincent Seller's house was right in the middle of a single borough, though I'm not sure this was really the case. The area outside our yard was its own community, as far as I could tell. I wanted to be a part of it.

As if to demonstrate that we were stuck-up or *too* good for the neighbors, a tidy chain link fence separated us from the grassy common area shared by all the neighboring houses and apartment buildings. It was like one big backyard everyone used--except us. For whatever reason, Dad just didn't fraternize with his neighbors. I felt a little like an animal at the zoo behind Vincent Seller's chain link fence. Being that we had only just showed up in June, Benny and I were the odd new kids. Benny longingly watched the boys play ball and marbles--almost in reach, but not really.

People congregated and had barbeques. Groups of Hispanic kids met to play in the shrubs and small trees and on the concrete. I'd try to watch what they were doing without them noticing. They were spraying each other with hoses and playing hopscotch and tag and horsing around.

While I tried to be inconspicuous about watching the neighborhood kids, for some reason they were completely unabashed about watching *me*. Dad bought us a little blue wading pool and when we went to fill it, a few kids came right up to our fence and just watched us play in it. I felt awkward and embarrassed. I turned my head away, but Benny seemed to *try* to show off for them, splashing around with added animation. I didn't know if I was supposed to invite them in or *not* invite them in.

"Why don't you invite them to play?" Dad asked one afternoon while he smoked a Kool on the back stoop.

I shyly walked up close to the fence in my bathing suit and asked the kids if they wanted to come in and play. The girl was a few years younger than me and the two boys were about my age. They smiled without saying anything and timidly walked in as I opened the latch on the fence. I realized right away they didn't speak any English. Within just a few minutes, Benny and I and those kids were splashing and laughing in the shallow blue plastic pool. The pool was too tiny for all of us, the sides bending as we pushed against them, the water spilling out onto the lawn. We had a great day, spraying each other down with the hose and drinking Cokes. We got to play with the kids a few more times After that day.

Gay Pride

Dad took us right away to see the Village People film, *Can't Stop the Music*, which was out in theaters that summer. We walked on either side of him on the way to the theater, each holding a hand. He was talking up the sexiness of the male actors, spelling out the word *men*.

"I am about to see some fine, beautiful M-E-N, people."

On the letter N, Benny and I snapped backwards as Dad took a half-step back and shook his butt. Dad liked to make his points with impromptu mini dance numbers like this, seemingly performing for an imaginary audience. Did he want me to say something? Was I supposed to shake my butt, too?

"Daaaaad," I whined, "give me a break."

I loved all the dancing and singing and the sexual tone in *Can't Stop the Music,* even if Dad was whispering hot this and beautiful that through the whole movie. The theater was full of mustachioed men with the one earring--some wearing handcuffs, some even chaps. It hit me that Dad was following a trend, that he was part of a fad. It seemed that Dad and the other men were in a constant celebration of Halloween, one of my personal favorite holidays.

The Village People were dressed in classic costumes—a fireman, a policeman, an Indian chief, a construction worker, and even a Navy officer. Similar to *The Rocky Horror Picture Show* craze, these characters were fashionably *in* that entire summer in New York City.

Some of the men in and around the movie theater were kissing or walking hand-in-hand. It was the first time I ever saw other gay men together, showing affection. I felt relieved to see it, knowing Dad wasn't the only one. I could tell Benny felt the same way, as he stared at the men unabashed.

The three of us sang the songs from *Can't Stop the Music* and did the dance routines for the rest of the summer. The film offered me an explanation for Dad's change in appearance. He wanted to be like his idols, which I could understand. I loved Sandra Dee and Blondie--I wanted to be like them and had acted out their routines. I certainly would have dressed like these stars if given the chance.

Dad took us to the movie theater a second time that summer to see *Dressed to Kill*. I was used to adult themes--on film and off--but this movie frightened me. I kept waiting for the mood to lighten, for Dad to start whispering remarks about the hot men, but it wasn't that kind of movie. There was suspense and bloody scenes with razors, but what stuck with me the most was a graphic scene, where a woman got into a taxi with a stranger and had sex with him. She was moaning like my mother.

Watching a graphic heterosexual sex scene with Dad was so much more uncomfortable than him cat-calling male movie stars; it was even more uncomfortable than seeing him with Tweety Bird Man. I felt an urgency to lie that I had no idea what was going on in that taxi scene.

"Why was that lady making those sounds in the taxi?" I asked Dad when we left the movie theater and stepped out onto the sidewalk, the muggy New York City heat hitting us the second we left the air-conditioned theater. He had stopped in front of the big Village People poster to light a Kool, little beads of sweat already starting to form on forehead. I was claustrophobic in the thick, sticky air, and instantly regretting my stupid question. Dad stared at me for a second with smoke slowly trailing out of his nostrils. I was squirming and unable to look at him, feeling regretfully coy and manipulative.

"She was doin' the nasty!" Benny chirped, seemingly proud that he knew the answer right away, grabbing hold of Dad's belt loop and looking up for approval.

I always wondered whether Benny truly understood about bone jumping, doing the nasty, and getting laid. The older he got, the more he chimed in at moments like these, but there was always an edge of playfulness in his tone, like he was simply just trying to fit in by saying the words. Did he *really* get it? Back in California--when he was six and I nine--when we lived in the Victorian house, he asked me if Mother was okay when she was moaning from her bedroom one afternoon.

"They're having sex," I answered, grabbing his arm and yanking him in his tracks to save him from the graphic discovery, as he made his way to the orange bedroom to check on her. "That's the sounds people make when the man puts his penis into the lady's vagina," I explained, reminding him about the book, *Where Did I Come From?* on bookshelf at the free school back in New York.

"Gross--" he responded, making a sour face. But he didn't look convinced--he still looked worried about our mother, who was sounding a bit like a wounded animal in the other room.

"Because she was feeling sexual pleasure," Dad explained outside the movie theater like he was teaching sex-ed right there on the New York City sidewalk, placing his hand on top of Benny's head.

I *really* wished I hadn't asked at that point. But then Dad continued in his typical way, thrusting his hips forward in a *cha-cha-cha*, adding, "That's right, Pooh, she was doin' the nasty." Benny laughed and hopped up and down, chanting, "Doin' the nasty! doin' the nasty!"

I thought about that taxi scene all summer. It was not like any love scene I had ever watched. There was nothing playful or flirty; there was no disco. I kept trying to make sense of how the woman acted so terrified, yet she was supposedly turned on. Dad said she was experiencing pleasure, but it looked more like she was in danger to me.

Dad also took us to what he called a gay pride march that summer of 1980, on the twenty-eighth of June. We had to switch a couple subways to reach the Manhattan location where the march was to begin. It was supposed to culminate in Central Park. The subway cars were full of gung-ho supporters, like excited kids riding the monorail into Disneyland.

Being eleven, this was my first march, which was sort of like the thing Mother called a "protest," but not quite. Because Dad said the word march, I had imagined batons, captain's hats, and a marching band. I imagined uniformed gay men, looking like marching soldiers in their white polyester slacks. They'd be going in an orderly, choreographed march right down the middle of the street, people cheering on the sidelines. The build-up to the event was stirring my anxiety, giving me the idea that this was not going to be any kind of usual parade.

"We'll all end up on the grass at Central Park," Dad reassured us, saying we would get deli sandwiches and have a picnic. But there was some kind of energy that I couldn't quite pin down––an urgency in his voice about the march. It made me think of those pins he wore on his shirt and also about that day with Mother in Golden Gate Park—us dressed as clowns.

The streets leading to the event were so crowded that I felt caught in the herd, swept up like a small gazelle. People walked with an obvious intention and force, though for what purpose, I wasn't entirely sure. Were they angry?

Dad held our hands tight at either side of him as he darted through the foot traffic like a shark, pulling our fingers and yanking our arms sharply to the right or the left to avoid hitting fellow enthusiasts. We snagged them anyway--over and over--their elbows hitting my temples, my face plowing into their sweaty middles.

When we finally reached the actual march, Dad pulled us through to the front lines, where rows and rows of men walked indignantly, clapping and with fists in the air. The energy and intensity of each individual was bleeding out and spreading to the others, forming into one big palpable shock wave or a force-field of gay men that might bounce me back if I stepped too close.

There were men without shirts, their hairy sweat-dripping chests thrust forward; there were ordinary-looking men who walked just as fast as the others, but didn't shout. There was leather and sharp mustaches, chaps, and earrings-a-plenty. There were wild colorful feathers and painted faces and big hats. Couples of men kissed and marched arm-and-arm. And, of course, there were plenty of men dressed as firemen, policemen, and Indian chiefs, waving their clubs and bows in the air. There were even men dressed up like women--something I had never seen before--their long gowns flowing behind them on the pavement. I thought of the time I coaxed Benny to wear the long yellow dress to the movie theater--the way Tom called it "drag"--and how well Benny would have fit in on this day, if we only had another dress for him to wear.

My head bobbed side-to-side, caught up in hairy forearms and damp chests. I clung to my father's big wet palm with both of my hands, but it still didn't feel like I had enough of him to grab onto. It seemed I would slip away from him any second, or that he would slip away from me. I was being smothered, infested, and taken by this stampede in which I had no place.

It seemed that my little brother had a place at the march more than I did, simply because he was a boy. This summer Dad had a new routine of shaking his hips and clapping his hands above his head, saying in Benny's direction, "He's the son of a faggot, folks." Sometimes he said it like a song, other times, he'd repeat it like a cheer, thrusting his pelvis with each word: "*The. Son. Of. A. Faggot.*" Benny smiled and bounced on his tippy-toes, throwing a punch in the air and shouting, "Yeah!" Dad swore that he would have a shirt made for Benny with the "son of a faggot" logo, saying wouldn't it be the best. "When? When?" Benny excitedly pressed. I was a bit jealous. But Dad never did get around to having that T-shirt made for Benny.

Where *I* fit in, I wasn't sure. But it did seem like the contagious energy of the march—of *gay pride*—was penetrating me somehow, falling on me like I was a domino in a line of dominoes. I put my face into my father's side and let out a cry that came from the deepest part of me, a deep wail that took me by surprise. I gripped his shirt in my fists and dug my heels into the sidewalk so that we jerked to a halt right there. Dad immediately dragged us out of there, grabbing me by my arm, and grabbing up Benny off the ground in his other arm. He was yanking and plucking us from the crowd like it was a Jell-O mold and we were the two cherries stuck in the middle. I cried hard as I hit the proud ones while Dad pulled, my feet tripping over their feet.

"Princess, I'm so sorry," Dad said tenderly into my ear when we got under the awning of a shop, away from the crowd. He knelt down on the sidewalk right there, tightly wrapping his arms around me. I looked over his shoulder at my little brother, the "son of a faggot," his arms crossed and his eyes glazed over, staring straight ahead.

Dad led us to the closest subway station and we headed back to his apartment. I felt bad that he didn't get to march all the way to Central Park like he had wanted to. But—more than anything—I just felt relieved that he *got it* that I had felt scared.

The Flushing Y

Dad still worked on Long Island as a social worker for troubled youth. Like the previous summer, he was able to take a lot of time off while we were there. He signed us up at the Flushing, Queens YMCA Day Camp so we would have a place to go when he did work.

I hated waking up so early for camp. Benny and I still had a hard time acclimating to New York time, which was three hours ahead. Because the kitchen was connected to the living room, which was also the bedroom, we woke bright and early to Dad making his coffee and smoking his first cigarette.

"Good morning, my darlings" he sang, placing an open box of Entenmann's donuts on the folding table. He always made sure to pour me a cup of coffee, adding a bunch of cream and sugar, just the way I liked it.

Once dressed, we did what Dad called *hustle*. We grabbed on to his belt loops while he led the way to the subway station saying, "Come on, come on people, let's hustle, your father must get to work."

Dad rode the subway with us to Flushing, where he hurriedly walked us into camp and signed us in before saying "I love you" and running out the door.

Benny and I were among the few white kids at the Flushing Y, which hadn't fazed us much, as we were used to being the minority. We did relay races and played tetherball, basketball and tag in the swampy heat at a nearby park.

The most memorable day at the camp that summer was the wonderful, marvelous trip to Jones Beach in New Jersey. We left first thing on a school bus, and spent the whole day at the beach, playing in the water and listening to music on a big portable boom box radio that someone had brought. Being at Jones Beach was like being right back in Centereach. The smells and the boom box and the East Coast sand ignited my senses in an almost disorienting way––disorienting mainly because everything had changed so drastically since Centereach days, so much that I felt as though I was a completely different person, yet I was still me. I think Benny felt the same, as he stared straight ahead with his mouth open much of the day, not leaving my side.

My status at Flushing Y camp went up a notch after Dad took me to a little hole-in-the-wall salon in Manhattan, where a young black girl put tiny braids in my hair. We went to a craft shop beforehand, where I eagerly chose beads for my braids. I wanted beads that would make a sound when I moved my head, so I tested them out by clanging them together in the shop. Dad patiently stood by while I selected the colors, cautioning Benny to stop mixing up all the beads with his fingers.

Rather than cornrows, the girl placed the braids intermittently in my hair. She had worked quietly and quickly, without the smiling and small talk of the usual salon experience. I loved the way the beads clanged together when I shook my head.

"Princess, you're a *ten*," Dad complimented, referring to Bo Derek, whom he had said I was going to resemble once the braids were in.

Benny was making a fashion statement of his own that summer—he was in the midst of his John Davidson phase. John Davidson was the host on the popular show that Benny and I loved to watch called *That's Incredible*.

Benny kept a comb in his back pocket, slicking his long bangs neatly to the side over and over, saying out loud that he wanted to look just like John Davidson. He stood before us in the apartment with his pretend microphone, naming off amazing feats and events with confident candor.

Dad took Benny to the Macy's hair salon because he was asking for a haircut, something Benny had never requested before.

"Sweetie, what are we doing with your hair today?" the stylist asked, running her long painted fingernails through Benny's stringy hair. She was looking at Dad with a big, lipstick smile.

"Like John Davidson on *That's Incredible*," Benny said flatly.

The stylist laughed and laughed at this, saying "How adorable," but the expression on Benny's face did not budge. He sat motionless in the salon chair, staring at his reflection in the big mirror.

"I want a shirt like the ones John Davidson wears," Benny announced earlier that day in the Macy's boys department.

"Pooh, you will look positively gorgeous," Dad declared right there in the aisle as he held a fancy light blue Izod polo shirt against Benny's front. I think Benny imagined that the haircut—put together with his fancy shirt—might give him the authentic John Davidson look that he was going for.

Raisins

Dad and I liked to sit on the cement steps of the back stoop in the evenings, when the temperature dropped just a smidgen. I sipped on a glass of Coke on ice and Dad smoked a Kool, adding to the crowded metal ashtray he kept out there. I loved the resonance of his voice and the way it seemed to go with the smell of hot pavement and the smell of food cooking coming from open windows. I rubbed my hand slowly along the underside of his forearm while we talked, a place that—honest to God—felt softer than the crease of a newborn baby's neck.

"I noticed you're growing breasts," Dad declared out of the blue on the stoop one evening. I hated when he tried to sound so afterschool special. Could he be more anatomical?

I had what I called raisin tits. I hated them. I felt that everyone could see the protruding buds through my shirt; I was convinced that everyone was surely making mental note that I was morphing. I was exposed and unable to escape my transformation. Stuck in the middle of it, I was half woman, half child. Yet, it seemed like men ignored the child me, only zeroing in on the woman part.

Men glanced at my shirt as they walked by on the street, holding their eyes in a way I never noticed before. My chest was like an invitation, a flyer in all caps: "UPCOMING ATTRACTIONS!" Was the world full of bad men? I was suddenly on high alert for lurking creeps.

To make matters worse, the raisins hurt like hell. My nipples throbbed, as if big tits were trapped underneath the little ones, trying to burst through the skin. My dad talking about them was mortifying. What he didn't know was that––for some reason––I felt as though my budding breasts were actually pulling me *further* away from boys.

"Soon you'll be dating boys."

"*Daaaad…*" I pleaded, dropping my head to my knees and covering my ears.

"Princess!" he announced excitedly, slapping his knee and putting out his cigarette, "I do declare it's time for your first bra."

It seemed only appropriate that it would be *Dad* who would take me out for the milestone event of the first bra.

When we entered the Macy's lingerie section, I expected the extended browse like usual. Instead, Dad strolled right up to the sales lady.

"Excuse me. My daughter is ready for a bra. Can you help us find the right one, please?"

Oh my God, could it get any worse? I felt that they might as well have announced over the intercom, "Raisin Tits on the second floor."

The sales lady was a staid, well-dressed woman in her fifties with graying hair wound tightly atop her head. She took a look at me and drew out a measuring tape lickety-split, holding it out in her manicured fingers. I got a strong whiff of her old lady perfume as she quickly wrapped the tape around my chest, bending her head down to squint at the number.

"She'll be a thirty two––" she said without inflection, moving her eyeballs right to left, then left to right, from one bean sprout boob to the other.

I caught Dad's proud eye. Was he picking up on my embarrassment, even a little?

"Ha, ha…" Benny snickered. He was sneering with his arms crossed, wearing those ridiculous tight terry cloth bands around his wrists.

"Shut up––" I snapped, giving my little brother the look that threatened to kill, but he was enjoying this too much.

"Boobs," Benny repeated under his breath, continuing to snicker, "boobs, boobs––"

"Pooh," Dad shot, "knock it off."

"Thirty two double-A, I'd say," the sales lady finally announced, seeming to ignore Benny.

She led us to the appropriate rack, pulling out a few little dainty bras and holding them up against my chest. I was sure that each and every passing individual was keenly watching this display.

"But then, you could also go with a *training* bra," she said, holding up a dinky yellow thing that looked a bit more simple, with less gadgetry, like a bathing suit top.

"These are appropriate for a first bra, or for women and girls with small breasts. They come in small, medium and large, rather than the cup size."

    I liked the idea of the training bra. The word training made it seem less committed and less of a giving in to the morphing boobs--like my mini tits were just in training, and maybe not even not real tits yet. They seemed to have their own little personalities, just beckoning me to open my shirt and whisper, "Psssst, can you girls slow down?"

    The sales lady had wanted to join me in the dressing room to help me with the fitting, but I lied that I would be all right. I fumbled with the bra clasps in front of the mirror--wondering if they were on correctly--fidgeting with the adjusting straps. It was ridiculous to me that those miniscule raisins would require some kind of seatbelt. It seemed that the straps--which would surely show under my shirts-- would only draw *more* attention. I hated the thought of people thinking that I took notice of my biological makeover, taking the time and trouble to add binding. I preferred to ignore my raisin tits for as long as possible, thank you very much.

    We ended up getting a few of each kind of bra. I had to admit that--once we got home--there was something exciting about my new bras. I tried them on over and over in front of the little bathroom mirror in the apartment, pouting my lips and making sexy poses.

Tracie

    Vincent Seller was having part of the outside of his house painted that summer, and had hired a couple from Brooklyn to do the job. This tough pair drove the thirty to forty minutes to Sunnyside every morning in their beat-up red pickup truck full of tools and paint. The rather haggardly looking husband and wife team climbed out of the truck in their ripped faded cut-offs and paint-splattered T-shirts with cigarettes hanging out of their mouths. Both had leathery skin that reminded me of the shriveled apples that my mother used to carve and let sit in the sun.

The couple often brought along their lanky ten-year-old daughter named Tracie. She slunk around the yard at first, sticking close to her parents, and not saying a word to me or Benny. We became buddies when I blasted my *Xanadu* record in the basement––she came out of her shell, telling me she loved the Olivia Newton-John song "Magic." Tracie and I spent days spraying each other with the hose out back or playing records while eating popsicles and drinking Cokes.

I went to Brooklyn with Tracie and her parents once for an overnight. We squeezed into the red pickup, the smell of body odor penetrating the cab like a lethal armpit smoke bomb had gone off.

Tracie raved about her older sister, Theresa. I was looking forward to meeting her because Tracie made her sound so sophisticated, bragging about how she went out late at night with boyfriends. Their parents had already promised that Theresa would take the two of us to pick up a pizza that evening.

I put my head right against the glass of the windshield when we crossed the Brooklyn Bridge. I wanted to get a better look at the tall arches and see if I could catch a glimpse of the railing that Tony and his buddies grabbed hold of in *Saturday Night Fever*.

We stopped in front of an industrial area. *Gray* would be the word for this place. Gray broken down buildings beside gray broken down warehouses––gray sidewalk, gray sky. I felt edgy standing in the street watching them confidently approach the small shabby doorway of one of the old warehouses.

"You comin'?" Tracie waved.

I wasn't terribly surprised that Tracie's residence was a warehouse, rather than an apartment or a regular house. The vast and unusual homestead was dark and dusty, the air inside stale with rusting pipes and old wood. The roof—or the ceiling—seemed miles above our heads, and was full of pipes and beams. Tracie didn't really have any *rooms* in her warehouse, just compartments that had been rationed out via plywood and curtains.

Tracie's makeshift room had a mattress on the cement floor and an old dresser covered in peeling stickers with a drawer missing. A large ceramic lamp without a lampshade sat on the floor next to her bed, and was attached to a long, thick orange extension cord that went to some other part of the warehouse. Clothes lay all around the surface of her room, spilling out past her curtain wall and into the main area.

Tracie was my kind of people. We didn't have to say a thing about the fact that she and her family were not exactly normal, and that I understood this fact so clearly because mine wasn't either.

"Is your dad a cop?" she had asked me once during the summer, referring to the hand cuffs that occasionally hung off of the belt loop of his tight jeans.

"Sort of. He likes to keep those on in case he sees any jerks doing crimes."

Tracie showed me over to the only part of the warehouse with any natural light, a place that must have been regarded as the living room. We sat on an old, scratchy, olive green couch with holes patched up with duct tape, the late sun coming in through a large high window. This single window had bars over it and had been clouded by weather and time, so that the buildings across the way were blurry blobs of gray and brown.

Seventeen-year-old Theresa sat cross-legged on a giant beanbag that was losing it's innards, white stuffing pellets on the floor around her periphery. She had a stack of small cards she was working on, writing something on the cards with some amount of precision and concentration.

"My business cards," she said with her chin in the air when I asked what she was working on, "come take a look."

Theresa handed me one of her little rectangle creations. Listed on what she called her business card were various sexual acts with prices attached, her phone number at the bottom. I giggled in embarrassment over the graphic menu: Blow Job, Fuck, Hand Job. I was drawn to the prices listed. To me, the amounts in tens and twenties seemed like a lot. I wondered to myself if I could pull off playing with some guy's wiener for that kind of cash.

I kept thinking: I was sitting in the same room with a real live, bona-fide hooker. I watched her habits like she was a famous spectacle. She kept pulling her long brown hair back over one shoulder--she bit on the end of her pen--and she took drags from her cigarette slowly, the smoke escaping through her nose, as she picked little pieces of tobacco off her tongue. Her red toenail polish was chipped. I took note of the fact that she seemed to love the singer from Meatloaf, and the way that the song "Two Out of Three" playing in the background seemed to suit her in a depressing kind of way. Another off characteristic that I found intriguing was Theresa's clothes. She was not dressed in the mini skirt, tube top, and high heels that I assumed a hooker might wear. Instead, she dressed a lot like her parents-- wearing a white T-shirt and dirty cut-off shorts.

Tracie and I walked several blocks to the pizza parlor with Theresa that evening. The mechanized feel of the neighborhood made the heat seem even thicker, as if the steel and the lack of anything pretty just sucked up any cooling breezes.

We turned a corner to find--to our delight--a fire hydrant had been opened, shooting water full-blast with thunderous force. Kids of all ages ran through the powerful spray, the braver ones getting up close and standing against the rush, some getting knocked to the pavement. The cold water seemed like a drug to the sweaty, hot kids--an aphrodisiac of sorts--and a cut through the thick layer of lard they were in. "These Are The Breaks" by Kurtis Blow was blasting from a boom box full-volume--my new favorite song. The loud music tipped the scene; this was a cut-loose celebration.

Theresa confidently walked over to the open fire hydrant and put her body into the strongest part of the blast, yelling "Whoohooo!" She put her head right against it so that her long brown hair flew and stuck to her back. I was a little stunned by the sight of her large braless breasts under her soaked white T-shirt--the way her dark nipples popped out in full view like she wasn't wearing a shirt at all. This made the males go from boyish water seekers to hungry men. Black, Puerto Rican, and Mexican guys gathered around, hooting and whistling while Theresa held her jugs in her hands, shaking them and twisting her thin T-shirt. She shook her butt to the beat of the African drums in "These Are the Breaks," her butt cheeks protruding out of the back of her cut-offs.

Tracie and I stayed a few feet behind Theresa, my clothes getting thoroughly soaked. I suddenly felt exotic as I shook my wet beaded braids in the blasting fire hydrant. If there were any white kids there, I don't remember them--I only recall being a minority, which was nothing new to me.

"Hey, spoiled rotten!" a shirtless adolescent black boy shouted my way, a mat of thick black hair bulging from each armpit.

I immediately regretted wearing the new light blue tank top I had picked out at Bloomingdales, which had the shiny and glittery *Spoiled Rotten* on the front.

Even though I kept my distance from the prostituting Theresa, I still felt like part of her sale. Being my mother's daughter, I was familiar with my role as the steak dinner side dish. I was terribly aware of my raisins and the way they hurt when shriveled up by cold water. I was glad my shirt wasn't white.

I thought of Theresa's business cards and imaged that my raisins would probably be worth less than her cantaloupes, and wondered if this made me *more* of a target—a discount deal. But the cold water was so refreshing and my favorite song was on. This was all fun, right?

The stakes were raised when a low-rider slowly passed by with tattooed Brooklyn guys hanging out of the windows, pursing their lips into exaggerated kisses and rapidly flicking their tongues. They reminded me of Ricky Perez, an association that always made my fear go up a notch, as I worried that there very well might be a secret communication line amongst tough, macho men--that stretched all the way from California to New York and back--that included a photo of me with the word *wanted*.

Theresa walked right over to the car and bent down to rest her elbows on the driver's window, her cutoffs riding up her ass like dental floss. This seemed to deflate the vehicle-less, sidewalk traveling dudes. "Awww, man..." they groaned, waving a hand into the air.

Tracie seemed oblivious to her sister's hazardous flirtations, laughing and pulling my arm to join her in the now vacant spot right in front of the open fire hydrant. The strong blast was distracting enough, but I kept turning my head to look over at Theresa and that car, her image foggy through the mist.

I wondered if Theresa was handing those guys a soggy card, or if she was simply telling the guys about her business. My stomach lurched with the thought that I would be in her warehouse that night, with males like these aware of *my* whereabouts.

"Did you hand out your card to those guys?" I asked Theresa when we walked away from the scene-- our bodies dripping and our sandals making squish-squash sounds.

"No, not *them*," she snapped as if I ought to know better, "those were *boys*. They don't have any money."

"Not even the guys in the car?"

"Naw. Thought of it, though."

Theresa and Tracie seemed completely oblivious of the male attention that continued all the way to the pizza parlor--men hanging out of their cars as they passed, yelling, "Hey babies!" "Come here sexy," and "Hey chicas!" It seemed like my Bo Derek braids and my miniscule raisins--and especially my soaking wet spoiled rotten tank top--were all unintentional welcoming flags for the soliciting males. I was surprised that *it* seemed to be working so well when I wasn't even trying. I wondered what Dad would say. Would he be proud? I imagined him encouraging, saying "Work it girl!" while shaking his butt and clapping his hands above his head.

Late that night, I laid wide awake next to the sleeping Tracie. Theresa had left after she scarfed down a couple pieces of pizza, her Meatloaf record left playing in her curtained quadrant. My mind raced with what Theresa was doing at that moment. The images made my stomach churn—I saw her with her handmade business cards and her cantaloupes, getting into a creepy man's car, going to an unknown destination to suck on his dick. In my mind, the man was asking for the tag-along, "*Where's the spoiled rotten one?*" He'd be led to me--my location traced with ease--where he'd put his greedy fingers on me. I would have been the one to unknowingly and stupidly let him in myself, in my desire to come to Brooklyn and to cool off.

It was a long, frightening night. I was hit with a pang of worry when I passed Theresa's curtain in the morning, and saw that it looked like she never came home--her unmade mattress empty on the floor. I scrambled back into the beat-up pickup, hung-over by fret and glad to be heading back to Sunnyside.

Dad's Boy

That summer Dad had a boyfriend named Eddy that he called *Boy*.

"I got me a boy," he boasted happily with a southern drawl while thrusting his pelvis out and shaking his hips, as if Eddy were some kind of trophy. *But Benny is Dad's boy.* How could Benny and Dad's boyfriend be the same?

Eddy worked for his parents, who owned a very nice jewelry store. He was twenty, so that made Dad more than double his age. A few times, Dad left us alone when he went out on a date with Eddy, often returning with a new flashy item—a gold chain, a bracelet, a ring.

"Look what my boy got me this time," he'd proudly report, showing off his sparkling gift, and mumbling, "It pays to have a boy in the jewelry business…mmm, mmm, mmm, yesss folks, it sure pays."

Dad and I were dancing one afternoon in the basement apartment to one of our favorite 1980 radio hits called "Take Your Time (Do It Right)" by S.O.S. Dad was rocking his hips and putting one foot forward, then back, singing along. He dipped his body toward the floor in one quick, graceful swoop and then back up again to the sexy, grinding chorus that went, "take the time, *do it right.*"

"Do it, do it, do it," Dad was moaning, seemingly unaware of me--running his hand through his hair and cupping his crotch like he was in front of an audience.

I was trying to garb his hand and follow his dance moves, but he was lost in his own world, all lit up about something. He danced over to the folding table and grabbed the Polaroid camera that he had bought me for Christmas.

"Princess, let's do a photo shoot!"

My heart was beating fast as he led me through the back exit of the basement apartment that led to Vincent

Seller's section of the house--a place that was off limits to Benny and I unless invited.

Dad handed me the Polaroid and removed his shirt before draping himself across the pullout sofa in Vincent Seller's bright guest room--his chest glistening with sweat from dancing.

"Take my picture," he instructed, as he rested his chin on an elbow.

When he unsnapped the top button of his jeans, a clammy fear came over me that he might take his clothes off completely. I was remembering the Centereach photo shoot and those nude photographs that I had found in the curio cabinet. But he left his pants *on*, not letting the zipper down all the way.

"These are for my boy," he said with a gleam in his eye.

I tried to hide the letdown on my face. My stomach went up in my throat and I felt the urge to throw the camera at him. *This is about Eddy.*

I held the first snapshot in my hand, blowing on it and waving it gently in the air, as I watched the picture develop. I thought *these must be his camera eyes* when I saw his image develop on that Polaroid snapshot, because they were not the eyes I ever saw on my father when he looked at me. Dad had the same faraway look in those Centereach photos.

I kept just one of those snapshots of Dad on Vincent Seller's pullout, sneaking it into my carry-on bag. I still have that photo today, with "1980" scribbled in ballpoint pen on the bottom right corner in my loose handwriting--evidence that I was really there.

We got to meet Eddy The Boy just once. He picked us up in his large air-conditioned car to take us to a big theme park called Great Adventure in Jackson, New Jersey. I got to take along a friend that I had made at the Flushing YMCA camp--a chubby girl with short brown hair named Trisha.

Dad's boy showed up bright and early, laden with cologne, gold chains, rings and bracelets. He was a pale-skinned chunky thing who seemed uncomfortable with himself right off the bat. In fact, I don't recall him making eye contact with me once that whole day. I think that he must have been newly *out*, pushing his comfort zone to the limits with my flamboyant father. The pair had gone out and had matching T-shirts made that each bore the word *HIS* in the upper left corner, and they wore these shirts to Great Adventure that day. I imagined them calling each other the night before to plan out their outfits.

Dad kept saying it was "hotter than a motherfucker"--one of his favorite things to say when the summer heat got particularly bad. We strolled around from one attraction to the next with the two of them side-by-side in their His shirts. I tried to shrug the looks of the sunscreened, visor-wearing moms as they stared in apparent horror as we passed by.

We took a breezy ride on the Ferris wheel--the kind that has two seats facing each other on each carriage. I sat in complete mortification as Dad and Eddy began kissing passionately right in front of us. I wanted to die. Benny seemed oblivious, wiggling in his seat and saying "Weeee!" I think he was just thrilled to be so high up.

I kept my face turned the opposite direction from Dad and his boy, my head leaning over the side to see the park down below.

"LOOK! LOOK!" I kept shouting, pointing to the various attractions, in attempt to get Trisha's attention off of the opposite bench. But, of all the roller coasters, tilt-a-whirls, sideshows and cotton candy stands, no attraction was more alluring than the one right there in the carriage with us. I wanted to physically pull her head away with my own hands. No matter what I did to try to defer her attention, Trisha kept coming back to my dad and his twenty-year-old boy on that Ferris wheel seat. A few times, I caught her looking at me in my peripheral vision, seemingly searching for my eyes. I didn't dare meet her gaze. It was the most embarrassed I had ever been over dad's gayness. I was aware of my shame over this, but *more* aware of my embarrassment, and my wish for a believable explanation for Trisha.

When the ride was over and we stepped out, I tried to drag my pace so we'd walk a ways behind Dad and Eddy. Trisha asked the question I was dreading.

"Why was your dad kissing that guy?"

I had a quick answer.

"That guy is my uncle. They're really close."

"What do their shirts mean?"

"They're on a baseball team called the 'HIS' team, those are their team shirts."

I was thankful that Trisha seemed to at least *pretend* to buy my lies. Needless to say, she never came back to Sunnyside again, and I was never invited to her place.

Fetch a Martini

Vincent Seller threw a fancy party that summer. It was a big to-do that spilled out from his house into the backyard, which had been decorated with strings of Christmas lights, even though it was summer. I don't recall the occasion.

We helped set up outside, sneaking handfuls of fancy olives from the caterer's trays. Besides the catered goodies, there was a hosted bar set up on the concrete patio. I was eyeballing the little red plastic stirrers, the pickled onions, and the maraschino cherries. Bottles upon bottles of booze were lined up on the long folding table. Dad started early, carrying around his favorite martini in a plastic cup—vodka with a dash of cassis, or gin with vermouth, straight up––one or the other.

People arrived by the handfuls throughout late afternoon. They stood in clusters talking and laughing and hovering around the outdoor bar and food tables. Jazzy music played on the big speakers that had been placed in the windows, facing the yard. By the time the sun was setting, the small backyard was packed, and I was only a miniscule particle among the crowd, able to weave in and out without anyone noticing. This is when I got the idea that would lead to my first drunken experience.

Dad was luxuriating in his high society mode, holding everyone's attention with his off-humor and shocking stories.

"Princess, would you *pleeeease* go fetch your father a martini?" he shouted to me over the noise, holding out his empty plastic cup, the little red stirrer and the green olive rolling around at the bottom.

"Gin!" he yelled after me as I took off toward the bar.

I walked up to the young harried bartender--his sweat-stained bow tie all crooked--and asked him for a gin martini. I thought it peculiar and playful how he splashed the booze all over the table while pouring it into the cup, his hands and the tips of his white sleeve all wet from ice and olive juice. He didn't even look up when he shoved that drink my way, and so I decided to wait ten minutes or so before ordering up one for myself.

"A gin martini please," I ordered again, my heart racing, sure he'd be on to me. But that flustered bartender made me up a second martini without batting an eye. I waited to take a swig till I was close to the chain link fence and away from the lights. I almost threw up from the intense sting that hit the back of my throat, sending me into a coughing fit. I inconspicuously took little tiny sips from then on.

Some of the neighborhood kids had filtered into the party, going as unnoticed as my little brother and me.

We sat eating our plates of hors d'oeuvres with our moist backs against the fence and our bare feet lined up.

I shared a long conversation with a fourteen-year-old boy from one of the buildings down the ally. I had been interested in knowing about him because he often wore a pressed shirt--and sometimes even a tie--regardless of what day it was. He told me of his family from India, and how he lived with his aunt, his Grandmother, *and* his parents, all in one apartment. He said that he would make lots of money as a man, and that he planned to buy his family a nice house some day. He described a very rigid school year wherein he was very focused on schoolwork, spending hours studying daily. I had never met anyone my age who talked like this--with *thoughts* like this. He talked smart and I didn't doubt for a second that he would eventually do everything he said he was going to do.

"Is that liquor?" he asked, giggling nervously upon noticing my martini.

"Yeah, I drink it all the time," I lied, "want one?"

I was trying my darndest to hold that martini just the way my father held his--with my pinky elegantly flexed. Not an easy task with a plastic cup without a stem. It took every facial muscle to hide my gag reaction from the strong burning taste of the gin, and even more difficult to appear as though I loved it.

After fetching a third martini, two for us and one for my dad, the Indian boy and I sat together and talked up a storm over our martinis. I was glad to see that he was taking tiny sips, too.

"It burns my throat," he said, coughing and laughing at the same time.

My buzz, the Indian boy, and the sparkly yard were tipped by the Earth, Wind and Fire "You're A Shining Star" blasting from the speakers. A warm tingling sensation pleasantly crept up my legs and into my belly, all the way to my scalp; my lips went rubbery and numb. He must have felt it too, because he started coming up with all kinds of crazy ideas. He turned his penetrating eyes on me.

"Have you ever done it?" he leaned in and asked through a tunnel he made with his hands, raising his voice over the music. *Did I hear him right?*

The few seconds that hung while I thought about fibbing felt like a very long time. I decided to tell the truth and confess: *no, I hadn't done it.* He continued talking through his hand, close to my ear.

"Do you want to get it over with before you go back to California?"

He pulled his face back to look me in the eyes. His face had such a serious look––his dark and full eyebrows almost touching, the color of his eyes nearly black. I would later think of his eyes when I saw the black stone Star Diopside for the first time. If you hold that stone just right, you can see a little *star* in the center of it, like a pupil. I had the feeling that he could convince me to do anything with those eyes and in that tie and pressed short-sleeved collared shirt.

"Don't you wonder what it feels like?" he asked––grinning and almost apologetic––like he couldn't help himself from asking.

I weaved my finger in between each of my dirty toes, biting on my knee. I had a terrible case of butterflies.

"Yeah––" I choked quietly, my face on fire. *Of course* I was curious. I wished I could say more, but no words would come out.

"It would be perfect," he continued through his hand-tunnel to my ear, "we could do it before you go back and then I wouldn't be a virgin and you wouldn't be a virgin. We'd know what it's like…we could tell all our friends."

I couldn't bear to look him in the eye, so I turned my head and watched the adults, who were laughing and hanging onto each other, their drinks splashing around.

"Where?" I practically shouted over the music, turning to face the boy. It was the first thing I came up with.

"We could go right now, back there--" he proposed, swinging his arm around to gesture toward the other side of the fence, out into the courtyard.

"I'll be really gentle," he promised, so close to my ear that I felt the tickle of his breath.

Gentle. This put my dizzy mind to the idea that he would actually be touching me down there. *I* hadn't even dared to touch that part of me--no one had since Mr. Perez. This realization led me to an incredibly embarrassing retching state. I wanted so much to have the guts to run off and do it with this prince of a young man, but the butterflies had suddenly given way to an urgent nausea.

"Tomorrow--" was all I could say through my hand. I immediately jumped up and made a beeline for the cement steps to Dad's apartment--running through the rayon and the silk and the Earth, Wind and Fire-- hitting elbows and hips. I made it to the bathroom just in time, where I violently threw up into the toilet.

I lay down on the linoleum bathroom floor for what seemed like a long time, feeling the sickening vertigo caused by my underage martinis and the Indian boy's gutsy proposal. When I finally made my way out of the bathroom, I staggered toward Benny to join him on the pullout sofa, plopping down and pulling Dad's pillow over my head. I hadn't even noticed Benny there watching TV with his head propped on his elbow when I first ran into the basement apartment to hurl.

"Stupid head," he shot without looking at me. Did he *know* that I had dipped into the martinis that night?

"It's your turn for the mat, get off," he ordered, trying to shove my floppy body off the bed, and grabbing Dad's pillow out from under my head.

"Come on Ben, *please*? Don't be an ass, I don't feel well."

"I saw you drinking the alcohol, it's your stupid fault." I couldn't argue with that.

He had no pity, forcing me to sleep on that floor mat. He even later shoved my head out of the way when he went to take a pee later on, as I kneeled in front of the toilet, barfing again. I felt as though I was on a boat that night, going up and down, one wave after the other. If I closed my eyes, the boat ride turned into a miserable upside-down carnival attraction, so I struggled to keep my eyes open. *How on earth do adults drink this stuff all the time?* I wondered. I vowed never to touch alcohol again.

After a while, Dad came down the cement steps and stumbled through the door, hastily making his way to the bathroom, where I heard the sounds of *his* retching.

"Daddy, I'm throwing up too," I confessed when he dropped his loose body next to Benny on the pullout.

"I'm sorry prinfess," he slurred.

We took turns puking all night.

Despite the heat, I remained in the basement apartment for several days after the night of the party, only going out if I absolutely had to, afraid that the Indian boy might see me and cash in on our arrangement. I hung my head low to the sidewalk when we left the apartment to go out with Dad, not looking up until we were well away from our street. The funny thing was, I thought about the Indian boy all the time. I was daydreaming about meeting him in the courtyard to kiss, imagining how I might manage his offer by telling him we had to wait just a little longer. How could I both want to see someone so badly *and* do everything I could to stay away?

Finally, after a week or so, I could not stand the muggy heat one more minute. I ventured out to our little yard to spray the hose with Benny.

I was screaming and laughing at the same time, running barefoot toward the chain link fence in my drenched shorts and tube top, as Benny sprayed my backside full-throttle. Out of nowhere appeared the Indian boy in his collared shirt, walking through the alleyway. I came to a screeching halt in the grass, almost falling over. *Don't look, don't look, don't look.* I turned to face the opposite direction, slowing my pace and pretending to have somewhere to go.

"Hey!" Benny yelled, turning the hose, "You can't get away!"

No, no, no, not now, don't spray me. I felt the cold spray hit the backs of my legs. I wanted to call my brother a fucker and tell him to stop, but I couldn't say anything. My whole body was shaking; I thought I might fall over. I was dreading the boy's hello. Any second I was going to hear the latch on the chain link fence open. He was going to enter my yard and I was going to have to turn around and face him. What was I going to say to him? How was I going to act? But seconds were ticking by as I made my way toward the stoop, where Benny wasn't allowed to spray, and I could make my exit. As I approached the steps, I shot a half-second glance toward the alleyway. The Indian boy had already walked right passed our yard––his back was turned. He never said hello and I never saw him again.

Rain, Finally

"Halleluiah! Praise the lawd!" we yelled with our faces turned to the night sky the one time it rained that summer of the infamous heat wave. The three of us had run up the basement steps and into the yard in our shorts and T-shirts as soon as we heard the first drops. We spun in circles and danced and clapped, our clothes quickly saturated.

"Daddy, you were right! You were right!" Benny yelled, climbing on Dad's leg.

Earlier that day, Dad predicted that it was going to rain because the leaves on the sparse trees had turned upside down.

"It's a sure sign of rain, people," he said like he was a weather reporter.

I loved the way Dad's skin felt that night. I clung to him—infantile in the comfort of his wet arms—dripping with the fusion of his sweat and cologne and rain.

The smell of that big rain on the hot pavement was pure, delicious, sticky, sweet city summer. Thirsty cracks in the barren sidewalk were revived. The rain seemed to impregnate a seed in my olfactory, with vine-like roots traveling straight to some cavernous part of me where blossoms finally sprung out.

The thick layer of dust that had collected on New York was rolling past and washing away—not the kind of dust on your mantle, but the kind collected from the recoil of cars and subways and from the industrial dryers of one-hundred laundromats.

There was something really extraordinary about getting the gift of rain in the middle of a heat wave––it was a fresh start, a clean break, a run for it. Other people also swarmed out of their apartments like gophers coming out of holes, raising their palms up to the sky, smiling wide and sticking their tongues out to catch the big, fat drops. Old ladies let their hairdos go kinky and kids kicked off their shoes. Everyone was friends. Everyone spoke the same language; all skins were drenched. If there had been the deposit of hard times, that was being washed down the gutters.

Dad was skipping shoeless on the cement patio, chirping, "I'm singin' in the rain," when the thunder clapped so loud that it scared me to death. I screamed and grabbed hold of Dad. I had forgotten the clap of New York thunder––it was nothing like the wimpy thunder in California. Rather than running inside, we stayed out in the yard, watching the spectacular thunder and lightning show.

Dad taught us how to get scientific about the storm. We sat on the stoop and counted between lightning flashes and thunderclaps, our warm, moist arms sticking together, our slippery knees lined up.

"One-one thousand, two-one thousand, three-one thousand…" we counted.

This would tell us how far away the storm was in miles. Like clockwork, there was a booming thunderclap some time after each spectacular lightning bolt. Each second that passed marked one mile, indicating the proximity of the storm. There was disappointment when the seconds between lightning and the thunder grew farther and farther apart, indicating that the storm was moving farther away––the lightning flashing over someone else's neighborhood, the thunder rumbling the dishes in someone else's cupboard.

I could still smell the mealy, earthy aroma of that rainfall the next day, like sweet, soggy moss in a damp forest, or dead leaves that have turned to mush.

Dad and I sat on the back stoop, him smoking a Kool and me drinking a Coke as usual, when he announced that he planned to go ahead with adoption proceedings in the upcoming year, in the attempts to get two children—a boy and a girl.

"I just miss having you and your brother around all the time," he confessed in a sad, defeated kind of way, flicking his ash on the concrete. I was trying to catch his eyes, but he was looking away.

"Your mother will only give summers."

I felt my pulse in my face. I pictured Dad begging Mother for more time and her saying no.

"Did you ask her if we could stay longer? *I* would stay, Dad––I would."

"I know princess, I know you would," he said wistfully, kissing the top of my head, "She said she would take me to court, and they will take you away for good because I'm gay."

Dad put out his cigarette and took my head under his chin, wrapping his arm tightly around me. I could hear his heartbeat with my ear to his chest. I felt the tears swell. How could Mother keep me from Dad? How could she be like all the other people who were hateful to gay people?

"I thought it would be really fun for you and Benny to have some other kids around when you come for the summers," Dad said, feigning cheerfulness.

Dad said he already had names picked out—Mercedes and Royce. He pronounced Mercedes *Mer-said-eez,* rather than *Mer-say-deez.* I had to admit that I liked the idea of a sister. It definitely *could* be fun to hang out with these kids. I imagined what they might look like, and wondered if Benny and I could have a say in picking them out––selecting their hair color, their height, their ages and their eyes, like shopping for siblings.

I was stuck on the names, though. Dad had never been big into cars, so why the car names? I didn't like that he would call them something so glamorous, chic, and sophisticated. My name was pretty dull, compared to Mercedes.

I thought of Dad's words in Centereach: "If it weren't for you kids, I'd be dead." Maybe Mercedes and Royce would keep Dad alive in the same way we had; maybe two-and-a-half months out of the year was simply not enough to keep him alive. If that were the case, I had to go along with it. Still, I wished it were *me* with Dad all the time––already jealous of Mercedes and Royce––and I greatly resented my mother for keeping me from him.

Throughout the next year, I thought of Mercedes and Royce––a pair of phantom children who could be handed to our dad by a judge at any time. Any day, I could get the phone call from Dad announcing that he had found them. I imagined the three of them skipping hand-in-hand down the steps of a big brick courthouse, after an intimidating, plain-looking judge brought down his gavel and signed the adoption papers. Dad would immediately take them shopping and to lunch and for haircuts, changing their ordinary names--probably something like Ann and Peter--to the jetsetters Mercedes and Royce. He would take them home then, where they would *surely* fall in love with him like I had, running their orphan palms down his soft forearms and over his rough whiskered jawline.

    For one reason or another, Mercedes and Royce never did materialize. Dad's intention to adopt was never mentioned again after that day on the stoop.

    When the summer of 1980 ended, I was a blubbering mess again and--although I do not recall the exact details of this emotional eruption--I know it happened. What I did *not* know was that this would be the last summer that I would shamelessly and publicly cry over saying goodbye to my daddy. After 1980, that infantile attachment to Dad was gone--something I mourned, if one could mourn the loss of mourning. I actually started to *fake* the blubbering, which brought on terrible guilt (aside from making me feel pretty silly).

    Our plane landed at night, the stars dotting the August California sky like promises. Mother showed up at the airport this time—a relief I got to enjoy before the plane even stopped on the runway.

    "Look! There's Mommy!" Benny cheered, pointing out the little round window.

    Right away, I saw her giant head of dark curls through the glass of the brightly lit terminal. I could see Tom's tall figure standing beside her, the two of them facing the giant window. They would be taking us to our new house. There would be a new bedroom, with some of our things missing--some things carried over--all carefully laid out by our mother. A new year; a new house.

Berkeley Macaroni

We would live in our new rental for two years, marking the longest record of living in one place for our family. The single-story house was nestled in a very nice North Berkeley neighborhood (further north than our last house), with two large and sunny front rooms. Welcoming mortared brick stairs led to the front door of heavy knotted wood. It was a very *regular* kind of house--with a fireplace, and even a bona fide breakfast nook. If it weren't for the large sign on the front door that read, "SUPPORT THE IRISH HUNGER STRIKES," one might assume we were yuppies.

That year I would turn twelve and Benny nine. We shared the large front room on the left, which was actually meant to be the dining room, with a swinging door that opened to the kitchen. For the first time, Mother got her own bedroom--with a foam mattress on the floor--though Tom usually slept in there with her. Tom also had his own room, which he designated as his "study," just as he had before.

Mother had broken down the bunk bed, so we each had a twin-sized bed that indicated whose side was whose, like in Centereach. Much to Benny's annoyance, my side of the room was perpetually a complete mess, while his was immaculate. He grew so tired of my clothes and records and papers bleeding into his area that he created an actual division with a roll of masking tape.

Benny was still scrawny, and I took advantage of this in our brawls by pinning him down with my knees on his arms. He became a wild animal underneath me--bucking and thrashing to get loose--his face scarlet purple and the big vein on his forehead sticking out. My favorite part was when he tried to spit on me and his airborne loogie just came right back down on his own face. This was my cue to spring off him and bolt through the swinging door to make a run for the bathroom, where I quickly locked the door behind me.

"Haha, stupid bucking bronco spit on himself!" I yelled, laughing.

"Fuckhead!" he yelled back as he pounded hard on the door.

If I wasn't quick enough, and he got hold of me before I reached the bathroom, I was the recipient of some ass-kicking charley horses and socks to the face.

However, all bets were off after lights-out. I lay in bed watching the reassuring rhythmic up and down and up and down of Benny's breathing in the glow of the streetlamp across the street. This brought on a longing for when Benny and I spooned on the old foam mattress. I gave in on some nights, and crept over to Benny and tried to get in his bed as motionless and as quiet as I could. It was almost as if Dad were right there when I spooned with Benny. Did Benny feel it, too?

Late one night, shortly after we returned from New York, Mother and Tom had one of their big blow-ups when Benny and I lay in our opposite twin beds with the lights out. It was a bit ironic to hear them fighting on this night because only hours before, I had felt like things were on the right track in an actual *Leave It to Beaver* kind of way because Mother had whipped up a bona fide macaroni salad for a potluck picnic.

The American combination of elbow noodles, mayonnaise, chopped celery, and onions had been so uncharacteristic of her. I wondered if this was a new start to something. Were hotdogs next? I had proudly walked beside her as we approached the outdoor picnic party (instead of walking several steps behind her, as I had started to do). I watched intently as she carried the big yellow ceramic bowl full of macaroni salad over to the large picnic table, scanning for reactions as she placed the bowl among the chips and dips and casseroles. I was *sure* that expressions would widen with amazement and approval over my Betty Crocker mother and then over me--perfect by default.

What was going on behind closed doors that night on our street was no *Leave It to Beaver* scene. Tom was full of graphic, new insults I had never heard before.

"That thing between your legs is a fucking gaping hole--you just spread em' and suck men right in!"

I put my head under my pillow. I was sickened by the image of my mother lying on her bed with her legs spread, revealing a gaping, cavernous hole. In my imagination, her hole was breathing and dark and sucking up the entire bodies of men in the same way that a giant anaconda eats a gazelle or a zebra.

Next came a giant crash from the kitchen, just outside our bedroom door. I felt its velocity through my mattress. Whatever it was shattered across the kitchen floor.

"That is the last time--" Mother warned, out of breath. "The last. Fucking. Time." I could see her finger pointing at him in my mind. "I'm never coming back."

My stomach lurched. I wondered whether I ought to try to stop her, hoping she wasn't serious. Sometimes she'd say she was leaving just to say it, and sometimes she'd really go. I took the pillow off my head to hear better, and heard the far-off sound of Mother going through her things in her room. There was a sliver of light coming from the kitchen through the crack in our swinging door.

"Benny?" I whispered in the dark. "Benny?"

After a sigh, he groaned, "She's *not* going."

"But what if she *does*?"

"Then she'll come back."

My heart was thumping inside my ears. Once again, I was wishing that I were tough like my little brother.

"You're a fucking liar," Tom spat. They were walking through the hall quickly, and I could tell by the footsteps that Mother was in front, and he was trailing close behind. I heard her open the closet that shared a wall with our bedroom.

I listened intently to Tom's muffled voice through our wall: "*Where* the fuck will you go--"

He sounded nervous. I hung in the silence like a hopeful gnat, but she wasn't answering. Next, I heard the faint jingle of her keys--she was opening the front door.

"Get the fuck out, see if I give a shit!" Tom yelled from the front steps so that his voice echoed off the church across the street and--most certainly--straight into all the neighbors' windows.

The sound of Mother's boots running down the front steps made me shoot up in bed. My heart sank when I heard the door open to the Bug.

"Ben?" I let a few seconds pass, "Ben?"

"Shut up--" he snapped, groggy.

I *knew* I should trust that she was coming back, just like Benny did. Why did I think she'd be gone for good every single time?

Then came the familiar rumble of the Bug starting up. I held my breath--panic-stricken--as Mother tore out of the driveway without warming up the engine as usual. *Why wouldn't she take us with her?*

The swell of uncontrollable out loud crying started. I felt like a toddler walking over to Benny's bed in my big T-shirt and underwear.

"Please--" I hiccupped.

He moved over and opened the covers for me to get in.

"But stop crying."

There was a warm rush of relief next to Benny's bony body--he even let me wrap my arm around his middle and bury my face against his back.

The next morning, I awoke to the sound of a broom sweeping up broken glass in the kitchen. I quietly opened our swinging door the tiniest crack to find Mother sweeping up yellow pieces of broken ceramic--it was that giant bowl that she had brought to the picnic the day before, in little pieces all over the kitchen floor. Scattered on the floor and stuck to the straw of the broom were macaroni noodles wet from mayonnaise.

A Room in the Basement

Sometime shortly after the macaroni fight, Benny announced that it was high time that he didn't have to share his bedroom with his annoying big sister anymore. Mother's answer to his request was to convert the basement into a bedroom for me.

"You'll be a teenager next year--it'd be a radical pad for a teenager," she declared.

Mother was good at converting non-living spaces into real living spaces. For instance, she had recently rigged up a small bed for herself in her closet.

"It will be *so* cozy," Mother said with her hands clasped under her chin as she stood in front of the long and narrow closet one Saturday afternoon, marveling that it seemed so perfect for a little bed (even though the closet would literally fit nothing *but* the bed). The closet even had a little window. I don't think she slept in that gnome bed very often--maybe she saved it for when she needed to hide out.

I was thrilled about my basement bedroom. Mother placed a large piece of plywood between a slab of concrete and a utility shelf to make a bed. It was a bit askew, but it worked so long as the downward slant was at my feet and not my head--otherwise, I'd wake up with a headache. We placed a foam mattress on top of the plywood and *voila!* my bed was complete.

The next matter at hand in making my teenage paradise a room was to deal with the fact that the crawl space under the house was right beside my sleeping quarters. The crawl space was a dark and damp area, with about two feet between cold, mildewy dirt and the concrete foundation of the house. There were a few small openings at ground level that were covered with chicken wire where some light came through. Otherwise, the crawl space was pitch dark, and reminded me of a scary cave because I couldn't see exactly how far back it went, or what kind of creatures were hiding there.

    Mother dealt with the issue of the spooky crawl space by hanging up an old bed sheet across the opening right beside my plywood bed. Her crafty partition didn't really create a true barrier between me and the dirt, it just gave me the illusion that there was a wall––at least I could *pretend* there wasn't a creepy crawl space right next to my bed.

    At night, I lay in the dark smelling the pungent odors of wet dirt, old wood and cold concrete. Sometimes I was scared to death by the startling sound of something scurrying about down there beyond the sheet. I kept stock-still, thinking of horror movies and ghost stories. If I were really brave, I'd dare myself to lift the corner of the curtain to scan that vast shadowy space. Once or twice, our cat gave me a horrible scare when I saw her large green eyes staring out from the dark.

    When fear got the better of me, I bolted up the cement stairs, and made a beeline for my old room that was now solely Benny's room, blasting through the swinging door as quietly as I could. Safe in the familiar streetlight glow, I took a gamble on attempting to crawl in his bed. On those nights, I'd gladly take the shame and embarrassment of begging my little brother to let me under the covers over being alone with the monsters in the basement.

    Mother draped a second sheet in front of the washer and dryer area in my basement room, saying she did this so I wouldn't be reminded that I was living in the laundry room. The in-and-out traffic of family members toting heaping baskets of dirty clothes was reminder enough that my room was also a laundry facility. I didn't mind. I found the washer and dryer to be a bonus feature, on account of not having to walk far at all to start a load. I got used to the rickety-racket of the old washer, and the clangity-clang of a coin or pencil tossing around in the dryer.

  I was glad there were electrical outlets in my basement room; I *had* to have a working socket for the little record player Dad had given me one year before. Tom gave me the new Blondie album *American Graffiti* for Christmas that December. I liked to lay on my plywood bed for hours, daydreaming while alternating records-- Blondie, *Rapper's Delight* by The Sugarhill Gang, Cheap Trick and the Kiss *Dynasty* album, which I snagged from Benny (it was the first full album he ever owned).

  I got used to the washer and the dryer and the underground area of my room. What I *never* got used to were the beetles that jumped on my head from above. The black critters had square heads and long bodies, and I called them "clicker beetles" because they clicked when they jumped. Knowing they were hiding out in cracks and crevices kept me at a constant low level of anxiety and alertness. I jumped when one landed on my head-- startled--screaming and shaking my hair furiously. The trouble was that their legs were sticky and strong like a grasshopper's. The tenacious little legs fought to stay put as I grabbed the clicker beetle tightly between my thumb and pointer finger and slide him down the shaft of my shoulder-length hair. It took many tries to get over the creepiness and not lose my grasp on him like a chicken.

  My underground niche was a good spot to be when chaos broke out upstairs. Shouts were almost completely muffled between the floorboards and my little record player--door slamming and body slamming registered as only small vibrations.

Mother's Purge

Mother's tongue was turning green from her diets. She swore to "eat" only juice from her juicer—mostly vegetable, and wheatgrass juice a-plenty. She jogged like a maniac. When she'd return from her jogs, I knew it was better to stay away--when her eyes were bugging out of her head and she'd get revved up and yell. It could be the dishes or that someone was watching TV, or the music was too loud.

One particular day stands out. The frustration was that she had blown too many years caring for everybody but herself. And *I* was the culprit. Perhaps I had made a mess of her LP records, or perhaps I didn't clean up my mess in the kitchen.

"Do you know all that I did for you!?" she screeched in my direction, appearing surprisingly fierce in her little running shorts and T-shirt--her behemoth fro out of place and protuberant against her skinny waif body.

She reminded me that I was a colicky baby--how she tended to my fevers and cuts--and of how fucking often she's *still* gotta pick up after me. That *it* never ends; that "where's the appreciation?"

She followed me through the kitchen as I made a dash for the basement. I jumped onto my plywood bed and ducked under the covers.

"I've had it with cleaning up after you--" she continued from the top of the stairs. "Get your shit together."

"Mom, stop. Just stop, stop!"

"Who ever takes care of *me*? No one!" she went on, "All I do is take care of other people!"

I never came out of the basement that evening. It seemed my mother had declared that she hated being my mother--that she wished that I had never been born. I angrily thought of that hot day on the back stoop in New York, when Dad told me that she wouldn't let him have us, that she'd take him to court if he tried. *She doesn't want me anyway.*

Later that evening, Mother timidly came down the cement steps and appeared before me as I knew she would—disheveled and puffy-eyed.

"Honey, I'm sorry for what I said. I didn't mean it." Her chin was quivering, tears all over her neck and hair. "I just feel so overwhelmed. I have no time for myself."

I had practiced all the things I was going to say to her in my head: *Well, that's just not good enough. You can't treat your kid that way. I don't want to talk to you. Apology not accepted. I'm going to live with my dad.*

But I took my weeping, skinny, green-tongued mother into my arms.

"It's okay Mom."

Mother did make attempts to seek help for her moods. For instance, there were the occasional jaunts for what she called therapy, when the three of us climbed into the Bug and headed to Sebastopol to visit with Dan, who was some kind of therapist. It seemed that such visits were on the leg of a particularly bad fight with Tom or after a run of Sally Days.

Mother called Dan's property a "cleansing place," she said just being on the property alone was healing. She said she liked to bring me and Benny because we might as well get a clean-out ourselves. We enjoyed his property full of brooks and insects and trees to climb.

"You need to get rid of the garbage first. That's the first part of the cleanse," Mother said in the Bug on the way to Dan's, holding up one pointer finger, "that's the purge."

We knew what *that* meant. Looking at her staring straight ahead at the road in the rearview mirror, I wasn't sure if she was talking to us or to herself.

The visit always started out nice enough, with pleasant greetings from Dan—a nicely dressed skinny balding man in glasses. Sometimes, he would offer Benny and I a snack and we would sit at his large kitchen table surrounded by houseplants. He'd talk to us about school or our latest camping trip. Once we were ushered outside, we knew that we were in for a do not disturb afternoon—no knocking on the front or back doors and no calling out for our mother. We were in for an indefinite time of frolic.

After a short while of searching for tadpoles or playing hide-and-seek, we heard angry yelling coming from Dan's house. Mother's shrill voice was cutting through the serene wilderness—horrible, blood-curdling screams ringing through the trees and the gardens.

"There she goes," I'd say to Benny from the limb of a tree. "Let's check it out."

We'd sneak over to the house, ducking past the windows to inch over to the sliding glass door in the back. Benny and I sandwiched together––my chin on top of his head––to get a peek into the room where Mother was having her "cleanse."

The room was large and without furniture, with big pillows scattered at the sides, and sunlight illuminating the bright blue wall-to-wall carpeting. Through the thick glass, we'd catch a glimpse of our mother in sweatpants, an old T-shirt, and no shoes, her whole body plunged into a cleansing regime. She was throwing pillows, punching, kicking; thrashing her head back and forth and sideways. She was screaming out insults at various so-and-so's (mostly men) with her face coiled in an ugly scowl and her large dark mane of frizz bouncing with her thrusts.

"Fuck you daddy!" she screamed loud and guttural the way she did when she was really laying into Tom.

"I'm not daddy's perfect little girl, *am I?!*"

Mother whipped around like a tornado, her face bright red and full of spit and sweat and tears. There was something fascinating about seeing my mother yelling at imaginary people with such tenaciousness and venom.

"Gooood, gooood Katherine," Dan coached with the same calm demeanor that he showed at greeting time. "Let it out--"

More than once, I imagined myself in that room and wondered whether I'd have the guts to scream and kick and punch. Who would I yell at? I couldn't imagine allotting myself such an indulgence. The arena for falling apart was my mother's. I couldn't understand just why she needed to fall apart so much, but I did get the sense that I'd better keep it together.

At the end of the afternoon, we'd get back in the Bug with Mother purged, cured and smiling.

"Whatcha' guys do out there today?"

Sometimes, Mother would surprise me with her reactions to things. She would act one way when I had expected her to behave differently. The news of John Lennon's death was a perfect example of one of Mother's contrary responses.

That year, the poetic, peaceful music man was shot in New York City by some lunatic on the eighth day of December. I was at school when I heard about it. Classes at the alternative school were disrupted with the shock of the news, our teachers in tears, hardly able to speak.

I knew that Mother was home that day and I didn't want to wait out the rest of the afternoon to get to her, I was afraid of how she might handle the news if she were all by herself. I wanted to be the one to break it to her. I went through several scenes in my head of how I was going to inform my mother that John Lennon—the walrus, the magical mystery tour guide, the dream weaver—was gone. I imagined how delicately I was going to present the news. I would take her hand in mine as I told her; I would sit her down. She would burst into tears, calling out, "*Why, why, why...*"

I flew through the front door that afternoon, out of breath because I had run all the way from the bus stop. I slowed my pace, scouting for Mother. I found her in Tom's room, with papers in one hand and a big peeled carrot in the other. I still had my backpack on my shoulders.

"Hi honey, did you *run*?" her head was cocked to the side, a concerned, quizzical look on her face. I looked at her eyes for a few seconds, trying to decipher whether she had heard or not.

"Mom, do you know?"

"What?" *I thought so. Here I go,* I thought, *I'm glad I made it in time.*

"I'm so sorry to tell you, Mom--"

"Oh, John Lennon?" she interrupted nonchalantly, taking a big bite off of her carrot.

"Well, yeah, I thought maybe you didn't know yet." I think I was disappointed.

"Who doesn't? It's awful, isn't it? So sad. Some crazy shot him."

Her eyes went to the papers in her hand. She was reading. Perhaps she had her meltdown when she first got the news, or perhaps she never had a meltdown at all--I'd never know.

That night and then in the days to follow, we heard about various people killing themselves out of deep sadness over the death of John Lennon, who had really been like a prophet or a teacher to some. The television showed images of crowds of people everywhere standing in front of piles of flowers and letters--piles so large that a bulldozer would eventually have to take it all away. The people were crying. But not my mother. This time, she went about business as usual.

Mother's Missions

Mother and Tom spent a lot of time with some high thinkers—folks that came around to sprawl out in our living room or on our front yard. Music played on our record player, spilling out into the quiet street--The Rolling Stones, Traffic, The Grateful Dead and Van Morrison.

Brothers Barry and Allen came over just about every weekend—a pair of heady, intellectual brain-o-maniacs who ran research at some kind of science laboratory. They were usually playing the guitar and having serious talks, but I liked to jump on them and try to get their attention any way I could. They'd tickle me and throw me in the air.

During these weekend gatherings at our house, joints were carefully and skillfully rolled on the kitchen breakfast nook like origami creations. These party favors brought on dancing and laughing and eating.

It was the snorting of the tidy, precise lines of white powder that stirred up particularly manic conversations full of heated ideas and opinions. It seemed that Tom was getting more and more into this sort of recreation. I had *always* felt anxious around Tom--mostly because I got the feeling he wished I weren't there--but the anxiousness doubled when he was snorting coke. He was unpredictable and talked fast and gestured funny, as if he had uncontrollable tics. He focused on certain little details that seemed to bother him much more than most people, and banned my favorite radio station on account of it being AM because he didn't like the "frequency."

I do have only one memory of Tom and I being on the same side. Out of the blue, Mother had brought home a group of homeless people because it was a cold night and she wanted them to be able to sit by the fire and have a warm meal. Without talking to anyone about it, she drove right down to People's Park and corralled a carload of them like they were stray dogs. I recall watching from the big living room window as she pulled into the drive with the Bug loaded to the hilt with downtrodden street people. They piled out of the doors like a circus act.

When they came into the house, I retreated past the hall so that I could listen, wondering just where was my mother's head. That's when Tom came slinking up beside me.

"What the hell is *this*?" he asked me, more like he was asking the greater universe.

"I don't know, they're like…bums."

The homeless crowd was gathering around the fire that Tom had made earlier that evening. They were rubbing their hands and rolling up their sleeves and putting their palms close to the fire. I drew my breath when one of them picked up Tom's precious guitar and started strumming.

"What the fuck––" Tom let out, again like he was talking to the greater universe, and walked into the living room, tensely asking Mother to come out to the kitchen. She walked past me with her nose in the air, with that *I'm on a mission* posture of hers. I stayed in the hall so that I could eavesdrop and peek around the corner.

"What the fuck is going on here?"

"What's your trip, man? You're *so* uptight." She had her hands on her hips, her head cocked to the side. I was a little scared of how he'd take this one. "You're lucky to have a roof over your head and food to eat. I'm just giving a nice evening to people who have nothing."

Next, she was telling Tom to get real. "Get real" was one of Mother's favorite lines, and implied a terrible lack of coolness.

"You don't know these people," Tom half-whispered, gesturing toward the living room, "they could rob us. Now they know where we live!" he paused with his head down, nodding and repeating, "They're *never* gonna leave. They are *never* gonna leave."

"You're so fucking paranoid," Mother spat, sounding disgusted.

But I was feeling paranoid, too. I was imagining the dirty guys taking note of everything in the house, including me. I could tell by the quiet, deflated tone of Tom's voice that he was actually *also* scared of them. Mother seemed to take instant advantage of this by indignantly going back into the living room to offer the unfortunate guests some food and drink.

It was an odd thing to be standing out in that hallway next to Tom, sharing with him the jaw-slacking disbelief over the audacity of my mother. I think our sudden alliance in our shared conservatism was strange for the both of us, to say the least. It seemed this was the only instance we ever saw see eye-to-eye.

Luckily, the homeless guys did *not* spend the night. After Tom had bugged her enough, Mother finally managed to usher them out––late. I imaged her driving them back out to People's Park and letting them out like wild animals set free.

Once the crew was gone, the blood curdling screaming started between Mother and Tom. I fell asleep to the fighting and woke up to it the next morning. I had crept into my brother's bed, of course, scared the homeless men were going to come back and find their way to my basement bed.

"I'm fucking done with you not respecting my space!" Tom yelled.

"*YOUR* space?! Where's *my* space? My fucking bed in a closet?! Is that it?"

It wasn't long before he gave her one of his favorites: "Go fuck yourself." It was a line that I found to be particularly odd and insulting, as I assumed it had something to do with masturbation.

I was in Benny's room, sitting on the edge of his bed, trying to catch onto what he was thinking. But he was being silent as always, going through his collections.

Suddenly, there was a loud crash and a big *thump* that sounded like a body slamming against the floorboards.

"Ben! Ben! Call 911!" Mother screamed.

Benny and I flew through the swinging door in a flash, and found our mother pinned to the hallway floor in Tom's grasp. She was curled in a ball with her head down, looking sideways at us with her butt in the air. Tom had her forearm twisted behind her back in a way that a cop might get a hold of a crook.

Benny grabbed the hallway phone, but stopped for a second, looking at the two of them disheveled and out of breath. He was probably wondering if he really had to do this.

I wondered to myself why she yelled out to *Benny* on first impulse. He was only nine. I was twelve––it should have been me. But Ben was the other male in the house, which put him up a notch in the saving category.

"Call 911!" she yelled again.

In a quick darting motion, Tom leapt off Mother and grabbed the phone out of Benny's hands and put it back on the base. Next, he lifted up his shirt to reveal long, bloody scratches all over his trunk.

"Look at this! This is what she did to me!" he said, panic-stricken and out of breath, his red face covered with dewdrops of sweat. "I had to protect myself! She was attacking me!"

Mother started defending herself from her spot on the floor, as she flipped over to a seated position. "You saw him, kids. He was on me! He was hurting me!"

Our eyes went from Tom to Mother, from Mother to Tom, and then to each other as we tried to judge who was right and who was wrong, and what was what. Benny had such a look. It was as though he had been appointed arbitrator and some big timer was ticking away while he wrestled with his decision and it was just about to go *Ding!*

The cops were never called that day. I don't recall how that scene ended, but it probably ended like the rest, with Benny and I retreating to our rooms, soon to hear the two laughing and then having loud sex.

Betty and Errol

Our neighbors, Betty and Errol, offered their home to Benny and I when the fighting got bad at our house. I don't recall the specific day that we became regulars at their home; we just blended into that couple like they had adopted us or something. When the screaming was loud enough to broadcast into the neighborhood, we could find Betty on her front stoop waiting for me and Benny.

We moseyed on up her steps, where she took us to the very back of her house, to a place called the pantry. I was completely awestruck by the fact that she had an entire *room* of food, even if it was only about the size of a large closet. I had never seen a pantry. Betty had all of the kinds of treats that we never had at our house—Oreo cookies, Swiss Miss cocoa, Ritz crackers. She let us pick out something to eat. I'd take my time, browsing the shelves for minutes at a time.

Betty taught me how to create miniatures, which was her personal hobby. She made real live tiny beds and dressers and kitchen sets that looked just like the real thing, only one-thousand times smaller. She had special glues, cutting materials and paints, which she shared with me for our special projects. She kept the projects on newspaper on her dining room table, never moving them in their half-finished states until I came over to join her.

Betty even took me to her Saturday miniature-making class at the craft shop, where she introduced me to all of her miniature-making friends—older plump ladies who wore glasses and brought along their own sets of favorite tools. These ladies seemed to love it when I joined the class, all pitching in to help me with my tiny creations.

Errol was into boats and bought small plastic model boats to make with Benny. The two took up their own spot at the craft table in the dining room, using their own tube of stinky glue.

Betty and Errol did not have any children. Betty confessed to me that she had wanted to have children, but could not. I liked to think that I was the daughter that she never had, or that she thought of me this way.

We ended up spending so much time with this couple that they took us camping, on day trips, and even to see their relatives. During these excursions, I liked to pretend that I really *was* their daughter and that Benny was their son.

Once, we took a long drive to a park with a small lake so Errol and Benny could test out their model boats. At the end of a day, the couple took us to a steak house. As we gobbled up our steaks, I wondered if all of the people in the restaurant were taking note of the perfectly normal nuclear family sitting at our table. I imagined the people saying things like, "Wow, would you look at that family? They look so nice! They must live such wonderful, ordinary lives."

Betty made me a jacket by hand that year for Christmas. It was of green satin with a red, green, and white floral quilted fabric on the inside. I wore it all the time.

Todd Tharpe

The year that I turned twelve, I constantly rode my slightly used beat-up white bicycle all around North Berkeley. I felt a freedom and exhilaration, pedaling fast and making sharp turns--as though I could leave anything behind. I'd hop on the floral banana seat and cut through town to Kim's with my hair whipping in the wind.

Kim and I were still two peas in a pod, even though we no longer attended the same school and we no longer lived right around the corner from each other. I felt bad about not seeing her as often, and wondered how she was doing in the day-to-day with her mean brother and her mother that kept to her bedroom.

One sunny afternoon, Kim and I rode to the bike shop for some cool bike decals. We had gone a few times, pining over the many profane and righteous decals, wishing we could get one. We finally had finally saved up enough money.

After browsing the many decals for quite some time––looking for the best ones––we decided on two. Mine fit just right on the frame of my bike and it said, "If you value your life as much as I value this bike, don't fuck with it." Kim's decal read: "QUITCHABITCHIN'"

Outside the bike shop, with our bikes propped up against the storefront, we excitedly peeled off the backs of the decals and placed them on our bike frames. We were laughing and cheering and really feeling like a couple of badasses.

It was my bicycle that wheeled me in the direction of Todd Tharpe. He spent every other week with his mother who lived just down the street. Though this already tall and pimply twelve-year-old boy went to my school, we had not exchanged so much as one word.

It was unusually warm the day I caught a glimpse of Todd's dark hair as I whizzed past him. I had been enjoying a no-hands coast down the gradual decent of our street when I recognized him on his blue dirt bike. I nearly had a head-over-handlebars disaster when my feet slipped on the pedals in attempts to slow down while turning my head around. I composed myself, watching Todd with a side-eye as he did figure-eights at least twenty yards behind me. I turned around and whizzed by him in front of his house without turning my head. I must have had my chin pointed so high in the air that someone might have said, "She sure thinks she's one hell of a big shot."

In my blurry peripheral vision, I could see that Todd was looking straight at me—I suddenly felt dizzy and like I couldn't catch my breath. I had the sensation of someone pouring a bucket of ice water down my back. I pedaled faster. My heart raced as I zig-zagged and did figure-eights in the middle of the street about one hundred feet from Todd's house. I continued to lack the audaciousness to glance straight at him.

I was riding fast through the gas station at the bottom of the street when I heard the familiar sound of someone else's bike tires behind me. This made me pedal faster––the wind whipping my eyes, tears pooling at the corners. I went off the curb with a thump that made my butt hurt. I simultaneously wanted to get away from him *and* wanted him to chase me––both. In only a matter of moments, Todd finally approached the side of my bike. I smelled Aunt Annette's fabric softener as he whooshed by. Todd didn't look as he passed me, he just cut quickly in front of me, so that I swerved and hit the brakes.

He pedaled standing up, using his weight to go faster, not even sitting down to coast. This was a boy's way of riding a bike. I could see the muscles in his back strain and flex through his white T-shirt when he ducked his head low to the handlebars.

Todd Tharpe and I must have spent at least an hour that day lost in the dance of riding-together-but-not-together. It was a battle of wills over who would look first.

Finally, Todd stopped at the bottom of a dead end street as I was coasting down the hill in his direction. He stood straddling the frame of his shiny blue bike with his arms loose across his silver handlebars. He was squinting, his eyes shifting from me, to the sky, and to the ground, over and over. *What do I do?* There were two choices—head straight in his direction, or turn around and peddle away like a chicken. I kept cruising awkwardly toward Todd, still trying to decide what to do by the time I was only two feet away. I couldn't wipe the stupid smile off my face as I dragged my sneakers against the cement to slow down.

"What does your sticker say?" he asked.

Todd was pointing to the profane warning that I had so cavalierly stuck to my bicycle. I wanted to die.

"It's nothing," I shot, quickly covering it with my leg.

"Na-ah, come on, I want to see."

Next, Todd threw his bike down on the sidewalk with a crash as he hopped off to move my leg out of the way. His hand was strong and made me want to fight to push it away while keeping it on me at the same time. I squealed over and over for him to stop. I was laughing, my bike falling halfway to the ground as I struggled to keep Todd from seeing my sticker.

"I'm gonna see it!"

Somewhere in the scuffle, I managed to get my foot back on the pedal and tear away from Todd, leaving him there at the bottom of that dead end with him hollering, "I'm comin' to get you! I'm gonna read that sticker!"

So this is how it started with me and Todd Tharpe. I don't recall whether he ever saw my sticker that day or not. I do recall that the following day at school, he sent me a note that I kept in my jewelry box for a very long time. It read:

Dear Astrid,
Would you go with me?
From Todd

And I sent him a note back:

Dear Todd,
Yes.
From, Astrid

I looked forward to the every-other-week when Todd was just down the street, when we spent the afternoons chasing each other on our bicycles and playing hide-and-seek around the church. He never went inside of my house and I never went inside his. We stayed outdoors, where there were good hiding spots and plenty of space for us to alternate being sought and chased.

One time at school, Todd bought me a candy bar at lunchtime and I got to be the envy of all my young friends. This was *going together*, a term that made me want to ask, "Where are we going?" but never did. We did *go* to the movies once, to see *Oh God, Book Two* at The Oaks Theater on Solano Avenue. In the dark of the theater––our knees barely touching––we shared a Coke with two straws, no kidding.

"Close your eyes," Todd said to me one afternoon beside the big hedge outside my house.
"Why?"
"Just close your eyes, come on."
When I closed my eyes, I felt Todd's breath against my upper lip. I pulled my head back a few inches.
"I love you," he whispered, close to my mouth.
The next thing I knew, Todd put his lips against mine, closing his eyes (I kept mine open). His lips were moist and full and staying put as one second turn into two and then three. Time had agonizingly slowed down. The next thing I knew, I was instantly pulling away from Todd without thinking. I ran as fast as I could up the brick stairs and through my front door, not looking behind me for even one glance. I bolted for my room in the basement.

As I lay staring at my bare toes against the wooden planks above my bed, I tormented over just what it was that made me run away from Todd. It had been my first real kiss. I had done plenty of make-believe sexy kisses with boys in New York when I was younger. But everything was different now because of my raisin tits and the fine downy hair that was growing around my privates. These new manifestations raised the stakes. Is this what Dad meant when he warned about boys jumping my bones? Todd's kiss didn't seem anything like what Dad had talked about.

The Pelvic Exam

Perhaps it was the next day, or the day after that, or maybe even the next week––I cannot recall just *how* soon it was after Todd Tharpe's kiss—my mother announced that I ought to learn the inner secrets of what she called *being a woman*. She took me to her doctor's appointment at the women's clinic.

"I've seen you outside with Todd a lot lately," she said in the Bug.

My stomach lurched. I imagined my mother watching The Kiss from the large front window—I had so hoped that no one saw. Long moments of silence went by. *Don't talk to me, don't ask me questions, don't even look at me.*

"You seem to like each other a lot. Have you talked about sex?"

"*Mommm!*" I groaned, crossing my arms and turning my head toward the window. Houses and stop signs and businesses whipped past. I was holding tight.

The women's health clinic waiting room was decorated like a living room, with an over-sized couch so big, I felt overcome by the cushions when I took a seat next to my mother. The uneven, over-fluffiness of it made me blend into her and her into me in a nuzzling kind of way. Even though I kept scooting away, we naturally migrated to the worn-out slump in the center, our hips touching.

I placed one of the big, old stinky pillows on my lap and started trying to read my Judy Blume book while Mother read her college book. My eyes kept straying to the walls, to the dozens of fliers—domestic violence, lesbian support groups, STDs, drug abuse, you name it.

In a matter of minutes, a heavy-set woman called my mom's name from behind a door.

"It won't be long," Mother said as she tapped my knee, closed her big book, and got up to leave the waiting room.

Ten or fifteen minutes later, the same woman poked her head into the waiting room again. "Astrid? Your mom wants you to come to the room."

I followed her through the hall, past several closed doors and posters of feminine art. I wondered why I was being called in, hoping that *I* wouldn't have to be examined.

The woman opened the door to a little exam room and extended her arm through the doorway in a welcoming gesture, like an usher who says, "Here's your seat." I don't recall what was on the walls or whether there was a window. I do remember the image of my mother lying on top of a small exam table.

Mother turned to look at me, smiling. Her head lay on a little pillow, and a white sheet covered the lower half of her body. She was in an odd position, with her legs exposed and spread eagle, her feet in some kind of foot pedals at the doctor's end. I watched the door close behind me as the woman walked out. A female doctor with grey short hair and glasses poked her head from around her spot in between my mother's legs, and instructed me to come stand beside her. I tentatively inched my way over, my legs shuffling awkwardly.

"Your mom wants me to teach you the female anatomy so that you can understand your own body."

My face started to throb and my mouth went dry. I didn't want to disappoint the doctor, who seemed to think that this was a marvelous idea. Her cheerful attitude made me suspect that my presence at my mother's vagina inspection must have been pretty usual, to boot.

"Come on honey, it's okay," Mother ushered, scooting her butt a little toward the doctor, white paper underneath her making crinkly sounds.

I stood next to the doctor as instructed, close to my mother's feet that pressed against those pedals like she was riding a horse. I imagined her holding some reins, saying in a slow, firm way, "Whooooaa, steady boy…"

I held my breath at the first glimpse of my mother's gaping privates. There was a metal gadget shaped like a duck beak stuck inside her, spreading her parts.

"This is the called a speculum," the doctor explained, her gloved hand on the handles of the metal doohickey. A bright spotlight amplified my mother's vagina, like it was some kind of Broadway star who might just break out in a song at any moment. The doctor pointed out the various parts of what she kept calling the female anatomy.

"These lips are the labia majora"

"These inner folds are the labia minora."

"This is the clitoris. This is where women feel a lot of sexual pleasure."

There was an odd assortment of vocabulary used to describe my mother's private insides. Occasionally, the doctor sounded like she was referring to a dark cave, saying things like "walls," "mouth" and "entrance." Other times, she talked about the privates like they just might have the ability to talk. I never did like the use of the word lips to describe the parts down there—I had lips and they were on my face, thank you very much.

The fleshy insides of my mother looked like pieces of raw meat to me, all red and pink and moist. I couldn't help my smidgeon of fascination, which was bringing on a level of shame. Were other kids being invited to look at their mother's privates? My stomach was twisting while I contemplated *normal*.

Looking at the adults in the room, the experience of The Pelvic Exam was quite customary. In fact, my mother was smiling from her strapped down place with that beak thingamabob stuck in her, as if this was just any old ordinary thing to do.

Aside from a pretty clear knowledge of the female anatomy, I came away from that exam room with this pledge: a doctor's visit like this would never be ordinary for me. Not ever, no sir.

As we made our way home, I thought of the car ride to the vagina appointment just an hour or so before--the houses and the trees whipping by the stock-still me. Mother had started the whole anatomy escapade with questions about Todd Tharpe. I wondered how on earth did my mother ever connected Todd Tharpe to the complete exposure of female anatomy. How did my hide and seek, bicycle riding and viewing of *Oh God Book Two* ever have anything to do with what I saw on that examination table? I decided that it must be true—Todd would surely lead to clinics and gaping privates. At least, people might think of those things when they saw me and Todd together.

Later that week at school, I gave my friend a note to pass to Todd Tharpe.

Todd,
I'm dropping you.
Astrid

I didn't watch Todd open the letter. I did sneak a look at his pale, straight face later that day and felt terrible and glad at the same time. I wasn't exactly sure just why I *had* to drop Todd. It seemed that there was a me before The Kiss and the vagina check-up and then there was a me afterward—a before and after that demarked a sharp cut-off of some sort. Todd was the cut-off.

Elmhurst, Queens: Anton

Dad brought his new friend with him to the JFK airport that June, when we flew in for the summer of 1981. I was twelve and Benny was nine.

"I've found the love of my life," he said on the phone a few weeks prior to our arrival in New York, telling us he had moved into Anton's apartment in Elmhurst, Queens.

"You and your brother get a bedroom this time, princess," he promised.

When Dad grabbed us at the gate, swooping us up in his arms, I looked over his shoulder at Anton—tall and a little heavy, with a dark mustache, thick dark hair and pale skin. He was shifting his feet and clasping his hands. He had big tears in his eyes. I had been nervous to meet this new boyfriend who might be taking up Dad's time. But Anton was obviously genuinely touched to see Dad as happy as he was when we stepped off that plane, which was a good sign.

"You two are going to simply love your room," Dad gushed in the taxi to Elmhurst, one arm around each of us, Anton riding in front.

Anton was thirteen years younger than Dad, but he was *not* referred to as "Boy." We clicked with him right away because he was so friendly—always laughing and joking, and truly interested in Benny and I. He brought about some kind of leveling out in our dad, turning him down a notch. Dad had dropped the handcuffs and the leather. The four of us were like a nuclear family that summer, only that there were two Dads. We did the normal things that most normal families do.

The 81st Street apartment was the nicest place Dad had lived in since Centereach. I knew Anton wasn't *rich*-- he took the subway to his business job at an office every day--but we sure did live better than we had the previous summer. I could tell things were looking up because of the large dining room table, the framed art on the walls, and the above-the-floor beds. My favorite part was the giant TV.

Anton owned a video game apparatus called Intellivision, which connected to the TV like Atari. Benny and I played Astrosmash, Space Battle, Horse Racing and Auto Racing all summer long. We spent our air-conditioned afternoons on the couch in our pajamas or shorts and T-shirts, eating Planters cheese balls out of a big container and drinking glasses of iced Pepsi (Dad had switched to Pepsi because Anton preferred Pepsi over Coke.).

Not only did Anton have Intellivision, he also had HBO. When we weren't playing the video games, Benny and I were watching HBO movies, especially late at night after Dad and Anton went to bed. *American Gigolo* was on that summer. We watched it with Dad and Anton first, and then watched it by ourselves about five or ten times after that.

"Mother of god, would you look at that one?" Dad cooed over Richard Gere. (At first I was worried about Dad's apparently unstoppable cat-calling at men on TV and in public. I wondered if Anton would get upset, but he just chuckled.)

Dad and I played Michelle––Lauren Hutton's *American Gigolo* character––all summer, holding up a pointer finger and looking desperate, saying, "Just one fuck."

Aside from *American Gigolo*, also playing on HBO that summer of 1981, were *Urban Cowboy* and *Moonraker.* The movies would play over and over, each at least once—sometimes twice—during the late night hours. So Benny and I watched the same movies again and again, sometimes until 3:00 a.m. We even knew most of the lines, acting out scenes or just talking right along with the actors. On the really lucky nights—usually sometime after 1 a.m.—a burlesque show came on, which we watched every time. There was only partial nudity, but we never missed a chance to see it.

Anton took us to meet his large extended Cuban family in a suburb of Queens. I was not prepared for the greeting we received upon arrival at his parent's home. Aunts, uncles, cousins and grandmothers came rushing at Benny and I from all sides, giving us full body hugs, kissing our faces and pinching our cheeks. They spoke back and forth in rapid Spanish, pointing to my hair, my eyes--grabbing up Benny's chin and then Dad's.

"Come, come, come!" Anton's tiny mother ushered. Maricella was only about four-foot-eleven, covered up by an apron, and dressed in a sleeveless top and shorts. We stepped through the big front door into her two-story air conditioned home. She led us into her busy kitchen where she had a pot on every burner. The smell was chili and pork and tomato, barbeque, garlic and sweet all at once. Anton grabbed a spoon right away and opened the biggest pot, scooping up the delicious rope villaha, saying, "See kids? I told you."

Maricella laughed and swatted his hand. I liked her immediately. She poured us each a tall Coke with ice and led us out to the yard, where the other family members were sitting on lawn furniture. All of these folks had come over from Cuba when Anton was a boy.

When Dad told the story of the migration of Anton's family, of how they "all came over on a boat," he talked about this thing called The Bay of Pigs. I had heard the term in the ramblings of Mother and Tom and their friends. The Bay of Pigs always made me think of wet, pink, squealing pigs bobbing around in a dark bay, drowning and looking for something to use as a float. What this had to do with *Cuba*, I wasn't quite sure. I just nodded my head.

Dad told us how Anton's father had gone through a long period of not speaking to him after he came out as gay. It had only been recently that Anton had reunited with his family. Dad said it was a big deal that they were so accepting of him.

"I think it helped that I have kids," Dad said, "Maricella could not wait to meet you two once she found out you were coming."

For some reason, Anton was their only child, so—in a way—we were the closest thing to grandchildren they were going to get.

Dad and Anton took us to Disney World and Ocean World in Florida that summer. I felt like we were a regular run-of-the-mill family—the four of us on the airplane together, driving around in our rental car, and sipping Pepsi's in our air-conditioned hotel room and by the hotel pool.

For the rest of the summer, the four of us sang the theme song to It's A Small World, and the Tiki Bird song from the Enchanted Tiki Room.

At Ocean World, Dad strolled us up to a little pool full of oysters where you could pay a price to try to find an oyster with a pearl inside it. We spent a good, long time trying to guess which oyster might contain the pearl.

"This one, Daddy?" I said as I dipped my hands in the water, pulling out one after the other.

"No, no, not quite right," he said, "Princess, the pearl will be in the one you don't think would have a pearl."

We finally selected an oyster—medium-sized and ordinary looking, with a rough, bumpy shell. We held hands and bounced on our toes when the man who worked there cracked the shell open.

"Looks like we've got a winner," he said, holding the plump shiny pearl to the sun between his thumb and pointer finger.

"Daddy! You were right! You were right!" I squealed.

"Well, I found you, didn't I?" Dad said, bending down to kiss my cheek.

Back in New York, Dad took our pearl to a jeweler, and had it placed on a gold ring for my right ring finger. The pearl was so big that it stuck way out in a way that was pretty kitschy. Just about every time I looked at it, I thought of Dad looking down into the shallow pool of oysters on that hot day in Florida—when he referred to me as a hard-to-find treasure.

Terrance and Cliff

Dad and Anton introduced us to their very best friends—Terrance and Cliff. Cliff had a trimmed beard and a tidy mustache and had been married to a woman before, like our dad. He even had a son. Terrance, on the other hand—both Jewish and Italian, according to Dad—had his thick, black eyebrows done and appeared to be wearing eye makeup.

Terrance and Cliff shared Dad and Anton's gushing excitement over the Royal Wedding that summer, when Prince Charles married Lady Diana. Over martinis or dinner, the four of them glowed with both anticipation and sarcasm as the date for the royal nuptials approached.

On that July twenty-ninth of 1981, every television channel was tuned in to the Royal Wedding. Charles and Diana were under a big magnifying glass for hours and hours.

"Princess, princess, look!" Dad gasped, clapping his knees. "They're re-capping on the royal wedding. Look at her, look at her!"

I watched reruns of the extravagant wedding while I ate my Golden Grahams. Diana arrived to the ceremony in a glass coach wearing her Emmanuel designed ivory taffeta gown, escorted by her father, Earl Spencer. This was a real live Cinderella scene. The awfully plain Lady Diana was being transformed into a princess by marrying a Prince. Dad said that she was selected because she was already royalty, *A Lady*. However, when *I* thought of royalty, I imagined crowns and purple velvet and thrones. This Lady Di was a teacher in ordinary clothes, and had short hair. I wondered how it felt to one day be teaching in a classroom and the next to be riding in a glass coach to St. Paul's cathedral with hundreds of thousands of people watching.

Later in the day, or perhaps it was a re-cap a few days later, Dad and Anton sat in front of the large coffee table drinking martinis and smoking cigarettes with Terrance and Cliff, full of animated remarks about the attire and the endless formal procedures.

"Ah, can you get a load of that Emmanuel gown…"

"The train's too long."

"For chrissakes."

I daydreamed about being made into a princess this way. I replaced Prince Charles with Todd Tharpe. It seemed that this kissing thing came easy for most, with kisses occurring on balconies, out on the streets and in movie theaters. Why did I run away? I vowed never to tell anyone how I ran away from Todd Tharpe on the day he kissed me.

We spent several evenings at Terrance and Cliff's apartment that summer, the four of them drinking booze and smoking cigarettes and laughing together until very late.

Terrance worked at a women's clothing boutique. Dad arranged to have—what he kept calling—a *fitting* for me right at Terrance and Cliff's apartment.

"It's a fashion show," Dad explained, "where you get to model clothes for us."

"I'll be *borrowing* the clothes for the evening," Terrance had said with one eyebrow raised, like he was putting one over on someone.

"You need a nice blouse," Dad kept saying that summer.

I did not like the word blouse for a top. I could see an old lady wearing a blouse with her *slacks*. But, none-the-less, a fitting sounded very movie star-ish and Royal Wedding-ish, so I was up for the event.

"Come, come, come!" Terrance cheered when I walked in the door of his apartment the evening of the big fitting, immediately ushering me down the hall. "In the bedroom, in the bedroom."

He walked behind me, steering me by my shoulders, Dad following us. "Look at this," Dad marveled, running his fingers through the display of fancy shirts. The shirts—or *blouses*—were on hangers, lined up and facing outwards in the large bedroom closet, the tags still on.

"This is my favorite for you," Terrance said, grabbing one with a beige print and shiny buttons and puffy-looking shoulders. He held it up against my front, looking contemplative at my chest and then my face. I didn't really like it.

"Go ahead and model these for us, princess, I can't wait," Dad said, turning his back and leaving the room with Terrance.

Alone in that bedroom, I sifted through the various blouses, laying them on the bed to get a better look at each one. I was very disappointed to find that each had large, bulky shoulder pads. I hated that shoulder pads were so *in*—I thought they resembled either some kind of military get-up or me trying to be more than I was.

I tried on the first puffy top and attempted to adjust the massive pads, looking at myself in the dresser mirror. I thought I looked simply ridiculous. What was worse, I had short shorts underneath.

I made my way slowly and sheepishly down the hall to the four of them. From the look on my father's face, he agreed that I looked a bit disproportioned in clothing size and in age.

"Ten-hut!" I saluted. Dad and Anton laughed. Terrance jumped up and went about the business of fluffing and adjusting those shoulder pads and straightening the buttons. I hoped this trouble was not making my father want to purchase the blouse.

I did enjoy the catwalk fashion show and, by the third garment, I was strutting with my chin in the air. I can only imagine what torture this charade was for Benny, who sat on the floor about a foot from the television.

"Oh, now we're getting somewhere," Dad said with his martini held high.

"She's gorgeous, Neil, simply gorgeous," Cliff complimented.

The four of them were taking votes over the tops for much of that evening. I don't even recall if we brought one home or not.

At the next visit to Terrance and Cliff's apartment, somewhere around their third martini, Dad got the idea of a white Russian for me like a light bulb had gone off in his head.

"You're gonna love this, princess, it's got cream and sweet coffee flavored liqueur."

I loved the white Russian so much that I drank down at least three of them that night, making my own after Dad showed me how to make the first one.

I did one *Chorus Line* routine after the other in my drunken state. I kicked my legs in the air around their living room, nearly missing the lamps and ceramic doohickeys on the side tables.

"Positively pre-teen," Dad chided to his friends, shaking his head and fanning his hand my way with a cigarette between his fingers.

During this summer of 1981, my theatrics—once adored by my father—were dismissed as what he referred to as "pre-teen." Looking back on it, his references to my being "positively pre-teen" were really quite humorous. Not at the time. I was infuriated when Dad announced his theory on my upcoming *brain tumor*.

Dad had warned me for two years already that the inevitable brain tumor was coming. He said it would start just barely sprouting at age twelve and would have completely taken hold by thirteen. Dad listed various afflictions related to the brain tumor. He said I would probably get what he called "boat feet," as well as blackheads and pimples. Dad said not to worry, that all this would magically disappear at eighteen, waving his hand in the air in a nonchalant way, as if to say *Ah, don't pay any attention.*

He loved to bring up my apparent neoplasm in front of his friends, saying, "Oh my gawd, she may be pre-teen today, but it'll be that brain tumor of hers tomorrow." This is exactly what he said when I took to kicking and singing Broadway style with my white Russians that evening. This got the small crowd laughing in a way that made my father the center of attention as the famous dry humored comedian.

"I'm not getting a brain tumor!" I argued with my arms crossed, feeling my face go hot.

"Like hell you're not, look at you *now.*"

I stormed out of the living room with a large lump in my throat. I felt betrayed by Dad and stubbornly imagined never talking to him again. I was misunderstood; I would never be understood again. I lay on the guest bed staring at the ceiling, thinking about the ways that my father did not understand me—he didn't understand how I wanted to dress or how I said things. He couldn't understand that I was inevitably part Katherine. The room was spinning as I counted the ways that Dad didn't *get me.* What happened to Dad? Why had everything changing? I started to drift off. That's when I heard the jokes going on out in the living room.

"How do you know when a woman's been in the room?" Dad said in his cocky way like he had a good one to make everyone laugh.

"How?"

"By the slug tracks on the carpet."

That really stuck in my mind.

Trashy Makeup

We took the train to Aunt Annette's beautiful Connecticut home three or four times that summer--for the weekend and even once for a whole week. I made a friend during our first visit to Aunt Annette's. I tried to be with Priscilla every chance I got during the visits, which wasn't too hard because she lived just one or two houses down the windy country road. Benny had befriended Priscilla's little brother Toby, so Benny spent a lot of time at

It seemed to me that Priscilla had everything. Her giant immaculate home included an actual "movie room" with huge leather couches and the kind of television that---in the 80s--was a rare commodity only the rich could afford. This TV was about five feet across and went with a projector that cast lights in primary colors. Just like at the movies, I disrupted the picture if I walked in front of the TV, my legs illuminated in reds and blues.

Pricilla and her little brother Toby had a pool in their backyard and a very large screened porch padded with bright green Astroturf. Their mother—who did not work outside the home—liked to spend afternoon hours on the porch, sitting on a lounge chair, reading a book. Their father was some kind of Wall Street hotshot and commuted to New York City every day. Dad said that he was a millionaire.

Priscilla, Toby, Benny and I spent entire afternoons playing in the pool or drinking Tang while sitting on the white patio furniture. When we'd tire of the many outdoor activities, Pricilla led me up her carpeted stairs to her pink, frilly bedroom. Toby had every toy any eight-year-old boy would want, so Benny was happy as a clam.

Priscilla and I went to the mall in Greenwich once that summer. We strolled around from store to store, trying on miniskirts and stopping at the café court to have fries and Cokes with the money Dad gave me to spend. We spent at least an hour browsing through the cosmetics aisle in the drug store, talking about the boys we were going to *get* when we started to high school.

I had no idea where I would end up going to high school. Whenever I imagined high school, I had no reference of a place, only a made-up school courtyard in my mind. I adopted the school scene in the film *Grease* to go with my occasional high school fantasies. I imagined sitting on bleachers and watching sweaty boys in sports uniforms. I imagined sitting with a gang of girlfriends at a picnic table, pulling out sandwiches from our brown paper sacks, laughing and chirping about the upcoming dance. In all of my castle-in-the-sky daydreams of high school, I saw myself in pink lipstick and pretty blue eye shadow. Somehow, in these scenes, Mother and Tom had been demoted to a place so far from the front line—so much, that they are almost forgotten.

By the time that Priscilla and I wandered up to the cashier with our makeup selections, my entire left arm was covered in every shade of pink and red, purple and blue from my raid on the testers. We went straight for the mall restroom, where we excitedly peeled off the plastic wrappers. We applied our new cosmetics thick and carefully, watching one another's reflections in the large mirror.

"Is this good?" I asked her as I puckered my lips. She showed me how to blot the tissue paper like a kiss to get just the right amount. We laughed at the prints of our lips on the tissue, and talked about how we wished we had boys to kiss.

"*I* had a boyfriend in California," I bragged about Todd Tharpe, "We were going together––he kissed me for a really long time and told me he loved me." I left out the part about me running away, and leaving him on the sidewalk.

I couldn't help but notice the looks we were getting from men as they walked passed while we waited in front of the mall for Aunt Annette to pick us up in her Saab. Men in cars turned their heads and craned their necks to catch a glimpse of us as they drove by. This sensation of being a commodity was becoming more and more familiar, as my raisin tits had turned into apricots.

Dad continued to complain that I ought to wear a bra, but I still felt that adding binding was only asking for more attention. Such inevitable bodily changes were leading me to places, like that examination table with foot pedals my mother had been strapped to, her privates spread out for all to see.

Dad was sitting in the passenger seat when Annette showed up in her Saab.

"Oh my gawd, the brain tumor has taken hold sooner than we thought," he taunted, jabbing my aunt with his elbow, which got her laughing.

"Shut up, Dad."

I shook my head and looked at Pricilla in ultimate embarrassment. I was already shamefully embarrassed by my father because Priscilla had commented about his earring that summer.

"Why does your dad have an earring?" she had asked one afternoon in her bedroom.

"I don't know, I guess he likes it."

"My dad says your dad is a homo and that Anton is his boyfriend."

"*What?*" I gasped, playing dumb. I pretended I didn't know what she was talking about, but I couldn't stop my face from going red. I couldn't breathe. It must have been the things I associated with Priscilla that made me so rotten with shame--it must have been her pool and her giant TV, and maybe even her tennis lessons.

"Anton is my uncle."

"Princess, hand your father that bag," Dad instructed from the front seat.

"Why?"

He was acting in a way that was new, a way that I couldn't sniff out, which made my palms feel sweaty.

"Just do as you're told."

"Oh my *God*," I said to Pricilla, rolling my eyes as I pushed the small brown bag into his shoulder. Dad slowly pulled out each cosmetic item for inspection.

"This is trash. Pure trash." He shook his head. "My daughter is *not* to wear trash, is that understood?"

"Dad, what are you talking about?"

I felt that Dad was switching personalities, that perhaps he was being someone he thought he ought to be. Back in California, I had grown accustomed to my mother's various faces; I had gotten better at adjusting to suit her tides. This new Dad seemed to correlate with my apricots and my pink lips and my thoughts of high school courtyards. I felt as though he was reeling me back into him, afraid I was slipping away.

"Let's get this clear. Drug store makeup is for tramps. There will be no cheap makeup in my presence. Cosmetics are bought at makeup counters from stores with class, thank you very much. I don't know what your mother does--I don't care."

"My mom doesn't wear makeup. She doesn't care what I do."

"I don't doubt that," he chuckled to Aunt Annette. She chuckled too, though I could tell that she thought he was being a bit harsh. Heck, her bathroom counter was loaded with God knows how many brands of makeup.

I stayed quiet in the backseat looking out the window for the rest of the way back to Aunt Annette's. I was envious of Pricilla, who held her little brown bag in her lap. My dad had confiscated mine. I thought terrible thoughts about my beloved father—that he was just jealous because he was a man and could not wear makeup himself. I thought about a framed photo that he and Anton kept in their living room, both of them dressed in elaborate flowing satin drag, with fake eyelashes and heavy foundation and bright red lipstick. What cosmetic brand were *they* wearing?

We each took a grocery bag into the kitchen when we got back to Aunt Annette's house. Dad held my little brown bag above the trashcan, my heart dropping.

"Sorry princess, trash is for trash and you're not trash."

With that, Dad dropped my new makeup right into the trashcan. I ran to the guest room where I cried over my lip-gloss and eye shadow, mad as hell to be giving in to the pangs of my growing brain tumor.

Dad made up for his purging of my trashy makeup. He took me straight to Macy's after our week in Connecticut, when we got back to New York.

"Princess, we're going to buy you some makeup with class," he declared, as we walked hand-in-hand off the subway, just the two of us. "You don't think I'd do something like throw away your god-awful tramp wear and not make up for it, do you?"

As we walked down the crowded street toward Macy's, Dad announced the dreaded, "Folks, my daughter is becoming a woman." Who was he talking to? I hated this line. I could swear that he was referring to those tiny hairs down there that had grown a bit darker and a bit more coarse through the year.

"*Of course* you want to wear makeup and look pretty," he said, not stopping his stride, "It's time for your first makeover, princess."

I loved Macy's. My feet tapped across the marble floor of the vast air-conditioned department store. It seemed that Macy's could make anyone pretty and clean and happy. I didn't doubt that my father could turn me into class, just like he was promising. He knew just where to go, waltzing up to the Clinique counter like a regular.

"My daughter is ready for her first makeup," he announced proudly to the young woman, who was adorned with drastic amounts of cosmetic caking herself.

"Oh, how fun!" she chirped cheerfully before scanning us back and forth for a second or two. I could only imagine that she was thinking *where's the mother?* before realizing that Dad was it.

Dad did most of the talking, as if he knew how to do the job better than this makeup extraordinaire.

"She'll need light pastels—soft pinks and powder blues because of her age."

"Definitely not a *lipstick*--too much, no. We'll go with a light gloss."

I sat on the stool in front of the mirror and closed my eyes while she brushed on various shades. I was thinking about Dad's entire bathroom shelf of *Clinique for Men*. I wondered if he underwent his own makeover to select those products, a snappy little makeup girl fussing over his complexion. I imagined that he would have loved such fawning.

When we were through, we walked away from that makeup counter proudly carrying a little white plastic bag that contained *high class* cosmetics—little opalescent light green cases that came with bona fide miniature brushes, and tiny mirrors on the inside of the lids.

"It may cost a fortune, princess, but it's what a girl's gotta do if she wants to have any class at all."

My father knew how to be a girl more than a girl knew how to be a girl.

Berkeley: Back at the Alternative School

Mother parked the Bug in the driveway next to Tom's Dodge van and cut the engine. The streetlight illuminated the house so much that the white paint was glowing. In all our airport pick-ups between New York and California, Benny and I were returning to a familiar house for the very first time. It would be our second year at the house with two front rooms.

"Home!" Mother announced with a sleepy smile.

I couldn't see the fog that night, but I could tell it was close. The chilly evening Bay Area breeze kissed my bare arms as I grabbed my bags out of the Bug. It was late August—there was a morsel of Berkeley summer left. I flashed to the thick muggy New York City heat––the *hotter than a motherfucker* heat. I was just there. How was this even the same planet?

I walked up the brick front steps and gladly pulled the thumb latch on the familiar heavy wooden door. *Home.* The smell was toast and the old large braided rug, Dr. Bronner's soap, and rosemary. This time, there was an unusual comfort and pleasure in returning to Mother's California. School was in California—friends and boys. And where was Dad and New York in my mind? It would be a few days in before it would hit me that I had hardly thought of Dad. I wasn't trying to push him out of my mind––he simply wasn't in it. I felt terrible guilt upon realizing this. I remembered when I once believed these thoughts might bring Dad an ill fate. That was gone, too.

I would be thirteen that coming winter. Not only had the importance of friends absolved the ache for Dad that was once overwhelming, friends were also rapidly encroaching on Mother's influence. She would soon no longer be the barometer for my state of ease. Friends could distract and consume and disappoint. My preteen forecast was in their hands.

I was happy to be returning to the alternative school that fall—no late registration, no switch-up, no being the new kid. I'd be joining the small group of girls I had left behind in June.

There were only a few of us girls in the school of thirty. There were no other mysterious cliques to stare at across a field or courtyard. We were it. Being apart from the mainstream school system, we had little idea of current trends other than kids we saw around town. We picked shirts and pants we all liked and sometimes wore matching outfits.

There were only a few boys at the school who passed as acceptable candidates for crushes. We wrote and then re-wrote formulas of lists—best pick boys, best homes to live in, best cars. We dreamed of having normal families and normal lives when we grew up—a husband, matching dishes and clean cars, jewelry and makeup.

We shared the commonality of having parents who—in their quest to be unlike their own parents—seemed to be in a constant state of adolescence. Our parents had emerged from the sixties and seventies still deciding just who they were going to be and what they were going to believe in. Having these evolving parents in common, we kids at the alternative school banded together like a troop of banshees. Over the next two years, we would form some very strong bonds. We were merging into our own adolescence in the shadow of all of our young-hearted parents. I think that our parents meant well in their hearts, they just didn't realize that sometimes they were driving with no headlights.

Benny would be graduating into double digits that year. He was very quiet and in his head a lot of the time, loosing himself in Space Invaders and Pac-Man at an arcade up the street from the alternative school called Silver Ball Gardens. At home, he quietly focused on Dungeons and Dragons.

Benny had begun running off in the middle of the school day. He would suddenly just disappear, the teachers fretfully walking room to room, saying, "Ben is missing again." It seemed my little brother just got the notion to take off on foot at any old time of day. Jeff was one of the teachers at the alternative school, and he had a real knack for finding Benny, and Benny really seemed to trust him. Sometimes Jeff would find Benny on Telegraph Avenue, some blocks from the school, or he'd find him on the church grounds next door. Occasionally, Benny headed all the way down Durant Avenue, toward the direction of our house, even though it would have taken him hours to get there on foot. Jeff always spent a good chunk of time talking to Benny when he caught up with him, calming him down in a way that no one else seemed to be able to do. I think Benny enjoyed Jeff's strong, compassionate male presence. Sometimes I wondered if he ran away partly to get Jeff's full attention.

Sometimes, Benny ran all the way to Mother's work at a childcare center off College Avenue before Jeff had a chance to find him. Mother would call the school to let them know he had shown up, and that she'd be keeping him the rest of the day. Benny desperately wanted his mother––that was obvious––and he wanted her *when* he wanted her and on his own terms.

Occasionally, the teachers caught Benny on his way out the door, which caused quite a commotion. This was when everyone got to see the flip side of the quiet and staid Benny. Just like at home, when Mother held him in a lock for a time-out, Benny hurled his body and fought like hell while the teachers held him against his will, thrashing all his extremities and calling out, "You fucker!" with his face all red. They'd put him in a room with a faculty member if they managed to contain him, shutting the door and calling Mother to come get him.

I was half-embarrassed and half-heartbroken when Benny acted this way. I knew that––aside from just plain wanting his mother––it was probably because of all the shit that was going down in our house. Ben's flip-outs seemed to be a physical manifestation of the chaos––he couldn't internalize it as well as I could. The funny thing was, he had always been the one with his arms crossed and his eyes glazed. I guessed he had his boiling point.

Aimee And Her Dad

Like most kids at the alternative school, my close friend Aimee's parents were divorced. In fact, I cannot recall one kid that went to that school whose parents were still together. Larry, Aimee's father, was very popular with all the kids and was always listening to 60s and 70s rock music. He was in his forties, with thinning, graying hair to his shoulders--stocky and not very tall--and always wearing tired T-shirts, and worn jeans with a big brass belt buckle. He went on all the school camping trips and donated his time to the school. Although she lived with her mother every other week, most of my memories involving Aimee are of being at Aimee's father's South Berkeley duplex.

A group of smiley people who called themselves *Rashneesh* lived in the unit below Aimee and her father. The Rashneesh people only wore red or orange, or variations of red and orange. This group had an immense amount of loud sex, which we would hear at any time of day. Sometimes, we'd hear the furniture smashing around in sync with the moans and screams. Within the Rashneesh clan, no individual seemed to be attached to any one or the other. Instead, they were like one big couple, all ten or twelve of them. One day we would see these two holding hands in the yard, the next day it was one of those and a third.

Larry had a cabin in Cazadero. Whoever got to go to the cabin was considered the lucky one. Shortly after returning from New York that year, I got to go to the cabin not once, but *twice*. This certainly classified me as Aimee's best friend.

The first time to the cabin, we went for the weekend with Larry and his lover, Irene. Irene brought along her daughter, who was entering high school in just one year. This tall, blonde, soon-to-be fourteen year old sat at the round wooden table in the downstairs of the cabin, sharing joints with her mother and Larry.

Irene's daughter had just gotten her first period, a detail of glorifying high status. She showed us her boobs about a hundred times on that trip. At the river, she threw off her clothes and perched on a rock like some kind of celebrity, where she schooled us on the varying changes of vaginal secretions throughout the monthly cycle. It seemed odd to me that any young girl close to my age would be so much like my mother.

It was early fall and the tall grass was dry and sharp like pointy twigs the color of oat. It stung my knees as I walked through it to get to "the shitter," which was an outhouse on the hill next to the cabin––the name of it calling attention to what you were doing inside, everyone well aware of who was needing to go. Every time I made my way up the path, I felt exposed, as if I were waving a flag, yelling, "Here I am! I'm just walking my way through the thicket up this here hill to the shitter! I must have to shit real bad!" For this reason, each and every time I had to go––whether it was number one or number two, or both––I made the announcement, "I'm going to the shitter to pee."

"Don't you ever *shit*?" Larry finally asked without smiling, like he really wanted to know.

Aimee and I spied on her father with his lover that weekend. The two had grabbed up a blanket, some food and a bottle of wine before they headed down the hill beside the cabin. We sneakily kept a distance so they wouldn't catch us, dipping in and out from behind trees and shrubs, and trying not to snap branches as we walked slowly.

Finally, they chose an open grassy spot that overlooked a small cliff. The smell was of cracked, hot dirt and fennel, and the only sound was the breeze rattling the dry leaves in the trees. We watched from our hiding place as the two lay out a blanket and started to undress from the standing position. Next, Larry lay himself face down on the blanket--his hairy back exposed--his ass cheeks in the sun. His robust blonde, pillowy Irene spread her legs and squatted on top of him with her back to us, straddling his lower back.

This woman went right into a vigorous massaging routine, kneading his hairy back like bread dough. I imagined the two must have done this before, as they had not spoken a word before going into the act—they just went straight for it. It was interesting to see them this way, as Larry and Irene were not very affectionate with each other. I wondered whether she enjoyed what she was doing, as she seemed like Larry's servant. Even though I was only twelve, I got the feeling that she was more into him than he was into her.

Aimee fought back her giggles--her face bright red--with her hand over her mouth.

"Her ass--" she whispered.

"It's huge," I finished.

The size of this woman's rear seemed monstrous. She was a wide-hipped woman anyway, and her rump was enormously accentuated in that squatting position. Their picnic massage looked disgusting to me—his hairy back and her huge ass. *I don't ever want to be an adult doing this,* I thought.

"Let's get out of here," Aimee said under her breath, sounding disgusted.

I quietly and disappointedly left the scene, repulsed and interested at the same time. We didn't talk as we walked single file through the tall grass back to the cabin. What was it like to have a Dad that was into women? I was a little glad that mine was into men.

Doobie Burrito

One of the girls at the alternative school, who was more of a peripheral friend, had access to marijuana through her older brother.

"Do you want some of this?" she offered, opening her closet door and pulling back a few boxes to reveal the hidden trash bag.

"Sure, I guess."

I watched as she stuffed an empty brown paper grocery bag full of—what looked like—dried up, dead plants.

"Ouch!" she spat, drawing back her arm and rubbing a scratch.

"That's not pot," I said, thinking of Mother and Tom's pot that looked like Italian spices.

"This is how it came," she explained as she continued to load my bag.

The pot leaves were still on the branches—this was dried up *twigs* of pot. I then remembered Tom's pot plants and recognized the shape of the leaves.

I toted the brown bag of dried up pot twigs the five or six blocks home in broad daylight like I was carrying any old thing. The scratchy branches stuck out of the top and poked out of the sides of that paper bag, scratching up my leg.

Once I got home, I stashed it behind the bed sheet covering the crawl space in my basement bedroom. Over the next week or so, I'd pull it out, open it up and take a whiff, or pull out a branch or two to place on my bed for a look. Smoking it really hadn't occurred to me. I associated the smell of pot and everything that goes with it with what I didn't like about my mother and Tom and all of their friends.

Finally, one afternoon after school--when my friend Ivy was over--I decided to do something with my grocery bag of pot twigs. Ivy and I had gotten close that year. She was only eleven, but you'd never know it. She looked and acted much older, and was just as offbeat as me. In Ivy, it seemed that I had found my soul mate, the person who could read my thoughts and I hers. We were always up for making life interesting, so it only made sense that we would try to roll ourselves up a doobie in my basement bedroom one afternoon.

Mother and Tom rolled up their oregano-looking stuff in little rectangular pieces of paper, making homemade cigarettes they called joints. Sometimes they stuffed it into pipes. So I was wondering just what I was supposed to do with these twigs of pot. How would I make a joint with it?

I looked around for the joint rollers Mother and Tom used. The little individual papers—which they called "rolling papers"—were about as thin as tracing paper and came in a nifty small mini-cardboard cassette thingy with the name ZIG-ZAG on the front. I had watched them rolling joints with the ZIG-ZAG's––they looked like they were making origami creations. But I couldn't remain inconspicuous while looking for the rolling papers. We went for what I *did* have in my basement bedroom, and that happened to be red construction paper.

"How should we do it with this paper?" I asked Ivy with a piece of the red construction paper in my hands.

"Kind of like a burrito?" Ivy guessed, shrugging her shoulders with her bright blue eyes mischievous through the big strands of her straw-colored hair.

So I placed a piece of construction paper on my bed, and put a bunch of the little branches in the middle of it, snapping some in half to make room. I then wrapped up the whole shebang like a big red pot burrito.

We sat side-by-side on my platform bed with our legs dangling off the edge, with me holding the giant doobie and ivy holding the book of matches.

"Here we go," I announced nervously.

I finally put the rolled-up construction paper to my mouth. It took Ivy several attempts to strike the match, so the paper was getting soggy in between my lips, my teeth holding it in place. I inhaled when Ivy put the little flame to the end of the giant doobie. The next thing I knew, I was coughing like I might throw up and the red construction paper was aflame, and burning fast toward my hand, the seeds popping like popcorn. We jumped off the bed squealing and making a dash for the big basin sink beside the washing machine, tossing the giant doobie burrito right in. I ran the water full blast, quickly extinguishing the flames. Smoke hung in the air, smelling like burnt cardboard and that familiar skunk stench that I had come to hate so much.

"Do you feel funny?" Ivy asked.

I had forgotten about my toke in the midst of the inferno. I was wondering if I was stoned. I stood still for a minute and looked down at my shoes and then up my legs and held my arms out. Was I any different?

"I think so," I said. *Maybe* I was––I couldn't really tell.

Next, Mother was coming down the basement stairs. As physics go, the smoke had risen up into the house. For a second, I wanted to hide everything, frantically fanning the air with my hands. Ivy said "Oh shit" and looked worried. But I quickly realized Mother wouldn't be mad. If I were hiding, it was only because I didn't want her to think that I wanted to be like her.

"I smell marijuana––" Mother said like she was talking to herself, scanning the air.

She stopped halfway down the cement stairs, noticing the smoke hovering at the wooden planks above my bed. She scanned my bed—the stack of construction paper, the matches and the brown paper bag with pot twigs sticking out the top. She looked a little stunned. She didn't seem angry, she just looked like she hadn't expected this quite yet.

"Sorry--" I said, not wanting to look at her. I couldn't think of anything else to say.

"No, no, no...don't be sorry. You don't have to *hide* to do this. I'd rather you just smoke it out in the open."

The next thing I knew, Tom and Mother were having a heyday with that brown paper bag, marveling at the *score* I had made. Tom had himself a good laugh over Ivy's and my joint rolling technique--he just couldn't get over that I had tried to smoke the whole kit-and-kaboodle. I couldn't remember a time I had won him over so well.

That day, I earned the status of being privy to the little ZIG-ZAG papers. I had a little problem with applying too much saliva on the side of the paper when it was time to glue it together, but I got better with that over time.

Mother's Lessons

A small room at the school had been allocated for Mother's pottery class, which she taught in exchange for a large chunk of my brother's and my tuition. Benny was glued to her hip for the most part when Mother was teaching her class, regardless of where he was supposed to be at the time.

I liked the way Mother looked so industrious with clay smudges all over her jeans and T-shirt. She may have been working with a bunch of snot-nosed kids, but she sure took her pottery seriously. She said *any* creation was a work of art. Many of us kids took this fact to a profane level, creating elaborate giant penises and boobs. We created some realistic looking piles of dog shit, which we sneakily placed on the sidewalk. We got miles of amusement watching from the second floor as the UC Berkeley students stumbled out of the way to avoid the fake dog shit (or even better, watching them step right into it). But my mother seemed to not even notice--lost in her world of vases, bowls and animal shapes.

Mother also took it upon herself to make sure that all the alternative school faculty and student body got their fair share of wheatgrass. Rows of wheatgrass trays lay placed alongside a large window in the downstairs of the school. Around the time that Mother planted those trays, she did a little informational talk in front of all the kids and the teachers. Benny and I sat beside her and, as a demo, I took a big handful of mature grass and chewed it up in front of my classmates. I showed off to everyone how it's done—to chew and chew on the wheatgrass in order to extract all the healthy juice, and then spit out the matted, chewed up wad.

Mother and I shared a miracle that year—we got to be part of an actual birth. I had decided I wanted to deliver babies when I grew up, and so I did my science report on the birth process. When I presented my report in front of the school, I was careful never to say the dreaded word vagina, not even once. Instead, I said "birth canal," which was almost as embarrassing, but not quite.

Simone, the school bookkeeper was pregnant and due in December. I had so marveled at Simone's huge round pregnant belly. My mother approached her, asking if I might be present at her birth, and Simone graciously said yes. This was such a priceless gift from my mother. I did nothing but fantasize about the upcoming birth.

"Astrid!" Simone called from the doorway of the tiny school office shortly after Mother asked if I might be present at her birth, "You're going to be there for the big day! I'm so glad."

Simone was a big, warm earthy mother--the kind of person you just wanted to hug. She always had such a happy disposition, with her big dimples and matronly clothes. Would she be the same when she was pushing out a baby? Would she scream?

Simone invited me to one of her prenatal visits with her home midwife. I counted the days till I got to go. On the drive there, with her two-year-old in the back, she listened attentively as I talked about my plans to become a midwife when I grew up.

I sat next to Simone on a big pillow and soaked up everything at that prenatal visit. I was in heaven. I got to listen to the baby's heartbeat through a special stethoscope and feel Simone's bare belly with both my hands. The midwife told me what to expect at the birth and asked Simone to think up a job for me. Simone said I could massage her feet. This seemed like an enormous privilege, and I could not wait. The midwife sent me home with a couple books on pregnancy and birth. I read them front to back and stared at the amazing photographs.

I was at Ivy's house for an overnight in December, when I got the call from Mother around midnight that Simone was in labor. I paced outside the front door for what felt like an eternity, waiting for Mother to pick me up. The night sky was black that night, with only a few stars. I stood in the winter cold, warm from the stirring feeling that I was about to be part of something really big.

When Mother and I walked into Simone's house, she lay sprawled naked on a big bed right in the middle of her living room, her body covered with sweat. Her husband was kneeling beside her, with his face close to hers, stroking her hair. Even though I had heard about and read about the noises that laboring women make, I jumped back and drew my breath when the surge started a minute or two after we arrived. Simone's sound was low and guttural and long. No one in the room did anything different. It appeared that this was just a normal sound to make, just like the books said. I wondered for a minute whether I might be out of place, but when the surge was over, Simone tilted her head in my direction and gave a little smile and a wave. I was glad to have a designated job—I went right to it. I kneaded and rubbed her feet, looking up at her giant belly.

When the little head began to emerge, it was covered with black hair. There I was—observing the miracle of birth from a front row seat. Simone sounded like a wild cat--hissing and shrieking--as she stretched in a way that I couldn't imagine ever stretching. The midwife held the black-haired head steady, the little face purple and wet, while the shoulders came out. That's when Simone spat, "It stings!" and then the whole body slid out like a fish. The wet, slippery baby was placed on her belly, the umbilical cord thick and ropey. With that cord still attached to the inside of her, I heard Simone announce weakly, "Another boy." It was her third boy—a ten and-a-half pounder at that—and he was wailing like a little bleating lamb.

It was between three and four o'clock in the morning when Mother and I stepped into the Bug to make our way home after the birth. The night sky had gone from a starless black to a marvelous deep blue, with stars in the northern hemisphere. We were hungry, so we pulled into the only place that was open—a Jack-in-the-Box on San Pablo Avenue. We sat in the parking lot there with big sleepy smiles on our faces, steam rising from the hot delicious fries we were gobbling up. We were talking about the boy who had just come into the world. I thought of Mother saying she wanted to teach me "the inner secrets of being a woman" when she took me to her pelvic exam. This time, my mother had led me to the most magnificent place in "the inner secrets of being a woman." I knew I'd be forever grateful.

Mother was still going to graduate school. She did housecleaning jobs to make extra money. She specified "FOR WOMEN ONLY" on her flyers, which she posted all over town.

Benny and I often came along with her when she went to clean houses and offices. One woman, who lived in a fancy house in the hills, had more shoes for one person than I ever imagined possible. Mother lost that gig because apparently the woman could tell that I had been in her walk-in closet, trying on her hundreds of shoes, along with her designer clothes.

She cleaned for a therapy office that had a huge pillow room like Dan the therapist, where I presumed people did anger therapy. Benny and I had fun jumping around on the pillows and got carob chip cookies at Nabolom Bakery, which was right around the corner.

The housecleaning client I remember most of all was an older lady named Eva. Eva led me to believe that—while my mother had plenty shortcomings—lack of respect for older folks was *not* one of them.

Eva had many varieties of little birds that she kept in a big cage. I watched in amazement as she fed her birds with her own mouth by sticking a cracker in between her lips, and letting them pick away at it.

"Just watch! This old lady feeds her birds crackers right out of her mouth! All day long, she does it!" Mother had carried on in the Bug on the way to Eva's house. But honestly, I did not think this even a bit more odd than anything *Mother* ever did.

Eva was a survivor of the holocaust. She had lost every single member of her family in concentration camps.

"Eva is one of the most brave people I've ever met," Mother said one day at the orange table, stirring her tea, "she's been through hell, and yet all she wants is to go to The House of Pancakes."

Eva wanted us to join her at The House of Pancakes on College Avenue, her treat. We had never been there, so it sounded good to me. Benny was in hog heaven, inhaling his greasy little sausage links and his tall stack of perfect pancakes dripping with melted butter and warm syrup. He hardly came up for air. The meal was rare and delicious--no doubt about it--but I was most consumed by watching Mother talk to Eva. Eva did something to my mother that I so adored—she brought out such a sweet voice, such a kind and soft tone. Mother talked about flowers and the weather and the changing tone of the city. She was reformed and civil for Eva, because Eva deserved it. I loved that my mother saw this.

Pillowcase Dreams

Mother's radical political stance sort of matched her emotional fierceness. Her crocheted purse was covered with pins that said things like *Reagan for Shaw*, *No Nukes* and *Question Authority*.

I was swept up in the adult's drive to make a dent in the apparent jail bars of our society evidently run by fascists and liars and assholes––mostly because I wanted to be part of the rebellion of it. The truth was, I understood very little about all the fuss. Sometimes, I swore they were talking about the book *Watership Down*, when they referred to sheep and pigs in their conversations about war and power.

I associated "nuclear power" with large missiles, sent out to kill thousands of people––women and children––set off any second by one man (all he'd have to do is push a big red button to start the end of the world).

The grown-ups were still distraught over Three Mile Island and the Arms Race. They talked about "nuclear plants" in their heated discussions. For some time, I imagined a giant dangerous houseplant with devastating, poisonous leaves that could kill people with one touch. Once I had somewhat of an understanding of the term "nuclear plant," the houseplant image was replaced with the image of a huge, menacing machine that was surrounded by a tall chain-link fence, housing a terrible poison, with a big sign outside that said "KEEP OUT."

The grown-ups fretted about this thing coming from the plants called a *spill*, which was apparently also called a "nuclear disaster." A spill invoked images in my mind of a terribly hazardous substance spewing out of the huge machine they called a plant--it would leave the grounds as a consuming, slow and thick maple syrup-like material. I imagined people running down the streets, screaming, "Run for your lives! It's coming!" as the nuclear ooze crept toward them at a pace that would eventually overcome everything and everyone, as in the movie, *The Blob*. I lay in bed at night afraid that the spill might happen, and hoping that--if it did--it wouldn't reach our house.

    Mother and Tom and their friends hung out in the living room, ranting this and that about the injustices of the world; about the potential for nuclear spills, and about how they wanted to shut down the nuclear plants. Sometimes, they hung out on the front lawn or in the backyard, *The Rolling Stones* and the smell of pot streaming through the air. The consumption of rolled up doobies was all part of the deal, as was the snorting of the carefully cut cocaine (though Tom seemed to do this behind closed doors at this point, where I couldn't see).

    Mother went to plenty protests--as she always had--toting me and my brother along from time to time. One such a protest that year involved bringing pillowcases to Lawrence Livermore Laboratory.

    The protest was to start at the crack of dawn, just as the sun was rising. I had been excited about the adventure in making a stance at such an hour--an added sacrifice. What dedication this would show!

    The night before the demonstration, Mother had handed me a white pillowcase and a fat black permanent pen.

    "You need to write a dream on this for the demonstration, honey," she instructed.

    She explained that people from all over would be writing dreams on pillowcases to display at the lab the following day. I don't recall an explanation as to *why* we were writing on pillowcases--I think she assumed I would get it. I went along with the project, proudly envisioning my pillowcase as a testament of my commitment to *the cause*. I associated "power" with a large mass of people all doing the same thing, so I felt solidarity in writing on linen just like the other protestors.

I sat at the breakfast nook table and carefully wrote out my most memorable dream with the extra large stinky black Sharpie. It was tricky, because the ink wicked, making the letters run together--I was worried my dream would be illegible. My dream was so lengthy; it took up one whole side of the pillowcase.

I was only five years old at the time I had the dream, but I had always remembered it. It started with the little Carle Place house in New York, with chunks of the sky started falling down and landing in the backyard, each piece covered with fresh green grass and bright, colorful flowers. I was both frightened and enchanted as I watched Dad out the kitchen window--he had run outside to dance amongst the fallen sky, picking flowers for a bouquet. Next in the dream, I continued to watch from the window as giant dinosaurs entered our yard. My mother stepped outside and lovingly began to feed them handfuls of grass from her hands. The dream then turned sour, with a great darkness falling, and people running for their lives. Benny--then two--had gone missing and we were frantically searching for him in the old clunker. We finally found him along the roadside, running in his P.J.'s. Mother pulled him into the car while it was still moving. The dream ended there, with the four of us speeding off together, the falling sky crashing behind us.

I wondered what the other protesters would think of my dream and whether or not they might consider it to be a voice against nuclear power. Mother frequently talked in metaphors, and searched for symbolic meanings. I thought of how she always offered her interpretations of my dreams, when we sat together at the breakfast nook table in the morning while she sipped her Peet's coffee with milk and honey.

"What do you think that means?" she sometimes asked, instead of giving her own ideas, and I'd try to interpret my dream myself.

"It's actually more beneficial for *you* to figure out your own dreams. Only you know the true meaning."

I imagined that perhaps the dream I etched onto my pillowcase might be viewed as a far out image of the world changing or ending.

I was not too thrilled with the reality of the crack-of-dawn protest, when I woke to my mother coming down the basement stairs and turning on the switch to the glaring hanging light bulb at 5:30 a.m.

"Good morning, Astrid," she said a little too perky and cheerful, before she continued in a sing-song voice, "We're going to the demonstration, remember? We need to get there early."

Forget it then, I thought, groaning.

"Come on, we'll eat in the car," she nudged as she threw some clothes on top of me.

I squinted one eye open and groggily looked her up and down. She was ready to go and in one of her favorite outfits––her faded Levi jeans rolled up to just below the knee, her orange and red stripped knee-high socks with her old blue running shoes, and wearing her embroidered shirt with a sweater hanging off her shoulders. Her hair was in curly wet ringlets, filling the basement with the lavender and coconut scent of the Berkeley Co-op all-natural conditioner.

Yawning, I sat up in bed and fumbled for the clothes Mother had tossed my way, as she headed back up the stairs.

"Let's go!" she sang out as she turned the corner to enter the kitchen.

I schlepped up the basement stairs after getting dressed, feeling the familiar uneasy sense of uncertainty in being a soldier in my mother's court. What would today bring?

The sun had just barely come up when we arrived at Lawrence Livermore Laboratory in the Bug. There were many, many people sprawled out in front of the fence that surrounded the lab. They were coming in vanfuls and busloads, carrying their pillowcases in their hands. Some appeared to have camped overnight, sitting on blankets with sleeping bags and pillows. Small groups of people had made little congregations for themselves with musical instruments, backpacks, jugs of water and food. Some were singing and playing guitar. Folks spilled out from patches of grass right onto the concrete, all facing the tall chain-link fence already laden with many pillowcases. It seemed--in my estimation--that there were hundreds of pillowcases already up. I stood for a minute by the Bug in the parking lot, staring at the fence. I could see that some pillowcases shown only a few words or a sentence, while others were very elaborate, with colorful paintings and many statements.
     We gathered our blanket and our backpacks full of food and art supplies, and headed to the grass to find a spot. Benny was going along with it, and had brought his own pillowcase--adorned with an elaborate drawing in black Sharpie ink.
     "Let's do it! Let's get these up there," Mother cheered as we claimed our spot on the grass.
     She was in one of her favorite roles as The Zealot. It seemed that I just shriveled up into some puny, tight-assed sidekick when Mother took on this level of manic defiance and dedication. Her upping the anti brought on an obligatory leveling in me, as if it was up to me to turn her volume down for everyone's sake. The protest at Laurence Livermore Lab being no different than any other time that my mother was unabashed in her passion, I was clucking calls such as "Slow down," "Don't get so excited" or "Just be calm, please…"
     I had been pretty proud of my pillowcase, but for some reason--upon our arrival to the lab--I tucked it into the crook of my arm. It suddenly felt far too personal,

and I was really wanting to get rid of it. I was sure that every individual was wondering just *what* was written on my pillowcase, and whether or not it was good enough for the fence.

Benny had eagerly joined Mother to make a dash for the chain link-fence, obviously excited to apply his pillowcase. But I slowly plodded some distance behind our vigilante mother--through the grass, and weaving in and out of protesters--until I finally stood alongside her and Benny, in front of the hundreds of posted dreams flapping in the wind. Benny didn't even search for a spot--he immediately took the clothespins Mother gave him, and fastened his pillowcase where the fence met the ground, partially obstructing someone else's pillowcase.

Mother was childlike in her obvious glee over choosing the perfect vacant spot on the fence. She chose a spot way up high--almost too high for her to reach. She stood on tippy-toes with her pillowcase in one hand--wooden clothespins in between her teeth--trying over and over to slip a foot in the fence to get some leverage. Finally, she managed to attach her pillowcase, and then stepped back a few feet with her arms at her sides, looking so happy and proud in her rolled-up jeans.

I felt as though elbowing a space for my graffitied linen was just about equivalent to making a speech in front of a crowd. Mother looked over at me and rolled her eyes.

"Come on!" she coaxed, smiling and touching my shoulder, "What are you waiting for?"

I fought back as she went to grab my pillowcase out of my arm, desperately clutching it to my chest.

"Give me a break," she scoffed as she found me a spot on the fence. "This will do, come on honey, your pillowcase it so great."

I knelt down to apply my dream to the fence, close to Benny's. I could swear there was one of those giant bright spotlights beaming down on me. Mother there, still smiling with her head cocked, immersed in reading the various dreams. I quickly stepped back, and began to read some of the others myself.

"I dream of living in a world with no war"
"I dream of living in a world of harmony"
"I dream of abolishing hate"

To my horror, I realized that my pillowcase was all wrong. Not a one pillowcase with a dream in the literal sense of the word *dream*. My heart sank and my stomach went into my throat. I pictured Martin Luther King at his podium, his fist in the air, professing, "I have a dream..." How could I have been so stupid? How did I miss the obvious? I looked at my mother sideways there, trying to see if she had caught on to the fact that my pillowcase was different than everybody else's. Her face was unruffled and beaming as ever. It was obvious that––to Mother––my dream was just fine and perfect.

Mother was as lovely as could be, standing in the early morning sun beside the pillowcase covered chain-link fence in front of Laurence Livermore Lab. She was happy as can be about our dreams. She didn't seem to care how my dream compared to the others––this probably didn't even cross her mind––she was just glad to be there with us, dreaming big about taking a stand.

Feathered

It was an odd time, being part adolescent and part child. My boobs hurt and I lay awake in my bed thinking about boys. I didn't want my mother to hug me or make mention of my bodily changes, yet I wanted her mothering so badly in an infantile way. How could I have *both*?

For as long as I could remember, Dad presented my entrance into adolescence like a Hollywood movie. I would be playing a part, like Kristy McNichol or Tatum O'Neal in *Little Darlings*, which I had watched with Dad in

New York. I imagined dim lights and glittery disco balls; wearing revealing outfits while animated young men tried to jump my bones and beckoned me to do the nasty.

The dawning of adolescence was nothing like Dad had depicted. I spent long hours alone in my room listening to my *Tattoo You* record. I rolled joints with Zig-Zags and played AC/DC.

I had just turned thirteen when I started going with Gabe, a freshman at a private high school, who had attended my school the previous year. Gabe was nothing like Randy in *Little Darlings*—he was what we called a "rocker." He was pimply and skinny with long and stringy greasy hair. I only liked him because he liked me, and because he was in high school. I decided it was my new haircut that made Gabe like me.

Mother picked me up from school one day in February, for a special date to celebrate my first ever period, which had finally arrived that week. We went out to lunch and then she took me for a haircut at the Supercuts on University Avenue.

"I want it feathered," I told the hairdresser.

I dreamed of having fine, straight, feathered hair that wisped to the sides perfectly. It was the *in* style of the early eighties. And I—for the life of me—could not get my hair to do it. From the doubtful, pondering looks of the blonde hairdresser, it seemed that she thought she might not be able to do it, either.

Just like Dad predicted when he carried on about my upcoming brain tumor, my first period seemed to bring on a bunch of other firsts—pimples, sweaty armpits, and widening hips. But, worst of all, my hair had gone from straight, shiny, and manageable to full and curly and almost as wild as my mother's. I hated it.

"You've got a lot of curl in your hair, sweetheart, but we'll give it a try," the hairdresser said cheerfully (who, incidentally, had perfectly feathered hair herself). I prayed silently for my hair to feather.

Amazingly, she pulled the curl right out of my hair after she created layers around my face. With a blow dryer and a brush, she worked those layers into the chic feathering flips that I so longed for.

"Close your eyes and hold your nose," she instructed before she sealed the look with a seemingly magic wand—a giant can of hairspray. I didn't even look like me when she was finished.

It was the end of the lunch hour when Mother brought me back to school. I was glad I had chosen to wear my favorite pants that day—a pair of rose pink corduroys from JCPenny. Gabe, who had come to the school for a visit, was leaning against the railing on the front stoop. His jaw visibly dropped when I walked up the steps. *Don't I look like Farrah Faucet* was what I was thinking, and I must have walked that way, too.

Gabe turned his long and lanky body to block me at the top of the steps so I couldn't pass him.

"You look so much better," he said, continuing to block the top of the stoop like he was waiting for a password. Was this a compliment? Next, he was asking me to go see *The Hobbit* with him and a group of his high school friends, along with a few kids from my school.

I really tried to have a crush on Gabe. Not only was he skinny as a rail (you could see the bones of his shoulder blades and spine through his T-shirt), he had too many pimples and his little mustache was weird and his long fly-away hair was kind of grungy. But we both loved AC/DC, and the other kids thought he was cool, and I liked the way he could play "Smoke on the Water" and "Stairway to Heaven" on his guitar. So, I thought it was okay when he went to hold my hand during *The Hobbit*. I kept thinking that, if I hadn't gotten my hair feathered that day, I wouldn't be sitting there in the movie theater right then.

A group of us took the bus to Gabe's house after the movie. He led us down a dark stairway to a moldy-smelling basement and turned on the light that was hanging from the ceiling. I wrapped my arms tightly across my front, feeling the damp chill of the basement that had been converted to a recreation area with a dartboard and a pool table. *Now this is what normal people do with their basements.*

Gabe thumbed through a stack of records on the floor and pulled out his *Back in Black* album and put it on the record player, turning up the volume almost to max.

"Check it out!" he yelled over the music as he reached in back of a shelf and pulled out a bottle of Jack Daniels. Everyone made hooting sounds. We all formed a semi-circle on the carpeted floor and passed the Jack Daniels around, taking quick swigs out of the bottle while we listened to the music.

The alcohol stung my throat pretty badly going down, so I tried to mime taking big gulps so no one would notice the tiny sips I was actually taking. This booze wasn't buffered with cream or soda water or cassis like the booze in New York. This straight stuff was like fire, and caused that warm tingling sensation to go right to my head fast.

Gabe held his guitar in his lap and played along with "You Shook Me All Night Long," his long hair covering his face entirely. Us girls sat in a line and I suddenly found humor in the fact that we were all wearing the same exact Nike sneakers. If we said anything, it must have not been very important, and it would have been yelled over the music. I don't remember any dialogue that night.

I let a week go by before I reluctantly washed my hair. I had struggled to keep the feathers fluttering, but they were curling up disobediently and going every which way but the way that I wanted them to go. After that first wash, it was all over. I stood in front of the mirror with my hairbrush and my blow dryer forever trying to get those sides to go into flips like that sassy blonde Supercuts hairdresser had been able to do. It was impossible. I actually *cried* over my hated curly hair. *No guy will ever want me and my untamed, frizzy doggone hair.* I cursed it a hundred times.

But Gabe still took interest in me. I had some friends over to my house one Saturday night, and he came along. In the back yard, he pulled me into him and bent way down to give me a kiss. It was my second-ever kiss; I was glad that I didn't run away as I had with Todd Tharpe. I was only about four-foot-eleven, and he was close to six feet, so we were quite a match.

I put my arms around his back, like in the movies, when Gabe opened his mouth wide and put his lips over mine like a suckerfish. I didn't know how I was supposed to kiss back with my whole face invaded. The coarse hairs of his new, budding mustache poked at my upper lip. He did not use his tongue—for this I was relieved—but he opened and shut his mouth around mine over and over. A thick film of saliva formed around the edges of my mouth. Just as I was praying for it to end, I felt his retainer go loose and bump my tooth.

In the bathroom, I washed my lips and around the edges of my mouth with soap. I brushed my teeth. Mr. Perez flashed in my mind as I stared at my reflection in the mirror. His image was so real; I could almost smell the motor oil on his workpants. I was thirteen, but my mind's image of Mr. Perez brought me back to when I was nine and ten-years-old at the Victorian, so much that I had to look away from my reflection. Dad was there too—I could feel him egging me on, approving of my metamorphosis. He was snickering about the grungy, lanky Gabe and teasing me about the sloppy kisses. Sometimes, the mirror was just too crowded.

Breaking Up While Living Together

There was an awful amount of turmoil going on at home that year--issues were coming to a head with

Mother and Tom. One afternoon, the two had a terrible fight in broad daylight, right on College Avenue. Benny and I kept several feet behind them as they screamed and yelled like no one was watching.

"Why don't you get fucked?!" Tom spat, an insult that lined up with his other favorite, "Go fuck yourself." It seemed he was telling her to go fuck someone else, which was embarrassing on a monumental level when aimed at your mother in front of strangers on College Avenue.

The fighting went on anywhere and in any place. Tom's cocaine use was often the topic of fights, with Mother yelling, "Everything goes up your fucking nose!"

He was getting rather maniacal, with poetry readings to no audience at all hours of the night—with choppy words and sentences that didn't seem to go together.

His big red nose had about doubled in size and was always running like a faucet. We watched his odd tick-like gestures get worse and worse, like his incessant zipping and un-zipping of his hoodie. And he was thinking that people were stealing his things. One night, at about two o'clock in the morning, he burst into Benny's room, turning on the light. I had crept into Benny's room that night when I heard all the yelling, so I was already awake. But Tom woke Ben up, and forced us both out of bed. He was holding up an empty carton of ice cream, yelling about the little pigs that had gobbled it all up.

The day came when I'd had enough. Once again, their fighting had progressed to body slamming and to shouting out terrible low-blows. I ran up the basement stairs and into Benny's room, where I found him sitting on his bed with his arms wrapped around his knees.

"I hate them," he said.

They were outside his window, in front of the house in the mid-afternoon sun, with their yelling broadcasting out to all of the neighbors. It had been a Peet's Coffee Sunday morning. Strong, freshly brewed Peet's poured into a man whose been doing lines of cocaine and a woman who's eating nothing but wheatgrass could only equal one thing, and that was a nervous disaster.

I looked at my little brother and felt a fire that I hadn't felt before. For the first time, I was ready to stand up to them.

"This is it, Ben. We can't take this anymore, we *have* to leave."

He looked up at me like I was crazy, like I was talking just like our mother.

"I have enough money to get us on the bus. Grab a couple things, we're going."

"Maybe I don't want to go." Benny was looking like he might cry.

"Then you'd be left alone. You can't be alone with *them*, Ben," I swung my arm toward the window, "you don't want to be stuck here. Come on, you're coming with me to Aimee's. They have an Atari."

I was back in Benny's room in just a few minutes to grab him after I got my backpack and a few dollars. He was pale and angry, dragging his backpack. My heart was racing as we went through the kitchen and the hall to the front door. The pent-up explosion was about to unleash—my whole body was shaking.

We walked through the front door and stood on the front stoop with the bright sunlight in our eyes. The two of them were screaming into the neighborhood. Tom had gotten into his van––the motor running––and Mother was standing by the driver's side door, threatening that he might as well never come back if he drives away, and he's calling her a fucking whore. For a second, I looked over at Betty and Errol's house, and had a flash in my mind of going to their house and into Betty's pantry to pick out a treat. *It's too late for all that*, I thought. I left Benny on the stoop and ran down the steps, flying right at them.

"I am so sick of your fighting!" I yelled, "I don't want my brother to be around this anymore! We can't live like this--we are moving out until it stops!" My whole body trembled; I thought I might fall over. I know I said more to them, but the memory of my speech beyond that is a blur. I was unleashed, uncensored, set free and unforgiving.

Mother and Tom were completely silenced for a moment or two, as they stared at me absolutely jaw-slacked. Suddenly, they were a united front.

"You think your *own* fighting isn't bad for Benny?" Tom argued from his van.

"Yeah, I don't think you have the right to say that, Astrid," Mother added.

"*You're* the adults!" I yelled back at them, something that I had wanted to say to those two for so long. "You're not supposed to act like this. We're going to Aimee's."

With this, I felt a pang of regret, as I had wanted to torture my mother by *not* telling her where we were going. I turned around then to motion to Benny *let's go* and saw that he had started to cry silently. I wished so much in that instant that his life was different, that he didn't have to put up with this. *He's only a child*, I kept thinking, unable to recall when was the last time *I* felt like a child.

We walked to the bus stop and Mother didn't run after us, and I didn't turn my head to check to see whether she was watching. I talked up a chatter about how this and that will be fun for Ben at Aimee's.

"Won't it be nice to not hear any yelling?" I said cheerfully.

But all Benny wanted was his room and his things, his bed and his yard. He didn't want things to change. I'm sure he certainly didn't want another female in his life saying, "Come on, let's get out of here." He wanted his mother--I mean, he *really* wanted his mother.

Benny stopped crying on the bus, halfway to Aimee's house. By the time we were walking through her front door, he had that stone-statue look on his face again, with his arms crossed in front of him, and I was showing him to the Atari.

I wondered how long we'd be at Aimee's, and I pictured days, weeks--even months. I felt like I might throw up. I lay on the green shag carpet in the front room, listening with Aimee to her new Clash *Combat Rock* record. I wanted to feel normal.

In only a few short hours, the telephone rang and it was for me. When I picked up the receiver, there was mother's hysterical hiccupping cry on the other end. I could hardly understand her.

"Please, please come home," she begged, "I promise I'll leave him. I'm sorry Astrid, I'm really sorry. I can't be here alone, I just *can't* be alone--"

How could I not fall for it? In less than an hour, our mother showed up at Aimee's front door to fetch us, her eyes all blood-shot and puffy. Benny's big move to Aimee's house had been nothing but a few hours of Atari after all.

Mother did keep her promise about leaving Tom. Over the next month, I wondered what was worse—the impending break up, or the miserable staying together? I lay awake at night pondering that one, as Tom sobbed out loud like a baby. I had never heard a grown man cry like that--and he did it over and over again. I never thought I would feel sorry for Tom, but I honestly did on those nights. I imagined how sad I'd be if *I* were losing Katherine forever. This thought even made me cry quietly to myself a few times when I heard his wailing.

The best it would get was when Tom took to singing The Rolling Stones song, "Miss You," seemingly just to get at our mother. Now *that*—though a bit creepy—I could manage. In fact, I found it kind of amusing to stop outside the bathroom door when he was showering, belting out the lyrics of that song. He sang it so passionately; I thought he sounded just like Mick Jagger. I especially liked it when he sang the part about bringing the Puerto Rican girls by around twelve. Mother looked at me outside the bathroom, rolling her eyes and saying, "It's not long, it's not long."

But if he wasn't wailing or singing "Miss You," then he was spewing out poetry at all hours of the night—poetry about her leaving or ruining his life or breaking his heart. I'd wake to rantings that went something like:

A dagger!
A dagger!
Right into my heart
Blasting
Blasting me apart
I'm dying!
Dying!
You're killing me now...

On and on, and so it went, with poor Mother begging, "*Please* stop, I can't take this anymore."

A few times, I'd hear her sobbing, too. Those were the nights she'd take him in her arms and console him and cry right along with him. I'd be afraid she would take him back, and we'd wake to the announcement that they were going to work it out. I recall creeping into Benny's bedroom one of those nights. He didn't budge.

"I know you're awake, you can't sleep through that," I said in the dark.

"Yeah, but I'm *trying* to sleep."

"Do you think they'll get back together?"

"Who fucking cares."

I sat on the edge of my brother's bed for a long time there, watching the streetlamp flicker on his hair. As always, I felt less anxious when Benny was right next to me. I imagined that--if I stayed awake--I could stop what I didn't want to happen.

We took off to New York that June with Mother's promise that Tom would be gone when we came back in August, and that we'd be in a new house. I was really proud of her for sticking to it--*really* proud. I could see that it was absolute misery to get through this business of living together while breaking up.

Like proof that it was actually happening, Tom's things were packed in boxes in his room. They would both be moving out of the house and I was sure as hell glad that we'd be away when the final leaving occurred.

Tom sat us down in the living room for a god awful chat the day before we left for New York. His talk was full of sentiments like "I know we never got along," and "I know I was hard on you," and "I know I've been difficult to live with," *blah, blah, blah*. Really, it was stuff that made me feel more guilty than anything, and I just wanted to get on that plane and fly away. And that's what we did.

Elmhurst, Queens: 1982

We returned to the Elmhurst apartment that summer of 1982. Dad was still with Anton and the two were as domestic as ever. Sadly, what I remember most about that summer was missing my friends something terrible and bargaining with Dad for just *one* more long distant minute, *please*. I knew that it hurt his feelings, but I just couldn't help it--I was thirteen.

"I have to say that I was surprised when I saw you step off the plane, after what your mother told me," Dad confessed in the kitchen while he was pouring us Pepsi's, only hours after we arrived.

"What did she say?" I gasped, shocked and curious about what my mother had to say about me.

"Well, actually, she told me you had gotten pretty fat. I was expecting a blimp. But you're not a blimp, princess." Dad kissed the top of my head.

I was mortified and furious. Along with my first period, I had put on a few extra pounds that year. In the midst of all that fighting with Tom, Mother had been trying to implement her diets on me. She said that rice cakes are a good thing to eat for lunch if you want to lose weight, and I'd open my brown bag to two rice cakes and an apple. If I got lunch money, it was only one or two dollars instead of three. I had starved at school. It seemed the starving was discipline, a means to change myself into someone I was supposed to be.

It was crushing to hear that Mother felt the need to warn Dad about the looks of me. That summer, I took to eating fruit smoothies while others ate solid food, and I came up with an exercise regime with goals in numbers of repetitions. I lost all the weight that summer.

This was the first summer I actually missed having a woman around. I blamed this on my stupid period. I had only had about three periods so far, but they had all been just dreadful. I thought I was dying the first time I felt the cramps. What was worse, I could not swallow whole pills for the life of me. Mother had crushed up the Tylenol and mixed it with yogurt, which tasted horrendous. But the hot water bottle was very nice. She had bought me a groovy book for teens called *Period*. It showed some exercises for when the cramps got bad, such as the pelvic tilt. So, it was no wonder that I missed my mother when my period came that summer.

I had planned a fun day at Jones Beach in New Jersey with a friend, Amelia, who was actually from the alternative school in Berkeley, but was visiting her grandparents in New York that summer.

Embarrassed, I confronted Dad with the unfortunate fact that I was on my period. How would I go to the beach in a swimsuit? I had hoped not to have to bring up my period with him at all (I had packed some Maxi pads so that I wouldn't have to ask Dad to buy some for me).

That February, Mother had written him to say that I had started menstruating for the first time. He called me on the phone and—in his dramatic, weepy voice—he declared the dreaded, "You're a woman now."

"Just wear a tampon, princess," Dad said about the beach dilemma.

I sheepishly explained that I had only worn a pad up to that point. So, Dad took me to the drugstore down the street to buy tampons. We had always walked hand-in-hand or with my finger in his belt loop—now we walked apart and separate, me with my arms crossed.

"We'll get the smallest kind they have," he said. Now, *that* was reassuring.

When we got back to the apartment, I went to the bathroom with the tampons and locked the door. I had remembered the diagrams in my *Period* book that illustrated how to insert those suckers. I hoped it would go easy.

"Is everything okay in there?" Dad asked quietly, gently knocking on the door after I was in the bathroom for at least twenty minutes.

No, it wasn't okay. I had been trying to put that doggone thing in me every which way and it would not go. It hurt too bad. I couldn't bear to tell Dad.

"It's okay," I said sheepishly.

"Are you sure?"

"Dad, go away!"

I sat on the toilet staring at the wall, wondering how come all these girls wore tampons and I couldn't get one in? Even poor Aimee used tampons, having been cursed with her period at age nine.

I finally stepped out of the bathroom, heading straight for mine and Benny's room, where I threw Dad's *Evita!* record on the turntable. I had coped it from the living room a few days before, because I so enjoyed the therapeutic effect of facing the window and singing my heart out to "Don't Cry For Me Argentina."

An hour or so later, Dad knocked on my bedroom door. I took the needle off the record and stared at the wall. He stepped into the room and closed the door behind him.

"I know you want to go to the beach. Let's go get you some lubricant to make it easier to insert those tampons," he said calmly.

We were walking to the little mom-and-pop drugstore again, and I hadn't even dared to ask what *lubricant* was, though I had a good idea. I walked about five feet behind Dad at the store, as he scanned the feminine product aisle, the diaper aisle, the medication aisle, until something utterly mortifying happened.

"Excuse me?" Dad was leaning over the counter to get the pharmacist's attention.

"My daughter is having trouble inserting a tampon," he said in a low voice, but I knew everyone could hear him.

"Can you tell me where to find some kind of lubricant for this?"

My ears rang. I felt my pulse pounding in my cheeks. I watched the pharmacist hand Dad a tube of KY jelly. I stayed in the middle of the aisle in front of the pharmacy booth while Dad paid. I thought my feet might not work when we went to leave. But the lubricant did work––a little.

I had a harrowing day at Jones Beach. The cramps and heavy bleeding hit so hard, I had to go to the medic station. Our beach day was cut short and Amelia's embarrassed, staid grandfather dropped me off in Elmhurst. Dad crushed me up some Pamperin in the kitchen right away. Next, he called up my Aunt Annette.

"Please. *Do* talk to your Aunt," Dad said as he dramatically handed me the phone receiver, extended his arm in my direction while looking at the floor.

After a good talk with Aunt Annette, I went to my bed and slept and slept and slept. I never thought I'd see the day when Dad admitted he wasn't woman enough to handle me. When I woke up, Dad had arranged for a visit out to Connecticut to see Aunt Annette because he thought I needed a woman around. Anton wasn't able to join us because he had to work.

"It's that brain tumor of yours, it's worse than I thought. Maybe your Aunt Annette can do something to help you."

Upon arrival, my lovely, cosmetic-filled bathroom, hair-in-rollers, blouse-wearing Aunt Annette took me to Macy's straight away. After hours of shopping, she took me to the Macy's restaurant. She went through a round of menstrual confessions like she was starring in an after-school special. But it felt good to talk to someone who understood the vast inconveniences of being female.
 We went to the Greek diner down the road from Aunt Annette's house because she had a big crush on a waiter there. That summer it was Greek Waiter this and Greek Waiter that. Dad had egged her on to ask him for a date.
 "Come on, would you get off your ass already and say something, for chrissakes?" Dad groaned.
 Benny and I sat listening in the back of the Saab as they planned out their crusade on The Greek Waiter.
 "He sure is one hot motherfucker," Dad cooed slowly, in the drawl that he put on when talking about anyone *hot*. "Hot motherfucker" was a big compliment, according to Dad.
 "Neil, *come on*," our aunt said laughing, slapping his leg.
 "You just have to say it like this," he said slinking down in the seat and spreading his legs while pushing up his imaginary tits with his hands, "Hey hot piece of ass...yes you, I'm talkin' to youuu. You want to take me home?"
 "Really, just like that, huh? *That* oughta go over just great," she giggled, shaking her head.
 "Do it! Do it! Do it!" I chanted from the back seat, grabbing her headrest.
 "I'm never gonna be able to do it *now*..." Aunt Annette complained.

"Here he comes, here he comes," Dad hushed with his head low to the table after we were seated.

I must have been blushing beet red when the poor sap took our order. I was sure that he knew what we were up to.

"How are you tonight?" Annette asked, her voice cracking. I looked at Benny with my cheeks puffed, trying to stop my laughter, as he kicked my shin under the table.

"Could you people be any *more* pubescent?" Dad snapped.

As we ate our burgers and Dad and Annette ate their Greek something-or-others, the invitation to The Greek Waiter was rehearsed and re-rehearsed. But every time she got close to doing it, Aunt Annette would say, "Wait, wait, just one more glass of wine first."

"She has to get shit faced to do it," Dad said to Benny and I, rolling his eyes, pointing his thumb at our aunt. "Hell, *I'll* do it. He's probably a faggot anyway, I already told you that. Maybe he'll go out with me if you're too much of a chicken shit."

Dad had been going on earlier about the chance that the waiter preferred boys, right down to the percentage. He had counted up the evidence—no ring, Greek, a waiter, soft spoken...such characteristics certainly put him into the 50/50 likelihood of being gay.

"Oh shut up, Neil, you're making me lose my confidence."

"Yeah Dad, shut up. Not every guy is gay, you know," I chimed in.

"Hey, nobody asked you and your brain tumor," He snapped back.

Finally though, my sloppy, slurring aunt popped the question right in front of us all. After about four glasses of wine, she *did* ask the Greek waiter out that night.

"I was wondering if you might like to have lunch with me sometime."

I could tell that she was trying to steady her voice. I was mortified for her, keeping my eyes on the gold rim that lined the Formica table. But the waiter shot right back in his sexy accent without a single pause.

"I'd love to, why don't you give me your number?"

With that, he pulled a pen from his apron. *Bingo!* I thought, *touchdown!* We all sat perfectly still and quiet while Annette jotted down her number for the waiter. When his back was safely turned the other way, I put my hand up for a high-five. She was smiling ear-to-ear and wiping her forehead with the back of her hand saying, "Phew, I'm glad *that's* over." But Dad coolly sat back with his arms crossed saying, "Good girl, good girl, told ya." I think he was jealous.

The Date was arranged as a frolic to the river by Aunt Annette's house. All of us were coming.

"It's safer that way, I don't know this guy," Annette had said, which I found odd. I had assumed she'd *want* to be alone with him. I thought she surely must have wanted to do it with him.

When the Greek waiter arrived (I know he had a name, which I cannot recall), we all sat in Aunt Annette's solarium for drinks—them white wine, Cokes for us kids. I wanted to slap my father. He sat in the big sunken chair all slumped down in his tight designer jeans with his legs wide open, sipping his wine slowly and talking incessantly about food preparation. He monopolized the entire conversation, with recipe this and recipe that. It seemed that he thought he might still have a shot at the waiter.

The single file walk to the river was awkward. And seeing a tight Speedo on the guy who took our order at a restaurant was even more awkward. About an hour after splashing around in the swimming hole, Aunt Annette announced that she and The Greek Waiter were going to take a walk. I watched them disappear into the muggy briar.

It must have been about two hours later that Dad, Benny and I walked into Aunt Annette's house from the river carrying our wet towels. We were surprised to see her sitting by herself in her living room, sipping a glass of red wine.

"Where is he?" Dad shot, stopping in the hallway with his arms out, scanning the room.

"He tried to maul me," Aunt Annette said shakily with her face wide like she was in disbelief. I wondered what *to maul* meant, but then it seemed clear.

"He pushed me into going to the bedroom with him and got on top of me. I couldn't get him off––I was really freaked out."

I wondered whether my Aunt was a prude. Didn't she want him to maul her? Wasn't that the whole idea? Dad agreed.

"He was hot. Did you get a load of that tiny suit? umm, umm, umm...*Girl*, you must be crazy to turn that ass down."

"I don't do that on the first date," she turned her head away from us, "I told him no and he kept pushing––"

Aunt Annette sipped her wine. I could see that her hand was shaking; she was rattled. I imagined my poor, sweet aunt in her fancy bedroom trying to fend off the big Greek Speedo-laden waiter who was probably sporting a giant erection. I felt sorry for her. I remembered Mother telling me that Aunt Annette was a fragile person. I imagined that she had played with fire when she dared to ask The Greek Waiter for a date, and then let her guard down by being caught alone with him. She should have trusted her first instinct.

Unlike the other summers, Dad worked for most of this one. Anton worked, too. Benny and I stayed home alone all day, with strict orders to never open the door for anyone. I was a bit afraid of the big city, and hoped that no one would try to break in.

I anxiously awaited the sound of Dad's keys in the door every evening. He had showed me to the little mini bar by the dining room table, teaching me how to make a gin and tonic just the way he liked it--measuring the gin with a tiny glass he called a shot glass, and adding just the right amount of bubbly tonic and ice cubes (I once tried tasting the tonic, thinking it was a type of soda pop--boy, was I wrong). He also taught me how to make him a vodka martini, using the contraption he kept at the bar called a shaker. It was a little challenging learning how to use the shaker the right way, spilling the first few times. I tried to time it just right so that his martini had just the right amount of chill when he got home. I stood there proudly holding out his drink when he'd come through the door all sweaty from riding the subway in the muggy heat.

"Oh!" he'd gasp, putting down his keys on the little entryway table and undoing the first few buttons on his dress shirt, fanning his forehead, "my darling daughter, you *do* know what your father needs."

This end-of-the-day greeting always made me think of that Sheena Easton song "Morning Train," where she's singing about her "baby" working nine-to-five and taking the morning train, how she's waiting for him when he gets home. I'd actually sing that godforsaken song out loud while fixing Dad's drink.

Toward the end of that summer, I guiltily went snooping around Dad's things one afternoon while he was at work, just out of sheer boredom. I found something that day that I wished I hadn't.

Buried deep in one of his drawers were letters from my mother. I froze when I saw her handwriting on the envelopes. It was the last thing I expected to find. The postmarks were dated 1978 and 1979--this was when we were living in the old Victorian, and I was being molested. I took the envelopes in my hands and sat down on Dad and Anton's bed. I spread them out on top of the shiny gold satin comforter and stared at my dad's name written in Mother's handwriting. What was inside?

I opened the first letter and pensively began to read. Mother's handwriting was loose and—as usual—on art paper, rather than lined paper. To my astonishment, Mother was urging Dad to take me to live with him. "All she wants is you," she wrote. She wrote that her heart was breaking because he was the only one I wanted. "I feel so helpless," she confessed. She wrote of Mr. Perez and of how I wouldn't eat and wouldn't talk to anybody. She said in her letter that I cried at night, "I want my daddy."

After reading the first letter, I opened the second one with the hesitancy you get when you're doing something you know isn't good for you but you can't stop yourself. I bit hard on my lip as I read more of the same. She was talking about money, and how she needs child support and "Astrid needs you." She was worried I was sick. "Astrid has a lump on her forehead that won't go away."

I sat on the bed for the longest time--those letters loose on my lap--with tears running down my face. How could this be? If I didn't have the proof right there in my hands--if someone had *told* me about the letters, I wouldn't have believed them. My mother hadn't kept me from Dad all along; she had tried to give me to him. He had said no. I kept repeating it in my head—*He said no.*

I thought that Mother must have written one of the letters that evening at the Victorian when I cried at the table and wouldn't eat her soup. She had said, "Fine, I'll send you to your father's like you want," and went into her room, crying out loud like a baby.

I thought—when she made the bold move to write the letter—it must have felt like she was diving off of a cliff. She'd be giving away something precious that she loved so much. I remembered feeling guilty that night in 1979 because I was so, so happy that she was finally going to put me on the plane, even though it was not summer. I resented her so much when the subject was dropped and we did not go to New York. I assumed she hadn't followed through; I'd thought she had planned to keep us out of selfishness. It turned out that this was untrue. Mother had been *selfless*—she could have confessed that Dad wouldn't take me, but she kept that all to herself to spare breaking my heart. My mind was spinning.

I thought of Dad on the stoop in Sunnyside, the day he announced his intention to adopt a girl and a boy named Mercedes and Royce. He said Mother wouldn't give him more than summers, and that she had threatened to keep us from him altogether because he was gay. He had lied. I had the proof in my hands. Why did he ever bring up the adoption story? What did he hope to accomplish?

It was a good while that I stayed put in Dad's room that day, sitting on his and Anton's bed, staring out the window at the tops of the neighboring buildings. Those pages burned in my hands when I went to fold the letters back up and return them to the envelopes—I didn't even want to touch them. I wanted to get rid of the letters; I never wanted to see them again.

I never felt the same about my father after seeing Mother's letters. Why had he even kept them? I tried to force my brain to forget the letters, or to scramble the words like I had gotten them wrong. It was a betrayal that I could not forgive. I spent the last few weeks of that summer waiting for it to end.

I wanted to get back to California and start my last year before high school. There was no plan yet of where I'd go to high school. But I saw the courtyard in my mind.

A Hotel With Dad

I was twenty-five in September of 1994, when I spent a weekend at a hotel near the San Francisco airport with my dad and my two small children. Our plan was for me to drive the 300 miles to come see him. I had been so relieved when he made the hotel reservation, as it was so difficult—nearly impossible—to stay at his home in Diamond Heights with my two small children. I had misunderstood, and thought the reservation was just for me and my children.

"Princess, I went ahead and booked a hotel for your visit," he said on the phone. I tried to conceal my relief that I would have a separate place to stay, with the ability to take in doses of Sick Dad little bits at a time. I imagined driving back to the sanctity of my hotel room after brief visits.

However, when I showed up at his apartment, Dad's suitcase sat next to the door. I tried hard to act as though it was all part of the plan for me and my two young boys to stay crammed into a small hotel room with my father who was actively dying of AIDS. I felt my hands go clammy, my stomach drop. *What do I do? What do I do? What do I do?*

"And there she is, the princess of the hour—" he said as I came up the stairs toting my two young sons behind me.

"My fine, beautiful daughter. Here she is, people—"

He was leaning most of his weight on a cane, one of his hands gesturing in a modified bow. I could never quite tell if Dad was putting one over on me, or if he was being genuine when he gave me these kinds of greetings. His voice sounded theatrical and insincere, like some kind of announcer saying, "Step right up."

"Ahhhh, the children—" he said in a sing-song voice, painfully crouching down to get closer to eye level with my boys--ages four and almost two--who immediately withdrew behind my back, their hands grabbing the backs of my legs.

"Boys, say hello to Grandpa, come on," I nudged, feeling a little bad because *I* would have been scared of his cane and white hair too, if I were little.

"Are we going to the hotel boys? Aren't you excited?" Dad cooed in his exaggerated preschool teacher voice. "We're going to have so much fun, so *very* much fun."

My four-year-old tentatively nodded yes with a shy, polite smile, his eyes crossing as he timidly focused on Dad. My stomach was in knots. I felt my boys' little hands clutching me, their heads of blonde hair at each hip. Two days in one room with my sick father.

My knuckles were white as I clutched the steering wheel. I could feel Dad staring at me from the passenger seat. I felt as though he had planned to trick me into believing the hotel room was just for me and my boys. It seemed as though it was another one of Dad's *Gotchas*. I smiled through my humiliation, but I must have been pale.

"The way you let your things fall out of your suitcase makes you look like a bag lady. I refuse to walk into the lobby with that."

We were standing at the back of my car with the hatchback open and my boys were bouncing off the seats to get inside of the hotel. Dad hobbled away from me with his cane, leaving me to tidy up my luggage, which was unzipped with clothes spilling out of the sides. He turned around and said in my direction, "I'm getting a bellhop. Have that Puerto Rican thing zipped before I get back."

We rode the elevator up the three or four floors with the bellhop. I was wondering if he thought Dad was my husband. Dad had reserved us a suite with two rooms separated by a french door. There were two queen beds in the bedroom—one for him and one for me and my boys. The other room had a bar, TV, a coffee table, a big chair and a loveseat. The suite was very dark, even though it was early afternoon. Aside from the starchy white linen on the beds, everything was a shade of brown or black. I immediately began turning on the lamps and opening the heavy curtains.

Getting settled in was awkward. Dad took a seat on the big chair, holding his cane between his legs and looking around. The boys began jumping on one of the perfectly made beds. I felt pressure to keep things calm for my dad, who looked gaunt and tired. He pointed to one of his bags and told me to open it because he'd brought gifts.

"Boys! Your grandpa brought you some presents!" They excitedly plopped down beside me, wiggling and craning their necks to look in the bag. Dad was smiling. I felt so happy that he had thought of them.

"So sweet of you, Dad."

I reached into his bag to find a couple plastic dinosaurs, their favorites.

"T-rex!" my oldest cheered. They immediately started acting out dinosaur battles on the carpet.

"Does that give you a little wet spot boys?" Dad said, drawing out the *wet* so it sounded like a hiss. As he glanced at me, he managed to rock his pelvis just enough to get the point across, his mouth in a crooked smile. My heart sank. I felt my cheeks go hot, my eyes uncontrollably blinking over and over. Anger and hurt swelled like a sudden high fever. Dad made remarks like this all the time when Benny and I were growing up, but it sounded so different and unbearable when directed at my own children. I tried to speak, but nothing came out, so I just pretended I hadn't heard him. I didn't take my eyes off the boys, scanning them for a reaction, but they kept playing happily, unaware of what Dad meant.

Both nights, Dad told me to order up whatever booze I wanted.

"Princess, we're approaching five," he said, looking at the imaginary watch on his wrist. "Drink for me."

He could no longer drink on account of all his medications. He had set up his astonishing array of pharmaceuticals by the bathroom sink. His day revolved largely around which medication was due next. None of those pills were any kind of miracle cure, especially the AZT. I wished I could lock that bathroom door from the outside in order to ensure that my little boys would not get into my father's medications, but I could only keep a close eye. When my oldest had to use the toilet, I did my best to find excuses to bring the boys out to the lobby, where we would use the public bathroom, my son staring up at me from the potty asking, "Mommy, why can't we go in *our* bathroom?" (my youngest was still in diapers).

"This is an adventure," I said back. "It's fun to try out different bathrooms."

I felt ashamed of my seemingly ignorant fear. I had taken a weekend seminar on HIV and AIDS in college, for one unit. *Ivory soap kills it* is what I kept repeating to myself. But all factual knowledge just floated out the window when it came to these two little innocent people who meant the world to me. After Dad used the bathroom, I found myself scrubbing the faucet and toilet handles with a starchy white washcloth that I had lathered up with a bar of hotel hand soap.

Both mornings that weekend, I woke to the sounds of my father retching into the toilet. This was his daily ritual. The rest of the day, he was in and out of naps. I wondered—why on earth would he want to go to this hotel with his daughter and her small children? I wondered if perhaps Anton needed a break.

The morning of the second day, while Dad was retching in the bathroom, my boys and I went down to the large buffet breakfast. He had stayed up in the room the previous morning, so I assumed he wasn't coming. I spotted him out of the corner of my eye as I sat drinking my coffee. He moved through that crowded patio court like a cross between a slithering snake and Greta Garbo, what with the way he *slid* over to the table, hardly lifting his feet from the ground. He wore his illness like a *style*, one that was even in vogue. In Dad's way, even terminal illness could be provocative.

"Look at my sexy cane," he purred as he cautiously sat down. People were happily talking about what they were going to do in San Francisco that day, or talking about their company or where they were going next. They seemed to slow their conversations as they eyed my father.

Dad rubbed his cane and talked incessantly about his acquisition of this cherry wood staff, which bore intricate, elegant carvings in the handle. I felt we were the sole representation of his AIDS culture of stigma, sickness and gloom amongst the cheerful vacationers and business people in that busy patio court. The way in which he showed off his ailings seemed to be a part of his identification as "The Dying Beautiful Faggot"--*his* words, not mine. That morning, he was the sole representative of the many afflicted who toted bubbling oxygen tanks and hoses, Kleenex boxes and vomit basins, canes, home care attendants, and vials and vials of medications. They all shared the same look—the sunken cheeks and the bulging yellow eyes, the thin, emaciated bodies. This may sound like it matches up with the look of cancer. However, the person dying of AIDS has a very distinct appearance, one that could be spotted fairly easily in San Francisco.

Though he was skin-on-bones and constantly battling nausea, Dad's worst complaint so far was about his peripheral neuropathy, a painful disorder common to people with HIV and AIDS involving damaged nerves in the feet. This sent him to screaming at his feet, "Motherfucker!" and, "Jesus fucking Christ!"

About the time that I was wondering if it might be too early for a drink, Dad rolled his eyes and announced, looking flippantly at my chest, "Sweet mother of God, those tits of yours could kill." The embarrassment and the sting were so much, I couldn't say or do anything. I pretended he didn't say it. *Please not in front of my boys,* I repeated in my head, feeling my teeth dig into my bottom lip, my hand clenching my fork. It was evident that Dad would say these kinds of things to me all the way to the end. Talking this way had always been part of Dad; I usually did my best to shrug it off. As a kid, Dad's razzing about sex and boys seemed lighter, and even fun. But his comments became more lewd during my adolescence. I anticipated a visit with anxiety and hope, not knowing what I'd get. He went back and forth between putting me on a pedestal and treating me like––what he called––pure trash.

Dad's tenderness receded and his vulgarity grew the more I became a woman, which was odd, because he had always seemed to lovingly and tearfully announce this fact when I was growing up, saying the then dreaded, "you're becoming a woman." Back then, it had seemed like Dad thought my becoming a woman was a milestone, and something to celebrate.

I wanted so much for him to be the way he was when I was little, so devoted and kind and fun. It was hard to imagine that he was the same man. I imagined the old Dad was just under the surface––almost in reach––I just had to figure out how to access him. For years I had been trying to say the right thing or act the right way or give the right gift. There were glimpses and moments of almost getting him back, only to be squashed by a derogative, sexual, or mean comment that I *knew* shouldn't be coming from my own father. I had hoped he would soften and perhaps become less unchaste as he grew sicker, anticipating both the irony and the comfort in his finally protecting me from harm and indecencies at his death. But he got worse. He had a free ticket to act however he wanted because he was dying. I missed my chance at ever confronting him. I'd share the pain of losing Dad with my disgust and disappointment.

That afternoon, while Dad rested, I found myself driving around Daly City with my children in the backseat. I was driving in circles, alternating TLC and En Vogue on the CD player. I was taking wrong turns and getting lost. The music was somehow magnifying the feeling of being an alien on my own planet. I was aware of how I used to feel elevated by the songs, but now the *never, never never gonna get it* and the *so I creep* felt off. Where was normal? I felt like there was a free, fun life out there and perhaps I would never get back to it. I changed the CD to The Rolling Stones *Goats Head Soup*, which seemed a little better, but really was almost equally disorienting.

I wanted to find a park--something green and pretty--but could not. We eventually ended up back at the hotel, where we jumped into the indoor pool for the third time that day. Anything to stay out of our room-turned-infirmary. When we went into the hot tub and turned on the jets, a businessman came in to join. We made small talk, and before I knew it, he was inviting me his hotel room that evening. My boys were taking handfuls of the hot bubbly water and dropping it on each other's heads, laughing.

"My kids...." I said in a small, shy way, hoping I didn't have to explain any further, hoping that he would infer the *But I am a mother, I have these little children, don't you see my wedding ring? How could you ask me that?*

"If you don't have anyone to watch them, you could bring them—" he volunteered.

It seemed that I had stepped out of reality and had entered a void where in my children and I were not safe from anything. No one had any decency; there were no rules. Everything was filth.

I talked to my husband on the hotel phone late that afternoon while Dad slept in the other room. I knew Dad would get a big bill for the call, but I didn't care. I had put the boys in front of the TV, turning on some cartoons. I did my best to keep my voice down and use code words. I was crying.

"I can't handle this," I was confessing.

I told him about Dad's comments and the sickness and the man in the pool.

"That's so awful," he sympathized. My husband was kind on the phone and mad at my father for me, but nothing he said could soothe the feeling that I was chasing something I had once loved so very much that had curdled.

After I finally got the boys to sleep later that night, I stayed up quietly talking with my dad, refilling my glass with the bottle he had ordered up for me. He swooped up his own imaginary glass, holding it elegantly in his hand the way that he used to. He brought it to his lips and pretended to sip, closing his eyes.

"Ah, to have a martini."

Like magic, my disgust for him turned to pity––a trick he often knowingly or unknowingly played on me. He began to talk about his funeral. This was one of his favorite topics. He had been talking about this personal revelry long before he was even diagnosed with AIDS. He was planning for his big shebang, a party full of style and theatrical drama in which he was the guest of honor. He had his guest list made out, and all the details mapped out––from white lilies to a small orchestra, plates of caviar and escargot, and a full hosted bar. He talked about the silk dress I would be wearing as I made *The Speech.*

"Why would you want to sit up here, having a depressing conversation with your dying father?" he asked in his sarcastic New Yorker tone, waving a hand in the air in a poo-pooing gesture.

Good question.

Dad pointed to the door. "You know, if you go down to the bar and have a drink, I can watch you."

The large hotel was built so that all floors were in tiers—the hallways balconies above the large open interior below that included a bar, a dining area and a small pond and garden. Dad explained that he could stand out on the balcony and watch me from high up. He said he'd keep the door to our suite open so that he could hear the boys if they should wake up. He was staring at me with his head tilted to the side, his arms crossed in front of him. I darted my eyes to the brown carpet.

"All those men down there. I could watch you work it."

Not only did my dear dying father want me to drink for him, apparently he hoped he might talk me into seducing men so that he could watch. I felt a stabbing sensation in my gut when he said it, a tightening in my throat. I wanted to say, "Why would you want that for me?" but I couldn't open my mouth. The only sound in the room was the squeak of my finger nervously running around the rim of my glass. I tried to pretend I didn't hear him say it. I didn't look at him, but I could feel him still staring at me, the familiar crooked half-smile on his face.

While I was so taken aback, there was a part of me that wanted to go lure men for him. Dad was the one who taught me just how a woman hooks a man. I remembered when I was a little girl, when he called it getting laid and jumping your bones, and doing the nasty. It seemed like a fun game back then––when he showed me how to say no way Jose, and how to swing my hips and wave my finger. There was a part of me that wanted to show him that I had gotten it right; I longed to engage him in a way that would get his full attention and really light him up like nothing else.

Later that night I lay in bed next to my boys, unable to sleep. I was picturing myself at the bar in a low-cut shirt with my tits that could kill, my father watching from above. I imaged him egging me on, licking his lips and rubbing his hands--so pleased. The thought made me ill. I hated the part of me that wanted to do it. I hated that he suggested it.

I put into my mind a good memory—when I was eight and Dad took me to Bloomingdale's in New York to buy me what he called a "moonbeam dress." When I stepped out of the dressing room, he had tears in his eyes. He walked up to me and took one of my hands and twirled me around as if we were going to dance right there in the department store.

"An angel," he said, cupping my face in his hand, "you're my angel."

When we got home from our Bloomingdale's trip, he removed a tiny box from inside the shopping bag. Somehow, he had managed to buy me a secret gift behind my back—a delicate ring for my finger that had a glass bead with a little yellow flower on it.

Next, I recalled when Dad referred to me as a hard-to-find treasure at Ocean World in Florida when I was twelve, when he and I picked out the oyster with a pearl in it. I felt so special when he had a gold ring made for me with that pearl in the center.

I repeated these memories over and over in my head that night, until I finally fell asleep.

Goodbye Dad

I was twenty-six in February of 1995, when Dad asked me to pick out a broach from his Joan Rivers Collection. It was just five days before he died, and the last time I ever saw him. I had to endure QVC jewelry showcases that afternoon, when Dad suddenly seemed more alert and more engaged than at any other point that entire three day visit.

"The Joan Rivers selection will come on," he mumbled my way, his sunken eyes fixed on the television.

"Ah, look at that one," he oozed over the fake gems. I did my best to match his enthusiasm. My once dazzling father was about to lose his battle with AIDS, and was nothing but skin on bones. His weak excitement over the Joan Rivers Collection would be the last time I'd catch a glimmer of his glamour and style. It would be the last time I felt like his princess.

He was rubbing his bony hands together like he was wishing on something during the Joan Rivers Collection showcase. That's when he asked Anton to fetch his private stash out of a drawer. Dad struggled to shimmy himself up toward the headboard, wincing and groaning along the way, as Anton returned to Dad's bedside with a black jewelry box in his hands.

"Here, here, here," he instructed Anton, pointing to a flat surface on the blanket. Dad opened the black box slowly, revealing its red velvet interior and the assortment of sparkling colorful costume jewelry inside. He pulled out each gaudy piece separately, laying them out in a tidy line.

"Princess, pick any one you want. All from the Joan Rivers Collection."

It was a bit of a strain to keep the *oy vey* off my expression. The broaches were kitschy as all could tell. What drew my father to collecting such costuming, especially at this point in his life? I imagined him lying in a coffin with a tailored Armani suit and a big fat Joan Rivers broach planted right on the lapel.

"Oh Dad, that's so sweet, thank you."

I picked up a few pieces, turning each one around in my hands, tracing the phony gems with my fingers. He had choppy stories to go with a few of them.

"Oh, that one was a steal. Really worth two hundred. I got it for twenty, last minute."

Finally, I chose a shiny, fire engine red cluster of cherries dotted with rhinestones.

"Very well," he said with a small nod before he carefully put each remaining piece back into that black velvet-lined box.

I held the broach in my hand, being careful to not get stuck by the small pin on the back. I rubbed the smooth glass-like surface of the cluster of cherries with my fingers and imagined that someday––and very soon–– I would remember that afternoon when my dad asked me to select a broach from his tacky collection. I thought of how I would remember his thin fingers reaching for the black box, and how he had so carefully assembled his treasures for me. I knew that, for many years to come, those rhinestone-laden cherries would give me a good laugh while reminding me of the good parts of my father. Of course, I still have that flamboyant broach today.

It was a brisk afternoon in San Francisco the day of Dad's funeral, in March of 1995. Several of us drove in a procession down Market Street. Anton and his friends rode in front in a Rolls Royce, their tribute to Dad. I could see the outline of their heads through the back window–– I could see that Anton was sitting in between two other men, and I wondered what they were talking about. My husband and I followed in our Honda station wagon, our two little boys in the back seat. In back of us were twenty-three-year-old Ben and his girlfriend in Ben's little souped-up sporty car. I kept turning around from the front passenger seat to make sure they were still behind us.

I had felt sorry for Anton when we stood awkwardly with his friends outside the apartment before getting into our cars. It was an obvious consensus to keep conversations to small talk. But just moments before, Anton had found me in Dad's closet, wrapped myself up in his things, crying.

"I know, me too," he had said with his eyes full of tears.

We congregated on the grass of the Columbarium off California Street. The wind whipped my dress at my shins, and I was wishing that I had a big coat. Big lofty clouds periodically covered the sun as they moved quickly over the blue sky. The historic Columbarium looked like a small palace--a place where perhaps only famous people were kept. I stared at the many stained glass windows and the dome-shaped roof. My little boys ran around the perfect, tidy hedges that covered the grounds. Ben stood quietly off to the side, holding hands with his awfully beautiful girlfriend with long golden copper hair and olive skin.

Dad's friends wore pin-striped tailored suits and shiny black patent leather shoes. Some wore their hair slicked back and gelled in a fifties kind of way. Being that it was the height of the AIDS pandemic, I knew most of them had been through this routine many times. Dad and Anton had lost so many friends already, including Terrance in New York, who had brought home all those shirts for me to model when I was twelve--he died early, in 1985.

Some of the people at Dad's service were even talking about their jobs, or what they were going to do the next day. *Another one bites the dust* was the feeling I got from them. This incongruity made me want to rip my dress off and run around on the grass naked, screaming and doing cartwheels.

We walked slowly into the echoing circular columbarium. Sunlight streamed through the stained glass images of angels and of Jesus. The feeling of being in an altered reality was magnified by the fact that it seemed I had entered Ancient Rome.

"Mommy!" my youngest called out, pulling at my finger. He was craning his neck and pointing to the magnificent glass pinwheel design on the oculus above our heads. Every inch of the towering pillars, the balconies, and the giant atrium were covered with statues and carvings, gold paint and Michelangelo-like images.

My high heels clapped against the mosaic floors as I made my way toward the area where several wooden chairs had been arranged. *Where is Dad?* I could hear Dad's voice—he was both cooing and heckling.

The four floors of the columbarium were lined with tidy square compartments called niches, each containing the ashes of those who had passed, some with special memorabilia and trinkets. I was glad that my dad would not be locked up in one of those cubicles; such a confinement would have been so uncharacteristic of him. Instead, his ashes would stay with Anton. Dad had bragged about a cowboy boot shaped urn labeled "Went out kickin'," but I wasn't sure if it ever truly existed.

The location was regal, but missing were all the over-the-top details Dad had bragged about for years. I felt terrible guilt over his mediocre funeral. I wondered if I had somehow unconsciously purposely jabbed him by not giving him the shebang that he had talked about for so long. There were no white lilies, no caviar, no sequined singers with large exotic red flowers in their hair––no piano player.

After a few words from someone from the Neptune Society, I was chosen to be the one to accept an exceptionally wrinkle-free, triangle-folded American flag––handed to me by a man who had seemed to pop out of nowhere. Dad and patriot certainly did not go hand-in-hand, but he had served in the military in his early twenties, none-the-less. The oddity in the sudden presence of this flag amongst the crowd of Dad's friends was so out of place that I was afraid I'd start giggling in front of everyone when I stood up to accept it. After I awkwardly took the flag, I went back to my seat between Ben and my husband and boys.

Next, silence hung heavy, the small podium empty. People started stirring in their seats and clearing their throats. *Come on, come on, someone get up and say something.* I looked at Anton a row over; his eyes were pleading with me. I then found myself returning to the podium to face the twenty or so mourners.

I had not written a big long eulogy like I had for my father-in-law a few years before. For some reason—of which I could not tell—I decided that I would improvise if I ended up speaking at my father's funeral. I was surprised at how long I was able to talk in this unorganized, unplanned fashion. I hoped to find a way to bring Dad out. I wanted to demonstrate that he was so much more than just another dead gay man in San Francisco; that he was not that Columbarium, that he was not just that day. It felt like he had been gone so long, there was relief in getting a venue to deposit my grief.

The well-dressed men sat slack-jawed as I recollected Dad's early days. These were untold secrets. I talked of how Dad once lived in rural Vermont and that this was where he met my mother. Part of me felt guilty about bringing up his former straight life––it's not something he would have discussed with his friends.

I spoke of him as once a gardener in clogs and a ponytail. It was as if Dad had lived many lives in one life and I was exposing all of him at once. His friends sat stock-still; you could have heard a pin drop. They were probably trying to match up the flashy Joan Rivers collector with the down-to earth hetero mountaineer.

I told the story of how, when Benny and I were very little, he delighted us with our very own personal Macy's Day Parade because we had missed the real thing that November. I described how the three of us marched in a single-file right through Macy's in downtown Manhattan clanging metal pots with big spoons, singing *Love Train* full bore. I could see that Ben was trying hard to keep his sobs from letting loose when I told this story—his face red and purple, the vein on his forehead sticking out. I couldn't help but feel like I had inflicted something on him by telling that story.

I could almost feel the sigh of relief when I then spoke of Dad as a dancer and a performer, and of how he could light up any room with his classy style and sharp wit.

"He could sing all the lines of every song in *A Chorus Line*," I boasted for him.

There was the story of the red disco dress and how Dad took us to One's Disco in New York City, how we just about took over the dance floor.

I described how Dad had helped many people as an RN, working with AIDS patients in San Francisco, and of how he tirelessly worked nightshift. He had found the career that resonated with him in the last ten years of his life.

"These are from his old co-workers in New York," I said, pointing to the large, beautiful bouquet of flowers sent by the agency for troubled youths in New York where he worked for years. "He changed the lives of many troubled teens as a social worker."

I had only dared to talk about the *good* parts of Dad, my childhood Dad. These were the parts of him I hung onto. There was no talk of doing the nasty or getting laid, or playing his father with the belt. There was no mention of our hotel stay seven months prior to his death. I kept Dad's demons out of that columbarium.

Dad's make-believe had sometimes been better than real life. As a kid, I fell for his make-believe hook, line, and sinker. Who was I without him? In so many ways he was long gone; I was used to mourning him. Yet, I was still redefining myself without him.

That day of his funeral, I had a flash of him in Centereach saying, "You'll hate me when you grow up, you'll see." I remembered protesting and arguing. But now--as an adult--I knew what he meant. He was afraid we'd see the *real* him and run away. *I'm still here Dad.*

When I finally made my way off the podium, just about every man and woman in the place had pulled out his or her little pristine folded hanky or their tissue from their pockets. The serendipitous event that happened next will forever be nothing short of a miracle.

After I returned to sit next to Ben, his girlfriend and my family, a woman from the back row stood up and made her way down the aisle toward the podium. She had straggly, greasy hair and wore old jeans and a worn-out sweater. *Who in hell is this and how does she know Dad?* I gave Anton a look and he shrugged his shoulders.

"My name is Becky," she announced, "Astrid and Ben, I was your babysitter on Long Island when you were little."

My stomach dropped. I had always remembered Becky--our babysitter after Mother moved to San Francisco--who tirelessly created one paper doll after the other. We walked beside the train tracks and went to the park. I grabbed Ben's arm.

"I remember you!" I yelled out without thinking.

If this was not a Lifetime Movie moment for us all, I don't know what was.

"Oh my God, can you believe it?" I heard someone gasp behind me. I could feel the astonishment amongst the rows of seats.

Anton shot me a cautious look--it hadn't occurred to me that she could be a phony. But then she knew so many details of our life on Long Island, she *couldn't* have been a phony. Becky explained that she was now a resident of San Francisco and had seen Dad's obituary in the paper. She talked of how our dad had changed her life, how she had been one of the troubled teens he helped at the youth services agency in New York.

"He proved he believed in me by giving me the job of watching his kids," she said.

Becky said he helped her believe in herself. She described Dad as being a shoulder to lean on when there had been no one else.

"I never forgot him," she said tearfully.

It was as if the universe had opened up so that this woman could be there that day as proof that those good parts of Dad were truly real. I sat with big tears dripping down my face as she spoke of a father I *knew* had existed, it wasn't all in my head.

I was thankful for the wine at the reception held at Dad and Anton's Diamond Heights apartment. My little boys were out of place as the only children there. They were eating cookies and flailing their little bodies around, laughing. My poor husband was trying to control them on his own. Ben seemed a little shell-shocked, sitting next to his girlfriend with his plate of crackers and cheese.

I had invited Becky to join us for the reception. I found her presence so reassuring; I sat so close to her that our elbows touched. I clung to her the whole time, asking one question after the other about my father back on Long Island in the mid-seventies. She brought the old Dad back in a way I never dreamed possible.

A month or two later, Becky wrote me a long letter detailing all those things she had told me that day, so that I could have it all in writing. Included were statements such as, "Your father was a good man," and "Your father changed my life for the better." Becky and I talked of getting together, but that never did happen. The way she left my life just as quickly as she reentered it gave me the idea that maybe she had been some kind of angel and that maybe there was someone—*something*—looking out for me and my brother. Perhaps no matter how much we doubted it, there would always be good. Maybe the good never left.

Outrageous Older Woman

It's a gray late morning in Northern California in September of 2006, when my mother and I sit across from each other at a little café. We live in close proximity to one another--she moved many miles just to live closer to me and my sons in the year 2001--but it has been months since we have had such a meeting, as my mother and I have struggled to define our relationship. The long absences and standstills have mostly come from me. I have not been able to forgive the past, at least not enough to carry on merrily in the present.

One wall in the café is red and the other is periwinkle blue, both covered with framed images of fish that have been stamped to the artist's paper like fossils. The one that hangs above our table displays a trout in orange. Every feature has been delicately pressed to the paper, leaving out not a single scale. Mother stares at the art with her head slightly cocked. I watch her, the way that she is studying that fish so intently.

"Aren't these beautiful? This is an ancient technique that is coming back. People used to make these hundreds of years ago. The artist has taken real fish and made prints of them. They look so fragile," she says, bringing her fingers close to the fish image, before withdrawing her hand, realizing she's not supposed to touch. I look at how she's aged—her hair, still full of kinky curl, is graying a bit at the roots. Her face reflects a woman who loved the sun. I think that she still looks beautiful.

I am proud of my mother for continuing to do her art. She currently has a piece in an art show downtown.

Our mochas are served in big Fiesta Wear mugs. Hers is brick orange and mine is mint green—they aren't from the same set, they are shaped differently. I think of how they remind me of the mugs we had when I was growing up.

"These would be in *Alice in Wonderland*!" Mother says, laughing like a child toward the waitress, holding up her mug in one hand like she's making a toast.

"One pill makes you larger and one pill makes you small," I chime in flatly with my eyes raised at the waitress, who chuckles before walking away.

I'm sure that we are quite a spectacle to the twenty-something girl, as my mother has placed a bumper sticker against the wall that meets our table that says "Outrageous Older Woman," a gift I got her on a recent trip. It is placed in such a way so that everyone at the café can see it, like an advertisement. She had bounced in her stool and clapped her hands when I pulled the bumper sticker from my purse and handed it to her that morning.

She has recently come back from a visit with her ninety-year-old mother in Delaware. During that visit she found some document while snooping around in her mother's files. The document is some kind of family tree, with two rows of names, one listed as the *Hebrew Line* and the other as a potpourri of wasp ethnicities, such as French, English, and Scottish. She had returned from her trip like a detective who had found the last piece of evidence.

"I *knew* we were Jewish! I knew it all along!" she beamed.

Just prior to meeting me at the café, Mother had a visit with a local Rabbi. She hoped that the Rabbi might solve this mystery for her, once and for all. Before she gets the chance to tell me what he said, I tease her.

"Mom, what's he going to do? Take a big rubber stamp and pound a certificate with a fat red JEWISH hallmark and say 'See ya' at temple'?"

We both laugh a bunch over this, though I know I've been a little bit cruel.

"He told me that everyone in the world probably has a Hebrew line, he said that he can't tell me anything." Her eyes look into her big mug while she traces the rim with her finger. "He said it's all up to me."

I know her so well. I know that "It's all up to you" is definitely *not* what she wanted to hear. My mother will be sixty-four this year, but she's still thinking about who she wants to be when she grows up—she's still coming of age, she's still searching for clues as to who she really is.

This trip to the Rabbi is par for the course for my mother, a quest to redefine herself once again.

I sit across the table from her and feel such a love for her. This visit feels different; I feel lighter. I am not threatened or annoyed by her eclectic, eccentric and compulsive ways. I think to myself that she reminds me of Maude in *Harold and Maude*, a character I find to be wildly lovable. I think that perhaps I can see her as separate from me; perhaps I can appreciate her for her sweetness, her artistic wackiness, and her capriciousness. I am pleasantly surprised at my true compassion for the part of her that will always seek, the part that never feels quite right. I can palpate her struggle at trying to come to terms with being neither young nor old. Though she has experienced some considerable challenge with every phase of her life, I honestly feel compassion in this one, enough to hold it as separate from all the others.

I am enormously grateful for her third husband—an incredibly intelligent, kind, yet introverted man who is eleven years her junior. He is devoted to my mother; I know he will never leave. Because of him, she does not have to work, and she can tend to her garden and her artwork. She can remain at home during her *off* times.

At the table, she tells me that she is still trying to figure out what to do with herself.

"Sixty-five," she says definitively with a sure nod, "I will know what I am supposed to do when I am sixty-five."

She pronounces that, for now, she is going through what she calls a "detox" from her visit with her mother. I know that this will go on indefinitely. She tells me that she went to bed the previous night at five p.m. and slept straight through until eight a.m. the following morning--always a standard feature of what she calls *detoxing*. I call it depression, but I don't say this to her. I know that this mood of hers is the flip-side to the good times, the other side of the moon. I know that in two weeks--a month, maybe two months--my mother will be making plans, doing art, buying things and showing up.

Mother's schedule of ups and downs and highs and lows was the timetable that had me in a vise grip when I was a girl—a clock always ticking way in the background that made me think, *time's almost up, get ready for the next trip.* Even though I am a grown woman on this day, there is a vague far-off sense of this timer that keeps on ticking, letting me know that my mother is about to expire. The worry, trepidation, and doubt are still inside like little stubborn roots that got missed.

We've been at the café for well over an hour now and people have filtered out, leaving the tables empty and full of dirty plates after a busy brunch rush. We step off of our stools and she pays the lunch bill and I leave the tip.

It feels like rain outside. We stroll up the block to a cute little clothing boutique and browse through the racks of very expensive dresses. They are replicas from the forties and fifties, many of fine silk and chiffon.

"Can you imagine?" Mother holds one up in front of her and pulls out the skirt, swaying her hips. I pull out the price tag—one hundred and sixty-eight dollars.

"Who around here can afford these?" I ask, pulling out a black cocktail dress with a very low neckline. "But wouldn't it be so great to own one?"

We laugh over panties that cost twenty-seven dollars a pair and *"Ah"* over thin, soft cotton T-shirts. I realize in the middle of this that I am experiencing a moment with my mother that I have longed to experience for quite some time: I am having fun with her and I'm not thinking about the past.

We go to another shop, a secondhand store. Mother tries on a long full black skirt with embroidery at the bottom. It's tight at the waist.

"What would I wear this with?" she asks, standing in front of the mirror with her head turned to the side.

"A body suit. You know, like a leotard," I tell her.

She doesn't buy the skirt. She puts it back on the rack and rubs her eyes, letting out a big yawn.

"Believe it or not, I feel like I need to go home and sleep," she says, laughing at herself, scratching her head.

But I do believe it. She will go home and sleep for hours again. I know that her light is fading out, she's retreating back into her safe place. She'll curl up in the safety of her bed, her cats, and her big dog--her kitchen, her garden, her homeopathic remedies. I don't think about how or when she'll return from her hibernation. I feel a pang of worry, wondering if she'll eat and whether she'll be suicidal. Then these thoughts are quickly dismissed. I am briefly able to turn off that timer inside of me; I'm able to forget my mother's mood schedule. I know that we've been at this place a hundred times and the outcome doesn't really change. I'm actually taken aback by my own detachment. I just feel warm all over with love for my mother who I'll never be able to change, and I'll never be able to save. I think that I am approaching some kind of forgiveness for the past.

It seems that I am finally what one might call successful. I have followed in Dad's footsteps in becoming a registered nurse. I have remarried, my husband a very *normal*, sensible man. We have had a child--my third son. I ask myself: Am I a real grown up now? Mother usually brings out the adult in me. Her spinning compass still seems to keep my dial straight.

With Mother tired—and it starting to drizzle—we end our lovely visit on the plaza in town.

"I know we didn't talk about all of that uncomfortable stuff. But it felt really good to just have a nice time and forget about all that for a while," I say into her ear as we share a sweet, earnest embrace.

"It was really nice," she says, looking into my eyes and holding my shoulders with her hands.

She stands on the sidewalk watching me as I get into my car. I am about to close my door when I stand up and get back out for a second.

"Don't forget to put your bumper sticker on your car!" I shout her way.

She startles with a big smile and lifts one finger in the air in an ah-ha. She pulls the *Outrageous Older Woman* sticker from her purse and holds it up high above her head with both her hands, wiggling it back and forth and swaying her hips, laughing. I blow her a kiss before driving away.

I keep an image of my beautiful mother in my mind and in my heart--it's the year 1969, and she's swaying to her *Nashville Skyline* record with me in her arms. She's looking out a big window at the Vermont snow while stroking my white barely-there newborn hair. Like most new mothers, she's dreaming about the big plans she has for me. She wants to show me nature and music and art; she wants to show me unabashed love and free expression. And that's what she did.

Taking Off

Ben and I are in our forties when we fly to Orlando, Florida together in 2015. I'm joining him on one of his business trips, something I've wanted to do for a long time. We are one again on this trip—sharing our private language and staying up late talking. He gets me like no one else in the world, and I him. Some say we seem as connected as twins.

Ben is successful at doing what he loves and—the icing on the cake—he gets to travel often for his work. He owns a lovely home in the Bay Area and has remained meticulously detailed and organized, as he always was as a child. He's never married or had kids, of his own choosing. I'm thankful every day that he's alive, as he came so close to losing his life during his train wreck of an adolescence.

Our trip together is one of the very best times of my life. I spend the days writing this very book in the fancy hotel room while he works. We go out on the town at night, choosing the best restaurants and breweries. We go out to dinner and to lunch with people from his company, and I finally get to put the faces with the names. They boast about Ben--how amazing he is, what a good job he does, how funny he is, and how they always look forward to his work visits. I'm so proud of him.

We are reminded of Anton when we go to a Cuban restaurant where you can sit right in front of a stage where dancers are performing in colorful, elaborate costumes. Sadly, Anton has dropped off the face of the earth. We talk about how kind and funny he was, and how much we loved his family.

"I love to meet people when I travel," Ben says, as he tries to explain that he prefers to sit at the bar when he eats out, rather than at a table. He says that facing someone at a table him edgy. I think of how we each walked away from our bizarre childhood with our own unique idiosyncrasies.

We go to Disney World and ride "It's A Small World," singing along the whole time, and marveling that the characters look the same as they did over twenty-five years ago. It feels like we've stepped back in time to when we visited Disney World with Dad and Anton in 1981, and I can almost feel Dad sitting beside us.

Too soon, it's time to fly back home to California. Sitting next to my brother on an airplane is surreal--I go right back in time to all those flights we took together when we were kids. I'm still afraid of the takeoff. Ben understands this, and takes my hand in his when the engine starts to roar. As the airplane takes speed and lifts off the ground, I look at his face instead of out the window. Benny is my constant. His presence authenticates all that happened—and he is living proof that we've made it in the world.

Made in the USA
San Bernardino,
CA